THE COMPLETE
Miniature Schnauzer

by ANNE PARAMOURE ESKRIGGE

THIRD EDITION

1985—Seventh Printing

HOWELL BOOK HOUSE INC.

230 PARK AVENUE

NEW YORK, NEW YORK 10169

In Memoriam
Frank Tatham Eskrigge, 1871–1967
A veteran of 55 years in dogs
as exhibitor, writer and judge

ANNE PARAMOURE ESKRIGGE

Preface to the
First Edition

IN 1935, *The Miniature Schnauzer* was published with some hesitation. There was considerable question whether interest in the breed was sufficient to make the venture worthwhile. The book had, accordingly, the financial backing of the American Miniature Schnauzer Club, itself barely two years old as a separate organization, and hence was in some degree an official publication.

Today the breed occupies a very different position. The old book is long out of print, and there is no question as to the demand for a successor. Hence this present volume, completely rewritten, is an independent venture. Though members of the Club have been whole-hearted in their cooperation during the unexpectedly lengthy process of writing it, the book stands on its own merits. Since individual opinions differ, I prefer to be able to express my own freely, without binding the Club to an endorsement of any statements with which some members might disagree.

From 1924 to 1939 I was closely associated with Miniature Schnauzers as breeder, exhibitor, breed correspondent, and secretary, first of the Schnauzer Club of America and later of the American Miniature Schnauzer Club from its formation in 1933 to 1938. Then for business and family reasons I became inactive until 1952. I knew most of the early dogs of any importance first-hand, since the breed was then confined to a comparatively small area. Now that Miniature Schnauzers have become so much better known and are bred in nearly every State, it is no longer possible to know all the good ones personally, while during the period from 1940 to 1952 I saw only an occasional winner.

The material included in this book is derived from a number of sources. Wherever possible I have used my own first-hand knowledge of the various dogs. Next come published records: studbooks, American, German, and others; the *American Kennel Gazette;* correspondence with the English Kennel Club; and clippings of show reports and breed columns in various publications. Recognized textbooks on genetics and breeding have also been consulted. Finally, breeders and fanciers both here and abroad have been more than generous in sending material and answering questions. Without their help I could never have written the book.

Statements regarding individual dogs, breeding trends, and genetic theories are my own considered opinions, derived from the aforesaid sources. When not based on actual records or my own knowledge, I have endeavored to qualify my statements, either by direct quotation or by adding some phrase to indicate the source. This is particularly true of the dogs shown during the 1940's, few of whom I knew myself, though I have, of course, their show and breeding records. Some sections which were first written several years ago have had to be revised and brought up to date. If any omissions or errors have been made, on this account or otherwise, I shall appreciate having them called to my attention.

From the many, many pictures which have been sent to me I have tried to select the most interesting from a variety of points of view. I have included some outstandingly important dogs, even though the available pictures were not all that might be wished. In general, however, I have preferred a clear, natural picture to a poor example with a big name. In addition, I have tried to illustrate all ages, a variety of countries, periods, and geographical areas, and to include views of the breed at home and in action as well as formally posed in the show ring. For many of us love the breed for their personality and charm above all, and many notable champions have been house pets as well.

My warmest thanks are extended to all, both here and abroad, who have patiently answered questions and supplied information, cuts, and photographs. I wish I could name them all, but the list is far too long. My special thanks are due Dorothy Williams of Dorem Kennels for her generous assistance on many points and particularly to her and to the Frederick Smiths for the wonderful illustrations on how to trim correctly. To Mrs. Dorothy Goldsworthy for reading and criticizing much of the rough draft, to Mrs. Vera Kantor and Mrs. W. N. Maguire for invaluable help in the study of color inheritance, to Mr. Vernon P. Fleming for statistics on puppy weight, to Mr. and Mrs. Carl Roth for information secured from German fanciers, to Mlle. L. de Tavel of Switzerland, to Herr Franz Leix and Herr Max Woch of Germany, Dr. Granata of Italy, Mr. S. E. Whitely, Mr. Donald Becker, Mrs. Doreen Crowe, and Mrs. K. M. Boubelik and Mrs. F. M. Milsom of England, and Mr. T. H. Wylie and Mrs. William Gottschalk of Canada for material on the breed in those countries; to Mrs. Evalyn Peterson for her drawings of Miniature Schnauzer type; to Mrs. Joan Dalton for her able work on the advertisements, and to Mrs. Emily Gaykan and Mrs. Kay Pumphrey for typing and retyping the manuscript. Also, my thanks to the *American Kennel Gazette* and *Popular Dogs* for their generosity in lending cuts, and to my family who have borne with me during the past three years when the work absorbed most of my leisure time.

Preface to the
New Edition

MOST of the statements in the first preface still apply. The long delay in the revision, which I regret extremely, has been due to lack of free time, health, and other causes. My thanks are due to the publishers for bearing with me, and my apologies to all who have been irked by the repeated postponements.

The tremendous growth of the breed during the past ten years has greatly increased the material to be considered and reduced proportionately the number of dogs which I could know at first hand. This, together with the unavoidable delay, has necessitated rewriting certain portions more than once, to bring the records up to date (there will necessarily be a time lag before the book actually appears). While every effort has been made to correct statements in the first edition which time has rendered obsolete, it should be possible to identify these from the context if they are contradicted elsewhere.

Again I must thank the many who have helped me with information and pictures. In particular, my thanks are due to Mr. John T.

Knight, who has become the "Mr. Statistics" of the breed. Without his generous assistance I could never have coped with the increased number of champions.

Miss Ann Corbishley has been foremost in supplying information and obtaining pictures of the breed in England, and Mrs. R. A. Rothe has supplied material from the early German studbooks not available in this country. To these and all the others who have aided me I cannot be sufficiently grateful.

A book of this sort, aiming at relative completeness, contains material intended for many different types of readers. I have started with a section for the novice, though I hope that others will also find the section on "What Makes a Good Miniature Schnauzer" helpful. Some will not be interested in the history of the breed in its early days, though I have found it fascinating myself, but it is included as a foundation and for those who will enjoy it. For the real student of the breed, the meat is in the bloodlines and the section on genetics and problems.

The listing of all AKC champions and their ancestors, as included in the previous edition, has been omitted. However, the complete list through December 1967 will be available separately. Information regarding this list can be obtained from the secretary of the American Miniature Schnauzer Club, c/o the American Kennel Club, 51 Madison Avenue, New York 10010.

Finally, to avoid confusion, since I have written books on the breed under three different names, the 1935 volume, entitled *The Miniature Schnauzer,* was published under my maiden name of Anne FitzGerald; the 1959 Complete Miniature Schnauzer under my married name, Anne FitzGerald Paramoure; while the current edition has been published under my present name.

ANNE PARAMOURE ESKRIGGE

Contents

Part I: The Miniature Schnauzer, Past and Present

1. Introducing the Miniature Schnauzer Puppy 15
2. What Makes a Good Miniature Schnauzer? 32
3. The Miniature Schnauzer Standard 46
4. Breed Origins 51
5. Breed Beginnings in America 93
6. American Producing Lines 107
7. Postwar Miniatures on the Continent 183
8. The Breed in Great Britain 194
9. Miniature Schnauzers in Canada, Bermuda, Mexico and
   South America 217
10. The Miniature Schnauzer in the Pacific, Asia and Africa 228
11. Miniatures in Obedience Work 235
12. Trimming and Grooming for Show or Home 244

Part II: Genetics and Breeding

1. Something About Genetics 259
2. The Practical Application of Genetics 286

3. Breeding Problems and Solutions 297
4. Color Inheritance 312
5. Puppy and Litter Size 336
   Bibliography for Genetics and Color Breeding 347

Part III: Black Miniature Schnauzers

1. The History of Black Miniature Schnauzers 351
2. The Genetic Makeup of Blacks 367
3. Breeding Blacks for Color and Type 381

Part I

THE MINIATURE SCHNAUZER, PAST AND PRESENT

1

Introducing the Miniature Schnauzer Puppy

THE owner of a new dog does not always have a chance to pick him out, nor even to choose the breed he prefers, for often the animal is a gift, selected by someone else. Often, too, chance decides. A passerby may fall for "that doggy in the window." A neighbor's litter may be too fascinating to resist. Or the purchaser may settle for his second or third choice because he is too impatient to wait for a first choice not immediately or locally available. So it often happens that the person who buys a book about a particular breed of dogs does so because he already has a dog of that breed.

Indeed, it is probably the exceptional person who makes up his mind on the choice of breed and studies the matter carefully before buying his first dog—though he will probably do so before acquiring his second.

Nevertheless, it is logical to start with the characteristics of the breed, and the reasons for choosing one rather than another in a

15

particular litter. And even the owner who already has his dog may want to find out if he has a typical specimen, or what he can reasonably expect his puppy to grow into.

Dogs, like people, differ greatly in appearance and character, even when they belong to the same breed. Upbringing, too, has a marked effect upon both. A normal Miniature Schnauzer is alert, friendly, intelligent, healthy, vigorous, and long-lived. Like his Schnauzer ancestors, he likes to hunt and will often catch mice, rats, or snakes, and sometimes squirrels, particularly when two dogs work together. On the other hand, it is usually easy to teach them to get on well with the family cat, and a puppy and kitten raised together should be the best of friends.

Miniature Schnauzers are active and enjoy long walks. They will follow a horse for miles, while two or more together run lively races with each other. Usually they like to swim, too. On the other hand, they can exist quite happily on a moderate amount of exercise and are therefore an excellent breed for city dwellers.

Most Miniatures like riding in cars and are seldom carsick. They are usually easy to housebreak or leashbreak. Many Miniatures, including both show champions and pet stock, have been trained for obedience classes and have performed well, for they are quick to learn.

Temperament naturally varies with the individual, and also with the way in which the dog is brought up. While sometimes criticized in the past as noisy, the breed should not be troublesome in this respect if raised and handled properly. Never encourage a puppy to bark without good reason just because he is "cute," nor allow him to go on barking indefinitely at other animals or at people. One of the most frequent comments of visitors regarding my dogs is that they are quiet. Sometimes one puppy in a litter will show signs of being unusually noisy. This may be due to the fact that it is alert and intelligent, noticing whatever goes on. Such a puppy can usually be trained not to bark. However, if a puppy appears nervous or hysterical you may have a problem, and such animals should not be used for breeding.

Provided they have not been teased or frightened, Miniature Schnauzers are usually very good with children to whom they are accustomed. I once had a bitch who would bark at small boys but paid no attention to little girls. The boys had pestered her on their

16

way to school until she had no use for them! Children should be watched carefully and be taught how to handle a dog. Little children do not mean to be cruel but they can hurt a puppy seriously, or ruin his disposition permanently. They must be taught to speak and move quietly, not to squeeze the puppy too tightly, pick him up by the legs, poke his eyes, or otherwise hurt or frighten him. And above all, not to continue to play until the young puppy is exhausted.

Miniature Schnauzers have good memories. They will recognize friends or former owners after a long period. Some are one-man dogs, and many show a definite preference for some particular member of the family. However, these characteristics seem less marked than years ago. If raised properly, most Miniatures are friendly, well-balanced, not excitable. Nevertheless, they do better in homes, or in small numbers, than in large kennels. Like bright children, they may become bored and get into mischief with nothing to do. Take your Miniature with you whenever you can. He will love it and receive plenty of admiration, both from those who know the breed and from those to whom it is a novelty. But teach him, also, to behave quietly when left alone, for there are always some places where dogs are not allowed or are unwelcome. If he fusses when left by himself, try turning the radio on low. This may make him feel he has company and prevent his crying or scratching the furniture.

In deciding whether to acquire a dog or a bitch, several things must be considered. If you plan to become a breeder, by all means get a bitch—the best you can possibly afford. Breeding opportunities for males are rare unless they are really outstanding, and it it is much more satisfactory to put your money into a good bitch and the stud fee to a first-class dog than to buy a pair.

When choosing a pet, many novices formerly took for granted that they should buy a male. This tended to keep the prices of males higher except for breeding stock. In an effort to offset this, breeders stressed the qualities of the bitch as a pet until the price differential has largely disappeared. Individual disposition is more important than sex in a pet, and males are very lovable.

Many owners maintain that bitches are more affectionate, quieter, less inclined to wander, and easier to train. A bitch comes in season twice a year, as a rule, and must be confined for two to

17

Too young to leave home—4 weeks and 1 day old.

Still in the rough—Quarrydene Freida and Quarrydene Fritzi.

18

three weeks, even if she is not bred. On the other hand, a male will be attracted by a bitch in heat any time during the year. A bitch may be spayed (not "spaded"). However, that not only eliminates the possibility of her ever having puppies, but also makes her ineligible for showing in breed classes, though not in obedience trials. When choosing a puppy for a pet, unless one has a strong preference as to sex, it may be well to let this be determined by what is available.

The other important decision to make is that of age. Many people prefer a puppy of weaning age or a little older. This has both advantages and disadvantages. Puppies are usually lower in price than older dogs of good quality, but there is always more uncertainty as to how they will finally turn out. Any well-bred puppy who is not a cull will be playful and attractive. He or she may prove to be an excellent specimen, even a champion. There is always the gambler's hope of picking up a flyer at a moderate price, for the younger the litter the less likely the owner is to be sure of retaining the best for himself. Then, puppies are fun. If you have the time, patience, and experience to raise one, you miss a lot if you do not do so. And if you know how to handle him properly you can bring him up your own way, with no bad habits. On the other hand, the puppy that is adorable at six or eight weeks may be just average by six months or a year of age. But by that time you may not care. He is your dog, and you would rather have him than a champion.

When you buy an older dog you can see how he has developed. A puppy, on the other hand, may grow too big, he may prove to be undershot when his second teeth come in, he may be too long in body, or develop other faults which did not show at a few weeks of age. Even an experienced fancier may be fooled. If you buy an older dog, you can tell more accurately what you are getting and you usually pay accordingly. Barring unusual circumstances such as illness, moving, or an urgent need for cash which may induce the breeder to part with a good one for less than he normally would, the price of the older dog is likely to reflect his quality more closely than does the price of the puppy. Or, to put it another way, you are not so likely to buy an older dog for less than he is really worth. Puppy prices are based on the general market price modified by pedigree, the breeder's estimate of future quality, and how anxious he is to sell. If he has a lot of puppies and the demand is normal, he

19

may prefer to make a sale at once rather than feed the puppy for several weeks or months. Unless he is a real show prospect, he may be harder to sell at four or five months of age than when he was eight weeks old. Even an increase in price may have been offset by the additional expense of food and care. A breeder with good stock and several bitches usually cannot keep all his outstanding puppies. The younger they are the harder it is to be sure which will really be the best. Still, though champions have been purchased at a couple of months old, it does not happen often. At a pet price you usually get a pet.

Some people hesitate to buy an older dog for fear he will not be happy in a new home and will pine for his old one. This is sometimes true if the dog is several years old or has been a very special pet. However, a dog which has been one of several and is not much over a year old should adjust without great difficulty if he is allowed to take his time. A more probable source of trouble is the kennel dog that has received little attention beyond having been given food and ordinary physical care. If untrained, he may be hard to housebreak, or he may have developed undesirable habits, such as barking. Even more important, like a child brought up in an institution instead of a home, he may be shy or unable to adjust himself to a different environment. Some breeds seem to do all right under mass production and kennel conditions. Other do not, and Miniature Schnauzers are among the latter. The brighter and more affectionate the puppy, the more he needs occupation, affection, and training. Sitting by himself in a kennel with nothing to do is bad for him.

The best advice in determining the age at which to buy is to consider all the circumstances involved. Do you know anything about raising puppies, or are you willing to learn? Have you the time and the patience to train one? And have you the facilities? You cannot expect to train a puppy properly unless he is with you. If puddles on the floor upset you, if you are away from home most of the time, if you cannot control your small children's behavior, if you live up several flights of stairs, do not try to train a young puppy. And when buying an older dog, look for one which has been raised in the family if possible, is friendly with strangers, behaves on a leash or in the car, and is in good health. One of the most satisfied customers I ever had bought a dog over a year old. He was whelped in the kitchen, raised with the children, and kept as a house dog until he grew a little too large to show. I hated to sell him, but I did not have room to keep him. While he missed me at first, he was very well behaved and settled down quickly in his new home.

The novice planning to buy a Miniature Schnauzer has various ways of locating what he wants, depending somewhat upon where he lives. There may be ads in the local paper. If there is a dog show in the vicinity the exhibitors often have puppies for sale themselves, or they may know other breeders who have. All-breed dog magazines, on sale at shows, may have advertisements of kennels within driving distance. Failing these, one can write to The American Kennel Club, 51 Madison Avenue, New York City, for the names of local breeders. Or one can buy by mail.

Buying by mail enlarges the range of possible choice, which may be a real advantage. On the other hand, both buyer and seller are dependent upon the reliability and knowledge of the other party to an even greater degree than in a direct sale. The buyer misses the chance to select the puppy that appeals to him personally. Even those from the same litter, with no great difference in quality, may vary in appeal. One buyer falls for the cute, bright little fellow, another for the big, good-natured clown. The most careful, written description cannot take the place of picking one out for yourself.

Moreover, the experienced seller can more easily size up his customer face to face. And customers do change their minds. They come looking for a six-months-old male and depart delighted with a ten-weeks-old bitch, or the reverse. Everyone concerned in the deal may be perfectly satisfied—yet a responsible breeder could not possibly have substituted one dog for the other when shipping sight unseen. A puppy may be entirely as represented and still not be at all what the novice buyer expects or actually wants. And the seller who really cares for his dogs does not like to think of their going to buyers who will not know how to care for them properly. The late Albert Payson Terhune of Collie fame used to refuse to sell to buyers unless they came for their puppies and took them home, thereby avoiding shipment by express.

While the mail buyer may sometimes receive a dog which is not as good as the seller claimed, the seller, too, faces problems. A dog which does not please the buyer and is returned for any reason may have contracted some disease in the course of the trip and infect others upon his return. Equally, of course, a dog may leave the kennel in good health and contract an illness on the road. Often neither buyer nor seller can tell positively which was the actual truth, although a veterinarian's health certificate before shipment is helpful. Since buyers are sometimes financially irresponsible, sellers with good reputations and established businesses are reluctant to ship c.o.d., and less reputable breeders may take advantage of the fact to boost their own sales.

So the best advice to the novice is to visit the kennel in person and select his own dog if possible. If you want a show dog, try to get the advice of someone who knows the breed and buy one old enough so that its quality is evident. You will pay more than for a puppy, but you will be surer of what you are getting. Have your veterinarian examine the dog *immediately,* so that there can be no question of his good health at the time of purchase. And remember that the wise breeder tries to keep his best prospects for himself.

If you are interested in a pet, you may, of course, later change your mind and desire to show. If you have bought a dog of show quality then you have no problem. On the other hand, the breeder of a first-class dog may be reluctant to sell to a customer who intends to hide his light under a bushel. To be known as the breeder of top quality stock is the best of advertising. But if one's top dogs are never shown, this advantage is lost. So the breeder may set his price higher by way of compensation. Or he may legitimately try to sell you one that is not a show dog, at a lower price. A dog that is a trifle too large or too small, not of the choicest color, too soft in coat or somewhat lacking in whisker, for instance, may have wonderful temperament and make the best of pets. If this is clearly understood by both parties the sale can be to the advantage of both. On the other hand, do not ask for a pet at a pet price and then complain loudly that your dog does not win in the show ring. And some breeders prefer not to sell culls at any price, on the theory that people who see them will think that the kennel produces poor quality in general.

Choosing a puppy from six to twelve weeks old is not easy, even for experienced fanciers, if show quality is desired. Healthy puppies are much alike at birth, varying chiefly in color and size. As they develop, differences become increasingly apparent. The best one or two in the litter may stand out, but even the most promising can change enormously, and poor food and care may spoil a prospective champion. The perfectly gorgeous puppy who finishes oversize is a heartbreak for the exhibitor but can prove a grand pet.

Good health should come first. The occasional runt which is small but otherwise good may respond amazingly to devoted, individual care, but the same care lavished on the best puppy is much more likely to pay off. And no amount of care can develop quality in a mutt.

Healthy puppies are bright-eyed, alert, and lively. They eat well, play hard, and flop down to sleep when they are tired. At birth, Miniature Schnauzer coats are rather short and smooth, but by six or eight weeks of age, the top coat has begun to grow out. This first puppy coat is usually much darker in color than the permanent one. Sometimes it is nearly black, but when the coat is turned back it shows gray underneath. The adult coat usually resembles this undercoat. Solid black Miniatures, which are growing in popularity, are black from birth, with black undercoats, while black and silvers have black bodies with cream or silver markings on the head, feet, and the root of the tail.

Puppies a few weeks old should have good bone. Their legs should be bigger around in proportion to their size than those of an adult dog. Their front legs should be straight when observed from the front. Viewed from the side the hind legs make an angle at the hocks, but a six-week-old puppy still tends to brace his hind legs under him a little, to support the weight of his body, which is heavy in proportion. Ears bend over close to the head until they are cropped (usually at eight to ten weeks old). An occasional puppy may have small ears which stand erect like a Scottie's at two to three months old, but the correct ear carriage for an uncropped Miniature is a drop ear, like that of a Fox Terrier. Cropping a puppy changes his expression very decidedly. Some idea of the effect of cropping, however, can be obtained by holding the ears up and together at the back of the head.

By six or eight weeks old a puppy's whiskers should be sprouting sufficiently to indicate that he will have a good crop. Unusually developed whiskers and fluffy body coat, however, are signs that the puppy is inclined to have a soft coat. A rather smooth, flat body coat at this age points toward a hard coat at maturity. If whiskers do

23

not show signs of sprouting and the body coat is unusually hard, the dog when grown may lack sufficient whisker. Or the end result may be a better quality coat which takes longer to develop. Big, soft whiskers and a soft body coat are much more common faults at the present time than lack of whiskers and furnishings.

The eyes should be dark brown, and not too large or round. First teeth should be cut by six weeks of age. A serious fault is the undershot mouth where the lower teeth protrude beyond the upper ones. The front teeth should not meet exactly, since they wear down too fast in that case. The upper teeth should pass outside the lower in a "scissors bite." If there is noticeable space between the upper and lower teeth when the mouth is closed the puppy is overshot, which is also a fault. Mouths should be examined, but it sometimes happens that a puppy with a perfectly good mouth as a youngster becomes undershot when his second teeth come through at about four to six months of age. Not much can be done about this, but it is well to pull the loose first teeth when the second teeth are coming through, since the root of the first tooth which stays in too long may force the second out of line. An undershot jaw is much more serious than a couple of teeth out of line.

In general, the younger the puppy the bigger his head and the shorter his legs in proportion to his body. After eight or nine weeks of age the legs grow longer, the body loses its puppy roundness and compactness. By three months old the puppy, already cropped, begins to look like an adult but on a smaller scale. From then on he grows bigger, and usually lankier up to about four or five months. Then he begins to fill out again and by six months is often practically grown, though he may gain as much as an inch or more in additional height. Small puppies usually mature more quickly than larger ones, and stop growing sooner. Consequently, they may well look more mature at six months. The larger ones still have a puppy look and need to tighten and harden. Their muscles are still soft, and less able to handle their greater size and weight. Miniature Schnauzers are sometimes shown in the puppy class at six months, only to grow too big later. However, a more slowly maturing puppy may prove better in the long run, and retain his quality to a greater age. Even at eight or nine years old some of these veterans make an impressive appearance.

Size is one of the most difficult matters to judge in young puppies.

Eight-week-old pepper and salt puppies.

Black puppies at eight weeks.

Grown Miniature Schnauzers vary considerably, the preferred shoulder height being about 13 to 13½ inches. However, many individuals grow larger, and sometimes become too big to show. Others remain small. Very small specimens, too, are not acceptable in the show ring, and the minimum set by the 1958 Standard is 12 inches. However, I have been told that in some sections of the country, small ones are popular in the ring.

Puppies vary in size at birth, depending to some extent on the size of the litter. Sometimes one puppy is distinctly larger or smaller than the others, and as they grow older the difference in size may become either more or less marked. On the other hand, some litters are very even. Such figures as are available indicate that 3 to 5 pounds is a fair weight at eight weeks, with the average a little less than 4 pounds. At three months a well developed puppy probably weighs upwards of 7½ pounds, with 10 pounds a bit on the large side. More data is needed, however, to corroborate these figures, which are based on only a few litters. (See more detailed study in Part II, Chapter 5.)

It will be clear from the foregoing that the age of the puppy makes a big difference in his size and general appearance, and must be taken into consideration. If there are several of the same age and they can be compared to each other, slight differences become more apparent. At six or eight weeks the body should be short and deep. The distance from the withers (the top of the shoulders) to the root of the tail is important. It seems to be easier to judge body length at this age than a bit later. At three or four months the puppy is at his lankiest, and may appear too long, yet he may have correct proportions after his body and legs have finished developing. Body length is a point to be watched. So is a well-developed muzzle, not too short in proportion to the skull. Low-set, heavy ears will tend to make an uncropped puppy's head look short and broad, but become less important when he is cropped. The skull should be of moderate width, neither very narrow nor thick and broad. If there is a pronounced bony ridge on the side of the skull between the ear and eye the head may be too thick when the dog is grown.

The tail should be cut quite short, so that it is not more than once and a half or twice as long as it is thick, and should be carried high and alertly. However, it should not be set and carried so high

Litter at 3 months, cropped. Third and fourth from left became champions.

that it becomes a "squirrel tail" pointing forward toward the dog's head. "One o'clock" is about right.

Temperament is important in both a pet and a show dog. When competition becomes hot, the best shower, with plenty of personality, has an advantage. The dog that is either sluggish and indifferent or shy and nervous will not get to the top in fast company. Naturally, a pet should have a pleasing disposition and some authorities rate the importance of good temperament at 90% of the whole.

One fault the novice often overlooks is monorchidism or cryptorchidism in a male. The Miniature Schnauzer standard has disqualified both for the show ring since 1953, and in 1955 the American Kennel Club forbade their exhibition in any breed. Cryptorchids have neither testicle descended and are sterile, while most fanciers are reluctant to breed to a monorchid, which has only one testicle descended.

When choosing a puppy out of a litter, watch what happens when you first approach the pen, or when the puppies are turned loose in the room where you are sitting. Normal, friendly puppies should make friends readily. If they are accustomed to people they are likely to be curious and eager to be petted. If they have seen few or no strangers, and have not been handled by the breeder, they are likely to be more hesitant. If the dam is with them, watch her behavior. If she barks or is afraid of strangers, the puppies tend to imitate her. If other dogs in the kennel bark on all occasions, puppies easily acquire the habit. The boldest puppy in a litter may simply be bluffing—barking because he is a little frightened and hopes to scare away the visitor. Or he may be just full of pep. The puppy who takes his time and looks things over first, but then comes to make friends, may be more intelligent than his headlong brother. If the whole litter hesitates, it may be nothing more than not being accustomed to strangers. But if one puppy holds back more than the rest, tries to tuck his tail between his legs, and seems definitely frightened, go slow. He may be really shy. If so, he is usually a poor bargain at any price. Beware of choosing him out of pity for his nervousness.

When judging temperament, however, be reasonable. Do not grab a strange puppy by the legs or the scruff of the neck and sweep him up into the air. Do not shout at him, stamp at him, or thump him down suddenly. Speak quietly, move slowly, give him a chance to sniff your hand. Pick him up gently, but firmly enough so he is not afraid of falling. Remember he is just a baby and needs time to grow accustomed to strange sights, sounds, and smells, and to find out what they are all about.

Finally, choose the puppy that you like, that really appeals to you, and that likes you. Then, if you possibly can, carry him home in your arms, where he will feel warm and supported, not completely uprooted and deserted by everything familiar.

The age of the puppy you select may depend somewhat on circumstances. The younger he is the more care he will require. Puppies *can* be taken very young and reared successfully, but it requires a great deal of care and attention and is hard on both owner and puppy. Unless for some special reason, such as the illness of the dam, six weeks should be the minimum and eight is much better. If the Miniature Schnauzer puppy is cropped before being sold, he is likely to be at least ten weeks old by the time he is taken to his new home. Ears take ten days or two weeks to heal completely. A puppy should *never* be sold immediately after cropping. He needs to recover from the operation and be fully back to normal before facing the adjustments of a new home. The age at which cropping is done varies considerably, however, according to the method. A local anesthetic can be used earlier.

The breeder should give the new owner written information in regard to feeding—the number of meals per day, as well as the kind and amount of food. Growth requires two or three times as much food as maintenance, and a puppy's stomach is small. He therefore needs all the food he will readily clean up at a feeding. Four meals a day at two months old and three at three months are advised. Toward six months of age puppies often lose interest in the midday meal and can be cut down to two per day. Fresh water should always be available, though puppies drinking milk do not always want it. A puppy's "papers" should include a memorandum of the date and kind of innoculations he has received. The buyer's veterinarian will want to know this. If only temporary shots have been given there must be an interval for the immunity to wear off before permanent innoculations will "take." Most veterinarians use permanent innoculations requiring at least two shots, and if the series has been started but not finished it is important to know exactly what has been done. If the puppy has been wormed the date and kind should also be noted.

Reliable breeders will supply a pedigree giving the puppy's ancestors for at least three generations. This is for the owner's information only. A litter of purebred puppies should be registered with the American Kennel Club, which thereupon supplies individual application forms for each puppy in the litter. Some breeders register all their puppies individually and put names and numbers in a kennel record. Once registered, a dog's name cannot be changed, but many dogs go by a "call name." When a registered dog is sold, the owner signs the transfer form on the back of the registration. The new owner must also sign it, and send the form to the AKC, who will send back a form with the new owner's name. If the puppy has not been individually registered the breeder signs a blue application form. The buyer should sign this also, filling in a choice of two names for his puppy, and send it promptly to the AKC. The puppy is not registered until this has been done, and if the application is lost it may be difficult to replace later on.

What does the new puppy need? A light collar and lead, even though he is not leash-broken, may help prevent his escaping where he may be lost or hurt. Breeders often supply a small bag or can of the food he is used to. His bed should be free from drafts; a box, basket or carton in a quiet place of his own, with a comfortable pad or old blanket. If you take him to bed the first few nights, until he feels at home, it will *not* mean you cannot train him to sleep alone later. If he must sleep alone, a clock with a loud tick may help.

Spend plenty of time with a new puppy, but let him make his own advances and do not try to make him "tough." Remember, he is still a baby. Let him take his time. Play with him, but let him rest when he becomes tired. If you want him to like children, don't let him be teased, frightened or hurt, even if no harm is meant. Don't disturb him while eating, but turn his dish or offer a bit from your hand occasionally. Then he will not be afraid you will rob him of his food. Some time it may be necessary to take away something dangerous he has picked up.

House-breaking is usually easy if done regularly from the start. Because a puppy eats often, he must be taken out often: the first thing in the morning, after a nap, after meals, and the last thing at night. Taking him out every hour for the first day or two will pay dividends in the end. As the puppy grows bigger he can wait longer. He will not want to soil his bed if he can help it. If confined to a small area, with newspapers on the floor, he can be accustomed to use the paper. This is gradually removed till it covers only a small space. If he is taken outside he will select a spot. Always go to this spot, praise him when he relieves himself, and soon he will associate the place with the idea. If he is forgotten and left too long, an "accident" is not his fault. Don't scold him for mistakes until he understands, and praise him when he shows you he wants to go out. By four or five months, if the puppy has been properly trained, he should have sufficient control to go for three or four hours without having to relieve himself.

2

What Makes a Good
Miniature Schnauzer?

IN order to assess accurately the quality of your own or other people's dogs it is necessary to read and interpret the breed standard. This requires experience. To the novice, Miniatures look much alike except for size and decided variations in color. Gradually, with study and familiarity, the differences become clearer and the finer points more evident.

It is difficult to give an accurate description of a breed in words so that the novice can form a correct picture of what his dog should be like. Actually, in the early days of a breed, the standard of perfection is likely to represent a breeder's ideal, striven for but not entirely realized. As the breed improves, through careful selection, the standard is sometimes revised. Or it may remain the same so far as words go but be interpreted more strictly. On the other hand, without any change in the wording of the standard, a different type of dog may become popular. This may be due to the influence of some particular dog who stamps his type on his progeny and whose outstanding wins influence both judges and exhibitors. Sometimes experienced breeders who have not exhibited for a considerable period, but then return to the ring, observe wide variation from the type to which they were accustomed.

The biggest asset a novice can have in learning the fine points of the breed is a good visual memory. Can you look at a dog and then shut your eyes and see a mental picture of him? If so, you are lucky. See as many good ones as possible, file them away in your memory, and you will soon develop a composite picture of how a Miniature Schnauzer should look. Compare your own dogs to this mental picture and you will be able to judge whether they are good, bad, or in between. But be sure that you study really good Miniature Schnauzers. Dogs may win in poor competition or under judges who are not thoroughly familiar with the breed. Or they may be so good in some respects that they win in spite of certain other faults. Be certain you know which qualities in a winner are good and which are not, and do not confuse the two. Remember, also, that skillful trimming and showing may emphasize virtues and cover up faults. Ask questions, and handle a dog yourself when possible. Visit kennels if you can, and become as familiar as possible with the breed. If you have a poor visual memory it will be harder and take longer to develop good judgment.

In order to fault your own dogs properly it will be helpful to show them in competition to obtain the opinion of knowledgeable judges and experienced breeders. Finally, if you can, go over your dog carefully alongside a really good one, comparing them point for point. Get someone else to pose and move your dog for you, so that you can see how he looks from ringside as well as from up close. Be honest with yourself; it pays in the long run. Far too many old-timers, and not merely novices, suffer from "kennel blindness." If you cannot see and recognize the faults in your own dogs and the virtues in other people's, or vice versa, you are not likely to reach the top, or to stay there for long if you do get there by chance. And beware of confusing a dog with his owner. You may dislike the latter, with or without good reason. To condemn a good dog on that account only reflects upon your knowledge and fairness, while to refuse to breed to a sire because of strained relations with the owner may be simply cutting off your nose to spite your face.

Nowadays, Miniature fanciers often speak of the "old-fashioned type" or of the "Schnauzer type" as opposed to the "Terrier type."

Poor head: wrong expression, ears low set
and badly carried.

Good head, profile view.

What is actually meant by these terms varies a good deal according to the person who is using them. As I look back over 40 years of Miniature Schnauzers in America it seems to me that there is often less change than people think. There are certainly some differences. The average is better and the quality more even, but many of the old dogs would still be good today.

One of the major changes is certainly size. The original American breed standard set a maximum shoulder height of 12 inches for both sexes. By 1934 this had been changed so that the rule read 10½ to 13½ inches for males and 10 to 12½ inches for females, but no male was to be disqualified for oversize unless over 14 inches, and no female unless over 13 inches. This difference reflected the fact that dogs average larger than bitches, and was more logical than the breed standard as now approved, which sets the size for both sexes between 12 and 14 inches, with the same disqualifications for both. Logically, a bitch close to 14 inches is very likely to have oversized sons, but since many brood bitches are not shown in any case, and bitches over 13½ are less likely to win, it is doubtful if this lumping together of the sexes makes a great difference in actual practice. Too small and toyish appearing dogs are not typical and should be penalized. After the 1958 revision both sexes were explicitly disqualified if under 12 inches. Nevertheless, some breeders prefer small ones and some judges do put them up. Unquestionably, the tiny puppies appeal to a certain group of the public, but since they occur from time to time in almost any bloodline they may be sold strictly as pets without deliberately deviating from the standard.

Within the standard range, individuals and local areas may have size preferences, which frequently vary from time to time. When there are too many big ones there will be a reaction in favor of a smaller type, while if this is carried to extremes it may produce a counterreaction.

To measure size by eye accurately is practically impossible. In a class of small ones a 13-inch dog will look big. In a class of big ones the same 13 inches may look small. Also, a heavy-boned dog looks larger than a light, leggy one. The only way to be certain is to measure with a scale which has a sliding arm that can be moved up and down. Even then, a dog closely stripped will measure a little less than when he is in heavy coat. I have heard it claimed by experienced breeders that most of the top sires in the East are very close to 14 inches if measured carefully, but I cannot vouch for such assertion. In other sections of the country smaller dogs are frequently put up, but this varies from time to time.

Color is another aspect of the breed which has definitely changed in the last 20 years or so. In the twenties there were many so-called pepper and salt dogs which were really almost reds, and the vast majority had a lot of red-brown or yellow in their coats. Later the silver gray, chinchilla, or "pure" pepper and salts, with the light portions of the hair pale cream or off-white, predominated in the show ring. The "bicolors"—solid black with silver, cream, or light tannish markings—are somewhat more common than formerly. This color has always been recognized by the American standard and still is. It was originally recognized in Germany, where I recall at least one bicolored Sieger (champion), but I understand that the present rule bars anything but pepper and salt or solid black there.

There have been several American bicolor champions, and personally I am sorry there are not more bicolors shown. Good ones are very flashy, and they provide variety on the bench and in the ring. A surprising number of the general public admire very dark pepper and salts, which as young puppies may closely resemble bicolors, and I think that if bred and shown in greater number they would broaden the appeal of the breed. Most breeders sell their bicolors as pets when they do appear in a litter from pepper and salt parents, and there have been very few recorded matings of two bicolors. Those of which I have detailed results produced all bicolor puppies. Recently interest has increased. Walsh's Frosty Charmer, a bicolor, finished in Canada in 1964, and others have done so since.

In Germany the solid blacks have their own classes and Sieger titles. They have always been popular, and a number of kennels breed them exclusively. Blacks occur in the early generations of all Miniature Schnauzers when the pedigrees are carried far back. Solid blacks have never been very numerous here. They had a bad start in the 1920's, for the few blacks imported at that time were poor in quality, inclined to be soft in coat, lacking whisker, and often undershot. Their deficiencies were blamed on their color. From time to time there have been attempts to popularize the blacks, but many judges, as well as breeders and the public in general, seem unaware that they are a recognized color. Since 1958 concerted attempts by the Black Miniature Schnauzer Fanciers' Association

Good front.

Out at elbows.

Wide front.

37

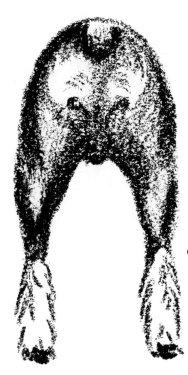

Good rear standing.

Cowhocked, low tail-set.

38

have begun to bear fruit, though there is still a long way to go. A few shows have divided the open classes by color.

Blacks may prove of real value in arresting the tendency which seems to be developing in some strains for lighter and lighter dogs. Not only did the standard declare that very light, whitish colors are a fault, and (since 1953) that pure white is a disqualification, but bleached-looking, faded color is unattractive. Very light dogs also tend to lose the dark face markings which add so greatly to a Miniature Schnauzer's expression.

Coat is, I think, undeniably softer than used to be the case. Leg furnishings and whiskers are more profuse, and this almost inevitably means a tendency to softer body coat. The really harsh, wire coats, which often went with sparse whisker and leg hair, have become scarce. There is a tendency to trim more closely on the body so as to minimize the softness which is less apparent to the eye when the coat is short, while some heads are left with so much eyebrow that the dog resembles a Kerry Blue. This is not the proper appearance for a Miniature Schnauzer. The remedy is twofold—a correct trim and more emphasis on breeding hard coats. The difference in leg furnishings 25 years ago can be judged readily from a study of the photographs of leading winners of those days.

Size can be measured and color described with reasonable accuracy. Conformation, however, is much more difficult to put into words. How is the novice to decide when a skull "fairly broad between the ears" becomes too broad, or when the neck becomes too short and thick or too long and light? When does the "sturdily built, nearly square proportion of body length to height" become too thickset on the one hand or too racy in outline on the other?

Since no living thing remains unchanged and breeders are always striving for greater perfection, there is in all breeds an inclination to exaggerate. Greater size, greater weight for the big breeds; tinier toys; short-legged dogs which practically drag on the ground; heads so big that natural whelping becomes nearly impossible; streamlining which smooths away a breed's character, these are some of the forms which the itch to improve upon nature may take.

In Miniature Schnauzers the trend has been toward an increase in "Terrier type." This has no historical basis, for the breed does not by descent or relationship belong to the same Group as the British Terriers. The Schnauzer began his recorded history as a yard

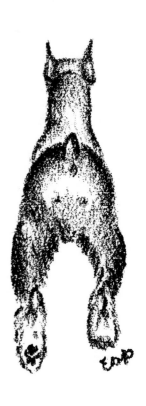

Good front moving.   Good rear moving.

40

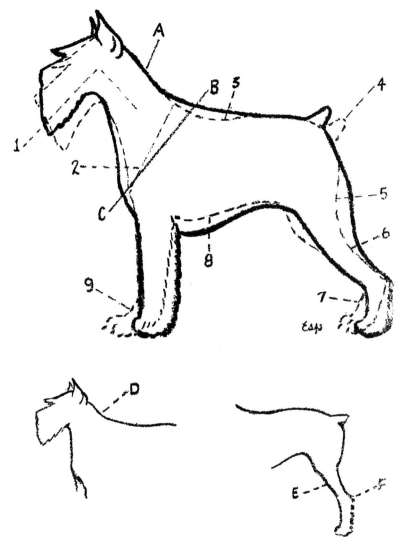

FAULTS, SIDE VIEW

1. Head set on badly
2. Upright shoulders
3. Soft-backed
4. Low tail set
5, 6, 7. Weak rear

8. Shallow chest
9. Weak pasterns
A, B, C. Good neck and shoulders
D. Short neck
E. Straight stifle
F. High hock

41

and stable dog, a great ratter and killer of vermin, with a substantial infusion of cattle droving blood.

The United States and Canada are the only countries in which the Miniature Schnauzer is classed in the Terrier Group. In England they are classed as Non-Sporting and in Germany as Luxushund. German breeders simply laugh when told that the breed is considered a Terrier. Originally, all three sizes competed in the Working Group here, and no one seems to know upon what grounds the change to Terriers was made. Later (1938, I believe) the Standard Schnauzers were moved back to the Working Group. The Miniatures remained among the Terriers because the American Kennel Club declined to put them into the Working Group again and the alternative offer of the Toy Group was firmly turned down. The possibility of a transfer to Non-Sporting was actively discussed in 1937 and the American Miniature Schnauzer Club actually voted at a meeting to ask the AKC to make this change of classification. However, the matter was later referred to a mail vote of the entire membership and no action was taken.

In the broader sense of general character and type, Miniature Schnauzers do resemble terriers more closely than any other Group. The Miniature Schnauzer is an excellent ratter and vermin killer. Probably he could and would "go to ground" as readily as any of the present day Fox or Scottish Terriers, though I have no knowledge of the breed being so employed. Certainly it is closer in temperament to the alert, active Terriers than to the gun dogs or Hounds. Nevertheless, a typical Miniature Schnauzer should exhibit a strong dash of working temperament, without the nervous, yappy disposition of some Terriers. And this "big dog" temperament is a decided asset in obedience training as well as for companionship in the home.

The Miniature Schnauzer originated in the attempt to produce a small scale Standard Schnauzer, indistinguishable from the larger breed except for size, but this ideal was never realized by the breed as a whole. During the 1920's and early 1930's, color, heads, and bone were usually sufficiently different to distinguish between the two breeds even when size was disregarded. Then, as color began to approach the Schnauzer norm, "Terrier type" began to play a part in the Miniature's development, while the Standard Schnauzer remained substantially unchanged.

The breed standard calls for a robust, cobby little dog, with a fairly broad skull, a sloping shoulder and a moderately broad chest. The ideal, in fact, resembles a little draft horse or Shetland pony rather than a race horse, and should give an appearance of solidity and strength, with nothing carried to extremes. This is emphasized again and again in the standard—"fairly broad skull," "moderately blunt" muzzle, "somewhat sloping" shoulders, chest neither too narrow nor too broad, tail set "moderately high," coat "neither smooth nor long" and "trimmed only enough to accentuate the body outline"—all stress the desire for balance and moderation.

Certainly the breed has improved in many respects during the past 15 or 20 years. At least in the show ring there are fewer weak backs, long bodies, lowset tails, and overbuilt rears. Snipey muzzles, heavy skulls and short heads are also less numerous. On the other hand, there has been a strong trend toward streamlining the Miniature Schnauzer until there is some danger that he may eventually become merely a pepper and salt Wire-haired Fox Terrier with cropped ears and a shorter tail. In order to compete with the Terriers on their own ground, the Miniature has tended to approach more and more closely those breeds in the Group which he superficially resembles most closely—the Wire-hair, the Kerry Blue, the Welsh Terrier. To carry this too far would sacrifice the very characteristics which make him unique. It would be well for breeders to take a good look at the best Standard Schnauzers at regular intervals, thereby refreshing their memory of the original Schnauzer type and correcting too great deviations.

The fact that at many all-breed shows a Terrier specialist judges Miniature Schnauzers along with the rest of the Terrier breeds, and then often picks the Group winner, is bound to have a strong effect upon type over a period of years. At best, such judges have Terrier background and point of view. They are not Miniature specialists, and even when they have studied the breed standard carefully they are likely to be influenced unconsciously by their mental picture of the Terrier ideal. So the sloping shoulder gives way to a "Terrier front" with its corresponding stilty gait. The Schnauzer spring of ribs yields to flatter, slab sides. The head becomes increasingly longer and narrower. And the breed constantly moves further and further from the basic Schnauzer type unless this tendency is corrected at intervals.

Under all-round judges, who are better acquainted with other breeds besides Terriers—including the Standard Schnauzer as seen in the Working Group—the typical breed character has a better chance to assert itself in the breed classes. When it comes to Group competition, however, another problem arises. The Terrier judge who has put up a Terrier type to Best of Breed is more likely to place such a dog in the Group than the Schnauzer type which the breed specialist or all-rounder may have selected. And so when competition for Best in Show is reached, judged by an all-rounder, he in turn may look somewhat askance at the Terrier judge's selection. I believe that more Miniature Schnauzers would go Best in Show if the breed competed in either the Non-Sporting or the Working Group, but this is only my personal opinion.

Understand clearly that I do not want to turn the clock back, but I think we have gone as far as we safely can in the direction of longer heads and Terrier type generally. To go further would be dangerous, for in the long run the Miniature Schnauzer would lose his individuality and character. If we study our breed standard and stick to it, however, this cannot happen.

Among the most prevalent faults at the moment seem to be poor rears, a problem that was disturbing breeders nearly 20 years ago and still seems to be unsolved. With breeding stock so generally related as most of it is, once one goes back three or four generations, special efforts should be made to take advantage of whatever individuals excel in this respect, both when planning matings and selecting puppies to keep. The drawings especially prepared to illustrate the various sections of the Miniature Schnauzer's anatomy show both faults and good points, and illustrate the dog in motion as well as when standing still.

For a thorough understanding of dog anatomy and movement, how the various parts interact, and the application of the facts described, breeders and judges should carefully study *The Dog in Action* by McDowell Lyon (Howell Book House Inc., 1966). In light of this, it would appear that certain items in the breed standard should be carefully scrutinized and probably reconsidered. The book includes far more than the title implies and explains much that even experienced breeders have failed to grasp.

By and large, temperament, too, has improved over the years, and its importance cannot be too highly stressed. There seem to be more happy extroverts and fewer reserved individuals. Regardless of show-ring success, no breed or strain will continue to be popular if its disposition cannot be depended on. When selecting breeding stock, therefore, temperament deserves prime consideration.

One mistake made by far too many breeders today is a tendency to force their puppies ahead too fast. Instead of showing in the Puppy Class and waiting until maturity to show their dogs in the Open Class, owners show their puppies in the Open Class and expect them to become champions by nine or ten months of age. As a result, many quick maturers go off badly later on and have to be retired when they should be in their prime. Yet, being champions, they are often bred on the strength of their show records. The dog who matures slowly, but holds his quality, is all too often discarded as a poor show prospect and sold as a pet. The result is an increasing tendency to quick maturing, flash-in-the-pan stock, which has a bad effect upon breed quality in the long run.

By way of final caution, I should like to emphasize two related points. A good dog is more than the sum total of many different parts. Look at him as a whole, while not forgetting to analyze carefully the various details. Does he strike you at first glance as a good one, typical of the breed and full of quality? And remember that real breed character and quality can outweigh a number of lesser faults, or even one or two big ones. A dog with no outstanding faults may be equally lacking in outstanding quality. He may be just plain mediocre. Some great dogs have had decided faults, but they were great in spite of them. Particularly in choosing breeding stock, go for quality first, and try to compensate for any faults by a choice of breeding partner or rigid selection in the puppies. But be sure the quality is there. Do not strain at a gnat and swallow a commonplace camel. With the present increase in breed popularity it is of the utmost importance to retain its quality and breed only from top stock.

3

The Miniature
Schnauzer Standard

DURING 1956 a committee of the American Miniature Schnauzer Club made a study of the breed Standard and
presented a revision, which was approved by a mail vote of the
members in the spring of 1957 and submitted to the American
Kennel Club for their approval. Various portions are reworded to
make them clearer. The principle differences are:

A change of eye description from "medium" to "small."

Inclusion of a detailed description of the proper gait.

Change of minimum size to 12 inches, maximum 14 inches, and
the ideal 13½ inches.

Stipulation that the short tail, typical of the breed, should be just
long enough to be clearly visible over the topline.

Omission of "very light, whitish or tiger colors" from the list of
faults.

Under *Color* the somewhat confusing statement in the last line
that "All the salt and pepper section must be black" means that
bicolors have black where the salt and peppers are darker on the

body, while both colors have light markings in the same areas on the head, legs and underbody. The color known as pepper and salt is produced by banded hairs with dark tips, a light portion, and dark again toward the root. The general effect is gray, varying from light to dark, but the banding should be definite.

THE BREED STANDARD OF THE MINIATURE SCHNAUZER
(approved May 13, 1958)

General Appearance—The Miniature Schnauzer is a robust, active dog of terrier type, resembling his larger cousin, the Standard Schnauzer, in general appearance, and of an alert, active disposition. He is sturdily built, nearly square in proportion of body length to height, with plenty of bone, and without any suggestion of toyishness.

Head—Strong and rectangular, its width diminishing slightly from ears to eyes, and again to the tip of the nose. The forehead is unwrinkled. The topskull is flat and fairly long. The foreface is parallel to the topskull, with a slight stop, and is at least as long as the topskull. The muzzle is strong in proportion to the skull; it ends in a moderately blunt manner, with thick whiskers which accentuate the rectangular shape of the head. *Teeth*—The teeth meet in a scissors bite. That is, the upper front teeth overlap the lower front teeth in such a manner that the inner surface of the upper incisors barely touches the outer surface of the lowest incisors when the mouth is closed. *Eyes*—Small, dark brown and deep-set. They are oval in appearance and keen in expression. *Ears*—When cropped the ears are identical in shape and length, with pointed tips. They are in balance with the head and not exaggerated in length. They are set high on the skull and carried perpendicularly at the inner edges, with as little bell as possible along the outer edges. When uncropped, the ears are small and V-shaped, folding close to the skull.

Neck—Strong and well arched, blending into the shoulders, and with the skin fitting tightly at the throat.

Body—Short and deep, with the brisket extending at least to the elbows. Ribs are well sprung and deep, extending well back to a

47

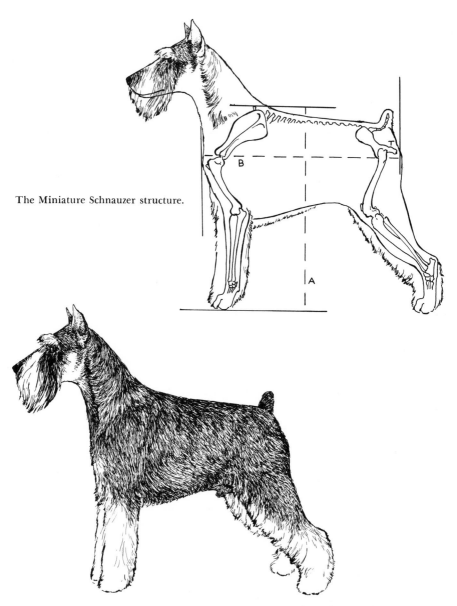

The Miniature Schnauzer structure.

Correct type. (This illustration and the one above by Lorraine L. Bush, from the *Illustrated Discussion of the Miniature Schnauzer Standard*, published by the American Miniature Schnauzer Club.)

short loin. The underbody does not present a tucked-up appearance at the flank. The topline is straight; it declines slightly from the withers to the base of the tail. The over-all length from chest to stern bone equals the height at the withers.

Forequarters—The forequarters have flat, somewhat sloping shoulders and high withers. Forelegs are straight and parallel when viewed from all sides. They have strong pasterns and good bone. They are separated by a fairly deep brisket which precludes a pinched front. The elbows are close, and the ribs spread gradually from the first rib so as to allow space for the elbows to move close to the body. *Hindquarters*—The hindquarters have strong-muscled, slanting thighs: they are well bent at the stifles and straight from hock to so-called heel. There is sufficient angulation so that, in stance, the hocks extend beyond the tail. The hindquarters never appear overbuilt or higher than the shoulders. *Feet*—Short and round (cat-feet) with thick, black pads. The toes are arched and compact.

Action—The trot is the gait at which movement is judged. The dog must gait in a straight line. Coming on, the forelegs are parallel, with the elbows close to the body. The feet turn neither inward nor outward. Going away, the hind legs are parallel from the hocks down, and travel wide. Viewed from the side, the forelegs have a good reach, while the hind legs have a strong drive with good pick-up of hocks.

Tail—Set high and carried erect. It is docked only long enough to be clearly visible over the topline of the body when the dog is in proper length of coat.

Coat—Double, with a hard, wiry outer coat and a close undercoat. The body coat should be plucked. When in show condition, the proper length is not less than three-quarters of an inch except on neck, ears and skull. Furnishings are fairly thick but not silky.

Size—From 12 to 14 inches. Ideal size 13½ inches. (*See disqualifications.*)

Color—The recognized colors are salt and pepper, black and silver, and solid black. The typical color is salt and pepper in shades of gray; tan shading is permissible. The salt and pepper mixture fades out to light gray or silver white in the eyebrows, whiskers, cheeks, under throat, across chest, under tail, leg furnishings under body, and inside legs. The light under-body hair is not to rise higher on the sides of the body than the front elbows.

The black and silvers follow the same pattern as the salt and peppers. The entire salt-and-pepper section must be black.

Black is the only solid color allowed. It must be a true black with no gray hairs and no brown tinge except where the whiskers may have become discolored. A small white spot on the chest is permitted.

Faults

Type—Toyishness, raciness, or coarseness. *Structure*—Head coarse and cheeky. Chest too broad or shallow in brisket. Tail set low. Sway or roach back. Bowed or cowhocked hindquarters. Loose elbows. *Action*—Sidegaiting. Paddling in front, or high hackney knee action. Weak hind action. *Coat*—Too soft or too smooth and slick in appearance. *Temperament*—Shyness or viciousness. *Bite*—Undershot or overshot jaw. Level bite. *Eyes*—Light and/or large and prominent in appearance.

Disqualifications

Dogs or bitches under 12 inches or over 14 inches. Color solid white or white patches on the body.

4

Breed Origins

THE Schnauzer (pronounced *Shnowtser*—the German z always sounds like *ts*) is a breed which lays claim to considerable age, for specimens have been identified in paintings by Dürer at the close of the fifteenth century (1492) and by Rembrandt in the seventeenth. The origin of the breed has been variously traced. *Life* magazine's dog genealogy chart (published January 31, 1949) begins with Tomarctus. From this prehistoric ancestor of the dog was derived *canis familiaris Inostranzewi* whence are descended, in successive steps, the Molossian, the Tibetan Mastiff, the Alaunt, the Mastiff, and the Brabanter. From the Brabanter came the still existing Bouvier des Flandres, and thence the Schnauzer (Standard size), which is said to be a source of the Doberman and the Manchester Terrier. On the other hand, Fitzinger, a Viennese zoologist (1802–1884), described the Wire-haired Pinscher (by which name the Schnauzer was then known) as a cross between the Dog of Boulogne and the Spitz. Reichenbach, in 1836, described

51

a dog which has been claimed as an early form of Wire-haired Pinscher, but the description and the name "Gryphus" seem to point, rather, to an ancestor of the Brussels Griffon. Perhaps, however, it was the Wirehaired Pointing Griffon's source.

The term *pinscher*, while said to be of English origin, was used by Weiss in 1852 in his German translation of Youatt's book to signify Terriers. During the 1930's a German-born American Schnauzer fancier reported that his grandfather remembered the dogs of about 1850 and declared that they came from a cross of wolf-gray Spitz and German black Poodle upon the old German Pinscher stock. These old Pinschers were described as black and tan, or fawn (*rehfarbig*), which might account for the tendency to fawn or reddish undercoat seen in many of the early importations. About 1900 Georg Goeller of Stuttgart is said by this same fancier to have exhibited real salt and pepper dogs, while keeping secret the means by which he obtained them.

In this connection it may be noted that Otto Goeller of Apolda is said to have developed the modern Doberman Pinscher upon a foundation of stocky drovers' dogs which had black coats with grayish-tan markings and thick, light undercoats. They were partly descended from cattle dogs brought from Württemberg by drovers. It is therefore probable that the Doberman, the Rottweiler, and the Standard Schnauzer had a common source in these Württemberg cattle dogs. The Rottweilers remained fairly close to the original type, while selection and crossing with Manchester Terriers produced the Doberman, and some other cross (perhaps Spitz and Poodle, as mentioned) gave the Schnauzer his characteristic color and coat.

At any rate, the Schnauzer's original vocation was that of a stable, yard, and cattle dog, a guard and ratter. He was never a Terrier in the English sense of a small breed used to bolt vermin from the earth, and has little or no true Terrier blood. German and Continental breeders consider the Schnauzer entirely misplaced in the Terrier Group in which the Miniature Schnauzer is classified by the American Kennel Club.

Wire-haired Pinschers were first shown at the Hannover show in 1879, at Aarburg in Switzerland in 1882, and at Zurich and Copenhagen in 1887. A breed standard was issued in 1880, but the first specialty show was not held until 1890, at Stuttgart in Württemberg, the cradle of the breed. The Pinscher-Klub, founded at Cologne in 1895, published the first independent Schnauzer stud-book, of which Volume I appeared in 1902. The Klub issued six volumes in all, and in 1918 joined forces with the Bayerischer Schnauzer-Klub, founded in Munich in 1901, which had published three volumes of a studbook between 1901 and 1914. The amalgamated organization still exists under the name of the Pinscher-Schnauzer-Klub 1895 e. V. The first volume of its joint studbook was published in 1924 and thereafter successive studbooks appeared annually until interrupted by World War II. The studbook has now been published through Vol. 44 (1966).

A few Standard Schnauzers in the first volume of the Pinscher-Zuchtbuch (commonly referred to as PZ) are recorded as having been whelped in 1879, but there seem to be no definite records before that date. In addition to the Standards, this volume registered a handful of Glatthaarige (Smooth-coated) Pinschers (a breed intermediate in size between Dobermans and Miniature Pinschers, now almost extinct) ; about 80 Miniature Pinschers (Zwergpinschers) ; and there were also 14 Wire-haired Miniature Pinschers, the breed subsequently known as Miniature Schnauzers (in German, *Zwergschnauzer*).

The oldest Miniature Schnauzer registered was a black bitch, Findel (281), whelped in October 1888. She was of unknown parentage and was owned by Max Hartenstein of the Plavia Kennels. Of the eight bitches registered in this first volume, three were black, three were yellow (*gelb*), one black and tan, and only one was described as pepper and salt. The six males included no blacks. Four were yellow of various shades, one was black and tan, and again only one was pepper and salt. Four of the eight bitches were of unknown breeding, and the sire of a fifth was also unknown.

There is little data to indicate how the Miniature Schnauzers originated, but the last decade of the nineteenth century was evidently an era of experimentation. Of the eight smooth-coated Pinschers registered in the same volume, five had both parents recorded as wirehaired. One Miniature Pinscher bitch is credited with a Standard Schnauzer dam, while the Miniature Schnauzer dog Käsperle vo Stuggert (279), had a Miniature Pinscher sire.

Emil Ilgner, who in 1902 published a book on German dogs called *Gebrauchs-und Luxushunde,* was not a Schnauzer specialist,

Jocco-Fulda Lilliput, 1899. The earliest picture of a
Miniature.

but he gives some interesting illustrations. Besides *Rauhhaariger Deutscher Pinscher,* or Wire-haired German Pinscher (as he calls what is now the Standard Schnauzer), he shows an old type Doberman which differs little save in color from his *Glatthaariger* (smooth-haired) Pinscher. The latter would seem to have had the Schnauzer color with the Doberman type of the day. The gray Spitz could well have contributed his color at some stage of the breed's development, while the contemporary ancestors of the German Shepherd (whose color variations appear to belong to the same series) might easily have played a part in the formation of the early cattle drovers' dogs, to judge by some studbook pictures before 1900.

Jocco Fulda-Liliput 16, whose picture is included in Ilgner's book, was the first Miniature Schnauzer registered in the PZ (where he is listed as a *Rauhhaariger Zwergpinscher*). There may have been earlier registrations in the DHSB (the German all-breed studbook), which I have been unable to examine. In any case, Jocco, though the first recorded in the PZ, was not the oldest. He was whelped December 6, 1898, and was younger than several others who were registered later. Although at least three of his sons were registered, there is no indication that Jocco's descendants carried down to later times, and Felix Ebner, writing in 1907, implies that Jocco's line was already extinct by that date.

Jocco's picture as reproduced by Ilgner differs very little from the picture of "Fritzle," owned by Georg Goeller, which he calls an Affenpinscher. Ilgner, indeed, lists Goeller as an Affenpinscher breeder, and his name is not included under Miniature Schnauzer breeders. But since Ilgner usually cites only one or two names under each breed, this means little. It does, however, suggest that Ilgner, not a Schnauzer fancier himself, associated Goeller with Affenpinschers rather than with Miniature Schnauzers, which at that date were few in number and not yet well established as to type. It is interesting to observe, nevertheless, that the first volume of the PZ (the only one I have been able to locate in this country) does not include any Affenpinscher registrations but does contain a picture of a pair, "Affi" and "Pitti," owned by Gräfin Larisch of Munich. These two were blacks and resemble the Affenpinschers of 20 years later more closely than "Fritzle" in Ilgner's book, yet Affi could easily pass for a Miniature Schnauzer and seems to resemble the latter breed the more closely. Since in 1907 Berta mentions Georg

55

Goeller as having bred Fritzli, "that widely known Zwickau dog and model for the breed," and above all, Champion Seppel, it is at least possible that Ilgner was mistaken in labeling "Fritzle" as an Affenpinscher. He may actually have been one of the first Miniature Schnauzers of which we have an illustration. On the other hand, names were frequently repeated, to the confusion and despair of the researcher; parents were often registered later than their progeny in the early studbooks, and when no registration number is given in a pedigree it is often impossible to be sure whether or not the same dog is meant.

Indeed, these early registrations are extremely difficult to make out, even when registration numbers for the parents are given. In an astonishingly large number of cases the date of whelping recorded for a sire or dam is later than the date given for their registered progeny. While at first glance this might seem due to a mistake in copying or printing, the mystery deepens when the dates of show wins, generally included, are also considered. These usually agree with the dates recorded for the parents, but indicate that in some cases they must have been shown and have won at seven or more years of age.

The usual theory regarding the origin of the Miniature Schnauzer is that the breed resulted from the crossing of Standard Schnauzers with Affenpinschers. The Affenpinscher is claimed to have been well known in Europe as far back as the seventeenth century, and to have been a progenitor of the Brussels Griffon, but I have been able to find no further information about its beginnings. Ilgner stated in 1902 that both Miniature Schnauzers and Affenpinschers were neglected in Germany at that date, when the interest in *Schooshundrassen* (which I take to be pet dogs) was very slight. The theory of the Affenpinscher cross seemed confirmed by the fact that so many of the earliest Miniature Schnauzers from which the descent of the modern breed can be established definitely were solid blacks. However, this theory has been questioned by some of the oldest German breeders still active, who state that in the early days there were more gray and yellow Affenpinschers than black ones. Even as late as 1924 the German standard for Affenpinschers, while listing blacks as first choice, allowed many other colors, including black and tan, yellow, red, gray, and various mixtures. The only color faults listed were very light colors, white, and white markings. Very, very few of the Affenpinschers registered in Volume I of the PSZ in 1924 were blacks.

One of the older German breeders points out that in the early days there was great variety, not only in color but in type of coat, including shorthairs, wirehairs, wavy coats, and even silky coats. A class for silk-coated Miniature Pinschers was actually offered at Berlin at 1902. Another indication of varied background is the ear formation observed before cropping. Some German Miniature Schnauzers are reported by this breeder to have Spaniel ears, Pomeranian (prick) ears, rose ears, and other variations. Many of the entries in the studbooks, even as late as the early 1920's, are marked "breeding unknown." While some of these may indicate records lost during World War I, we can do little more than speculate as to the origins of such individuals. The door must have been wide open for experiments of all sorts, some of which would seem to have left traces still cropping up now and then today.

One very definite source easily available to early German breeders was unquestionably the Miniature Pinscher. In 1924 the height standard was 28 cm. at the shoulder for both breeds. The preferred color for Miniature Pinschers was black and tan, but yellow, red, and roebuck, as well as brown (chocolate?), or blue with tan or yellow markings were all permitted. Since solid black was not a Miniature Pinscher color and was always extremely rare among Standard Schnauzers, we must look elsewhere for the origin of the solid blacks. It is clear that blacks were popular and numerous at an early date. There are said to have been 14 entered at the Leipzig show in 1909. Separate classes for blacks were soon provided, and are still the rule in Germany and elsewhere on the Continent, while separate championship titles for blacks are awarded.

Various indications point to the possibility that the black color may have been derived from the Toy Spitz, otherwise known as the Pomeranian. Ilgner illustrates a group of these, all blacks, owned by a Heilbronn kennel, and Heilbronn has long been a center for black Miniature Schnauzers. If the larger Spitz was used in the development of the Standard Schnauzer, as claimed, it would be logical to make use of the Toy variety when attempting to produce a miniature version. One of the oldtime German breeders mentioned above mentions Pomeranian (prick) ears as occurring, while another reports a definitely Pomeranian-type puppy as recently as 1944 in a litter by a Miniature Schnauzer Sieger. This same breeder names Miniature Pinschers, Affenpinschers, Pomeranians, and even Fox Terriers and Scottish Terriers as breeds which actually or possibly played a part in the development of the Miniature Schnauzer around the turn of the century. No doubt breeders experimented with various crosses when attempting to improve bone, body, head, and coat. If Fox Terriers were actually used, this may account for the occasional appearance of particolors in pure-bred litters of Miniature Schnauzers today. On the other hand, in 1924 the Miniature Pinscher standard listed particolors as permissible, and this may well have been the immediate source. Nevertheless, although particolored Miniature Pinschers were allowed, they certainly were not common, for a check of 1,500 Miniature Pinscher registrations before 1924 reveals no particolors, few chocolates, and a mere handful of blues. The vast majority were either black and tan or solid red, both of which are colors occurring frequently among Miniature Schnauzers of the same period.

It is interesting to observe that the dog Michel Chemnitz-Plauen, whelped in 1920 and registered as a Miniature Pinscher, was sired by a Miniature Schnauzer Sieger, Trumpf Chemnitz-Plauen, out of a Miniature Schnauzer bitch Resl Chemnitz-Plauen. Both parents played important parts in early Miniature Schnauzer pedigrees. From these facts one may assume that at least up to about 1920 smooth-coated puppies might appear in Miniature Schnauzer litters and were sufficiently close to the Miniature Pinschers of that day to be registered as the latter. Indeed, I can recall a number of puppies in the middle 1920's in this country that had almost smooth coats and practically no whiskers. Bitches of this type when bred to dogs with plenty of furnishings often produced outstanding puppies with wonderful, hard coats.

In the early volumes of the Swiss all-breed studbook before World War I, there are several cases where puppies from the same litter are registered some as Miniature Schnauzers and some as Affenpinschers, or some as Standard and some as Miniature Schnauzers. Individual type would appear to have counted as much as did breeding. In Germany the records show that Heinrich Schott of the Affentor Kennels and Georg Riehl of Dornbusch, both located in Frankfort on the Main, bred Affenpinschers as well as Miniature

Schnauzers. It would therefore have been extremely easy for either or both of these breeders to experiment with an Affenpinscher cross. Riehl was breeding Miniature Schnauzers at least as early as 1904.

I have been able to locate in this country only one German studbook registering Miniature Schnauzers during the period between 1902 and the end of World War I, Volume IV of the Pinscher-Zuchtbuch, which contains registrations through August 1913. Although the older German breeders have been very cooperative, few of them remain and many records were destroyed in the blitz. Add to this the language barrier and the many "breeding unknown" declarations and it becomes impossible to form any but a very general idea of the descent of most dogs which appeared during that period. We come to firmer ground only with the emergence of three important sires from whom all present day Miniature Schnauzers are descended over innumerable lines.

The oldest of these, Peter v. Westerberg, PZ 604 (DHSB 862 E), was whelped in November 1902. He was owned by Herr Max Woch of the Werneburg Kennels, then located in Weimar but later in Munich. Herr Woch described Peter, a solid black, as "a foundling without pedigree." However, he believed that there was no Miniature Pinscher blood in Peter, since the latter, he said, never sired a smooth-coated puppy, nor, on the other hand, any longhairs. Whatever Peter's breeding, Herr Woch declared that he always produced black puppies regardless of the color of the bitch, but this statement seems open to question. There is only one puppy by Peter, Mucki v.d. Werneburg (PSZ 8) in the first volume of the Pinscher-Schnauzer Klub studbook, but she is recorded as yellow. Another German correspondent also states that Peter produced many yellows in addition to blacks. He was certainly a popular sire in his day, being used as far away as Switzerland, and retained his vigor to a good old age, for Mucki v.d. Werneburg was sired when he was 12 years old. He is recorded by the PSK as having sired 55 litters. A line drawing by Richard Strebel shows Peter at the age of five. Berta describes him at that time as having "good length of head, no longer recalling the Affenpinscher in form or expression, with heavy, close coat, sound bone and harmonious appearance." Evidently Berta, an outstanding early authority on the breed, accepted the fact of an Affenpinscher cross before 1907.

Peter was a successful show dog and his owner claimed that he

S. Peter v. Westerberg, oldest of the
"big three" sires.

S. Cito v.d. Werneburg, by Peter, whelped 1907.

always defeated Prinz v. Rheinstein when they met. At any rate, Peter doubtless played an important part in the popularization of the solid blacks. However, because of the gaps in the records already mentioned, I have definite information on only a few of his progeny. These include a Swiss litter bred by Herr Tschudy out of Rauricas Pia (by Lord out of Kuni v. Schussental, who may have been a Standard), and three daughters and a son who can be traced at the back of many modern pedigrees. Indeed, I doubt if there is a single Miniature Schnauzer today who does not go back to Peter v. Westerberg a great many times over. These four producing get of Peter's were Lilli Lehrte (1115), Mucki, Mohrly, and S. Cito v.d. Werneburg (953).

Herr Woch began breeding about 1903 and stated that many of the foundation bitches were blacks of unknown pedigree. He cited the entry of 14 blacks in 1909 as an indication that the color at the beginning was black. This hardly accords with the fact that only three out of 14 Miniatures registered in Volume I of the PZ, all whelped by 1901, were blacks. It may well, on the other hand, show the popularity of Peter himself and his outstanding son S. Cito, who was whelped in 1907.

The second important sire who profoundly affected the development of the breed was Prinz v. Rheinstein, whelped July 12, 1903, some eight months later than Peter, and bred by Herr Kissel of Frankfort. Prinz is described as a very sound dog, black with yellow-gray markings. Herr Woch said that he, too, was a "foundling," but that his appearance indicated a faultless mixture of Affenpinscher and Miniature Pinscher. His son S. Gift Chemnitz-Plauen is reported to have sired many Miniature Pinschers, though whether this means they were actually so registered or were merely smooth puppies that lacked whisker is not clear. The drawing of Prinz done by Strebel in 1907 certainly shows no great amount of whisker, but his contemporaries do not seem to have had much more.

Prinz was owned by Herr Trampe of Berlin and apparently died young, for Berta spoke of him as already dead in 1907, while praising him as an epoch-making sire whose worth was already recognized and whose loss to the breed was lamented. Prinz's picture indicates a sturdier build and heavier bone than Peter v. Westerberg displayed, with hard coat, high withers, medium-sized dark eyes and a good head (the last a point in which his descendants were to excel). His get were seldom solid black (probably only when out of a black dam) but were often yellow or yellowish gray. Evidently his worth was quickly realized by Herr Stacke of the Chemnitz-Plauen Kennels. He was used with local bitches of a small, gray, rough-coated Pinscher type (not, it is said, of Schnauzer character), which were found in Saxony and Thuringia. These helped tremendously in the establishment of the salt and pepper color, while Prinz, described as a model Miniature Schnauzer when he made his show debut, presumably improved the type.

While Prinz v. Rheinstein can hardly have been a complete foundling if his breeder was known, his pedigree certainly seems to have been doubtful. The Dutch studbook registered a daughter, Mauschen (NHSB 3183), whelped in 1905, with a three-generation pedigree which gives Prinz's sire as Poppi (by Bubi out of Hexe) and his dam as Lottchen (by Moritz out of Lolla). On the other hand, two registrations in a later volume give his parents as Seppel v. Rheinstein and Minnette v. Rheinstein. Berta in 1907 commented on the likeness between Prinz and Ch. Seppel (Goeller) as though there were a relationship which he did not make clear. Since the kennel name was frequently changed when a dog was sold, particularly if he was unregistered, Seppel v. Rheinstein might easily be identical with Ch. Seppel (Goeller), a fact which lends this pedigree a certain degree of probability. Moreover, the Swiss studbook records the registration of a Seppl (Gütsch) (2617), bred by Goeller and whelped July 10, 1902, who may well have been Prinz's sire.

Seppl (Gütsch) was by Fritzle out of Mäusle, and Fritzle appears to have been by Käsperle (SHSB 1954), whelped in 1897 and also bred by Goeller. This Käsperle's sire, another Käsperle, was probably identical with Goeller's Käsperle vo Stuggert (PZ 279) (whelped in 1892), whose sire, Alli-Göller (PZ 294) was a Miniature Pinscher whelped in 1889, which carries us back very close to the beginnings of the breed. The dam of Seppl (Gütsch) may easily have been the same Mäusle as Fritzle's dam (who was by Benno out of Betty), which would make Seppl the result of a dam and son mating. Such close inbreeding was common, and if a fact, would help to intensify the qualities possessed by Prinz v. Rheinstein and account for his success as a sire.

Berta, in his little pamphlet on the Miniature Schnauzer written

S. Lord v. Dornbusch, youngest of the "big three."

Prinz v. Rheinstein, tail male ancestor of all American champions.

63

in 1907, mentions that Swabia, the cradle of the Standard Schnauzer, unquestionably played an important part in the development of the Miniature as well. He cites Käsperli Stuttgart of 1887 (perhaps a misprint for Käsperle vo Stuggert, whelped in 1897) as almost the foundation dog. While tracing no line of descent from Käsperli, Berta goes on to mention Fritzli, "that widely known Zwickau dog and model for the breed," and "above all Ch. Seppel," whose resemblance to Prinz v. Rheinstein he points out as evident in their pictures. It is therefore at least possible that the Miniature Pinscher Alli-Göller was the direct male ancestor of Prinz v. Rheinstein and of nearly all American Miniature Schnauzers today. Alli, like Prinz, was a black and tan, and Alli's son Käsperle vo Stuggert was red and tan; both these colors occur frequently in the early generations of the Prinz line.

Although not more than four years old when he died, Prinz sired at least three champions, Perle v.d. Goldbach (also called Perle Chemnitz-Plauen) , S. Gift Chemnitz-Plauen, and Michel v. Chemnitztal, while five or six known litters by him are mentioned.

The youngest of the "Big Three" among the early sires was S. Lord, whelped November 2, 1904, and variously known as Lord (v. Dornbusch) , Lord v. Riehl, or Horburg's Lord. He was a yellowish gray in color, distinctly the lightest of the three, and undoubtedly played an important part in the development of the pepper and salt color, as well as of the Dornbusch type.

Lord was owned by Herr Georg Riehl of Frankfort, who is said to have bred Miniature Schnauzers from about 1890 to his death during or shortly after World War II. Shown at Frankfort in 1906, Lord defeated Peter v. Westerberg, Stift v. Chemnitztal, and four others in a hot class, and his picture by Strebel was done the next year. Berta commented with enthusiasm on his square build, unsurpassed coat and bone, and wonderful balance. In his whole appearance, whether standing or moving, as well as in temperament and expression, Lord offered a typical picture of a Schnauzer, and his beaming owner, Berta declared, refused an unheard-of offer for him. Nevertheless, not all breeders were equally enthusiastic, for Herr Tschudy of Switzerland is said to have bred several bitches to Lord and reported particolored puppies by him.

Lord's breeding is uncertain. Various early pedigrees give his sire as Bubi or Möbi and his dam as Guss, or (more probably) Süss (by

Poppi out of Lottchen). Poppi and Lottchen were the parents ascribed to Prinz v. Rheinstein in an early Dutch pedigree, as mentioned above. This may indicate a relationship between the two dogs, or only a copyist's error. Since Poppi's parents are there given as Bubi and Hexe, it may be that Lord was inbred to Bubi. Whatever his breeding, Lord attained a respectable age, for he continued at stud until almost eight years old and perhaps even longer. He left three producing sons, Frick v. Dornbusch, Räuber v. Dornbusch, and Fritz v. Lohr, who founded male lines, and five known daughters, three of them producers who occur at the backs of modern pedigrees.

In 1935 I reported that the Peter v. Westerberg male line was virtually extinct in the United States and rapidly disappearing abroad. While it is still true here, the position seems to have altered somewhat in both Germany and England. In the latter country, Ch. Chorltonville Quintin Bonus goes back in the third generation to Zarewitsch v. Leixenstein, a son of Irrwisch v. Leixenstein. Quintin's sire, Axel v. Neubau, and grandsire, Dorn v. Batzenberg, have many descendants in Germany. Irrwisch v. Leixenstein's paternal grandsire, Yula v. Leixenstein, went to England during the 1930's but his son Moorland Black Knight is now represented only through daughters. It is interesting to note that this entire line, though tracing to Peter v. Westerberg, has lost the black color and is now pepper and salt.

Peter's only male line which survived World War I in Germany came through his Sieger son Cito v.d. Werneburg (953), whelped September 24, 1907. He was awarded first at the big Berlin show when only six months old. Berta described him as a dark iron gray in color, but his picture indicates that he was black like his sire. Possibly he had a sprinkling of a few light hairs, but his breeder-owner, Herr Woch, not only spoke of Cito as black but also attributed much of the early popularity of that color to his quality. If Cito was actually a dilute black, and other Miniatures registered as *eisengrau* were also in at least some cases actually black or blue, it would explain several instances where the mating of *eisengrau* to *gelb* (yellow) individuals resulted in black puppies in the litter.

Cito surpassed his sire in general appearance, with a sound body, faultless front and rear, and a head which Berta considered a model. His picture indicates that he was larger and heavier than

Peter, and in his day he was certainly a landmark for the breed. Cito's dam, Röschen v.d. Werneburg, was apparently more of a brood bitch than a ring performer. She was a dark pepper and salt with an excellent coat, whelped June 7, 1905, and bred by Guido Flache of Hohenstein. Röschen's dam was Grethel v. Hohenstein (510) whelped March 16, 1902, and an important factor in early breeding. She was bred by Herr Krappatsch of the Goldbach Kennels at Hohenstein-Ernstthal and owned by Herr Flache. Through their use of the Prinz v. Rheinstein line, Krappatsch, Flache, and Ernst Stacke (of the Chemnitz-Plauen Kennels) must be credited with major parts in the development of the breed during the first decade and a half of the century.

Grethel v. Hohenstein was evidently well esteemed by her owner and produced at least seven litters between 1903 and 1910. She has carried on through three daughters, Mohrly v.d. Werneburg by S. Peter v. Westerberg, Mücke v. Hohenstein (PZ 2184) by Benno v. Hohenstein, and Röschen v.d. Werneburg from the first of two litters by the Standard Schwipps v. Gladbach (PZ 631). Schwipps sired the black Standard S. Schwarzer Stropp v. Schillerplatz, who has important Standard descendants at the present time. Cito v.d. Werneburg's greater size and bone compared to his sire was no doubt due to the fact that he was one-fourth standard.

Berta comments on the fact that breeding results depend on the hereditary makeup transmitted through the chromosomes rather than on external appearance, and declares that Mohrly v.d. Werneburg apparently had everything which Peter v. Westerberg lacked, while plain Röschen brought nothing to the mating. Nevertheless, it was the latter who produced S. Cito, though it is Mohrly whose tail female line has continued via Amsel v.d. Werneburg, her daughter by Prinz v. Rheinstein. That Röschen's contribution was no light one is borne out by the fact that when mated to her son Cito, she whelped on May 10, 1910 a dark pepper and salt dog, Pucki v.d. Werneburg (PSZ 12), through whom all the present Peter male lines trace.

Mucki v.d. Werneburg, the yellow daughter of Peter v. Westerberg and Gretel v.d. Werneburg (PZ 1530) was whelped in October 1914 when Peter was just short of 12 years old. The mating of Mucki, a Peter daughter, to Pucki v.d. Werneburg, a Peter grandson through his sire Cito, produced Peterl v.d. Werneburg (PSZ 11), whelped June 2, 1916. Peterl (Little Peter—the final *l* or *le* is a diminutive, shortened from the form *lein*) was a solid black and sired many of that color. (This is one of the cases where a "dark iron gray" and a "yellow" produced black.) His popularity at stud must have been great, for there were 47 litters by him registered in the PSZ—an extremely large number for that period. They range in date from December 1917 to December 1925, the last when Peterl was nine years old, indicating that he carried on the family tradition of longevity.

All the Peter and Cito male lines trace back to Peterl, and both also come down through several daughters. Amsel Chemnitz-Plauen, by Cito out of Perle v.d. Goldbach (PZ 2026) was the most important, but her breeding record really belongs with the Prinz v. Rheinstein line. She should not be confused with the Mohrly-Prinz daughter Amsel v.d. Werneburg, mentioned above. The latter was the dam, by Cito, of Mira Lehrte. Although Peter v. Westerberg had failed to produce satisfactorily with his daughter Mohrly, he did better with Amsel v.d. Werneburg. Their daughter Lilli Lehrte (PZ 1115) became the dam of S. Prinz Lehrte and his sister Freya Lehrte, both by S. Gift Chemnitz-Plauen. Freya was mated to Flock Lehrte, a son of her brother Prinz out of Mira Lehrte (the daughter of Cito and Amsel v.d. Werneburg) and produced Siegerin Wala v. Hopfenberg, who combined seven lines to Prinz v. Rheinstein with four to Peter, three to Mohrly, and two to Nettel v.d. Goldbach. Sn. Wala was bred back to her grandsire, S. Prinz Lehrte, and produced Prinz v. Kohinoor, the sire of Dutch Ch. Ador v. Rheinstolz (PSZ 973). Ador was the first Miniature Schnauzer at stud in England, where his descendants are still numerous in female lines.

Mira Lehrte, the Cito v.d. Werneburg daughter, besides being bred to Prinz Lehrte, had a litter by Brunsviga's Bube, a strongly inbred Gift Chemnitz-Plauen grandson. Their daughter Jette Lehrte was the great-granddam in tail female of Alma v.d. Zukunft, a black bitch imported in the 1920's and the founder of one of the five American bitch families to be discussed later.

Jette Lehrte's daughter Mara Lehrte (from a litter by Prinz Lehrte) was mated to the black Mohr II Lehrte (whose name signifies African and indicates his color). Mohr was a son of Peterl out of Biene v. Hopfenberg, an older full sister to Prinz v. Kohinoor, and carried six lines to Peter v. Westerberg, four of them through Lilli Lehrte. Nevertheless, he had even more—seven, in fact—to Prinz v. Rheinstein. Indeed, if there was any such intense inbreeding to the Peter v. Westerberg line as there was among the descendants of Prinz, it must have been unsuccessful, for it does not appear in the pedigrees of dogs which have carried on.

In addition to Amsel Chemnitz-Plauen and Mira Lehrte, Cito v.d. Werneburg sired another producing daughter, Lore v. Lohr, out of Zecke (PZ 1677). In March 1915, when he was $7\frac{1}{2}$ years old, Cito also sired two bitches out of the unregistered Nettel. They were Annemarie and Anneliese v. Finkenberg. Anneliese was a solid black and Annemarie a black and tan. The latter was the dam of Biene and Bremse v. Finkenberg. A Biene son, Eitel v. Rheinstein, appears in the fourth generation of the 1932 black Sieger Fred (Terhörst) (PSZ 4106a). Another Biene son, Dutch Ch. Abs v. Cleverhof, sired Am. Ch. Billy v.d. Zonnenheuvel, a really nice dog who left no surviving progeny so far as I am aware.

The best son of Peterl v.d. Werneburg was perhaps the black S. Claus v. Lutherpförtchen, whelped in July 1925 in his next-to-last recorded litter. The dam of Claus, likewise black, was Puppi Heinzelmännchen, a daughter of Arpad v.d. Künstlerkolonie (whose dam was a Peterl granddaughter) out of Mücke Lehrte, a sister to Mohr II. Claus therefore carried considerable Peter v. Westerberg blood, and his male line may still exist in Germany. He sired three Siegers—the black Astor v.d. Bergischen Höhen out of a black Siegerin, Dohle v. Intzeplatz, and the litter brothers Egon and Edler v. Mümlingtal out of Sn. Heidy v.d. Hermannsburg. Both Edler (a pepper and salt like his dam) and the black Egon were subsequently sold to Switzerland, but Egon, in particular, left many German descendants. His most successful son, the black S. Oswien v. Königseck, carried on his male line, chiefly in Austria. Egon also appears through his daughters, particularly Pia v. Stolzenburg, the granddam of S. Zarewitsch Heinzelmännchen, and Estra Lehrte, the dam of Schlau Lehrte. Zarewitsch appears in recent British dogs through Ch. Chorltonville Quintin Bonus, Dondeau Favorit Heinzelmännchen, and Amor v. Ohsen Emmerthal, while Amor has a further Egon line through Schlau as well.

Edler v. Mümlingtal went to Switzerland earlier than Egon and most of his descendants are in that country. He carried on through his son Mutin du Jorat and the latter's son Swiss Ch. Artaban du

WS. 1935 Artaban du Jorat (Swiss).

Dutch Ch. Hummel van Duinslust.

Jorat, the World Sieger (actually Continental champion) winner in 1935. Egon left 24 litters in Germany.

Two other Peterl sons of secondary importance were Sepp v. Steinheim and Baldo Wichtelmännchen, both blacks out of Peterl granddaughters. Sepp's dam, Brunhilde v.d. Hermannsburg, was by S. Rudi v. Lohr out of Cilla v.d. Werneburg (whose dam, Struppi v.d. Goldbach, was by Muck v.d. Goldbach, a brother to the great producer Ch. Perle v.d. Goldbach, out of Nixe v. Reichenbach). Sepp's daughter Loni v.d. Weichselwacht was the dam of American Ch. Giron v. Feldschlösschen, whose name appears in pedigrees of many recent dogs here through his granddaughter Ch. Kathleen of Marienhof I. Baldo's dam, Liese Heinzelmännchen, was by Swiss Ch. Lackl Chemnitz-Plauen out of Mücke Lehrte (already mentioned). Baldo mated to Cilli Wichtelmännchen (also a Peterl daughter, out of Gera Wichtelmännchen) was the sire of Meta Wichtelmännchen and grandsire of her son Axel v. Freyersheim. Axel was bred to a black Egon v. Mümlingtal daughter, Hexe v. Jägertor, and produced the black Sn. Bärbele v. Burg Heldenstein, World Siegerin in 1935 and dam of Triple Champion Annerl v. Hohentwiel, owned by Frau Pfahler of Switzerland. Annerl, sired by Giff v. Abbagamba, carried 14 lines to Peterl.

The litter brothers Arno and Arco (sometimes spelled Arko) Heilbronnia, both blacks, were by Peterl out of Liese Heilbronnia (PSZ 280). Liese may have been a Peterl daughter, for her unregistered parents were given as Peterle and Hexe v. Oedheim. Arco, the only Peterl son I ever saw (when he was 10 years old), was a very compact little dog of excellent quality, and from him descends one of the two Peter v. Westerberg male lines which are still producing today. He also comes down through his daughter Asta v. Hahnwiese (DHSt 3863), the dam of Benno and Blitz v.d. Gottlobshöhe, who played prominent parts in the development of the Leixenstein strain, now one of the oldest and most scientifically bred in Germany. Benno and Blitz were sired by Kasperle Weiss, a son of Arco's brother Arno Heilbronnia, and their parents were therefore first cousins. The second male line from Peter that is still producing comes from Arno via Benno and continues through Axel v. Leixenstein, Alex v.d. Irpfel, Nauke v. Leixenstein, and Yula v. Leixenstein. Yula, who went to England but left important German progeny, carried at least two other lines apiece to both Benno and Blitz,

Sn. Lenchen v. Dornbusch, first AKC
champion.

Sn. Isa v.d. Werneburg, 1920–1933.

Arco Heilbronnia, 1920–1933.

as well as a line to Mirzl Lehrte, a Mohr II daughter, and his pedigree shows deliberate and careful line breeding. Another English import, at stud there in 1935, was Rex Heilbronnia. He was straight Leixenstein on his sire's side and an Alex v.d. Irpfel great-grandson, but I have found no record of living descendants except in Germany, where his litter sister likewise left progeny. An early American importation, Morle v.d. Ludwigshöhe, whom I do not recall ever seeing, was a Peterl son, but was sold in Canada in 1927 and does not seem to have left any get whatever in this country.

The most interesting, and in many ways most important of Peterl's get were his seven litters out of Pussel v. Ruhrtal, who does not seem to have been bred to any other sire. Pussel and her sister Mora v. Ruhrtal were by S. Fritschen (by Hans out of Fippy, otherwise unknown) out of Hella v. Ruhrtal. Hella was a double granddaughter of S. Gift Chemnitz-Plauen, and her dam, Dohle Chemnitz-Plauen, was further the result of a sire-daughter mating of Gift and his daughter Gustel Chemnitz-Plauen. (Gustel's dam, Hexe Chemnitz-Plauen, is the source of the second most important bitch family in the United States.) Pussel v. Ruhrtal was a pepper and salt who became the mainstay of the Werneburg Kennels; her sister Mora was apparently sold after a single litter. Pussel's get by Peterl consisted of 30 registered puppies, including two Siegerins and seven other producers. Of these nine, eight were bitches.

The first litter contained Sn. Braga v.d. Werneburg, dam of Brigitta van den Zonnenheuvel, a Dutch bitch whose daughter Pia van den Zonnenheuvel came to the United States and appears in several Wollaton pedigrees with descendants still winning. Braga's sister Biene v.d. Werneburg carried down to some of the black Königseck strain. The next Peterl-Pussel litter contained Dohle and Dora v.d. Werneburg, both very important producers. Dora was the dam of S. Friedel v. Affentor, ancestor of many of the Dornbusch strain through his son S. Don v. Dornbusch and his sisters Lore and Litta, as well as the less important Friedel v. Eishof. Outside the Dornbusch Kennels, Friedel v. Affentor sired S. Cito v.d. Künstler-kolonie and his litter sister Cleo (dam of Erik v. Treuewald), and also Anni v. Dingshaus out of Rosl (1113). Erik and Anni were the parents of the two Dutch champion sisters Bella and Bärbel v. Dingshaus, the latter one of the foundation bitches of the prewar Enstone Kennels in England. Friedel sired a total of 47 litters.

Another Friedel v. Affentor daughter, Affi v.d. Hollerhecke, out of the black Rappi v.d. Feste Coburg, was the dam of Claus v. Schönhardt and Nora v. Schönhardt, both blacks. Nora, sired by Axel v. Freyersheim, a son of her half brother Claus, was the dam of Am. Ch. Hupp v. Schönhardt, the first solid black male to win an American title and the ancestor of many leading German blacks of recent years. Finally, Friedel v. Affentor sired Sn. Heidy v.d. Hermannsburg out of Dohle v.d. Werneburg, litter sister to his dam, Dora. Heidy has already been mentioned as the dam of Siegers Egon and Edler v. Mümlingtal, and was the dam of Nette v. Mümlingtal, the first Canadian champion. Besides Heidy, Dohle was the dam of Brigitt v. Mümlingtal, whose son Am. Ch. Bodo v. Schillerberg played an important part in the development of the breed in both the United States and England, as will be explained later. Bodo's full brother Ari v. Schillerberg was the sire of Nette v. Mümlingtal. Dohle v.d. Werneburg produced another champion in Sn. Ansa v.d. Hermannsburg, the dam of S. Cita v.d. Künstlerkolonie by her cousin Friedel v. Affentor, who was thus the sire of three champions. Ansa's litter brother Arko was of minor importance, producing only when bred to Cilla v.d. Werneburg, a daughter of Peterl and Struppi v.d. Goldbach. One of their sons, Coco v.d. Hermannsburg, appears in the fifth generation behind Dolf v. Kleinvilliers, and Carlo, bred to the double Rudi v. Lohr granddaughter Gretel v. Dornbusch, sired Strolch v. Einsiedel, the sire of Brigitt v. Mümlingtal. Another Brigitt son was Eros v. Schillerberg, by S. Zecher v. Dornbusch.

The third litter by Peterl out of Pussel was their largest, but of the seven puppies only Hella v.d. Werneburg seems to have carried on, though her brother Hoter sired a number of registered litters. Hella's daughter Afra v.d. Falkenhöhe (by the Baltischhort-bred dog Peter Baltia) was the dam of Austrian Ch. Fritzel v.d. Falkenhöhe, whose sire was Afra's own grandson, Clown v.d. Falkenhöhe. Both Clown and Fritzel were blacks, and the former's descendants include the recent black S. Sam v. Liethberg.

Sn. Isa v.d. Werneburg, whelped April 6, 1920, was one of the foundation pair at the Abbagamba Kennels, where I saw her with Arco Heilbronnia, her half brother, in 1930. Both were then hale and hearty. They died in 1933, within a few weeks of each other, at over 13 years of age. Isa was from the fourth litter and the fifth has

73

left no recorded progeny. Perhaps none survived to maturity. Satanati v.d. Werneburg, from the sixth, was also owned by Abbagamba. Majak v.d. Werneburg, from the seventh, was the only male of this breeding with any claims to success as a sire, through his daughters Hexe (2344) and Marga v. Matildenstolz and son Ried v. Rheinstein. Marga was the granddam of Fratz v. Stahl, who sired Sn. Fee v.d. Schwalenburg. Hexe was the dam of Sn. Adda v. Mazeppa and another daughter, Blanka v. Mazeppa. Blanka's black son, Jimmi v. Utbremer Ring was a popular sire in the 1930's who still appears occasionally through female descendants in Germany. A Hexe son, Achim v. Kaiserhain by Bubi v. Intzeplatz, was the sire of S. Fred (Terhörst), another black who is found in many modern German pedigrees. Majak's son Ried v. Rheinstein sired Bob v. Barop, who was mated to Hexe (2344) to produce Sn. Adda v. Mazeppa. Adda, with two lines to Majak, left a daughter Fricka v. Mazeppa, with a third line to Majak through her sire. There are still many German registrations which carry this Mazeppa blood, some of them through Fricka's grandson Bubi v. Osning.

In all, 20 of Pussel's 30 puppies were solid blacks. She was whelped August 6, 1914, but does not seem to have whelped her first litter until December 28, 1917, while her seventh was four years later, in December 1921. Braga, Dora, Hella, Isa, Satanati, and Majak were all blacks. Biene was a pepper and salt and Dohle a black and tan.

Sn. Isa v.d. Werneburg and her younger sister Satanati were the foundation bitches at the Abbagamba Kennels, which specialized in blacks for a number of years. Many of today's outstanding German blacks are descended from them. Satanati was bred to her sire, Peterl v.d. Werneburg, and their son Brumbies v. Abbagamba was mated to Bagatelle v. Abbagamba, a daughter of Arco Heilbronnia and Isa v.d. Werneburg and consequently a double Peterl granddaughter. Doris v. Abbagamba, out of this litter, with four crosses to Peterl and only two to Pussel, seems to have been a homozygous black, for her two litters by the pepper and salt S. Fatzke Baltischhort produced 12 black puppies with no other color. Among them was S. Eros v. Abbagamba, from whom a large proportion of today's German blacks descend in tail male. The Eros son Heliaster v. Abbagamba went to California, where he was the cornerstone of the Bambivin Kennels, oldest breeders of blacks in the United States.

74

His first champion descendant since 1936 was the salt and pepper Ch. Windy Hill Jiminy Crickett, who finished in 1961. Hence Heliaster was not included in the list of imported foundation sires in the first edition. He also appears three times in the pedigree of Sambo of Cobb, UDT, and more recently in Ch. Howtwo's Henry Higgins.

S. Crocus v. Abbagamba, a full brother to Bagatelle, was mated to Cariama v. Abbagamba, daughter of Nipon Baltischhort and Satanati, to produce Dutch Ch. Discina v. Abbagamba. Cariama is recorded as a black with gray and brown markings. Eros and Discina were the parents of S. Guril v. Abbagamba and Sn. Hedera v. Abbagamba in different litters, and Eros sired a third winner in S. Gero v. Abbagamba, out of a Satanati daughter, Eschidena v. Abbagamba (who was by S. Marko Baltischhort). Doris v. Abbagamba, the dam of Eros, was also the dam of Sn. Florida v. Abbagamba (sired by Diamant v. Abbagamba, a brother of Discina). Doris was likewise the granddam of Sn. Haliplana v. Abbagamba, by Crocus out of Gloriosa, the latter a younger full sister to Eros.

All these early Abbagamba winners combined inbreeding to Peterl with crosses of Baltischhort. This latter linebred strain was famous for type and coat but inclined to a reddish salt and pepper color. The solid black of the Abbagamba foundation stock proved dominant over the Baltischhort infusions, which undoubtedly contributed valuable elements. The fact that both kennels were located in East Prussia, at a distance from many other breeders, made the use of each other's dogs natural and easy. During ten years of activity Abbagamba bred no less than eight German Siegers and Siegerins plus a Dutch champion.

The litter by Eros out of Discina contained six puppies, all of them subsequently used for breeding, but the most successful sire was not S. Guril but his untitled brother, Giff v. Abbagamba. A pepper and salt sister, Gaja, went to Switzerland, from whence her great-granddaughter Ukase du Jorat came to the United States. Another pepper and salt sister, Galera v. Abbagamba, was the dam of the American importation Bässi v.d. Rissener Heide. Bässi's daughter Affschen of Ravenroyd was the first Group winner in California and her sister Troublesome Lady v.d. Aal has many descendants there. Gimri v. Abbagamba, a black male, sired Sn. Biene Hummel Hummel, the dam of Apollo v. Liethberg, who has

75

many descendants still winning in Germany. Apollo's sire, Imago v. Abbagamba, was by Arco Heilbronnia, whelped when Arco was nearly nine years old, out of Hilaria v. Abbagamba. He therefore belongs to the Peter v. Westerberg male line. Hilaria was an Eros daughter out of Filanda, a litter sister to Sn. Florida. Hindrin v. Abbagamba, a brother to Hilaria (and also to Heliaster), was the sire of Rajah v. Leixenstein, who also has descendants.

Giff v. Abbagamba had at least four producing sons. Besides Hupp v. Schönhardt there were Hasso v. Kleinvilliers, Harri v. Burg Heldenstein, and his namesake Giff v. Freyersheim. The blood of Peterl v.d. Werneburg is strong in these black lines today, although Giff traced in male line to Prinz v. Rheinstein (via Eros' sire, Fatzke Baltischhort). The only male line of blacks from Peterl is the one through Arco, Imago, and Apollo, and from Claus v. Lutherpförtchen in Austria. The Arno line, via Zarewitsch v. Leixenstein, is now pepper and salt.

S. Lord (von Dornbusch) was apparently never registered. He was the youngest of the three foundation sires and must have been still active up to nearly eight years of age, at least, for one of his sons is recorded as having been whelped September 2, 1912. Lord sired the bitch Zoe Zizlmann out of Sn. Eva Zizlmann, whose breeding was unknown. From the mating of Zoe to S. Gift Chemnitz-Plauen came S. Zeno Zizlmann, who consequently belongs to the Prinz v. Rheinstein male line but is found almost exclusively in Miniatures with Baltischhort blood through his son S. Marosch Baltischhort and grandson Adasch Baltischhort. Lord is reported to have sired a number of particolors and it is possible that his daughter Zoe was responsible for transmitting this color tendency to some of her descendants, though the evidence is inconclusive.

Two Lord daughters, Möbi v. Untersberg (out of Lotti v. Untersberg, by Troll v. Hohenstein ex Flinka v. Hohenstein) and Trudl v. Untersberg out of Bärbel v. Untersberg (by Ch. Michel v. Chemnitztal out of Lotti v. Untersberg) occur together in British and German pedigrees. Möbi's son Peter v. Steiermark (by S. Fips Chemnitz-Plauen) was mated to Trudl, and their daughter Litty v. Steiermark was the dam of Trudl v. Saalach (by S. Fips v. Annen-hof). The younger Trudl had at least three litters by S. Borzel v. Dornbusch, and one of their daughters, Ursel v. Schloss Burgeck, went to England before World War II. Two Borzel–Trudl sons,

Schnull and Tann v. Schloss Burgeck, were popular sires in Germany and may be found in numerous Contintental pedigrees during the 1930's. Tann's daughter Bärbel v. Grafen Eckhardturm was the dam of RS. (Reichssieger) 1941 Zarewitsch Heinzelmännchen, whose record of 202 litters is tops for the breed in Germany. This Zarewitsch (quite a different dog from Zarewitsch v. Leixenstein, with whom he should not be confused) was one of the top German sires of the 1940's. Two British importations, Dondeau Favorit Heinzelmännchen and Amor v. Ohsen Emmerthal, trace to Zarewitsch in male line, while Amor's dam, in addition, was a double granddaughter of Schnull. Gerti of Worth, dam of the important producing bitch Quarrydene Gelda and others in England, was granddaughter of Ursel v. Schloss Burgeck, but I do not recall any of this line in the United States, where few postwar importations have been shown. Frick (sometimes misspelled "Trick") v. Dornbusch (PSZ 347) was out of the unregistered Betti v. Dornbusch and seems to have been the last puppy registered by Lord. Frick left several daughters out of Mäuschen v. Dornbusch (PSZ 462, by Bobi out of Aeffchen), including Berwel v. Dornbusch (PSZ 476), the dam of Sn. Vinesse v. Dornbusch and Am. Ch. Viktor v. Dornbusch. Another bitch of the same breeding as Berwel was Lotte v. Dornbusch, (PZ 4088). Lotte's daughter Hexe v. Dornbusch (PSZ 349) was the dam of Lenchen v. Dornbusch, the first AKC champion Miniature Schnauzer and herself the dam of Ch. Don v. Dornbusch. A third daughter of Frick and Mäuschen was Betty v. Dornbusch (PZ 4003), the dam of Hupp v. Dornbusch. There is no record of any Frick sons, but his daughters and granddaughters were freely used for line breeding in the Dornbusch Kennels, and he was still siring puppies at 10½ years of age.

The second Lord son, Räuber v. Dornbusch, was out of Nidi (or possibly Nixi) v. Dornbusch. He, too, must have remained vigorous to a good old age, for a son, Rigo v. Dornbusch (black with gray markings), was whelped in September 1919 out of Ella v. Dornbusch, a sister to Mäuschen. Rigo's daughter Lenchen v. Dornbusch, mentioned above, carried four lines to Lord and is to be found in nearly all later Dornbusch pedigrees. It is through Rigo's son Axel v. Dornbusch (PZ 5382) that most if not all the tail male descendants of Lord at the present time are derived. They are not very numerous, for the Lord male line has declined steadily during

77

the past 20 years and appears to be extinct in the United States and England. In Germany ten generations bearing the Dornbusch name ended with Nickel and Othello v. Dornbusch, both grandsons of Wisko v. Dornbusch. Wisko was by Kaspo, son of Stuss, son of Triple S. Zecher v. Dornbusch, by the Axel son Hupp v. Dornbusch. Nickel, whelped in 1947, was the last Dornbusch male with sons, and his line appears to end with Ingo Rumpelstilzchen, whelped in 1953, and Kobold and Kiebitz Rumpelstilzchen, whelped in 1955. Ingo, Kobold and Kiebitz were all by the Nickel v. Dornbusch son Astor v. Ginheimer Stolz. There are still seven litters registered in 1952, all from Zecher. Two were via Wisko and four were from Jux v. Schlossberg via Finke's Quick, Goxi v. Batzenberg, and four of the latter's sons. One was from Ago v. Herrenalb via Männe v.d. Fallerburg, Flink v. Bad Ilmenau, Dixi v. Wiesenweg to 1953 KS. Dolf v. Schloss Burg, apparently the last Sieger of the Lord line, whelped in 1946. Dolf's son Bert v. Ronsdorfer Eck sired several litters, and another son, Derb v. Königshof, sired Bubi v. Abteihof in 1959. Bubi has sired five litters, the latest whelped in 1965.

A third Lord son was Fritz v. Lohr, out of Zecke (PZ 2907), a light bitch whelped in 1908. Zecke had three known litters. Lore v. Lohr by Cito v.d. Werneburg, bred to her half brother Fritz v. Lohr, produced Strupp v. Lohr. S. Rudi v. Lohr (PZ 2907), whelped April 7, 1912, was by Strupp out of his double granddam Zecke. Rudi, inbred to Zecke, was one of the leading sires of his day. He sired S. Friedel v. Affentor, Sn. Ansa v.d. Hermannsburg, and Am. Ch. Amsel v.d. Cyriaksburg, the foundation bitch of the Marienhof strain and source of the most productive tail female line in the United States. Hexe v. Dornbusch, dam of Ch. Lenchen, and her sister Hella v. Dornbusch, dam of Axel v. Dornbusch, were Rudi daughters, as were Dirndl Heinzelmännchen (out of Mücke Lehrte), an important early Heinzelmännchen producing bitch, and her sister Dorle Heinzelmännchen. Dorle's granddaughter Sn. Freifrau Heinzelmännchen played an important role in the development of the Sharvogue and Dorem dogs in the United States through her son Flieger Heinzelmännchen, and was later imported herself. Rudi v. Lohr also sired Brunhilde v.d. Hermannsburg, the dam of Sepp v. Steinheim, whose grandson was Am. Ch. Giron v. Feldschlösschen. Asta v. Lindenau, still another Rudi daughter, was the great-granddam of Balzer v.d. Zwick. One son of Balzer, RS.

78

Major Heinzelmännchen, has numerous winning descendants in both Germany and England, while another son, Opal Heinzelmännchen, became a prominent American champion, though as a sire he failed to approach his record in the ring.

Rudi must have been highly regarded in his day, for during the 27-month period from July 1919 to October 1921, when he was from seven to nine years old, 29 litters by him were registered. Amsel v.d. Cyriaksburg was among the latest. Rudi sons not previously mentioned included Arko v.d. Hermannsburg (litter brother to Sn. Ansa), Astor v. Treuewald (out of Luci, PSZ 186), Fififax, 939 (out of Hexel v. Kurhessen, PSZ 321) and Axel Heinzelmännchen (out of Sn. Wala v. Hopfenburg).

The most important of Rudi's get, with the possible exception of Amsel, was S. Friedel v. Affentor, whelped February 27, 1920, and already mentioned in connection with his dam, Dora v.d. Werneburg. Friedel's last recorded litter was whelped when he was only 5½, in marked contrast to others of this line, suggesting an abrupt end to his career. For during 1922 and 1923 Friedel averaged two registered litters per month, with a total of 47 for the entire period.

The male line of Rudi and Friedel continued for several generations. Friedel's son Bazi v. Dornbusch, a double Rudi grandson, sired Bodo v. Schillerberg, whose descendants played an important part in both America and England. So did the Friedel son Don v. Dornbusch. Don's German get included Viktor v. Dornbusch (incorrectly given in PSZ as by Friedel v. Affentor), who went to America young and made his title there, and Sn. Vinesse v. Dornbusch, his sister, who remained at the Dornbusch Kennels. Viktor's German son S. Borzel v. Dornbusch had American descendants through his son Jörg v. Dornbusch, and a Jörg daughter, Gretel of Allsworth, went to England. Jrma v. Dornbusch, a sister to Jörg, remained in Germany, and a second Viktor son there was S. Asgar v. Dornbusch. Borzel v. Dornbusch sired Hahlo v. Schlossberg, sire of Räuberle v. Helluland Dallacker and grandsire of S. Bingulf v. Helluland Dallacker. Bingulf's descendants were numerous and a male line from him through Zenith, Schnurps, and Wachtreu v. Helluland Dallacker may still survive. A final son of Friedel v. Affentor was Friedel v. Eishof, mentioned with his daughter Affi v.d. Hollerhecke under Peter v. Westerberg.

It is, however, from the last of the "Big Three" sires, Prinz v.

79

Rheinstein, that the great majority of male lines can be traced today, although he died at the comparatively early age of four. Prinz was the chief rival of Peter v. Westerberg in the ring and at stud, and along with local Saxon and Thuringian bitches established a salt and pepper strain. Only a few of his get can be definitely traced in the early pedigrees, but these included several of prime importance and at least three champions. Prinz's daughter Amsel v.d. Werneburg (out of Mohrly v.d. Werneburg) has been mentioned as the dam of Lilli and Mira Lehrte. There is no information available on Prinz's litter out of Grethel v. Hohenstein (PZ 510), but Mäuschen, out of Betty v. Chemnitztal, went to Holland.

Nettel v.d. Goldbach, described by Berta as Herr Krappatsch's oldest and most productive bitch, was typical in body, coat and color, but not the best in head. Her litter by Prinz, December 14, 1904, contained Ch. Perle v.d. Goldbach, also known as Perle Chemnitz-Plauen. In the same or a later litter she also had Stift v. Chemnitztal, Alli v.d. Goldbach, and Muck v.d. Goldbach (whelped in 1906). Muck was bred back to his dam, and he also sired a litter out of Nixe v. Reichenbach, which included Struppi v.d. Goldbach (PSZ 30); and from Flinka v. Hohenstein, possibly Nettel's dam, he sired Benno v. Hohenstein, sire of Mücke v. Hohenstein and Dienel v.d. Goldbachhöhe (994).

Ch. Perle v.d. Goldbach was mated back to her sire and produced S. Gift Chemnitz-Plauen, a black and tan like Prinz. In German "Gift" means poison, but the name was not an apt one, for all the present day Prinz male lines come through Gift and his influence must have been enormous. Although he may have carried an appreciable amount of Miniature Pinscher blood and apparently sired a good many smooth-coated puppies, Gift sired at least seven champion sons and one daughter. In addition, there were ten non-champions who carried on, three sons and seven daughters, from a total of 40 litters.

Besides the litters by her sire (Prinz) and Cito v.d. Werneburg, Perle v.d. Goldbach had a litter by Fritz v. Blankenau (by Putzi out of Aeffel) whelped February 10, 1907, which contained Fritz v. Sonnenhof and Ch. Seppel v. Sonnenhof, the latter also called Seppel Chemnitz-Plauen. Seppel apparently carried on only through his daughter, Ursel II v. Sonnenhof, dam of Finte Kleinpfeff. Finte comes down through Hedda Horsa, Kobold Horsa, and

The Chemnitz-Plauen team in 1911. S. Gift (second from left) and get: Taps, S. Fips, and Sn. Mirzl.

Ch. Trumpf Chemnitz-Plauen, a Gift son and source of his tail male lines.

S. Zeno Zizlmann, ancestor of Balti-schhort and Abbagamba lines.

81

Fips v. Hohndorf to Alma v.d. Zukunft in American pedigrees. Alli v.d. Goldbach, sister to Ch. Perle (not the same Alli v.d. Goldbach who was the dam of Grethel v. Hohenstein, 510), was bred to Gift and produced Brunsvigas Mäuschen, dam of Brunsvigas Asta and granddam of Brunsvigas Bube. Bube's daughter Jette Lehrte was the great-granddam of Alma v.d. Zukunft on her dam's side.

Shown at Chemnitz under Herr Berta when six months old, Gift was described in the judge's report as "an inquisitive fellow; typey, strong bone, solid if somewhat narrow front, good coat, very good in head and expression, full muzzle, luxuriant whiskers, excellent carriage and temperament." Strebel's picture indicates that Gift was lighter in color than his dam, Perle, who seems to have been almost pure black with grizzled whiskers. Gift's progeny included the champion litter brothers Trumpf and Turko Chemnitz-Plauen, as well as five other Siegers: Prinz Lehrte, Fips Chemnitz-Plauen, Zeno Zizlmann, Michel Piccolo Kleinpfeff, and Michel v. Chemnitztal, plus Siegerin Mirzl Chemnitz-Plauen. In addition there were the non-champion producers Bendor and Prigo Chemnitz-Plauen (full brothers to Trumpf and Turko) ; Ulbs and his sister Elster; the two sisters Motte Chemnitz-Plauen and Mücke v. Goldbachtal; Dohle Chemnitz-Plauen and her dam Gustel Chemnitz-Plauen (both by Gift) ; Maus Kiki Kleinpfeff (a full sister to Siegerin Mirzl Chemnitz-Plauen) ; and Monche Kleinpfeff.

From Hexe Chemnitz-Plauen, dam of Gustel, comes one of the important producing bitch lines in this country today. Gustel's daughter Dohle Chemnitz-Plauen (by her own sire) was mated to the Gift son S. Fips Chemnitz-Plauen (out of Nelly, by Scherry out of Aeffchen), and this half-brother–half-sister mating produced Hella v. Ruhrtal, the dam of Pussel v. Ruhrtal. The latter's seven litters by Peterl v.d. Werneburg have already been discussed. Bitches of this family line that have winning progeny in the United States include Bässi v.d. Rissener Heide, Can. Ch. Nette v. Mümlingtal, and Pia van den Zonnenheuvel. Also tracing to the same family was Sn. Gaudi Baltischhort, whose granddam, Goldjungfer Baltischhort, was a Gift double granddaughter, by Fips out of Gustel.

Sn. Mirzl Chemnitz-Plauen, the only bitch among Gift's champion get, was another who produced by her half brother Fips. Their daughter Resl Chemnitz-Plauen (PSZ 21) was the dam of Racker

Chemnitz-Plauen II and so the granddam of Am. Ch. Cuno v. Burgstädt, a very important sire of whom more will be said later.

Fips Chemnitz-Plauen seems to have been most successful with his half sisters. Mücke v. Goldbachtal and Motte Chemnitz-Plauen were both by Gift out of Mücke v. Hohenstein (by Benno v. Hohenstein out of Grethel v. Hohenstein, 510, the granddam of Cito v.d. Werneburg). Motte was the dam (by Fips) of Ch. Moeve Baltischhort, one of the foundation bitches of that important kennel. Mücke v. Goldbachtal and Fips were the parents of another Motte (Motte v. Goldbachtal), who was bred to the Gift son Trumpf Chemnitz-Plauen and produced the extremely important sires Linus and S. Heinerle Chemnitz-Plauen.

Maus Kiki Kleinpfeff, bred to her half brother S. Michel Piccolo Kleinpfeff, produced Pfieke Kleinpfeff. Neither Michel nor his son Pfieke, despite considerable use at stud, proved of much permanent value, but Michel, who sired 19 recorded litters, did carry on through his daughter Finte Kleinpfeff (out of Ursel II v. Sonnenhof, a S. Seppel v. Sonnenhof daughter) in the fifth generation back of Alma v.d. Zukunft. Alma's sire, Fips v. Hohndorf, was also the paternal grandsire of Bärbel v. Dingshaus of the Enstone Kennels in England before the last war. Fips also, through his son Erik v. Treuewald and the latter's daughter Sn. Bärbele v. Burg Heldenstein, has many German descendants today.

Prigo Chemnitz-Plauen, one of Gift's less important sons (out of Amsel Chemnitz-Plauen), was mated to Resi Plavia, and their son Prietzel v. Hohndorf sired Hedda Horsa, the dam of Kobold Horsa (Fips v. Hohndorf's sire). Bendor Chemnitz-Plauen, a brother to Prigo, sired Bendor v. Beutenberg out of the "unknown" bitch Fritzi. The elder Bendor appears seldom and formerly seemed of slight importance. In recent years, however, his male line has become one of the most important producers of blacks in Germany. As a Cito v.d. Werneburg grandson, Bendor was very likely a black himself, as his younger full brother Turko Chemnitz-Plauen was. Bendor v. Beutenberg was certainly a black. The latter was mated to Erda v. Beutenberg, his half sister on the sire's side and a double granddaughter of Amsel Chemnitz-Plauen with a further line to Gift through her maternal grandsire, S. Turko Chemnitz-Plauen. Erda whelped three blacks, including Heinz and Horst v. Rheinstein. Mated to an unpedigreed black bitch Schwarze Hexe, Heinz

v. Rheinstein sired S. Fred v. Düsselstein (PSZ 982). Fred sired one Austrian and four German Siegers, three German Siegerins, and three Dutch champion bitches. Furthermore, he left no less than four sons whose male lines are still producing in Germany: the full brothers Kurt and Fachschaftssieger Koni v. Düsselstein, S. Benno v. Intzeplatz, and Austrian S. Dietz Elektron.

S. Zeno Zizlmann, a Gift son out of a Lord daughter, has been mentioned under his dam's sire. Most of the Baltischhort strain traced in male line to Zeno's son Marosch Baltischhort (ex the unregistered Mausi Baltischhort) and the Marosch son Adasch Baltischhort (out of Marosch's daughter Ayesha Baltischhort, whose dam, Assy Baltischhort, was by Peter out of Fippy II). Adasch, whelped in 1917, was still brisk and active when shown in the veterans class at the Königsberg Jubilee Show in 1932. S. Marko Baltischhort, who went to America in the 1920's but was killed before leaving any get there, was a son of Adasch and Sn. Mirzl Baltischhort (a Marosch daughter out of a Moeve Baltischhort granddaughter). Marko's best son was S. Fatzke Baltischhort, whose dam, Putzi (Jensen) (PSZ 1140), came from a full brother and sister mating. (Putzi's parents were Ali and Pussel Baltischhort by Marosch out of Allaska Baltischhort, a double granddaughter of S. Fips Chemnitz-Plauen). Although himself a pepper and salt, Fatzke was frequently used by the predominantly black Abbagamba Kennels, and a large proportion of present day blacks trace in male line to his son S. Eros v. Abbagamba.

Another Adasch son, Nipon Baltischhort, is also found in Abbagamba pedigrees, chiefly through his daughter Cariama. He therefore has American descendants through the imported bitches Bässi v.d. Rissener Heide and Hadrosa v. Abbagamba (the latter the granddam of Ch. Moses of Wollaton). Adasch was also the great-grandsire, on the dam's side, of Ch. Giron v. Feldschlösschen and Ch. Dolf v. Feldschlösschen. Dolf was the first Miniature Schnauzer to win the Group. An Adasch daughter, Sn. Gaudi Baltischhort, was owned by Halowell Kennels in Delaware in the early days. Her dam, Grille Baltischhort, was by Akiba, a Marosch son, out of a Fips Chemnitz-Plauen daughter. Gaudi left her mark on the breed through her daughter Ch. Halowell Vega (by Viktor v. Dornbusch). Vega's son Ch. Virgo of Tassac Hill was by Vega's own grandsire, Don v. Dornbusch. As the sire of Jill of Wollaton II (the foundation bitch of the Dorem Kennels), Virgo introduced this line into the great majority of modern American pedigrees.

On the whole, however, the Baltischhorts have played a minor role in both America and England. None of the more important foundation stock in this country carried a substantial amount of Baltischhort blood, while in England only Gerti van Duinslust and Yula v. Leixenstein (great-grandchildren, respectively, of Adasch and his son Arrak Baltischhort) have carried down to the postwar period. In Germany the strain was systematically and carefully bred to produce a definite type, easily recognizable. The kennel bred 11 prewar title winners, the last in 1931. They were renowned for good type and heads, together with hard coats, but were strongly inclined to reddish or brownish color. As the vogue for clear pepper and salts with more furnishings increased, the Baltischhorts tended to be absorbed into many strains, to which they undoubtedly contributed many of their good qualities. Moreover, about 1932, Dr. Frommer, the owner of the kennels, seems to have suspended breeding (I believe for reasons of health). His concentrated line breeding accordingly ceased and he could not attempt to improve the strain by crossing and selection while retaining its best features. In 1943 and 1944 several Baltischhort litters were again registered, but I am uncertain whether the same Dr. Frommer or some other member of his family was the breeder. However, the kennel, which was located in East Prussia, a district now included in Poland, seems to have discontinued operations thereafter, doubtless because of the war. The marked longevity of this strain was again shown, however, by the 1930 S. Fra Diavolo Baltischhort, whelped early in 1929, who sired a litter whelped in 1942.

S. Fips Chemnitz-Plauen, whelped June 6, 1911, was unlike his sire Gift in that he carried on almost wholly through daughters rather than sons. He sired 29 recorded litters, as compared to his sire's 40. Fips' one Sieger son, Urian Chemnitz-Plauen, left no mark as a sire; Pfeff (Müller) (830), whelped in 1914 out of the Gift daughter Mücke v. Goldbachtal, left a son Bubi v. Schlossberg and grandson Drall v. Schlossberg, but a litter by Drall in 1937 seems to mark the end of this line. Fips' daughters have mostly been discussed already. They included Sn. Moeve Baltischhort (out of Motte Chemnitz-Plauen), Motte v. Goldbachtal (out of Mücke v. Goldbachtal), Resl Chemnitz-Plauen (out of Ch. Mirzl Chemnitz-

Plauen), Hella v. Ruhrtal (out of Dohle Chemnitz-Plauen), Brunsvigas Asta (out of Brunsvigas Mäuschen), Annele Baltischhort (out of Assy Baltischhort), and Goldjungfer Baltischhort (out of Gustel Chemnitz-Plauen), certainly an outstanding list. A son, Brunsvigas Bube, by Fips out of his own daughter Brunsvigas Asta, also carried on to some extent through a daughter, Jette Lehrte.

In nearly all cases the producers from Fips were strongly inbred to Gift, with several of them double granddaughters. One is left to wonder whether outcross matings were tried without success or whether all the bitches sent to Fips were of similar bloodlines. His picture indicates that he was a medium salt and pepper, probably red or yellowish. His daughter Goldjungfer (Golden Girl) and son Goldjunge (Golden Lad) bore names suggesting the tawny yellow color characteristic of many Baltischhorts. Yellow or red was also found in many of the near descendants of Fels v.d. Goldbachhöhe and Cuno v. Burgstädt, who were both unusually strong in Fips blood.

One other Gift son whose only producers were daughters was Ulbs (PZ 1514). He was out of Rose v. Plauen (by Flock out of Ibbette) and sired the bitches Lore Plavia and Resi Plavia. A Dutch champion son, Zamperl (218) does not seem to have produced.

Since S. Prinz Lehrte has already been mentioned under Peter v. Westerberg, there remain only the two most notable Gift sons, the litter brothers Trumpf and Turko Chemnitz-Plauen, whelped March 21, 1912, and both Siegers. Turko, according to the Austrian studbook, was black, and his dam, Amsel Chemnitz-Plauen, was also black like her sire S. Cito v.d. Werneburg. Turko's daughter Cilla Chemnitz-Plauen (out of his own dam, Amsel) was the dam of Erda v. Beutenberg, who was discussed under Bendor Chemnitz-Plauen. Stüber Plavia, a black with a white breast spot, was also by Turko out of Lore Plavia (daughter of the Gift son Ulbs). Stüber was mated twice to his dam's half sister Resi Plavia and from this breeding came the black and tan Peppi I v. Hohndorf (dam of Am. Ch. Amsel v.d. Cyriaksburg) and her younger full sister Ch. Grille v. Hohndorf (dam of S. Dynast v. Annenhof and the outstanding sire Bolt v. Annenhof).

Of the four full brothers, Trumpf, Turko, Prigo, and Bendor Chemnitz-Plauen, Trumpf was by all odds most important. From him comes practically every male line that traces to Prinz v. Rheinstein at the present time, with the exception of those Abbagamba descendants from Fatzke Baltischhort who go back to S. Zeno Zizlmann. Trumpf is also of interest because he sired the first litter registered in Volume I of the PSZ, the combined Pinscher-Schnauzer Klub which issued its forty-third volume in 1966. Volume I contained few entries whelped before 1918, so only six litters by Trumpf are entered there. The last was whelped in 1920 when he was 8½.

Trumpf sired at least three litters out of the Fips daughter Motte v. Goldbachtal, including Swiss Ch. Kalle, and Linus and Heinerle Chemnitz-Plauen. Linus Chemnitz-Plauen was whelped when their sire was not quite three, and his full brother S. Heinerle Chemnitz-Plauen more than four years later, in 1919. Although not himself a Sieger, perhaps because of wartime conditions, Linus was the more successful sire of the two. It is reported upon good authority that after Linus appeared upon the scene, the famous Heinzelmännchen Kennels virtually scrapped their existing stock and began over again. Certainly the highly successful strain bred there was strong in Linus and Heinerle blood, consistently linebred. However, the bitch lines go back to Mücke Lehrte, Sn. Wala v. Hopfenberg, and Sn. Ansa v.d. Hermannsburg and thus carry a good deal of Peter v. Westerberg. The most prepotent early bitch in this kennel seems to have been Grille Heinzelmännchen, who was by Linus out of Dirndl Heinzelmännchen (by Rudi v. Lohr ex Mücke Lehrte).

Linus' most notable son, Bolt v. Annenhof, was whelped April 27, 1920, and sired 26 litters during the next 9½ years. Bolt's get included the double Linus grandson Fels v.d. Goldbachhöhe, a potentially great sire who seems scarcely to have been used in Germany and may have died young. His son Mack v.d. Goldbachhöhe and daughters Ch. Lotte and Lady v.d. Goldbachhöhe were cornerstones of the breed in America. Bolt also sired Gertha v.d. Goldbachhöhe (dam of Mack, who was Bolt's double grandson), Kobold Horsa (sire of Fips v. Hohndorf), S. Dynast v. Annenhof (sire of the American-owned Pia v.d. Zonnenheuvel), Dirndl v. Annenhof, S. Fips v. Annenhof, Käthe v. Annenhof (the last four out of Bolt's own dam, Sn. Grille v. Hohndorf), Sn. Mücke Heinzelmännchen and her litter brother Mampe (whelped two months before Bolt's ninth birthday), and Balzer v.d. Zwick (whose dam, Alice v.d. Zwick, carried three lines to Bolt and one to Heinerle). S. Fips v. Annenhof left some descendants in the Mazeppa Kennels through a black son, Fratz v. Stahl (who also sired Sn. Fee v.d. Schwalenburg) and appears in the Schloss Burgeck line through his daughter Trudl v.d. Saalach. Dirndl v. Annenhof was the dam of Affi v. Feldschlösschen, sire of Ch. Dolf v. Feldschlösschen and Ch. Giron v. Feldschlösschen, who came to America. Giron comes down through his daughter Ch. Kathleen of Marienhof I, among more recent descendants being Ch. Karen of Marienhof II and her son Ch. Benrook Buckaroo.

In spite of his early success as the sire of two Siegers, Bolt's value to the breed does not seem to have been generally recognized until late. This was perhaps because neither of his best producing sons, through whom his male line has carried on, were themselves Siegers. Moreover, Mampe Heinzelmännchen was not whelped until 1929, and although Balzer was two years older, his reputation seems to have been established only with the triumph of his son RS. Major Heinzelmännchen in 1934. Another Balzer son the same age as Major was Am. Ch. Opal Heinzelmännchen. Opal was a handsome, light gray dog who did a lot of winning in this country but seems to be carrying on only through his daughter McLuckie's Opal's Gal, the dam of Ch. Karen of Marienhof II and her sister Krista of Marienhof. RS. Major has many British descendants through his son Crowsteps Hasty (whelped in quarantine), including all postwar champions who trace in male line to prewar stock. Another Balzer son, Nimrod Heinzelmännchen, has American descendants through Herzbub Heinzelmännchen and appears occasionally in German pedigrees.

The big majority of postwar pepper and salt Miniature Schnauzers in Germany, two out of three German exportations to England during the same period, and a few American importations during the middle or late 1930's trace in male line to Mampe Heinzelmännchen. Mampe's son Husar and Husar's full sister, the great producing bitch Waffe Heinzelmännchen (dam of three Siegers and an English champion), were out of the Linus daughter Grille Heinzelmännchen. Mampe's own dam was a Heinerle granddaughter and great-granddaughter, Afra Heinzelmännchen. Husar was bred to Sylva Heinzelmännchen (daughter of his dam, Grille, and by Ass Heinzelmännchen, litter brother to Mampe's dam, Afra), and the resulting litter contained RSn. Holde Heinzelmännchen (sent to England, where she whelped Crowsteps Hasty), Eng. Ch. Hilvaria Heinzelmännchen, and the prepotent sire Hupp Heinzelmännchen. By Hupp out of his sire's sister Waffe came RS. Zar and his litter brother RS. Zeus Heinzelmännchen, plus the producing bitch Zamba. Hupp also sired RSn. Arie Heinzelmännchen out of his dam, Sylva. Although Zar and Zeus both died in 1937 at a very early age (Zar was poisoned), Zar was in such demand that he sired more than 40 litters during 1936, his only full year at stud, and his blood is widely distributed. Most of the present male lines to him come down through RS. Zarewitsch Heinzelmännchen.

S. Heinerle Chemnitz-Plauen, full brother to Linus but four years younger, has the same number of registered litters, 21, and both seem to have ceased their activities at stud in 1924, when Linus was nine years old but Heinerle only five. Probably World War I restricted Linus' opportunities, for his first recorded litter was not whelped until 1919, the year in which Heinerle was whelped. Heinerle's sons included Arpad v.d. Künstlerkolonie, Puck Heinzelmännchen, and Racker Chemnitz-Plauen II. Racker, whose dam was the double Gift granddaughter Resl Chemnitz-Plauen, left few German get, the only one of importance being Am. Ch. Cuno v. Burgstädt. Cuno's dam, Asta Gablonz, was a Linus daughter out of the unpedigreed Lotte Gablonz, and the recorded portion of his pedigree was intensely bred to Gift Chemnitz-Plauen, having four crosses in the fourth generation, four more in the fifth, and in addition two to Gift's dam through one of her daughters. Cuno was by all odds the most important sire in his influence upon the breed in the United States during the early years, and his male line quickly ousted all others. Although most successful in America, Cuno left eight litters in Germany. Five were from his own dam, Asta Gablonz. One from Grille v. Annenhof included a Siegerin, Mücke v. Annenhof, and one out of Lotte v. Beutenberg included a producing daughter, Medi v. Beutenberg, and a notable son, S. and Am. Ch. Marko v. Beutenberg. Marko's American get will be considered later on. While in Germany he sired three Sieger sons, Urian Thuringia, Ador v. Goldgrund, and Dieter v. Sachsen, and two Siegerin daughters, Dilli v. Sachsen and Ursel Thuringia. His sister Medi v. Beutenberg was the dam of Sn. Blanka v. Sachsen (by the Linus son Ammon Schnauzeltreu) and of Asta v. Sachsen, the dam of Dieter and Dilli. Dina v. Sachsen, litter sister to the two last named, was the dam of World Sn. Medi v. Sachsen and of two winners of the rare ICS international championship, Marko and Mona v. Sachsen, all three in a single litter by S. Eros v. Schillerberg. Dieter's daughter Lydia Heinzelmännchen left descendants in Germany, some of them exported to both England and the United States, and his son Etzel Heinzelmännchen was still represented in 1952 in male line with a litter by Illo v. Agaheim. Aside from this one litter, however, the Cuno–Marko male line seems to have vanished from the recent German studbooks. Dieter was strongly inbred to Cuno v. Burgstädt, for Asta v. Sachsen was by Fips v., Burgstädt, a son of Cuno from his own dam, so that Dieter was by a Cuno son out of a Cuno double granddaughter.

The other important Heinerle sons did not carry on in male line. It would seem that both must have died early. Puck Heinzelmännchen sired 22 litters within a period of 17 months, ending when he was only 2½ years old, while Arpad v.d. Künstlerkolonie sired 17, the last when he was but a year older. Puck carried on through his daughters Mücke v.d. Rosenhöhe I and Elektra Heinzelmännchen, Mücke being of greatest importance as the granddam of Mampe Heinzelmännchen. Elektra was the dam of Sn. Freifrau Heinzelmännchen, whose son Flieger Heinzelmännchen had an important influence in America about 1930. Freifrau's daughter Verra Heinzelmännchen went to Switzerland and became the dam of Ch. Artaban du Jorat there. Flieger Heinzelmännchen was by Falk Heinzelmännchen, who, like Freifrau, was by Ass Heinzelmännchen, a litter brother to Mampe's dam, Afra. Ass, Afra and a second sister, Amsel Heinzelmännchen, were all sired by Arpad v.d. Kunstlerkolonie. Another Arpad daughter, Puppi Heinzelmännchen (out of Mücke Lehrte), was the dam of the black S. Claus v. Lutherpförtchen, from one of the last litters by Peterl v.d. Werneburg. Still another Arpad daughter, Gera Wichtelmännchen (whose dam, Liese Heinzelmännchen, was by Swiss Ch. Lackl Chemnitz-Plauen, a Linus son, out of Mücke Lehrte), was a black who comes down to the present time through the Freyersheim and Burg Heldenstein stock. Muckerl v.d. Rosenhöhe, a son of Arpad and Grille Heinzelmännchen, sired the early American importation Christel v.d. Fallerburg, who still has many descendants and comes into the Dorem strain through her granddaughter Judy of Wollaton.

Among the less important get of Linus Chemnitz-Plauen were the sons Ammon Schnauzeltreu, Affi v. Feldschlösschen, Blitz v.d. Feste Coburg, Lümpli v. Rheinstein (found in Dutch pedigrees), Lump Chemnitz-Plauen and his brother Swiss Ch. Lackl (both out of Resl Chemnitz-Plauen), and the daughters Gretel v.d. Goldbachhöhe and Alix Schnauzeltreu. Grille Heinzelmännchen, dam of Sylva, Husar, and Waffe, was probably the most important Linus daughter.

The present day Miniature Schnauzers are descended from the foregoing individuals over numerous lines, some of them so often repeated that the cumulative effect cannot help but be great. In a few cases it is possible to trace back to Standard Schnauzer crosses, but this can seldom be done in the pedigrees of the top producers. Having discussed the sources of the modern breed we shall now proceed to study its development in the United States during the past 40 years.

Ch. Amsel v.d. Cyriaksburg.

Ch. Moses Taylor, the first American-
bred champion.

5

Breed Beginnings
in America

A few Standard Schnauzers were imported before World War I, but there is no record of any Miniatures in this country before the 1920's. Late in 1923 Mr. W. D. Goff, of Concord, Massachusetts, imported a pair consisting of a male who died without leaving descendants and a bitch, Hella v.d. Goldbachhöhe. Hella was not registered for two or three years, and though she produced at least two litters in 1927 and 1928, her line did not carry on. The real beginning of the Miniature Schnauzer in America came in the summer of 1924 when Rudolph Krappatsch, who had exported the earlier pair to Mr. Goff, sent over four Miniatures to Mrs. Marie E. Lewis, Zeitgeist Kennels, South Lincoln, Mass. Better known to the fancy as Mrs. Slattery (of Marienhof Kennels), she is still breeding Miniature Schnauzers after 40 years, with a list of home-bred champions to her credit which must be close to 100, although not all of them bear the Marienhof name.

Amsel v.d. Cyriaksburg, whelped June 12, 1921, and her two puppy daughters, Lotte and Lady v.d. Goldbachhöhe, whelped July

7, 1924, and sired by Fels v.d. Goldbachhöhe (the sire of Mr. Goff's Hella), were imported together and became the foundation of the breed in America. It is safe to say that there is no American champion today that is not descended from them many times over, with the possible exception of the one or two title winners imported from Europe since World War II. Amsel was also the dam of the first American-bred litter, whelped July 15, 1925, which contained Ch. Affe of Oddacre (originally Affe v. Zeitgeist).

During the early days, Miniatures were not accorded recognition as a separate breed, and even the Standard Schnauzers were known as Wire-haired Pinschers. They were originally all shown in the Working Group. The Wire-haired Pinscher Club of America was formed in 1925, with George D. Sloane as president, Mrs. Morgan Belmont as vice-president, C. E. F. McCann as treasurer, and Morris Newton as secretary. Later, Monson Morris was secretary for a number of years, acting in that capacity until 1932. About 1926 the name of the breed was officially changed to "Schnauzer." Miniatures were shown in the class with Standards for a brief period before being recognized by the American Kennel Club (AKC) in the fall of 1926, when they were first granted registration. Separate classes were first provided in February 1927 at the Combined Terrier Clubs Specialty Show. Both Standards and Miniatures were soon moved from the Working to the Terrier Group in 1927. The Standards were transferred back to the Working Group in August 1945. Up to 1931 there were awards for Best Standard Schnauzer and Best Miniature Schnauzer, with representatives of each breed competing in the Group. Then the AKC changed its rule and allowed only one "Best" until the spring of 1933, when separate awards were again provided.

The first Miniature Schnauzer registered by the AKC was Monson Morris' imported bitch Borste v. Bischofsleben, who left no champion descendants. After registering Miniatures as a separate breed from 1926, the AKC suddenly decided in 1933 that a specialty club could cover only one breed. Since the Schnauzer Club of America included both Standards and Miniatures, this ruling made them all Schnauzers without distinction and would have permitted the crossing of the two varieties. Although this had been done in Germany during the early years of Miniature development, it would have been highly undesirable at this later stage; as a result, it was decided to dissolve the Schnauzer Club of America, or more accurately, to form two duplicate clubs with the same officers and membership. As a further means of distinguishing between them, the new organizations became the American Miniature Schnauzer Club (AMSC) and the Standard Schnauzer Club of America. At the close of the year 1933, members were given their choice of continuing in either or both clubs, which henceforth were entirely independent.

The first officers of the American Miniature Schnauzer Club, which officially began its separate existence on August 19, 1933, were Mrs. Isaac W. Jeanes (Mardale Kennels), president; Monson Morris (Woodway Kennels), vice-president and AKC delegate; and Miss Anne FitzGerald (Anfiger Kennels), secretary. The Board of Governors consisted of 12 members, three of whom were elected annually to serve four years. The original membership, according to the first annual report, was 32. A surprising number of the charter members were still on the rolls and actively interested in the breed in 1957. They included Mrs. J. W. Slattery, Marienhof; Mrs. Leda B. Martin, Ledahof; Mrs. R. N. Pierson, Edgeover; Mrs. Dodge Sloane, Brookmeade; Mrs. Joseph Sailer, Twells; Richard A. Kerns, Wollaton; and Mrs. Anne F. Eskrigge, Anfiger. Mrs. H. L. Woehling, Normack Kennels, and Mr. G. Harrison Frazier, former Standard breeders, have both now joined the AMSC, Mrs. Woehling in 1937. Mrs. Sloane, though no longer active, was the only member of the Schnauzer Club of America in 1927 still a member of the American Miniature Schnauzer Club at her death in 1964. Although not a member of the club until later, Mr. Frank Brumby handled Miniatures for Brookmeade Kennels as far back as 1927 and has been a steady supporter of the breed. Both Mrs. Sloane and Mrs. Slattery exhibited at the first Terrier Breeds Specialty in 1927, when Sieger and Am. Ch. Don v. Dornbusch, owned by the late Frank Spiekerman's Hitofa Kennels, went Best Miniature. Don's dam, Sn. Lenchen v. Dornbusch, owned by Mrs. Sloane's Brookmeade Kennels, was the first Miniature to complete an American championship and was also, apparently, the oldest of the breed imported, having been whelped October 17, 1920, some eight months before Amsel v.d. Cyriaksburg, although the latter was imported earlier. The first American-bred champion was Mrs. Slattery's Ch. Moses Taylor, a son of Ch. Affe of Oddacre, one of the first American-bred litter (who finished after Moses), and a double grandson of Ch. Amsel v.d. Cyriaksburg. Moses tied with Don v. Dornbusch for the honor of being the first male champion of the breed, as both finished on the same day but at different shows in 1927.

In the early days, the breed standard called for a maximum height of 12 inches at the shoulder, and some good dogs were measured out or not shown on that account. The limit was gradually raised to the present maximum of 14 inches, while the German standard now allows 35 centimeters, which is the equivalent of 13.78 inches.

We pride ourselves today on the breed's record in Group and Best in Show wins. However, the first Group win was made way back in 1928 by J. M. Brown's Czechoslovakian importation, Ch. Dolf v. Feldschlösschen. The first American-bred and first bitch to win the Group was Ch. Aennchen of Marienhof, at the North Carolina State Fair in October 1930. Aennchen, one of the truly great bitches of the first decade, was bred by Mrs. Slattery. She made her debut at Westminster in 1929, where she went Reserve Winners' at 11 months old, owned and handled by the writer, who had never shown at Westminster before. This was one of the thrills of a lifetime. Aennchen was afterwards sold to Mrs. Jeanes' Mardale Kennels, under whose ownership she compiled a record which included Best Miniature at Westminster in 1932 (something no other bitch accomplished until 1938) and Best Miniature over an entry of 52 at Morris and Essex in 1934 when past six years old, just a couple of months before her sudden death. She remains the only bitch, and until Ch. Dorem Display in 1949 the only Miniature, to go Best of Breed at both Westminster and Morris and Essex. That she never won the Associated Terrier Specialty is probably due to the fact that Miniature Schnauzers participated in this event only once during her show career, when in accordance with the AKC rule at that time no award for Best Miniature was made. In 1933, 1934, and 1935, Morris and Essex was considered the club specialty.

Aennchen was one of the nine champions in three litters by Ch. Cuno v. Burgstädt out of Ch. Lotte v.d. Goldbachhöhe, a bitch who still holds the breed record as the dam of 12 champions by three different sires, only recently tied by Ch. Sorceress of Ledahof, who now also has 12 AKC champion progeny plus one Canadian cham-

Ch. Jeff of Wollaton.

Ch. Cuno of Wollaton.

Ch. Moses of Wollaton.

97

pion. Two of Aennchen's full brothers, Ch. Cuno of Wollaton and Ch. Mardale Rudi, both bred by Mrs. Slattery, also went Best Miniature at Westminster—Cuno in 1930, when he was the first American-bred to do so, Rudi in 1931, when he also defeated the Best Standard Schnauzer.

Another Cuno daughter, Ch. Mehitabel of Marienhof I, was considered even better than Aennchen, but died whelping her first litter in 1930. Her daughter Mehitabel of Marienhof II, equally outstanding, was never officially a champion. Her wins were cancelled because she was shown cropped during the period when this was forbidden by the club standard (1930–1934) and she died before she could re-win the title. A pure gray pepper and salt at a period when this was rare, she was the best bitch of her day, and as the dam of Ch. Marko of Marienhof and granddam of Ch. T.M.G., profoundly influenced the breed.

Still another early first was Mardale Kennels' imported Ch. Urian Thuringia (a son of Ch. Marko v. Beutenberg), who won the Club's first annual trophy in 1933, while his record of Best Miniature at Westminster in two successive years, 1933 and 1934, stood untouched until Display won in 1947 and 1948. Two other dogs won Westminster twice, Ch. Sandman of Sharvogue in 1944 and 1946 and Ch. Bursche v. Hessen in 1953 and 1954. In 1935, Mrs. Slattery's Ch. Marko of Marienhof was the first Miniature Bred-by-Exhibitor to go Best at Westminster.

Mardale Kennels' Ch. Opal Heinzelmännchen was Best at Morris and Essex in 1935, and in 1936 (under the ownership of Jack Crockett) won both Morris and Essex and the Terrier Specialty. He was the last imported male, and Normack Kennel's Sn. Quarte Heinzelmännchen I (PSZ 6051) who won the Club Specialty held at the Baltimore County K. C. in 1938 and Westminister in 1939, was the last imported bitch to win one of the major shows. Quarte, a daughter of RS. Zar Heinzelmännchen, was a truly great show bitch, though she seems to have left no winning progeny. Another Quarte Heinzelmännchen (PSZ 14067) left German descendants. She should, of course, be Quarte II.

Ch. Jeff of Wollaton, bred and owned by Mrs. Richard A. Kerns, Jr., won the club annual trophy in 1934 and 1935. This trophy was won outright the following year when it was won for the third time by Mrs. Kerns with Ch. Wollaton Sheik. One of the youngest dogs ever to go Best of Breed at Westminster, Sheik was only three days over six months old, and he finished his championship in three weeks, while still under seven months.

The first Miniature Schnauzer to place in the Group at Westminster was Ch. Sandman of Sharvogue, who was fourth in 1946. His full brother Ch. Stylobate of Sharvogue had been Best of Breed there in 1941, and their full sister Ch. Heather Honey of Sharvogue, in 1943. Since Sandman also went Best in 1944, this established a record of four Westminster Bests by three individuals of the same breeding (from two different litters). Another brother, Ch. Wingless Victor of Sharvogue, won Best at Morris and Essex in 1940 and the club trophy the same year.

Among the club's outstanding achievements should be mentioned its first specialty show after the dissolution of the old Schnauzer Club of America. Held at the Century of Progress in Chicago in 1933, at very short notice, it was won by Ch. Porgie of Marienhof. The second specialty of the new club, at Morris and Essex in 1934, had an entry of 56 Miniatures, then probably a world record. In 1948 the Morris and Essex entry under Judge R. A. Kerns, Jr., was 82, won by Ch. Dorem High Test, a mark which stood many years. Montgomery County in 1962 had an entry of 102, with 73 competing. The first official regional specialty of the AMSC, in conjunction with the American Miniature Schnauzer Club of Southern California, at the Harbor Cities K. C. show in July 1963 benched 78 out of an entry of 87. At Montgomery County in 1963 Ch. Saladin of Ledahof was shown in the Veterans Class at the age of 16.

The marked increase in top placings awarded to Miniature Schnauzers during the past two decades, especially during the forties and fifties, testifies to the wider reputation of the breed as well as to the quality of the dogs being shown. With the exception of Ch. Dolf v. Feldschlösschen, the early Group winners were bitches. After Ch. Aennchen of Marienhof came Ch. Mehitabel of Marienhof III, who also won Best Brace in Show with her half sister Ch. Charity of Marienhof I at Denver in 1934. Mehitabel III was also the first uncropped Miniature champion to win the Group during the period from 1929 to 1934 when the club standard disqualified cropped dogs.

The fourth Group winner was Ch. Mehitabel of Marienhof IV, a

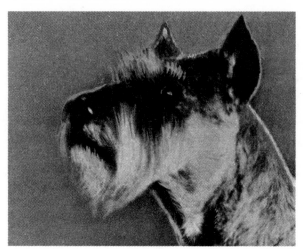

Ch. Marko of Marienhof.

Ch. Mehitabel of Marienhof IV.

Ch. Joshua of Marienhof.

100

daughter of Mehitabel III, at Charlotte, N. C., in 1936, under the noted all-rounder Charles G. Hopton. A champion at 11 months, Mehitabel IV had all the quality and showmanship of the previous Mehitabels, her dam, granddam, and great-granddam, each an outstanding winner in her day, but unfortunately she, too, died young, only a few months after her second birthday.

In 1937 Ch. Affschen of Ravenroyd became the first Group winner in California, at the Berkeley show. California also lays claim to the first solid black champion, Cunning Asta of Bambivin, who finished in 1936. (Two other solid blacks, both imported, also finished. These were Crystal Kennels' Ch. Hupp v. Schonhardt in 1942 and the Feldmans' Ch. Dirndl v. Schloss Helmstadt in 1950.) A long interval followed during which the occasional Group placements never reached the top until Ch. Dorem Display won at Westminster in 1947 and placed second the following year. This gave the breed impetus which it has never lost, and Group wins have become increasingly common.

The long-awaited achievement of Best in Show was slow in coming. Back in 1934, Ch. Mehitabel of Marienhof III was runner-up at Denver, but it was Ch. Dorem Display who finally accomplished this feat at Lackawanna in 1946. Display's overall record of five all-breed Bests, four Specialty Bests, and first in the Group at Westminster is still noteworthy.

The first bitch BIS winner was Ch. Sorceress of Ledahof at Quebec in 1948. Then came Ch. Hans of Sharonhof II in 1949 at Oklahoma City. In 1950, Ch. Charlena Sho-Nuff became the only Miniature to win Best in Show at Honolulu and later, after his arrival in the United States, became the first Hawaiian-bred AKC champion of the breed. (Strangely enough, his Massachusetts-bred son, Tarquin of Gregglee, returned to Hawaii to become the first all-Hawaiian champion in 1957.) Ch. Hit Parade's Lamplighter won a Canadian Best in Show in 1951 and several Groups as well before his early death in a kennel fire. Then came the banner year 1952, in which Miniatures scored no less than three BIS, won by Ch. Meldon's Ruffian, Ch. Forest Nod of Mandeville (the first bitch to go BIS at an AKC show) and Ch. Kalenheim Arno. In 1953 the breed won five Best in Show awards and 26 Group firsts, while in 1954 the count was four Best in Show wins and 35 Group firsts at all-breed shows. The top winner in the former year was Ch. Bursche v.

Ch. Phil-Mars Lucy Lady (1954) , winner of 2 BIS.

Ch. Phil-Mars Lugar, sire of 22 champions.

Hessen, with two BIS in 1953 and one in 1954, plus a total of 11 Group firsts and Best of Breed at Westminster in both years. Ch. Forest Nod of Mandeville and Ch. Meldon's Ruffian each added a second BIS in 1953; and the fourth BIS winner was Ch. Phil Mar's Mister John.

Three other Phil-Mar homebreds, Chs. Gay Lady, Gay Knight, and Gentleman Jack, won Group firsts in 1953, while in 1954 Ch. Phil-Mar Lucy Lady won two BIS plus a Group first and was the breed's top winner for that year. Ch. Hit Parade's Blacksmith Blues in 1954 was the first to win the Group on successive days.

Other top winners of the 1950's were Ch. Benrook Randy, with two BIS and 40 BB; Ch. Bursche v. Hessen, who died late in 1966, with three BIS; Ch. Perci-Bee's First Impression, with four Group firsts and 52 BB; and Ch. Marwyck Pitt-Penn Pirate, with one BIS and 75 BB.

In 1960 Helarry's Dark Victory went BIS at three successive shows in four days, from the classes, and won nine Group firsts and 15 Bests of Breed out of 17 times shown. His son, Ch. Helarry's Harmony, won his fifth BIS in 1964 and became the first of the breed to equal Display's record in this respect. Starting with Display, the line of BIS winners from father to son extends for five generations, through Ch. Meldon's Ruffian, his son Dark Victory, the latter's son Harmony, and the two Harmony sons, Chs. Franzel's Quick Silver and Blue Devil Sharpshooter (the latter from the classes in 1966).

Bitch winners of Best in Show have been comparatively few. Ch. Abingdon Heidi (from the classes), Ch. Victoria of Mary-O, and Canadian-bred Ch. Oak Gables Modiste scored one each. Ch. Phil-Mar Lucy Lady and Ch. Forest Nod of Mandeville tied for the record with two each for nearly 12 years, until Ch. Winsomor Miss Kitty gained her third BIS in 1966.

Ch. Mankit's Signal Go established a new record by winning his eighth specialty plus his twentieth group and third best in show in 1967. Two Miniature Schnauzers have won best in Show at Montgomery County. Ch. Dodi's Dimitri was first with a win in 1955 and Ch. Mankit's To The Moon took this coveted win in 1968 and again in 1969.

Today's competition has reached a point where a dog must not only be outstanding to break records, but must be consistently campaigned in top form over a long period. Ch. Fancyfree Fancy

Package compiled his record of 102 BB at some 300 shows, reportedly to prove that a Miniature Schnauzer could win 100. Ch. Phil-Mar Lugar, with two BIS and 71 BB, was a close rival to Ch. Yankee-Pride Colonel Stump, with three BIS and 72 BB during the late 1950's and early 1960's. In 1967, Lugar was the top living sire of the breed at stud, with a record of 22 champions in his 11th year. Though two years younger, Ch. Helarry's Dark Victory has a show record of five BIS and has already sired 24 champions (as of December 1967), giving him a slight edge over Lugar. They are the only two sires still active who have sired 20 or more champions.

Handful Kennels' team of four, including Ch. Benrook Bona and three of her progeny, was the first to go Best Team in Show at Westminster and Boston in 1955.

I have tried in vain to secure a complete list of the winners of the annual trophies formerly offered by the American Miniature Schnauzer Club. The following list is as full as I have been able to make it. Due to changes in AKC rules, these annual trophies have now been discontinued.

Year	Dog	Owner
1934	Ch. Jeff of Wollaton	Mrs. Kerns
1935	Ch. Jeff of Wollaton	Mrs. Kerns
1936	Ch. Wollaton Sheik	Mrs. Kerns (won outright)
1939	Ch. Minquas Marko	J. M. O'Connor
1940	Ch. Wingless Victor of Sharvogue	Mrs. Sailer
1941	Ch. Beulah's Job	Beulah L. Sullivan
1942	Ch. Cockerel of Sharvogue	Mrs. Sailer
1943	Ch. Heather Honey of Sharvogue	Mrs. Pierson
1944	Ch. Neff's Luzon	Mrs. Sailer (won outright)
1950	Ch. Dorem Inspiration	Dorothy S. Williams
1952	Ch. Benrook Bona and Ch. Diplomat of Marienhof	Gene Simmonds
	Ch. Kenhoff's I'm It and Ch. Kenhoff's Katy Did Too	N. A. Austin (Group wins)

During its nearly 35 years of existence, the American Miniature Schnauzer Club membership has grown to over 400, located in 36 states, Canada, and South America, with increasing representation from all sections of the country. Numerous regional clubs have also been formed, with the object of educating and encouraging local breeders, exhibitors, and owners. The first of these was the Potomac Miniature Schnauzer Club, which held its first specialty show in October 1945. It has since been superseded by the Mount Vernon Miniature Schnauzer Club, formerly the Chesapeake Miniature Schnauzer Club, formed in October 1953, which held its first match June 12, 1955. After a preliminary meeting at the Pittsburgh Show in 1945, the Penn-Ohio Miniature Schnauzer Club was founded in 1946, with a charter membership of 46. Its membership, not limited to local residents, totaled 290 in 1954 and it issues a mimeographed monthly news bulletin.

Other local clubs include the Chicago Miniature Schnauzer Club, which held its first specialty on April 3, 1954; the Miniature Schnauzer Club of Michigan, holding its first specialty on October 10, 1954; the Paul Revere Miniature Schnauzer Club, founded in October 1953; and the Miniature Schnauzer Club of California in 1956. A Hawaiian club, formed in 1957, has since disbanded. In 1966 there were three local breed clubs in California, two in Florida, and one each in Georgia, Alabama, Colorado and Missouri.

The addresses of these clubs, which change whenever new officers are elected, may be secured through the AKC or the American Miniature Schnauzer Club. The parent club is endeavoring to keep more closely in touch with breeders and exhibitors in every area. By supporting local groups and keeping members informed about breed events throughout the country through regular news notes and official club reports, it hopes to help fanciers maintain high quality as the breed's popularity increases.

The gain in popularity of the Miniature Schnauzer during recent years has been phenomenal. Starting from scratch as complete unknowns in 1924, Miniatures ranked eighth in number of AKC registrations in 1966 and seventh in 1967, for a total of 26,001 individual registrations the latter year—an increase of 23.7 percent over 1966—and their number is increasing. This is not an altogether happy situation for any breed. Inevitably, many of these puppies are bred by people who know little about the breed and are frequently more interested in making money than in producing top quality dogs. New owners eager for information and help find that such breeders have little real knowledge, and thus often they do not know where to turn. Moreover, the large demand for puppies leads to the use of many inferior animals for breeding. Sooner or later the supply exceeds the demand, prices fall, and the really serious breeders, who know and love the Miniature Schnauzer and are unwilling to cut corners, may find themselves unable to compete.

The American Miniature Schnauzer Club now has an Education Committee engaged in supplying copies of the breed standard and other information to newcomers. Since the name and address of the club secretary changes from time to time, those who wish to know it are advised to write to the American Kennel Club, 51 Madison Avenue, New York 10010.

Ch. Cuno v. Burgstädt.

6

American Producing Lines

DURING the first ten years of Miniature Schnauzer breeding in the United States (from 1925 to 1935), 108 dogs and bitches were imported from the Continent, nearly all from Germany, and were registered with the AKC. Some additional individuals are known to have died without being registered, and there were some further importations between 1935 and the beginning of World War II. All the American-bred Miniature Schnauzers now registered annually are, with very few exceptions, entirely descended from these dogs and bitches of 30 or 40 years ago; in fact, for the most part they trace to only a small portion of them.

Nearly two-thirds of the early importations have disappeared completely from modern champion pedigrees. Some of them were never used for breeding, either because they died early, were kept only as pets, or did not prove attractive to bitch owners. Some, although bred, left no surviving progeny, and still others produced stock which failed to meet the tests of competition and eventually gave way to more successful or luckier lines.

By 1935 all 54 American-bred Miniature Schnauzer champions that had finished up to that time traced to ten imported dogs and 11 imported bitches. Today the list of champions has increased to hundreds, with 90 winning the title in 1966, but the list of imported foundation producers has changed surprisingly little. Since their names will recur again and again they are listed below in the order of their approximate importance as indicated by the records of their descendants. A few individuals who had champion progeny during the early years but have had no descendants winning titles since 1940 have been omitted entirely or (if they are known to have registered descendants whelped in 1950 or later) have been included in a secondary list.

Imported Foundation Stock

(With descendants winning titles since 1940, in order of approximate importance based on records of their descendants)

Dogs	Bitches
Ch. Cuno v. Burgstädt	Ch. Amsel v.d. Cyriaksburg
Mack v.d. Goldbachhöhe	Ch. Lotte v.d. Goldbachhöhe
Ch. Marko v. Beutenberg	Lady v.d. Goldbachhöhe
Ch. Don v. Dornbusch	Christel v.d. Fallerburg
Ch. Viktor v. Dornbusch	Sn. Gaudi Baltischhort
Ch. Flieger Heinzelmännchen	Pia van den Zonnenheuvel
Ch. Bodo v. Schillerberg	Hadrosa v. Abbagamba
Ch. Qualm Heinzelmännchen	Käthe v. Annenhof
Jörg v. Dornbusch	Bässi v.d. Rissener Heide (black)
Ch. Amor zum Schlagbaum	Alma v.d. Zukunft (black)
Herzbub Heinzelmännchen	Can. Ch. Nette v. Mümlingtal
Ch. Giron v. Feldschlösschen	Tanta v. Dornbusch
Schnapp v. Dornbusch	Ch. Mücke Heinzelmännchen
Ch. Opal Heinzelmännchen	Ch. Walküre Heinzelmännchen
Ch. Urian Thuringia	Chenni v. Dornbusch
Ch. Fels Heinzelmännchen	Citti v.d. Goetheburg
Heliaster v. Abbagamba (black)	Krabbe Heinzelmännchen
	Ukase du Jorat
	Mira v. Liebenfels
	RSn. Dame Heinzelmännchen
	Heimia v. Abbagamba (black)

Dogs	Bitches
Ch. Hupp v. Schönhardt (black)	Ch. Polka Heinzelmännchen
	CzSn. Elfe Schnauzerheil
	Ch. Diana v. Feldschlösschen
	Dora v. Feldschlösschen

In the several cases where an imported dog or bitch has carried on only through imported progeny, he or she has not been included above, since the final results would have been the same had the animals in question never been imported. There have been few importations since World War II and as of November 1951, those imported had produced only one American-bred champion, although the black bitch Dirndl v. Schloss Helmstadt did complete her own title in 1950. Elfe v. Brentanopark appears once in the fourth generation behind Ch. Flosshilde v. Brittanhof. The French-bred male, Couza de Roc Fort (from German parents) now has two champion daughters, and Vesta Heinzelmännchen appears in a few pedigrees.

In 1953 I analyzed the pedigrees of five champions. One was Ch. Dorem Display, whelped in 1945, who was selected because of his outstanding show record and his ever-growing importance as a producer. The other four, Chs. Franz v. Elfland, Benrook Buckaroo, Suniland Hellzapoppin, and Salt 'N Pepper Sampler, were chosen from dogs who had finished their titles during the previous year and were bred in different sections of the country, from Massachusetts to California. My object was to discover whether geographical location resulted in substantial variations in pedigree. I checked this by counting the number of times each imported foundation dog or bitch appeared, and the proportions varied surprisingly little, as the list on p. 110 will show. This is admittedly a rough test, since it takes no account of how many generations intervene, but as all but two of the importations had arrived here by 1936, and the two exceptions in 1937 and 1939, respectively, the entire group dates back to a period covering little more than ten years.

The five pedigrees included among them 14 out of the complete list of 16 imported sires. Six of the 14 were represented in all five pedigrees, and with the exception of Cuno v. Burgstädt, they in-

Pedigree Analysis Showing Lines to Imported Stock

Importation	Display	Franz	Buckaroo	Hellzapoppin	Sampler
Amsel v.d. Cyriaksburg	68	45	129	161	586
* Affe of Oddacre†	28	9	52	43	240
* Lady v.d. Goldbachhöhe	22	9	43	39	193
* Lotte v.d. Goldbachhöhe	16	21	27	66	124
* Fiffi of Marlou†	2	6	3	13	27
* Jemima of Marienhof†	0	0	1	0	2
(Fels v.d. Goldbachhöhe) ‡	64	39	124	148	541
Mack v.d. Goldbachhöhe	28	9	52	43	240
Cuno v. Burgstädt	32	40	66	138	228
* Marko v. Beutenberg	11	9	26	24	95
* Urian Thuringia	0	0	1	0	0
Don v. Dornbusch	20	9	33	49	133
* Viktor v. Dornbusch	15	9	24	39	100
. . . .					
* Jörg v. Dornbusch	2	0	4	2	15
Flieger Heinzelmännchen	12	0	19	12	82
Bodo v. Schillerberg	5	12	16	27	55
Opal Heinzelmännchen	0	0	1	0	0
Qualm Heinzelmännchen	0	0	0	0	1
Giron v. Feldschlösschen	0	0	2	0	0
Amor zum Schlagbaum	0	1	0	0	0
Herzbub Heinzelmännchen	0	1	0	0	0
Christel v.d. Fallerburg	3	6	5	24	18
Gaudi Baltischhort	3	3	5	11	16
Alma v.d. Zukunft	0	0	1	0	2
Pia v.d. Zonnenheuvel	0	6	0	23	2
Nette v. Mümlingtal	0	1	0	0	2
Hadrosa v. Abbagamba	0	6	0	19	2
Käthe v. Annenhof	0	2	2	4	0
Bässi v.d. Rissener Heide	0	2	0	4	0

* Progeny of previous unstarred sire or dam and included in their total. Given to show the division between sublines, whether imported or American-bred.

† American-bred.

‡ Not imported himself, but influential through 3 imported get.

cluded the dogs which stand at the head of the list: Marko v. Beutenberg, Mack v.d. Goldbachhöhe, Don v. Dornbusch, Viktor v. Dornbusch, and Bodo v. Schillerberg. Two more appeared in four of the five pedigrees—Flieger Heinzelmännchen a significant number of times, but Jörg v. Dornbusch not often enough to be of comparable importance. None of the remaining six occurred more than twice, nor in more than a single pedigree, so they may be considered negligible. It is, however, worth noting that Fels v.d. Goldbachhöhe, who never came to this country himself but had a son and two daughters who did, occurs more often than any male actually imported.

The foundation bitches show much the same basic pattern of distribution as the dogs, with some variation. The leading three, Amsel v.d. Cyriaksburg and her two daughters Lady and Lotte v.d. Goldbachhöhe (the two latter accounting for the high record of their sire, Fels v.d. Goldbachhöhe, in great part) far outrank all others and occur in all five pedigrees. Christel v.d. Fallerburg and Gaudi Baltischhort are also found in all five, though well behind the leaders. Though not much behind Gaudi in total representation, Pia van den Zonneheuvel and Hadrosa v. Abbagamba each appear in only three out of the five pedigrees. The remaining four bitches, though of minor importance, all occur more often than the male dogs in the lowest group.

Three of the five pedigrees, those of Franz, Buckaroo, and Sampler, show 18 imported individuals apiece. Hellzapoppin has only 16 and Display 13. The latter fact is at least partly due to Display's being the oldest by several years. Every additional generation either doubles the number of appearances of all the names in the pedigree or introduces some new ones. In the case of a strongly line-bred dog such as Display, the number of imported ancestors is correspondingly low. Here the list of bitches is the most restricted and Display's pedigree actually contains only the top five.

In comparing the other four dogs, one notes that Buckaroo's pedigree has the greatest number of individual sires and (next to Display) the fewest dams. Hellzapoppin has the fewest sires, Franz the most dams, and Sampler, the youngest, shows by far the greatest total of appearances. This would naturally be expected, and with an increased number of generations this method of comparison quickly becomes unwieldy.

111

The two California-bred dogs, Franz and Hellzapoppin, do indicate some slight local variation. They are the only ones in whose pedigrees Lotte v.d. Goldbachhöhe substantially outranks her sister Lady. Franz, the only dog completely lacking Flieger Heinzelmännchen, is low in Dornbusch lines but high in the related Bodo v. Schillerberg. Hellzapoppin is relatively strong in both Dornbusch and Bodo, while correspondingly weak in Flieger lines. Through Ch. Job of Wollaton both Franz and Hellzappopin are also comparatively strong in lines to Christel v.d. Fallerburg, Pia van den Zonnenheuvel, and Hadrosa v. Abbagamba.

The constant selection which operates within a breed is well illustrated by the fact that out of 39 Miniature Schnauzer males registered by May 1935 only 21 left registered descendants and of these only 12 remain on the list of producing sires. All, of course, belonged to the three male lines which made up the breed in Germany, but only two of the nine imported representatives of Peter v. Westerberg had registered get, and among the 17 foundation sires on the list in 1966 not a single one goes in tail male to Peter.

The Lord v. Dornbusch line boasted only six representatives with registered descendants in 1935, of which five are on the list of foundation sires. However, none of the five has carried down in male line to the present day. For more than two decades all American-bred champions have belonged to the Prinz v. Rheinstein male line. There have been no male champions of the Lord line registered since 1941, and the last champion bitch was Martha of Bonalee, whelped in 1944, who finished in 1947. Twelve of the 17 foundation sires belong to the Prinz line, but this includes three imported between 1935 and 1939.

Nothing in the chromosome theory of inheritance as we know it today fully explains the undoubted fact that when dogs, cattle, horses, or other animals are selectively bred over many generations one male line almost invariably absorbs the others until it finally reigns supreme and unchallenged. The most plausible explanation is that certain qualities producing an outstanding sire may be carried in the Y chromosome, handed down directly from father to son. Whatever the reason, today's Miniature Schnauzer champions in this country all trace to Prinz v. Rheinstein, and with almost equal unanimity to Cuno v. Burgstädt.

Four of the five foundation sires belonging to the Lord v. Dornbusch line were inbred or line-bred von Dornbusch. The fifth, Bodo v. Schillerberg, was Dornbusch on his sire's side and carried closely related Werneburg blood on his dam's. The male line is given below, with the importations underlined.

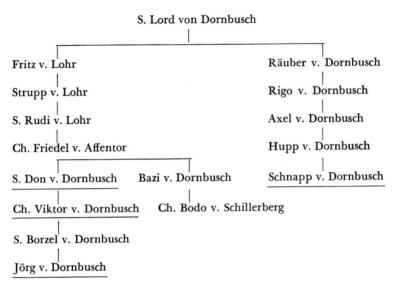

S. Lord von Dornbusch

Fritz v. Lohr — Räuber v. Dornbusch

Strupp v. Lohr — Rigo v. Dornbusch

S. Rudi v. Lohr — Axel v. Dornbusch

Ch. Friedel v. Affentor — Hupp v. Dornbusch

S. Don v. Dornbusch — Bazi v. Dornbusch — Schnapp v. Dornbusch

Ch. Viktor v. Dornbusch — Ch. Bodo v. Schillerberg

S. Borzel v. Dornbusch

Jörg v. Dornbusch

All these dogs were actually closely related. Not only was Don the sire of Viktor, who was in turn the grandsire of Jörg, but Bodo's sire was a half brother to Don. Though Schnapp was less close in tail male, his dam was a full sister to Don, and his sire, Hupp, out of a full sister to Viktor's dam. Jörg's dam was by Hupp, too, out of a litter sister to Viktor, and Borzel, in addition to being a Viktor son, was out of a full sister to the latter's sire, Don.

Because of their small size, good color and short bodies, the Dornbusch dogs were popular and were probably used more extensively outside their own kennels than any other studs of the early period in this country. Among the leading breeders and exhibitors of the late 1920's were Mrs. Dodge Sloane, Brookmeade Kennels, and Mr. Frank Spiekerman, Hitofa, who died some years ago. The first Miniature Schnauzer to become an American champion was Mrs. Sloane's Lenchen v. Dornbusch, handled by Frank Brumby, now of Havahome Kennels. Lenchen was an excellent shower, with

113

typical Dornbusch body and color but not as strong in head as the Goldbachhöhe dogs of her day. She was a German Siegerin as well as an American champion and was bred several times in this country. Her American progeny left no descendants among modern champions, but she influenced the breed through her imported son Don v. Dornbusch of Hitofa.

Don's imported son Ch. Viktor v. Dornbusch was owned by Mr. Harry G. Haskell, Halowell Kennels (Delaware), who a little later owned Ch. Bodo v. Schillerberg. Don left a Siegerin daughter, Vinesse v. Dornbusch, litter sister to Viktor, in Germany, and sired three American-bred champions. Nevertheless, Don's male line ended quickly, for Viktor was his only son to carry on except through daughters. Viktor's son, Fritz of Wollaton, is today represented only through his daughter, Ch. Asta of Wollaton, and Playboy of Marlou likewise through a daughter, Sue of Marlou. Viktor, however, left a son, S. Borzel v. Dornbusch, in Germany, whose son Jörg v. Dornbusch, whelped in 1929, was imported about 1930. Jörg was seldom shown and never became a champion. He was little if ever used outside the Allsworth Kennels of his owner, Mrs. Fred Hicks, but there he was mated to two champion bitches, Gretel and Nixe of Marienhof II, by Cuno v. Burgstädt. He left four producing daughters, one of them a champion, and a son, Allsworth Jorge, with whom the Don v. Dornbusch male line ends. Allsworth Jorge, bred to his half sister Allsworth Pandora, sired Nixe of Reklaw, the granddam of Ch. Vance of Palawan.

Aside from these Allsworth descendants, Viktor is represented through three daughters, Ch. Halowell Vega, Galloper of Marienhof, and Heidi of Wollaton. Halowell Vega, out of Sn. Gaudi Baltischhort, was mated back to her grandsire, Don v. Dornbusch, and produced Ch. Virgo of Tassac Hill, the sire of Jill of Wollaton II, from whom nearly all the modern Dorem dogs, including Ch. Dorem Display, are descended in tail female. Galloper of Marienhof also played an important part in the development of the Dorem strain, while Heidi of Wollaton is now of interest almost solely as the granddam of Ch. Moses of Wollaton and his sisters.

In addition to Viktor v. Dornbusch and Virgo of Tassac Hill, Don v. Dornbusch left a son, Hitofa Lon, whose imported dam Chenni v. Dornbusch was herself a Don granddaughter through Sn. Vinesse v. Dornbusch. Consequently, Lon was straight Dornbusch

114

on both sides and inbred to Don. He was mated to Judy of Wollaton, a granddaughter of Ch. Cuno v. Burgstädt, and their daughter
Ch. Salz of Tassac Hill became the dam of Ch. Wollaton Sheik.
Sheik's sire, Ch. Rudy of Wollaton, was a grandson of Hitofa
Regina, a Don daughter out of a Dornbusch bitch. Both Rudy and
Salz were the result of outcross matings which combined Dornbusch
with Cuno v. Burgstädt–Amsel v.d. Cyriaksburg stock. Perhaps this
is the reason that Sheik, despite an impressive show record and
considerable use at stud, produced only two champions, Gem of
Sparks and Mabo, and is most strongly represented today through
his daughter Cairnsmuir Sally, who was line-bred to the Cuno–
Amsel line. As the dam of Havahome Princess Carol, Sally is found
in the pedigrees of several champions, including the Eng. Ch.
Rannoch Dune Randolph of Appeline.

Out of Don's three American-bred champions only Virgo carried
on, and his non-champion daughter, Oddacre Wendy (out of Ch.
Amsel v.d. Cyriaksburg), was the only Don get to produce two
champions. Wendy's son Ch. Oddacre Tex carried on through two
non-champion daughters, Mardale Betzi and Mardale Sieglinde,
both out of Ch. Aennchen of Marienhof, but this line has been of
little importance. All things considered, it is surprising to find that
Ch. Dorem Display traces 20 times to Don—more often than to Ch.
Marko v. Beutenberg—and that Don equals or slightly exceeds
Marko in all four of the other pedigrees analyzed.

In comparing Don's record with Marko's, which will be considered in detail later on, it should be borne in mind that Don was
imported in 1926 at the age of two. Although popular at stud, he is
principally represented through the get which he left in Germany.
Marko, though little over two years younger, did not come over
until he was six and left more title winners in Germany than Don.
Nevertheless, Marko was very little used outside his own kennel and
his production record is in the main due to his American get, while
all but a handful of today's American winners are descended from
him in male line.

Schnapp v. Dornbusch, though he sired two American and one
imported champion, had only one granddaughter who finished her
title and carried on only through the daughters of his son Ch.
Oddacre Tex.

Halowell Kennels' Ch. Bodo v. Schillerberg was more successful than Don as a sire of champions, with five to his credit, plus 15 grandchildren. Nevertheless, he ranks below Don in four of the five pedigrees analyzed, Ch. Franz v. Elfland's being the sole exception. Whelped in 1928 and imported late in 1929 or early in 1930, Bodo was a light pepper and salt dog of good type and bone, with a better head than Viktor, his kennel mate, but a trifle light in eye. He was predominantly Dornbusch in breeding and resembled that strain in type. However, his sire was a double grandson of S. Rudi v. Lohr, the sire of Ch. Amsel v.d. Cyriaksburg, and all his champions were out of bitches strong in Amsel blood.

Bodo's last champion, Halowell Bausond Baume, was whelped in 1936 when his sire was eight years old, but appears to have no descendants. Ch. Porgie of Marienhof and his sister Ch. Priscilla of Marienhof II were out of Fritzi of Marienhof, a double Amsel granddaughter, and both proved good producers. Priscilla was the dam of four champions and Porgie sired three, all of his being sons. Bodo's other two champion daughters, Jean and Joan of Wollaton, were both out of Ch. Jemima of Wollaton, an Amsel granddaughter, and both were the dams of champions. Mehitabel of Marienhof II should have been Bodo's sixth champion, but her wins were canceled on a technicality and she died without finishing. She was out of Ch. Mehitabel of Marienhof I, a daughter of Ch. Cuno v. Burgstädt and Fritzi of Marienhof (the latter dam of Porgie and Priscilla II) and was in my opinion the most outstanding bitch of her day, as well as the dam of four champions, including Marko of Marienhof and Mehitabel of Marienhof III. Bodo's non-champion daughters Halowell Mücke and Halowell Kitty were both out of Ch. Mücke Heinzelmännchen, an imported daughter of Bolt v. Annenhof, closely related to the Marienhof bitches from whom Bodo produced successfully. Kitty's great-grandson was Ch. Rufus of Marienhof II.

It seems rather surprising that Ch. Porgie of Marienhof, who left six producing sons (three of them champions), and eight producing daughters, including the dam of Ch. T.M.G. of Marienhof, should not have carried on beyond a generation or two in male line. His two best sons were litter brothers, Chs. Josiah and Joshua of Marienhof, out of Abigail of Marienhof. (Josiah of Marienhof, AKC R-98285, whelped 1951, is quite a different individual and should properly be Josiah of Marienhof IV.) Josiah, who remained

116

at Marienhof, left three champion daughters, all rather on the small side, one of them the Group winner Ch. Mehitabel of Marienhof IV. Joshua was sold to Charlie Ruggles, the film star, in California, where he sired two champion daughters and three other producers. Joshua's descendants were rather strongly inbred, with apparent success, but his only producing son was Beulah's Aman, mated with a litter sister, Ch. Beulah's Anna, to produce Beulah's B.B.B., the sire of the producing bitches Judith of Oakridge and Lady Starr. Ch. Beulah's Anna was, however, most notable as the dam of Ch. Beulah's Ich Fiehl, by Ch. Job of Wollaton. Ich Fiehl sired eight champions (the record for a California dog until the 1960's), six of whom were males, in addition to two producing bitches. From Ich Fiehl and Top Bid (by Joshua out of a Ch. Moses of Wollaton daughter) came Ch. Beulah's Job, the sire of four champions. Although the male line of Ich Fiehl and Beulah's Job goes back to Ch. Cuno v. Burgstädt, the line breeding to Joshua is carried further in Ch. Siegmund v. Nibelheim, whose dam, Susie Q. of Yarbro, was by Fretz of Marienhof, a litter brother to Joshua. Siegmund, who was whelped in 1943 but completed his title in 1949, was, I have been told, a dog of tremendous substance, lovely blue-gray color, and steady, quiet disposition, his faults being flat feet and a poor gait. He sired four champions, his son Franz v. Elfland finishing in 1952 when nearly four years old. This would seem to indicate that this line retains its quality to a good age and perhaps matures slowly, in contrast to some strains which mature quickly but deteriorate equally fast.

It is the lines to Joshua of Marienhof which account for the unusual number of occurrences of Bodo v. Schillerberg in the pedigree analysis of Ch. Franz v. Elfland and other California-breds. It is also through them that Porgie is most heavily represented, for his eastern descendants carry little if any inbreeding to him.

Porgie also left a non-champion son, Charitable of Marienhof, from the only litter out of Ch. Charity of Marienhof. A Marko v. Beutenberg daughter line-bred to Cuno v. Burgstädt, Charity was an exceptionally nice small bitch who won Best Brace in Show at Colorado in 1934 under Hopton, paired with her half sister Ch. Mehitabel of Marienhof III. Charitable was mated to Heidy Anfiger, a double Marko v. Beutenberg granddaughter, so that the resulting litter carried three crosses to Marko and five to Cuno.

117

Trumpf Anfiger (a son of Charitable and Heidy) sired the dam of Ch. Vance of Palawan, Nixe v.d. Frevolyburg, who appears to have been the only puppy registered out of the two litters he is known to have sired. Trumpf was on the small side, with big furnishings and wonderful temperament, but the male line from Porgie ends with him.

In addition to the above, Porgie sired a dog and a bitch out of Gretel of Allsworth who were whelped in England, in quarantine, and both left numerous champion descendants there in later generations. These were Simon of Offley and Offley Becky Sharp. Simon's male line, too, has disappeared.

Unquestionably, however, Porgie's greatest claim to influence on the modern breed is through his daughter Tyranena Pansy of Marienhof, an older full sister to Chs. Josiah and Joshua of Marienhof. Their dam, Abigail of Marienhof, was a black and silver notable for her large litters (she formerly held the breed record for two litters of ten, all successfully reared). Abigail was by Ch. Marko v. Beutenberg out of Fiffi of Marlou, a black and cream daughter of Ch. Amsel v.d. Cyriaksburg and Cuno v. Burgstädt, a line which was notably successful with Bodo v. Schillerberg blood. From the mating of Abigail and Porgie came a total of two champions and five other producers, with eight champion grandchildren. Pansy herself produced two champions, which is not a remarkable record in itself, but one of them was Ch. T.M.G. of Marienhof. Whelped in 1936, T.M.G. sired 20 champions and this record stood unequalled for more than a decade until surpassed by his descendant Ch. Dorem Display.

Since T.M.G. belongs to the Cuno v. Burgstädt male line, he will be discussed there rather than at this time. It is interesting to note, however, that doubling up on Bodo or Porgie showed a tendency to produce very small size among the outstanding individuals. This seems to have been offset by additional lines to Marko v. Beutenberg in the East, while in California Ch. Job of Wollaton contributed the tremendous bone and substance of his sire, Ch. Moses of Wollaton.

All the imported foundation sires belonging to the Prinz v. Rheinstein line are descended from his son Ch. Gift Chemnitz-Plauen. They trace through Gift's son S. Trumpf Chemnitz-Plauen and thence from one of the full brothers S. Heinerle Chemnitz-

Leading Imported Sires

(And their descendants in male line with 3 or more AKC champions. Omitted generations indicated by dotted lines; sires of less than 3 champions in italics)

	Champions
LORD v. DORNBUSCH LINE	
Ch. Don v. Dornbusch of Hitofa	4
Ch. Bodo v. Schillerberg	5
Ch. Porgie of Marienhof	3
Ch. Josiah of Marienhof	3
PRINZ v. RHEINSTEIN LINE	
Linus Chemnitz-Plauen Branch	
Mack v.d. Goldbachhöhe	2
Ch. Affe of Oddacre	5
WS & Ch. Qualm Heinzelmännchen	3
Ch. Rufus of Marienhof I	3
.... Ledahof's Sentry (grandson)	4
Heinerle Chemnitz-Plauen Branch	
Flieger Henzelmännchen	5
Ch. Flieger of Edgeover	5
Falcon of Sharvogue	4
.... Ch. Vance of Palawan	8
Ch. Dewey of Kenhoff	4
Jonaire Dapper Dan	4
.... Ch. Mister Chips of Mulberry	3
Ch. Cuno v. Burgstädt	14
Ch. Cuno of Wollaton	4
Ch. Jeff of Wollaton	7
Hans of Wollaton II	3
Ch. Moses of Wollaton	3
Ch. Job of Wollaton	3
Ch. Beulah's Ich Fiehl	8
Ch. Beulah's Job	4
Ch. Siegmund v. Nibelheim	4
Ch. Marko v. Beutenberg	9
Ch. Marko of Marienhof	13
Ch. T.M.G. of Marienhof	20
Ch. Happy of Marienhof	4
.... Ch. Trumpfhund v. Stortzborg	3
Ch. Kubla Khan of Marienhof	8
Ch. Minquas Bimelech	4
Ch. Neff's Luzon	4
Ch. Cockerel of Sharvogue	5

119

Ch. Jonaire Little Boy Blue 3
Ch. Stylobate of Sharvogue 5
Ch. Dorem Spotlight 6
Ch. Sandman of Sharvogue 5
Ch. Tweed Packet of Wilkern 15
Ch. Wilkern Reveille 6
Ch. Wilkern Mr. Jackpot 5
....Ch. Dorem Display
(great-grandson) 42

Plauen and Linus Chemnitz-Plauen. While the Linus line was outstanding in Germany, Heinerle's has surpassed it in this country and nearly all modern American-bred champions belong to the latter.

These importations fall into several related groups. The descendants of Linus Chemnitz-Plauen are nearly all through Bolt v. Annenhof. Though numerous, for the most part they have failed to establish enduring male lines, although there are a few individuals who might still reverse the trend. Ch. Dorem Delegate, whelped in 1946, and Ch. Saladin of Ledahof, whelped in 1947, were both by Ledahof's Sentry and trace to WS. Qualm Heinzelmännchen, who was imported just before the war. I believe Qualm was the last importation who exerted any considerable influence on the breed.

Another member of the Bolt line, going back to much earlier days, was Mack v.d. Goldbachhöhe, a son of Fels v.d. Goldbachhöhe. Both these dogs are so closely associated with Amsel v.d. Cyriaksburg that they should be discussed as a group. Amsel's most important producers were the daughters Lotte and Lady, by Fels, imported with her, and her son by Mack, Affe of Oddacre. Had Mack lived long enough to have had any real opportunity at stud, he would undoubtedly have had a great influence on the breed, for he was a dog of excellent type and a remarkable producer. He resembled his grandson, Ch. Moses Taylor, but was smaller, being under 12 inches, dark pepper and salt with cream markings, somewhat reserved in temperament, but with a splendid head. Imported in 1925, Mack died of distemper only a few months later after siring only four litters, from which five puppies survived. Among them were Ch. Affe and Ch. Brookmeade Amsel, the latter out of Ch. Lotte v.d. Goldbachhöhe, Mack's half sister on the sire's side. The breed was then so weak numerically that after Mack's death there

120

MALE LINES FROM PRINZ TO FOUNDATION SIRES

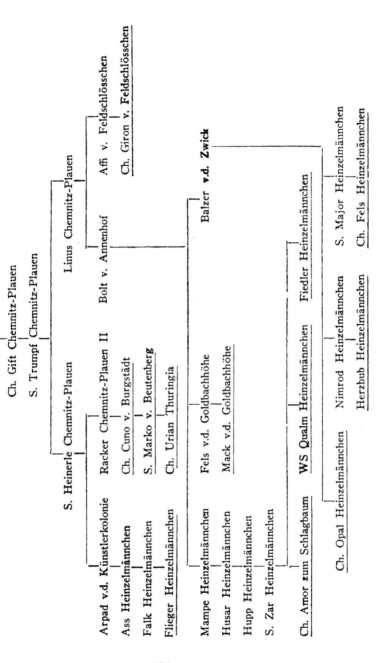

Prinz v. Rheinstein

Ch. Gift Chemnitz-Plauen

S. Trumpf Chemnitz-Plauen

Linus Chemnitz-Plauen

Affi v. Feldschlösschen

Ch. Giron v. Feldschlösschen

Bolt v. Annenhof

Balzer v.d. Zwick

S. Heinerle Chemnitz-Plauen

Racker Chemnitz-Plauen II

Ch. Cuno v. Burgstädt

S. Marko v. Beutenberg

Ch. Urian Thuringia

Fiedler Heinzelmännchen

S. Major Heinzelmännchen

Ch. Fels Heinzelmännchen

Arpad v.d. Künstlerkolonie

Ass Heinzelmännchen

Falk Heinzelmännchen

Flieger Heinzelmännchen

Fels v.d. Goldbachhöhe

Mack v.d. Goldbachhöhe

WS Qualm Heinzelmännchen

Nimrod Heinzelmännchen

Herzbub Heinzelmännchen

Mampe Heinzelmännchen

Husar Heinzelmännchen

Hupp Heinzelmännchen

S. Zar Heinzelmännchen

Ch. Amor zum Schlagbaum

Ch. Opal Heinzelmännchen

121

was no other stud dog available in America until 1926, when Hitofa Kennels imported Ch. Don v. Dornbusch, to whom Amsel was bred, while Affe was used at stud on his half sisters Lotte and Lady. All Mack's surviving descendants came from his son Affe, as the other lines eventually died out.

Amsel v.d. Cyriaksburg was an excellent dam, caring for her daughters' puppies if she happened to have none of her own. Her personality, style, and many good qualities were passed on to her descendants and undoubtedly have helped to popularize the breed. She was small even for her day, when 12 inches was the maximum, and never had large litters. Although she produced only three champions, Affe, Lotte, and Innocence of Marienhof (by her double grandson Moses Taylor), several others might have won their titles had they been shown sufficiently. Affe's litter sister, Woodway Raggedy Ann, went Best American-bred at the first specialty show in 1927, and was the only Amsel daughter who lived to maturity that did not produce a champion. In all, Amsel left 22 champion grandchildren including two double grandsons, plus a producing son, Lenz v.d. Goldbachhöhe, who remained in Germany.

Affe, the son of Mack and Amsel, was bred by Mrs. Slattery and shown unregistered as Affe of Marienhof before being sold and registered as Affe of Oddacre. Whelped July 15, 1925, he was one of the first American-bred litter. Unlike Mack, Affe lived to a good old age and was still siring puppies when ten years old. However, for most of his life he was owned by Woodway Kennels in South Carolina, where he was not available at public stud and hardly any of his puppies were shown. Three of his five champions dated from his first year, while the other two were not whelped until he was 8½. None of his three champion sons carried on in male line, so that Affe is represented today principally through his non-champion daughters, Fritzi of Marienhof and Gray Girl of Marienhof, both out of his half sister Lady v.d. Goldbachhöhe, and through two daughters of his son Ch. Medor Strupp, who was out of Ch. Lotte.

Affe was under the 12-inch limit of those days, and was a rather dark pepper and salt, with dark face and whiskers, characteristics not infrequently found among his descendants. He was still in good health when past 12 years old. That he did not leave a producing male line was probably due to circumstances, for his best son, Moses, was too closely bred to be used in his home kennel and other breeders considered him too large, for he matured at 12½ inches. Moses' brother Medor Strupp did fairly well with limited opportunities, and his daughter Cairnsmuir Wistful was the dam of Falcon of Sharvogue, who died before his fourth birthday leaving four champions. Three of Falcon's get appear in the pedigree of Dorem Display, who traces to Affe 28 times.

Ch. Lotte v.d. Goldbachhöhe, one of Amsel v.d. Cyriaksburg's imported daughters, held the breed record of 12 champions for 25 years until it was equalled by Ch. Sorceress of Ledahof in 1959. They came from five different litters by three sires. One other litter was wiped out by distemper while still very young, and her last litter, by an inferior dog, was the only mating which did not produce a winner. Lotte's first champion was by Mack, her next two by Affe. The remaining nine were by Cuno v. Burgstädt. All five of the last litter by Cuno (Marienhof-bred but whelped after Lotte was sold to Mardale Kennels and carrying that kennel name) completed their titles. I believe this is still the only instance of five champions in one litter. None of the five, however, proved important as producers, though Mardale Rudi carried on through a mating to the daughter of his full sister Ch. Aennchen of Marienhof, which produced Bramall Wilma, the granddam of Ch. Normack Fiedler.

Ch. Aennchen was the outstanding show bitch of her day, although she was originally considered outclassed by her half sisters Ch. Geisha of Aramink, who died young, and Ch. Mehitabel of Marienhof I, who died in 1932. Widely shown under the ownership of Mardale Kennels, Aennchen was the first American-bred Miniature to win the Group. As a puppy she was almost black and cream, but became grayer as she matured, though always retaining a strong reddish tinge derived from her dam. Aennchen had a beautiful head and expression, and was a natural shower with a lovely disposition. As the first really good one I ever owned, before she was bought by Mardale, I have always had a very warm feeling toward her, and she had a long memory for her friends.

As a producer, Aennchen fell short of expectations, perhaps because of being so strenuously campaigned. Her two recorded litters contained only one champion, Mardale Benjie, and she appears today only through her two daughters by Ch. Oddacre Tex. Mardale Betzi was the dam of Bramall Wilma, previously mentioned, and her sister Mardale Sieglinde, bred to Ch. T.M.G. of

123

Marienhof, produced Sieglinde v. Neff. Through Sieglinde's granddaughter Neff's Risque, the dam of Ledahof's Sentry, this line carried down to Ch. Sorceress of Ledahof. Neff's Risque was also the dam of two champions and additional producers.

Ch. Gretel of Marienhof, a litter sister to Aennchen, was larger than her sister, a trifle long in body and red in color, but excelling in head and furnishings. In three litters by Jörg v. Dornbusch she had four producers, including Ch. Allsworth Gossip (the granddam of Wild Honey of Sharvogue), Allsworth Pandora (the granddam of Nixe v.d. Frevolyburg), Allsworth Vinesse, and Gretel of Allsworth, the latter exported to England.

Ch. Lotte's best producing daughter and sons were from the litter after Aennchen and Gretel, whelped in October 1928. Ch. Cuno of Wollaton, the most successful American-bred son of Cuno v. Burgstädt, sired four champions and six other producers. His brother Joris of Wollaton sired only one litter before being sold as a pet and taken out of the country. Joris was the larger of the two, but I preferred him to Cuno, and his daughter, Maggie of Wollaton, was the dam of three champions and a producer of major importance. Finally, Ch. Jemima of Wollaton, sister to Cuno and Joris, was the dam of three notable champions and a daughter, Judy of Wollaton, to whom many of the leading bitch lines of today can be traced. They are discussed more fully under the Cuno and Bodo male lines.

Lady v.d. Goldbachhöhe, litter sister to Lotte, was very different in type. Where Lotte excelled in head and furnishings, was rather low-set, with a slight tendency toward length of body and softness of coat, together with reddish color, Lady was darker and grayer, though still not a chinchilla pepper and salt, was not so short on the leg, and had an extremely hard coat, almost entirely lacking in whisker. Few of her puppies were top show dogs, the best being Ch. Geisha of Aramink, who died young leaving no progeny. However, Lady's daughters have a remarkable record as producers, passing on hard coats, good color, and superlative showmanship. Lady produced another champion in Hermione of Marienhof, who closely resembled Lotte, her aunt. By her half brother Affe, Lady was the dam of Fritzi of Marienhof and Grey Girl of Marienhof, through whose descendants she appeared 22 times in the pedigree of Ch. Dorem Display, and through whom Affe is most often represented.

124

Fritzi of Marienhof resembled her dam in coat and color. By Ch. Cuno v. Burgstädt, Fritzi was the dam of Ch. Mehitabel of Marienhof I (dam of Mehitabel of Marienhof II), already mentioned under her sire, Bodo. Two other champions, Porgie of Marienhof and Priscilla of Marienhof II, were also by Bodo out of Fritzi. Porgie has already been discussed. Priscilla, the dam of four champions, has influenced the breed in England through her great-granddaughter Minquas Harriet, dam of Eng. Ch. Dondeau Hamerika.

Grey Girl of Marienhof, an older full sister to Fritzi, was the first light chinchilla gray to appear at the Marienhof Kennels. This may have been derived from Zecke, described as light gray, who was the granddam of Ch. Amsel v.d. Cyriaksburg, Grey Girl's double granddam. The latter was of good type, with excellent hard coat, but was not shown because of a slight touch of chorea following distemper. Her champion daughter Nixe of Marienhof, by Cuno v. Burgstädt, was the great-granddam of Nixe v.d. Frevolyburg and appears together with Allsworth Pandora in the pedigree of Ch. Vance of Palawan. Grey Girl's litter by Viktor v. Dornbusch was of notable importance to the development of the breed. From it came two daughters, Primrose of Marienhof and Galloper of Marienhof. Primrose, small, very hard coated, with scant whisker, short body, and a white front foot but otherwise good color, had a champion descendant in Joaq Whizz-Bang, finished in 1952, and her line is still carrying on. Galloper was larger than her sister, with better furnishings, and was a producer of rare quality. It was indeed unfortunate that she was run over after whelping her only litter.

One of the problems which breeders faced in the late 1920's and early 1930's was color. Bicolor puppies (i.e., black with cream or silver markings) occurred frequently in litters from pepper and salt parents. These were, and still are, allowed under the standard, but there seemed to be a general feeling that judges were less likely to put them up, so they were usually sold as pets. Attempts to produce light, clear grays by breeding the darker pepper and salts with reddish or yellowish intermixture to the Dornbusch dogs often resulted in bicolor puppies in the first generation or more. Today the bicolors, though they still occur, are much less common. There was a bicolor bitch, Fee of Edgeover, in Grey Girl's litter, who might have been the first champion of her color but was killed when lacking only a point or two. The first black and silver champion did not finish until 1938, when Inka of Aspin Hill made his title. He was a handsome, flashy dog, who left a producing daughter in McLuckie's Queen Alice. Inka reportedly turned gray as he grew older, which frequently happens. This makes it difficult to ascertain exactly how many bicolor champions there actually have been, particularly if the puppies were registered at an early age. I have found six which were registered as bicolors, but several may have changed. The six are: Halowell Bausond Baume (another male) in 1938, Dearborn Minuet and Gretchen v. Harter in 1940, Lady Gildae in 1946, Clairedale Compensation in 1949, and Marnan's Hi Jinks in 1952. Gretchen at least, retained her color to an advanced age.

The pepper and salt puppies in Galloper of Marienhof's litter numbered four future champions, Flieger, Fips, Freifrau, and Floerchen of Edgeover. They were sired by Flieger Heinzelmännchen, a line-bred dog from the Heinzelmännchen Kennels, then just establishing their great reputation, who traced in male line through S. Heinerle Chemnitz-Plauen to Prinz v. Rheinstein. Flieger was chosen carefuly late in 1929 shortly after the death of Cuno v. Burgstädt. The specifications included small size (for the 12-inch shoulder height was still in force), gray color, a pedigree suitable for use with Cuno daughters, and a whelping date before December 31, 1929, as a change made in the breed standard a short time before (but rescinded in 1934) disqualified cropped dogs whelped after December 31, 1929. Herr Walther complied with this request by sending Flieger to Rome, and in the spring a friend took him to Boston, where he reached Mrs. Martin of Ledahof in May 1930. He was a charming little fellow, with good general type, though not exceptionally strong head, and a friendly, outgoing temperament which he passed on in full measure to most of his descendants. He was presently sold to Mardale Kennels, but unfortunately died of blacktongue after only six months at stud, leaving eight litters from which came five champions. Besides the four out of Galloper of Marienhof, Flieger sired Ch. Abner of Marlou from Jemima of Marienhof, a daughter of Cuno v. Burgstädt and Amsel v.d. Cyriaksburg. Abner, a small, stylish gray, left three producing daughters. One of them, Pepper of Marlou, was the dam of Ch. Shaw's Little Pepper, the first of the breed to win a CD title in obedience work (1936). Flieger's descendants have included many good obedience workers. Pepper of Marlou's litter sister, Ch. Pal of Marlou, was the dam of three champions and granddam of five. From her daughter Amarantha of Ravenroyd, bred by the well-known judge Alva Rosenberg, came Ch. Lucky of Marienhof, the ancestress of such successful producing bitches as Ch. Rachel of Marienhof II, Ch. Karen of Marienhof II, and Ch. Dody's Rhapsody. Amarantha was also the dam of Ch. Rosalie of Marienhof, the dam of Ch. Rufus of Marienhof I.

The majority of Flieger Heinzelmännchen descendants are from his son Ch. Flieger of Edgeover, some of them in conjunction with the latter's sister, Ch. Freifrau of Edgeover, both owned by Ledahof Kennels. This mating was strong in Rudi v. Lohr blood, derived from Flieger Heinzelmännchen (who carried six lines to him) and from Galloper of Marienhof, who received it both from her sire, Viktor v. Dornbusch, and her dam, Grey Girl, whose double grand-dam, Amsel v.d. Cyriaksburg, was a Rudi daughter. The best of an exceptional litter, Flieger of Edgeover was a small dog of good color and unusual bone, with a lovely disposition. His worst fault was a slight thickness in skull. Unlike his sire, he lived to be 11 and was always popular at stud. The first of his five champions was sired when he was a year and a half; the last of his eight non-champion producers, six years later. Before carrying this line further, however, it is necessary to return to the early days of the breed in this country, to discuss other dogs which played a major part in its development.

Amsel v.d. Cyriaksburg's producing daughter Oddacre Wendy, a small silver gray bitch by Don v. Dornbusch, was included under her sire. The remaining Amsel daughter of importance was Fiffi of Marlou, by Cuno v. Burgstädt, who was a black and cream full sister to the rather reddish Jemima of Marienhof. Fiffi, like her daughter Abigail of Marienhof, produced very large litters, and was most successful with her half brother Ch. Marko v. Beutenberg.

Two years after Mack v.d. Goldbachhöhe's death in 1925, Mrs. Slattery imported the three-year-old male Cuno v. Burgstädt, who was to make breed history and to have a more far-reaching effect upon the development of the breed in this country than any other imported sire. His record in the Pedigree Analysis speaks for itself, and his get included top show winners and outstanding producers in both dogs and bitches. Although he gained his American title, Cuno was not an exceptional individual. He was a dark pepper and salt with cream markings, short in body, with a big beard and furnishings. The last was a characteristic he passed on to his get in a day when hard coat often accompanied sparse whiskers and leg hair. Not very heavy in bone and standing well up on the leg, Cuno looked smaller than his 12 inches at the shoulder. He sired few litters outside his own kennel and was killed in a fight with a Setter before his value was generally realized. The record of his German get has been given in an earlier chapter. In this country he was used with Ch. Amsel, her daughters, and her granddaughters.

Cuno sired 14 American champions, a record which stood until it was finally broken by his great-grandson Ch. T.M.G. of Marienhof. In addition are his German winners and nine non-champion producers, in a day when the breed was still numerically weak. His daughters out of Amsel, Fiffi of Marlou, and Jemima of Marienhof have already been mentioned. Fiffi progeny included Ch. Agatha of Marienhof, sister to Abigail, and a son, Playboy of Marlou (by Viktor v. Dornbusch), who was the maternal grandsire of Ch. Pal of Marlou. Fiffi's daughter Abigail left numerous producers, the most important being the dam of T.M.G.

Another Cuno daughter, Raggety Ann Ganahof (litter sister to Ch. Mehitabel of Marienhof I), was bred back to her sire; their daughter Mira of Burgstadt produced Cairnsmuir Wistful by Ch. Medor Strupp. Wistful appears in many later pedigrees, both through her son Falcon of Sharvogue, by Flieger of Edgeover, and through Cairnsmuir Strupp's Maria, from her mating back to Strupp. Maria's daughter, Cairnsmuir Sally, is found in the pedigrees of several champions, among them Ch. Rannoch's Rampion and his son Eng. Ch. Rannoch-Dune Randolph of Appeline.

Of the Cuno sons, Joris of Wollaton and his brother Ch. Cuno of Wollaton, both bred by Marienhof Kennels, have been mentioned. Kester Anfiger, from the first litter bred by the writer, was out of the imported Käthe v. Annenhof, whose dam, Sn. Grille v. Hohndorf, was a full sister to Amsel's dam and produced a Siegerin to Cuno in Germany. Käthe was a somewhat long, low bitch of good color but short in muzzle. Temperamental and a poor whelper, she was one of the very few Miniature Schnauzer bitches to require a Caesarian. Her son Kester was somewhat reddish in color and a trifle large in that day of the 12-inch maximum (1928). Nevertheless, he sired the first Group winner in California, Ch. Affschen of Ravenroyd (out of the imported Bässi v.d. Rissener Heide, a black), and a litter sister, Troublesome Lady v.d. Aal, dam of four champions, whose descendants include such West Coast winners as Ch. Tobias of Oakridge II, Ch. Adam v. Elfland, and the Best in Show Int. Ch. Hit Parade's Lamplighter from Oklahoma. Another Kester daughter, Helmar Ganahof, was the dam of Ch. Charity of Marienhof, while his litter brother, Kunz Anfiger, smaller than Kester and better in color but with less bone, still has descendants, the latest champion being Martha of Bonalee.

Ch. Cuno of Wollaton was his sire's most successful American son and certainly the one with most opportunity at stud. A small, compact dog whelped in October 1928, he was used with a variety of bitches and bloodlines and sired four champions, three of them sons. His only champion daughter, Carmel of Marienhof out of Ch. Priscilla of Marienhof II, was from the last litter of which I have a record, whelped when he was 6½. Carmel died young leaving no progeny, but her litter sister, Carmelita of Marienhof, left a champion son and grandson.

Cuno of Wollaton's sons Ch. Chevvy of Wollaton and Ch. Agar of Wollaton were both out of daughters of the imported Christel v.d. Fallerburg, a bitch whose breeding closely resembled Flieger Heinzelmännchen's. However, it was largely through the non-champion Arno of Wollaton, out of Christel herself, that the Cuno of Wollaton male line carries down. Arno sired Hans of Wollaton II, out of Heidi of Wollaton, a Viktor v. Dornbusch daughter whose dam was the Dutch bitch Pia van den Zonnenheuvel. Pia appears to be the only Dutch Miniature who left producing progeny in this country, though Ch. Billy van den Zonnenheuvel, from the same kennel, was an early specialty show winner.

Hans of Wollaton II bred to Maggie of Wollaton (by Cuno of Wollaton's litter brother Joris out of the imported Hadrosa v. Abbagamba) sired a litter with three champions and an additional producer, from which have come many winners. It is interesting to observe that this important litter came from non-champion parents and grandparents, with no champions till the third generation, when there were four. Of the three bitches, Mollie of Wollaton (dam of Ch. Inka of Aspin Hill) and Ch. Millie of Wollaton (dam of Ch. Mitzie of Roxbury and granddam of Brookmeade Misstep) were most successful. However, their brother Ch. Moses of Wollaton was the most outstanding member of the litter and a really prepotent sire. Among his get were three champion sons and three producing daughters. Ch. Shaw's Little Pepper was the first of the breed to win a CD and Cora of Wollaton became the dam of the first Canadian-bred champion, Bendigo of Clearbrook. Roxena of Roxbury, California-bred, appears in many West Coast pedigrees and was the dam of Ch. Beulah's Anna and the producers Beulah's Aman and Top Bid. Roxena's dam, Julie of Wollaton, was by Ch. Virgo of Tassac Hill out of Devontre Duchess (a daughter of Cuno of Wollaton and Ch. Joan of Wollaton). Moses' best son was Ch. Job of Wollaton, a dog I greatly admired and considered one of the best of his day. Sold to Roxbury Kennels (California) as a puppy, Job had an excellent show and stud record there, but lacked the opportunities he might have had in the East with more good bitches available. He resembled his sire, Moses, in general type, both of them excelling in bone. Though his dam, Ch. Jemima of Wollaton (a sister to Cuno and Joris) was small, Job was a tremendously strongly built dog who gave the impression of being larger than he actually measured. From Job came the only important Cuno of Wollaton male line still winning down to 1957. Job sired three champions, and his son Ch. Beulah's Ich Fiehl sired eight, a high record in that day. Ich Fiehl's son Ch. Beulah's Job won the American Miniature Schnauzer Club trophy in 1941 and sired four champions, as did Job's own son Ch. Siegmund v. Nibelheim. One of Job of Wollaton's daughters, Stockdale Mischief Time, the dam of Ch. Beulah's Job Junior, appears in numerous champions of the Oakridge, Elfland, and Hit Parade Kennels. Another, Berwel Anfiger, through her daughter Berwel Anfiger II (by Flieger of Edgeover) is at the back of most Kenhoff and some Marwyck pedigrees, including Ch. Queen Mona of Silver Oaks and Ch. Silver Belle of Kenhoff.

Ch. Jeff of Wollaton (club trophy winner in 1934 and 1935) was the most outstanding son of Ch. Cuno of Wollaton. He was small, of good color, a great showman, and a very popular sire. His picture bears a striking resemblance to his modern descendant Ch. Diplomat of Marienhof. Jeff's dam was Jean of Wollaton, the first uncropped champion and a daughter of Bodo v. Schillerberg and Jemima of Wollaton (the dam of Job). Jeff was therefore strongly bred to the Cuno v. Burgstädt–Lotte v.d. Goldbachhöhe mating which had produced nine champions. Jeff himself sired seven champions but none of his four sons approached his own record and he failed to carry on as well as expected. His grandchildren included one Canadian and seven American-bred champions. Jeff's best son was Ch. Rudy of Wollaton, sire of the outstanding show winner Ch. Wollaton Sheik, and of the Can. Ch. Bendigo of Clearbrook, with a total of four. Sheik went Best of Breed at Westminster in 1936 as a puppy barely six months old, probably the youngest Miniature ever to perform this feat, and won the club's annual trophy for the year. His dam, Ch. Salz of Tassac Hill, was by a Dornbusch-bred dog, Hitofa Lon, out of Judy of Wollaton, a Ch. Jemima of Wollaton daughter (making her a half sister to Chs. Job, Jean, and Joan of Wollaton) by the Cuno of Wollaton son Arno of Wollaton (Moses' grandsire). Judy was later to achieve importance as the dam of Jessie and granddam of Jill of Wollaton II, the latter the foundation of the Dorem Kennels.

Rudy of Wollaton's dam, Rosie of Wollaton, was by Ch. Agar of Wollaton, Jeff's half brother, out of Hitofa Regina, a Don daughter with straight Dornbusch on both sides.

Wollaton Sheik sired two champion sons, one of whom, Ch. Mabo, still has some descendants. Sheik's only male line, however, was through the non-champion Heather Ale of Twells, who was out of Freifrau Heinzelmännchen, the imported dam of Flieger Heinzelmännchen. Heather Ale sired two champions, Elgarjon Bampy and Signalton, and the latter's son Ch. Elgarjon Sonny finished in 1954. Sheik's daughter Bojean was out of his half sister Wollaton Countess, a Rudy daughter whose dam was a Moses of Wollaton granddaughter. Bojean had several litters and appears in a number of pedigrees. Her daughter Geelong Peggy, by Ch. Sandman of Sharvogue, was the granddam of Ch. Patricia of Ledahof, a double Group winner and a champion at 11 months. Patricia's dam, Minquas Pamela (by Ch. Minquas Bimelech out of Geelong Peggy) was also the dam of Minquas Vivacious, the dam of two champions. Vivacious' producing daughter, Minquas Melita, by Ch. Meldon's Merit, is herself the dam of five champions. Several top producing bitches of Family III, including Ch. Blythewood Merry Melody, trace to her in tail female line. Another Bojean daughter, Geelong Starlight, is behind Ch. Geelong Playboy.

131

Ch. Blythewood Merry Melody: 8 champions.

Ch. Minquas Alicia, dam of 5 champions.

More important to the breed than any of Jeff of Wollaton's sons was his daughter Dorem Diva, a litter sister to Ch. Dorem Dilletante and to the Crufts Challenge Certificate winner Dorem Domino. Diva was a daughter of the Dorem foundation bitch Jill of Wollaton II (by Ch. Virgo of Tassac Hill, through whom she carried a Baltischhort line, and out of Jessie of Wollaton, a daughter of Ch. Marko v. Beutenberg and Judy of Wollaton, mentioned previously). It is to Diva and her half sister, Jill's daughter Ch. Dorem Dubonnet, that all the recent Dorem winners trace in tail female. I believe that more producing bitch lines today come through Jill than through any other member of Family I.

The most successful male line for the past 30 years comes from Cuno v. Burgstädt's imported son, Ch. Marko v. Beutenberg. Marko was over five years old when he arrived late in 1931 or early in 1932 at the Marienhof Kennels, and died in 1937 at the age of nine years. He was larger than any of the sires previously discussed, with a strong head and excellent expression which were to do much for the breed. While he was a double grandson of Racker Chemnitz-Plauen II (Cuno's sire), Marko was also a grandson of Corna v. Schönau, a daughter of the famous Standard Rigo Schnauzerlust. To Rigo he probably owed his head and expression, while inbreeding to Racker, plus additional Linus Chemnitz-Plauen through Cuno's dam, gave a very prepotent pedigree. Marko left three Sieger sons and two Siegerin daughters in Europe, a record unequalled by any other importation. Nevertheless, perhaps because 13 inches was large for those days, in spite of a revision of the breed standard, he was little used outside his own kennel. Later descendants of his German get reached England as well as this country but have not been included in the pedigree analysis because several generations intervened. However, his Czech Sieger son, Urian Thuringia, became one of the top show winners of his day for Mrs. Jeanes' Mardale Kennels.

Marko v. Beutenberg sired nine American champions, eight of them American-bred, a record excelled only by his sire, Cuno, at that time. Marko's imported son Urian, in spite of his show record, was never popular at stud, perhaps because of his somewhat reddish color and a coat so hard that his puppies may have lacked furnishings. Urian's only American champion was Rosel v. Neff, though he left two Siegerin daughters abroad and appears twice in Brookmeade's imported Citti v.d. Goetheburg. Citti left champion Brookmeade descendants and through Brookmeade Zipper comes down to Ch. Jonaire Clarchen, the dam of four champions.

Marko's American sons included Ch. Kingswood Jubilo (out of Ch. Joan of Wollaton), Ch. Mussolini of Marienhof, and the latter's brother Ch. Marko of Marienhof (out of Mehitabel of Marienhof II). Both Joan and Mehitabel were by Bodo v. Schillerberg out of Cuno v. Burgstädt daughters. Jubilo's litter sister, Kingswood Jacqueline, was also a champion and the dam of Ch. Kingswood Dollfuss as well as several other good ones who met untimely ends before they could finish. The Mehitabel II litter contained four champions in all, the bitches being Melissa and Mehitabel of Marienhof III.

This Marienhof litter produced a number of "firsts." Mussolini was the first Miniature Schnauzer shown in obedience and won the Novice Class at Philadelphia in 1935. He was not much used at stud because of his large size, but appears way back in the pedigree of a 1954 champion, Marwyck Maid of the Mist. Mussolini's sister, Ch. Mehitabel of Marienhof III, was the first uncropped Group winner and runner-up for Best in Show in 1934. Her daughter Ch. Mehitabel of Marienhof IV was also a Group winner, and this was the first instance of both dam and daughter winning the Group. Finally, the other male in the litter, Ch. Marko of Marienhof, was the first American-bred to sire more than ten champions, and of Marko v. Beutenberg's get was by all odds the most influential upon the future of the breed.

Marko v. Beutenberg's producing daughters included Abigail of Marienhof, decidedly the most important as she was the dam of Chs. Josiah and Joshua of Marienhof and five producers, among them Tyranena Pansy of Marienhof, the dam of Ch. T.M.G. Another Marko daughter, Felicity of Marienhof (out of Allsworth Vinesse), became the dam of Ch. Neff's Duchess of Marienhof, dam of the Urian Thuringia daughter Ch. Rosel v. Neff. Pussel Anfiger (out of Can. Ch. Nette v. Mümlingtal) was no show bitch but her daughters Heidy Anfiger and Isolde Anfiger (double granddaughters of Marko v. Beutenberg and sired by Marko of Marienhof) appear in many modern pedigrees with Kenhoff and Palawan lines.

Marko of Marienhof, Best of Breed at Westminster in 1935, was a dog of outstanding quality and temperament, with his sire's unsurpassed head and expression. His record of 13 champions equals the American-bred get of his grandsire, Cuno v. Burgstädt, and includes five sons. In addition, he left 12 non-champion producing daughters, the most successful being Amarantha of Ravenroyd, dam of three champions. Susan of Marienhof produced Ch. Minquas Marko, top winner in 1939 for Norcrest Kennels, and Minquas Harriet, who went to England. Heidy Anfiger, already mentioned, was the dam of Ch. Welf Anfiger, Best of Breed at Westminster in 1940. Ch. Hope of Marienhof, by Marko out of Ch. Priscilla of Marienhof II, produced four champions, Hosea of Marienhof by her own sire, and the producer Ch. Minquas Bimelech by Ch. Kubla Khan of Marienhof.

It is through his son Ch. T.M.G. of Marienhof that Marko stands out as something more than just another good sire and becomes a link in a chain which has made breed history. T.M.G., named for the well-known handler, Thomas M. Gately, was whelped in 1936, the eleventh of his sire's 13 champions. He was a dog of perfect size and balance, excelling in head and expression, with a small, dark eye, good coat, color, and depth of body, excellent temperament, and natural showmanship. In 1937 he won Best at Morris and Essex over the largest entry of the breed up to that time. The get of T.M.G. included 20 champions, the largest number for a single sire until Ch. Dorem Display, and a record surpassed only by the latter and his two sons, Tribute and Diplomat (all of whom were T.M.G.'s tail male descendants) until 1959. T.M.G. also left 11 non-champion producing daughters and at least 46 champion grand-children. His most successful producing daughters were Ch. Gracon's Canis of Kenhoff, dam of five champions, Ch. Imprudent of Sharvogue with three (including Ch. Dorem High Test), and Tamina of Marienhof with two American and one Canadian champion.

It is a remarkable fact that ten out of T.M.G.'s 11 champion sons were producers and that five of them were the sires of four or more champions. This is still more impressive because in his day there were fewer shows and less campaigning of dogs by professional handlers, plus the fact that his best sons were handicapped by war-time travel restrictions. The highest individual record among T.M.G. sons was made by Ch. Kubla Khan of Marienhof with eight American champions (three of them also Canadian) and one

Canadian. Two of Kubla's five sons, Ch. Minquas Bimelech and Am. & Can. Ch. Neff's Luzon (winner of the club trophy in 1944), each sired four American champions, while Luzon sired one Canadian also, but the male line seems to have ended with their sons. Another Kubla Khan son, Ch. Kismet of Marienhof, sired two daughters who are both producers and are out of McLuckie's Opal's Gal. One of them, Krista of Marienhof, was the dam of the first Hawaiian-bred Miniature champion, Charlena Sho-Nuff. Her sister, Ch. Karen of Marienhof II, includes among her total of four American and one Canadian champion three successful sires—Ch. Benrook Buckaroo, Ch. Benrook Beau Brummell and Ch. Benrook Basil. The fourth Kubla son, Khengis Khan of Marienhof, also sired two champions but has not carried the male line beyond his son Ch. Delightful of Marienhof. Three Kubla daughters, Kathie of Marienhof, Kathie Khan of Marienhof, and Katydid of Marienhof, were all Canadian champions. Katydid was a Group winner with an outstanding show record, both she and Kathie being American champions as well. Nevertheless, none of Kubla Khan's sons has as yet approached his record and to date his male line ends with his grandsons.

Another T.M.G. son, Ch. Kampfhund v. Stortzborg, sired two champions, one of whom, Ch. Trumpfhund v. Stortzborg, sired three, two of them sons. Ch. Michelob v. Huertgenwald was a double grandson of Kampfhund, but this male line went no further. However, Trumpfhund's daughter Ch. Sporschon v. Stortzborg is the dam of 1952 Ch. Joaq Whizz-Bang, by Ch. Meldon's Merit. Mrs. Margaret C. Perkins carried on during the war in a unique manner, breeding and showing in widely scattered sections of the country as she followed her Army husband from post to post with her "kennels on wheels." Her record of at least eight Stortzborg champions compiled during this period is an achievement which shows what can be accomplished under difficulties. Portable folding pens and a one-wheel trailer helped to solve some of the problems recounted in "Hitting the Road" in the *American Kennel Gazette* of April 1943.

Ch. Happy of Marienhof, a T.M.G. son out of Ch. Priscilla of Marienhof II, sired four champions, three of them daughters, and three non-champion producers. The son, Ch. Gesundheit v.d. Westen, was out of Carolina of Marienhof II, a Marko of Roxbury

Ch. Vance of Palawan, sire of first UDT winner.

Ch. Charlena Sho-Nuff, BIS 1950.

Ch. T.M.G. of Marienhof (center) with Handsome of Marienhof (left) and Ch. Kubla Khan of Marienhof (right).

daughter and double granddaughter of Marko of Marienhof. When almost nine, Gesundheit sired Fritz of Gordon's Farm, who finished in 1953 when almost six years old. Fritz's dam, Madchen v.d. Westen, was out of a litter sister to his sire, Gesundheit, while on her sire's side Madchen was by Skipper's Sohnone (son of a brother to Ch. Beulah's Ich Fiehl out of a sister to Ch. Beulah's Job) giving a combination of two strongly inbred lines.

Another sister of Gesundheit, Ch. Blumchen v.d. Westen, was mated to her sire (Ch. Happy of Marienhof) and produced Gretchen of Hargrahof. Gretchen in turn was mated back to Happy, her sire and grandsire, to produce Jeep of Hargrahof, the non-champion sire of Ch. Stockdale Spitfire and two other producers. Both Spitfire and Stockdale Jeep-o-lette were out of Dorem Starlight (a sister to Display's dam). Spitfire produced two champion daughters, one by Ch. Siegmund v. Nibelheim, the other, Fledermouse v. Rogar, by again breeding back to Happy of Marienhof. Jeep's other producing daughter, Jinx v.d. Westen, was out of Pearl H. v.d. Westen (by Ch. Beulah's Job out of Liebschen v.d. Westen, one of the Happy–Carolina II daughters). Jinx bred to Gesundheit, brother to her granddam, Liebschen, was the dam of Schoenie v.d. Westen. Schoenie produced Ch. Franz v.d. Westen by her half brother Eulenspiegel v.d. Westen (a son of Liebschen by Ch. Dorem Sparkler). This group of California pedigrees is of interest as a study of the lengths to which inbreeding can be carried. The last champion in the male line from Happy of Marienhof seems to be Fritz of Gordon's Farm.

Returning to T.M.G. of Marienhof we find three champions in a litter from his half sister Amarantha of Ravenroyd. The two bitches, Lucky and Rosalie of Marienhof, were both successful producers, Rosalie being the dam of Ch. Rufus of Marienhof I. Another successful T.M.G. litter was out of Berwel Anfiger II (by Ch. Flieger of Edgeover out of the Job of Wollaton daughter Berwel Anfiger). This litter, with four crosses to Marko v. Beutenberg and seven to Cuno v. Burgstädt, included Ch. Gracon's Galahad, Ch. Gracon's Canis of Kenhoff (dam of five champions), and Gracon's Galatea, dam of Ch. Lady Gildae (dam of four champions).

Although the get already mentioned would entitle him to a high rank among the top sires of the breed, T.M.G.'s greatest claim to fame is as the sire of eight Sharvogue champions in two litters out of the non-champion bitch Wild Honey of Sharvogue. The matings produced 14 puppies, five whelped in July 1938 and nine in March 1940, with four champions in each litter. There is nothing to indicate that their dam was ever mated to any other stud, and the kennel seems to have ceased active breeding during the war. Short Wave and Symphony of Sharvogue, the two bitches in the 1938 litter, do not appear to have been used for breeding, but the other six all left champion descendants, three of which were Best of Breed at Westminster in different years. The T.M.G. male line continues through Ch. Sandman of Sharvogue, and to it belong the great majority of today's winners.

At this point is is necessary to go back and pick up the descendants of Ch. Flieger of Edgeover, since the Flieger line played an important part in producing the modern breed, particularly the Dorem strain.

Flieger of Edgeover carried on principally through two sons and three daughters. Of the latter, Ch. Dorem Dubonnet, dam of two champions and five producers, is notable as the granddam of Display. Berwel Anfiger II, mentioned above, and Ch. Brookmeade Zuzu (daughter of the imported Citti v.d. Goetheburg) each produced two champions. Flieger's two best sons were Ch. Normack Fiedler and Falcon of Sharvogue. Fiedler was out of Miss Flash of Bramall, a daughter of Ch. Amor zum Schlagbaum and Bramall Wilma, an inbred Cuno v. Burgstädt bitch. Amor, an imported son of RS. Zar Heinzelmännchen, resembled Flieger of Edgeover in type, though he was slightly larger, and excelled in body, bone, coat, and temperament, while he could be faulted a little in skull. His only champion son, Welf Anfiger, was little used at stud. Both Welf and his older brother Valentin Anfiger are represented only through daughters. An Amor daughter, Vanessa Anfiger, appears in a number of Elfland champions in California, but Miss Flash of Bramall, through her son Normack Fiedler, is his most important get.

Normack Fiedler sired the first CDX winner, Dorem Extra, owned by Mrs. Redmond McCosker and out of Ch. Dorem Dubonnet, while the first UDT winner, Playboy of Kenhoff, was his grandson. Extra's son Ch. Dorem Reporter left three champions and six producers, most successful of the latter being Dorem Serenade, the dam of five champions, but none of his sons have as yet carried on in male line. The Fiedler son Ch. Sentinel of Ledahof (out of Susi v. Neff, a T.M.G. daughter) died of leptospirosis when barely three. He sired two champions in Norcrest Sentry and Mister Chips of Mulberry. Mister Chips went BOB at Westminster in 1950 when almost seven years old, but his three champions were all daughters.

Flieger of Edgeover's male line was represented until 1966 only through the Fiedler son Ch. Vance of Palawan. Vance carried excellent temperament on both sides and his descendants have included many obedience winners. His dam, Nixe v.d. Frevolyburg, excelled in coat and color and derived her unusually good temperament from her sire, the Ch. Porgie of Marienhof grandson Trumpf Anfiger. Vance was the most successful sire of the early 1940's, with a record of eight champions and 12 producers. Only Ch. Kubla Khan equalled this number in the years between T.M.G. and Display, while in champion grandchildren Vance leads decidedly, having 24 against Kubla Khan's 15.

Most successful of the Vance matings were his two litters from Ch. Gracon's Canis of Kenhoff, also a Flieger of Edgeover grandchild and in addition a T.M.G. daughter. Canis produced five champions, including Ch. Sassy Sue of Kenhoff, dam of four champions (one of them by her sire, Vance). Ch. Dewey of Kenhoff also sired four, two of them out of his full sister Sassy Sue. Dewey's male line continued for three more generations through Jonaire Dapper Dan (the non-champion sire of four), Ch. Jonaire Laddie, and Ch. Jonaire Frivolity (finished in 1950). Ch. Dorem Sparkler, a Vance son out of Display's dam, Ch. Dorem Searchlight, also left a non-champion son, Eulenspiegel v.d. Westen (out of Liebschen v.d. Westen), whose son Ch. Jaxon of Stockbridge finished in 1952. The Vance son Ch. Palawan Tuffy was whelped when his sire was seven. Vance is widely represented today through his daughters and granddaughters. Ch. Kenhoff's Double Threat, who finished in 1953, was out of Ch. Pandora of Kenhoff, a bitch by Vance out of his own daughter Sassy Sue. Ch. Hit Parade's Black Magic was by a non-champion Vance son, Whiffenpoof of Hit Parade, and there are many others.

Actually, perhaps even more important than Ch. Normack Fiedler as a sire was another Flieger of Edgeover son, Falcon of Sharvogue, bred by Cairnsmuir Kennels. He was an excellent individual

140

who failed to finish his championship because of a slipped kneecap and died when less than four years old. Falcon left four champions and a producer behind him. During the period from about 1934 to 1940, Dr. and Mrs. Briggs (Sharvogue Kennels) exhibited a number of champions, not all of their own breeding, and produced a group of dogs and bitches which were of major importance in developing today's Miniature Schnauzers. They were all closely bred to Ch. Flieger of Edgeover and his litter sister Ch. Freifrau of Edgeover, who were both owned by Mrs. L. B. Martin (Ledahof Kennels). Freifrau's son Ch. Timothy of Sharvogue, and her daughter Woots of Sharvogue, were both by Falcon and bred by Ledahof Kennels. Ch. Bleuboy of Sharvogue was also a Falcon son, out of Ch. Allsworth Gossip, a daughter of the imported Jörg v. Dornbusch and Ch. Gretel of Marienhof. Falcon's dam, Cairnsmuir Wistful, was by Ch. Medor Strupp (half brother to Gretel on the dam's side) out of an inbred Cuno v. Burgstädt dam. Wild Honey of Sharvogue, the dam of eight champions, was the result of a mating between the Falcon son, Ch. Bleuboy, and his half sister Woots, whose dam, Ch. Freifrau, was a sister to their double grandsire, Ch. Flieger. Wild Honey, as mentioned earlier, was bred to Ch. T.M.G. of Marienhof, who carried the same lines found in Gretel of Marienhof and Cairnsmuir Wistful, and was likewise related further back to Flieger and Freifrau's dam, Galloper of Marienhof.

The six producers from T.M.G. and Wild Honey were all champions. Sandman of Sharvogue was retained by his breeders. He and his brothers Stylobate and Cockerel of Sharvogue were all outstanding winners as well as sires. Wingless Victor of Sharvogue, the fourth male, left no champion get but had four champion grandchildren, one of them the Am. & Can. Ch. Neff's Luzon, winner of more than 40 Bests of Breed. The two bitches were Imprudent of Sharvogue, dam of three champions, and Heather Honey of Sharvogue, the granddam of four.

Ch. Timothy of Sharvogue sired two champions, Dorem Exclusive and Dorem Escapade, out of Dorem Diva, and the producer Dorem Elect out of Ch. Dorem Dubonnet, but all his producers were daughters. Bleuboy's male line also disappeared after a couple of generations. Brookmeade Zipper, another Flieger of Edgeover son, also left daughters, so the Flieger male line, represented through Normack Fiedler, has now disappeared.

141

Before examining the Dorem line, it would be well to consider and compare the records of the three brothers, Sandman, Stylobate, and Cockerel of Sharvogue. Stylobate, owned by Mrs. Charles Gleason, Long Island, N. Y., was considered by many fanciers the best individual. Not long after going Best of Breed at Westminster in 1941 he was accidentally killed when less than three years old. His stud opportunities had been restricted by his having been owned as a pet instead of heading a kennel. Nevertheless, he sired five champions and five producers from four different bitches, all but two of them being daughters. The most successful mating, to Ch. Dorem Dubonnet, included his only producing son, Dorem Spotlight. However, through his daughter Ch. Dorem Searchlight, the dam of Display, Stylobate is of the highest importance.

Sandman, on the other hand, had a long career, siring a Canadian champion who was whelped after his ninth birthday. He was still living at the age of nearly 14 as was his brother Cockerel, while their sister Heather Honey lived to past 15. While this proves Sandman's virility and staying power, it is difficult to make a fair comparison with Stylobate, whose early death curtailed his opportunities and whose established reputation must certainly have helped popularize his younger brothers. Sandman's five American champions included four sons. Ch. Dorem Parade achieved great renown as the paternal grandsire of Dorem Display. Ch. Tweed Packet of Wilkern (the Display daughter Ch. Debutante of Ledahof) was by far his most successful son, with a record of 14 champions in some four years at stud, for he was not whelped until 1948 and an injury halted his breeding activities in 1953. One of Sandman's non-champion sons, Stockdale Sandman, sired the first Best in Show winner after Display, Ch. Hans of Sharonhof II. Ch. Kenhoff's Double Threat, whelped in 1949, also sired champions. Sandman of Sharvogue's daughters include Annie Laurie of Wilkern, sister to Tweed Packet and dam of Ch. Wilkern Ado, as well as Ch. Dorem Liberty, dam of the notable Ch. Enchantress.

The third brother, Cockerel of Sharvogue, sired five American and two Canadian champions but left no producers at all comparable to his brothers'. The most successful were Ch. Jonaire Little Boy Blue (dog) and Can. Ch. Princess Pat of Marienhof (bitch).

The Dorem Kennels of Miss Dorothy Williams began breeding about 1934 and their first home-bred champion, Dorem Dilletante, whelped in 1935, was a litter brother to Dorem Diva, by Ch. Jeff of Wollaton out of Jill of Wollaton II. Although she never completed her championship, Jill was good enough to go Best of Winners at the Associated Terrier Specialty in 1936, when she defeated Ch. Wollaton Sheik and at least one bitch who subsequently became a champion. She was about 13 inches high, which was rather large for those days, with excellent color and a good head but perhaps a trifle long in body. Two years after the litter by Jeff, Jill was bred to Flieger of Edgeover and produced Ch. Dorem Dubonnet. Both Diva and Dubonnet were bred to Timothy of Sharvogue. In Diva's case the mating was not a close one for three generations back. The only individuals appearing more than once on Timothy's side, Flieger Heinzelmännchen and Galloper of Marienhof in the second and third generations, were not in Diva's pedigree at all. Further back, however, were 12 lines to Amsel v.d. Cyriaksburg and seven to Cuno v. Burgstädt.

Ch. Dorem Escapade, from the Timothy–Diva litter, was retained for breeding, as was the Dubonnet daughter Dorem Elect. The latter, with three lines to Flieger and Freifrau of Edgeover, was bred to Ch. Sandman of Sharvogue, who was closely related on his dam's (Wild Honey's) side. The line breeding was carried further by mating a male from this litter, Ch. Dorem Parade, to Ch. Dorem Escapade from the Timothy–Diva litter.

Ch. Dorem Dubonnet was also bred to Ch. Stylobate of Sharvogue, Sandman's brother, producing a remarkable litter of seven including two champions and three other producers. Among them was Dorem Spotlight, whose record of six champions was the highest of the breed for a sire not himself a title holder, until surpassed in the 1960's by Fanciful of Marienhof with ten. Spotlight's daughter Ch. Enchantress rivals Wild Honey as the dam of eight champions and until 1957, when the eleventh champion out of her daughter Ch. Sorceress finished, was excelled only by Ch. Lotte v.d. Gold-bachhöhe with 12. The bitches in this litter included Ch. Dorem Highlight, dam of four champions and granddam of 15, and Ch. Dorem Searchlight, dam of three champions including Dorem Display.

Ch. Dorem Parade (son of Ch. Sandman of Sharvogue and Ch. Dorem Escapade) was the paternal grandsire of Display and carried down the male line from T.M.G. Whelped six weeks after Pearl

Harbor, he does not seem to have been much used at stud. His only champion was the bitch Havahome Freshie, dam of two champions, who appears in the pedigree of Eng. Ch. Rannoch-Dune Randolph of Appeline. However, his non-champion son Dorem Cockade achieved renown as the sire of Ch. Dorem Display.

So far as I know, Cockade was shown only once, as a puppy, when he went Best of Breed, and was sold thereafter. He is described by his breeder as a very short-bodied dog, with all the qualities toward which she had been working carried almost to excess. He was used at stud only once before leaving the kennel and this mating to Ch. Dorem Searchlight produced Display and a sister, Ch. Dorem Shady Lady, the latter the dam of three champions and the foundation of the Phil-Mars Kennel. By the time Display's great show record called attention to Cockade's potential value as a sire, he had disappeared from the ken of breeders and it was too late to make use of him.

Dorem Display, whelped April 5, 1945, was one of those rare individuals who are preeminent as both show winners and producers. His show record has been given in another chapter. As a sire he outstripped the breed record of 20 champions previously held by his great-great-grandsire Ch. T.M.G. of Marienhof. And he carried on to later generations through an impressive list of producing sons and grandsons. Line breeding to Display was extensively employed. There are pedigrees in which he appears five times in five generations, and two champions came from a Display son bred to a double granddaughter. He died in 1959 shortly before his fourteenth birthday.

As an individual, Display was about 13 inches high, with a very dark undercoat when stripped, which became a lovely pepper and salt gray in full coat. This dark undercoat seems to appear fairly often in his get. He had a short back, good coat, excellent head and neck, and first class temperament. During his active show career Display was owned by Mr. and Mrs. Phil Meldon, who sold him in 1952 to Benrook Kennels.

Display's unique position in the breed was the result of various factors. Whelped just at the close of the war, when breeding and showing were rapidly increasing, he embodied the trend toward a more streamlined "Terrier type" which was an advantage in Group and Best in Show competition. Widely campaigned, he brought the breed to the attention of a broader public to whom it had been but little known. And to the reputation gained by his great show record was added early success as a sire.

Display was only ten months old when his first champion son, Dorem High Test, was whelped; Ch. Dorem Tribute followed in July and the litter brothers Diplomat and Delegate of Ledahof in October of the same year. This at once established him as a successful sire while he was still making his big wins. To this should be added the fact that his pedigree represents careful and experienced selection and line breeding, resulting in exceptional prepotency. From this combination of individual quality, prepotent pedigree, and show reputation came greater opportunities to prove his worth as a sire than any Miniature Schnauzer had previously enjoyed in this country. The only comparable record I know is that of RS. Zar Heinzelmännchen in Germany, who in 1935 sired 40 litters out of a total of 170 registered for the breed.

Display's impact on the breed was already apparent in 1957, but can now be better appraised and the relative standing of his leading sons analyzed. Altogether, he sired 42 AKC champions, of which the last, Ch. Gladding's Bie Bie, dam of ten champions, was whelped when he was 11 years old; his last litter, with the non-champion producer Storyland's Conquistador, was whelped when he was 12. Of his 26 champion sons, 16 sired at least one champion. Eleven non-champions and a Canadian champion also sired AKC title-winners. By 1950, when he was five years old, Display had sired 16 champions. During 1946 he sired six who finished, and during 1947 he sired ten. In 1952 seven of his get finished, including Ch. Meldon's Ruffian, whelped in 1950 and the youngest of his top-producing sons. Although five of his champions were whelped in 1953 he sired only two more. The 1953 group included Ch. Flirtation Walk Tiara, dam of six champions and his third-highest producing daughter. The second, Ch. Benrook Bona, was whelped in 1950 and produced nine champions.

Whereas Display's best daughters were whelped in his later years, his leading sons were older. Dorem Tribute, Diplomat of Ledahof and Dorem High Test were all whelped in 1946, and Benrook Beau Brummell and Meldon's Merit in 1947. Meldon's Ruffian came in 1950 and Gengler's Drum Major in 1951. Altogether, ten Display sons sired four or more champions each. They fall into three

Ch. Dorem Display, who won 5 BIS and sired 42 champions.

Ch. Dorem Favorite, sire of 16 champions.

Ch. Dorem Tribute, a Display son with 41 champion get.

groups: the top three, Tribute (41), Diplomat (29) and Ruffian (26) ; a middle pair, High Test (15) and Benrook Beau Brummell (13) ; the remainder, with less than ten, Ch. Meldon's Merit (9), Ch. Gengler's Drum Major (7), Ch. Delegate of Ledahof (5), Ch. Benrook Zorra (6), and Dorem Chance Play (4). While male line descendants of several of the others are still carrying on, only one has yet reached two figures who does not trace to the first three— Ch. Cosburn's Esquire, of the Beau Brummell line. Of dogs still ten years old or younger (i.e., whelped in or after 1957) with four or more champions there is one to Beau Brummell and one to Ch. Delegate of Ledahof. This does not mean, of course, that one of the other lines may not suddenly produce a truly outstanding sire, but it does indicate that the dominating male lines for the past decade have traced to Tribute, Diplomat, and more recently to Ruffian.

Ch. Dorem Tribute, Display's second oldest champion, was whelped when his sire was 15 months old, out of Ch. Dorem Silverette, the dam of five champions by as many different sires. Although his final record was 41 champions, he made a rather slow start. He had been sold young to the Meldons, who also owned his sire, Display, and his older half brother, Dorem High Test, both of whom were promoted in preference to Tribute. When he was bought back by Dorem Kennels only two of his get had finished. By 1951 he had sired only eight, but no less than nine finished the following year, and eight more in 1953. Five champions finished after Tribute was ten years old, the last one whelped just before his twelfth birthday. Among his best daughters were Ch. Winsome High Style, a Group winner twice before she was a year old and the dam of six champions; Ch. Meldon's Mañana and Ch. Phil-Mar Lady Love, each with five; and Ch. Phil-Mar Gay Lady (also a Group winner, and out of Display's litter sister), who produced two BIS winners in one litter.

Tribute's son, Ch. Meldon's Seabiscuit, sired all his five champions before he was six years old. Ch. Dody's Daguerreotype, potentially a great sire with three champions to his credit and three more who died before finishing, changed hands and was withdrawn from stud. Ch. Phil-Mar Tributary, his sire's youngest champion, is the sire of four title winners, all daughters. Other Tribute sons are still carrying on in male line, but all those with four or more champions as of 1967 come down from either Ch. Benrook Bucka-

147

roo or Ch. Dorem Favorite. Buckaroo was himself the sire of 17 champions, eight of them sons. The leader, Ch. Benrook Randy, with two all-breed BIS and 40 Best of Breed wins, sired ten champions, seven of them sons, including a BIS winner, Ch. Melmar's Random Rain. The latter sired five champions, including Ch. Melmar's Jack Frost who already has a record of 12 champion get.

Buckaroo's son, Ch. Jonaire Pocono High Life, sired Ch. Jonaire Pocono Rock'N Roll, with a record of 11 champions, and Rocking Heart Chipper, a non-champion who has sired four. High Life's full brother, Ch. Jonaire Pocono High Mount, sired Am. & Bermuda Ch. Jonaire Pocono Top Hit, whose son Am. & Can. Ch. Jonaire Pocono Gladiator is the top sire of Canadian champions with a record of 14. Another Buckaroo son, Ch. Benrook Rego, sired three champions including Ch. Benrook Brandy. Brandy is the sire of four American and one Canadian champion, all sons but one, and at least five grandsons in male line.

Ch. Dorem Favorite, himself the sire of 16 champions, has at least 20 tail male descendants who have sired four or more. Of his four leading sons, both Ch. Dorem Original and Ch. Perci-Bee's First Impression died comparatively young, still at the height of their power. Original, whelped when Favorite was 14 months old, sired 13 champions, 12 of them daughters. However, his son from his first litter, Ch. Geelong Playboy, is carrying on through Ch. Geelong Little Sargent who already has seven and Ch. Geelong Royal Playboy with three. After Original came First Impression and a few days later Fanciful of Marienhof, whose record of 10 is tops for a non-champion. Fanciful sired Ch. Yankee-Pride Colonel Stump, sire of 15 champions, four of them sons. Other Fanciful lines give promise of carrying on, but none have yet achieved four champions. Ch. Mankit's Adam, now the sire of nine, is five years younger than Original and decidedly the youngest of the Favorite producers.

Adam's son Ch. Trayhom Tramp-A-Bout bid fair to be one of the outstanding sires of the breed. Unfortunately, he died of an acute virus infection before he was two, leaving the impressive record of seven champions out of a total of 21 puppies sired. Of these, the non-champion Mankit's Hector already has six to his credit at the age of five, and Ch. Winsomor Critique, who died in a freak accident when only three, left four champions including Ch. Fancway's Tom

Display Male Line Producers

(Including dogs with four or more AKC champions. Dogs with less than four, included to show line of descent, are given in italics.)

	Male	Female	Total
CH. DOREM TRIBUTE	17	24	41
Ch. Benrook Buckaroo	8	9	17
Ch. Benrook Randy	7	3	10
Ch. Melmar's Random Rain	3	2	5
Ch. Melmar's Jack Frost	7	5	12
Ch. Adford's Bob White	1	3	4
Ch. Benrook Rego			3
Ch. Benrook Brandy	3	1	4
Ch. Jonaire Pocono High Life			1
Ch. Jonaire Pocono Rock 'N Roll	4	7	11
Rocking Heart Chipper	1	3	4
Am. & Ber. Ch. Jonaire Pocono Top Hit			2
Am. & Can. Ch. Jonaire Pocono Gladiator			1*
Ch. Dorem Favorite	4	12	16
Ch. Perci-Bee's First Impression	7	8	15
Ch. Phil-Mar Lugar	10	12	22
Ch. Blythewood Main Gazebo	4	9	13
Ch. Blythewood Chief Bosun	1	3	4
Ch. Dorem Denominator	3	3	6
Ch. Mankit's Eager	2	2	4
Ch. Mankit's Moon Shot	3	2	5
Ch. Mankit's Signal Go	6	5	11
Ch. Mankit's Xerxes			4
Ch. Phil-Mar Emmett	4	5	9
Ch. Phil-Mar Thunderbolt	5	1	6
Ch. Phil-Mar Impressive Lover	1	3	4
Dorem Minuteman	3	1	4
Ch. Dorem Original	1	12	13
Ch. Geelong Playboy			2
Ch. Geelong Little Sargent	4	3	7
Ch. Blythewood Blue Salute	3	1	4
Fanciful of Marienhof	5	5	10
Ch. Yankee-Pride Colonel Stump	5	10	15

* Plus 14 Canadian champions.

149

	Male	Female	Total
Ch. Mankit's Adam	1	8	9
Ch. Trayhom Tramp-A-Bout	2	5	7
Mankit's Hector	4	2	6
Ch. Winsomor Critique	3	2	5
Ch. Fancway Tom Terrific	1	5	6
Ch. Meldon's Seabiscuit	2	3	5
Ch. Phil-Mar Tributary	0	4	4
CH. DIPLOMAT OF LEDAHOF	13	16	29
Ch. Delfin Janus	19	15	34
Ch. Windy Hill Defiance	8	3	11
Ch. Mutiny I'm Grumpy Too	5	5	10
Ch. Mai-Laur Devilish Duke	3	1	4
Ch. Jonaire Pocono Smart Money	3	1	4
Ch. Diplomat of Marienhof	7	4	11
Ch. Handful's Bantam	5	5	10
Ch. Handful's Blue Winged Teal			3
Ch. Handful's Pop-Up	6	2	8
Ch. Trayhom Talleyrand	1	3	4
Ch. Asset of Ledahof	5	4	9
Am., Can. & Mex. Ch. Marwyck Pitt-Penn Pirate	20	24	44
Ch. Allaruth's Joshua			3
Ch. Allaruth's Jericho	1	6	7
Ch. Marwyck Scenery Road	5	4	9
Ch. Applause of Abingdon, CD	3	3	6
Ch. Marwyck Brush Cliff	5	2	7
Am. & Can. Ch. Marwyck Penn Hurst	3	2	5
CH. MELDON'S RUFFIAN	14	12	26
Am. & Braz. Ch. Helarry's Dark Victory	15	9	24
Ch. Helarry's Harmony	5	8	13
Ch. Helarry's Ruff Stuff	4	0	4
Ch. Helarry's Danny Boy	0	5	5
CH. DOREM HIGH TEST	8	7	15
Ch. Meldon's Mignon	3	2	5
Ch. Benrook Basil			3
Ch. Benrook Banning	2	7	9
Ch. Bursche v. Hessen	2	2	4
CH. BENROOK BEAU BRUMMELL	8	5	13
Cosburn's Admiration			1
Ch. Cosburn's Esquire	10	3	13
Ch. Andrel's Viceroy	3	4	7
CH. MELDON'S MERIT	6	3	9
Ch. Kenhoff's I'm It	6	2	8
Ch. Salt 'N Pepper Sampler			3

150

Ch. Glenshaw's Gadget	2	5	7
Ch. Glenshaw's Johnny Appleseed	3	1	4
Ch. Handful's Me Too of Marienhof	2	2	4
CH. GENGLER'S DRUM MAJOR	5	2	7
Ch. High Potentate of Gengl-Aire	3	2	5
CH. BENROOK ZORRA	4	2	6
CH. DELEGATE OF LEDAHOF	3	2	5
Ch. Dorem Tempo	3	3	6
Ch. Phil-Mars Gay Knight	5	4	9
Ch. Phil-Mar Dark Knight	7	5	12
Belvedere's Andy			2
Ch. Belvedere Gay Boy	1	4	5
DOREM CHANCE PLAY	0	4	4
DISTINCTION OF MARIENHOF			1
Ch. Charlena Sho-Nuff	2	2	4

Terrific. Terry, at five years old, is one of the youngest sires in the breed to have six to his credit. Another Tramp son, the non-champion Winsomor Dubbl 'R Nothin, while not on the top producer's list, is the paternal grandsire of Ch. Winsomor Miss Kitty, the top-winning Miniature Schnauzer (Phillips System) for 1966 and top BIS-winning bitch of the breed.

The greatest number of producing sires of the Favorite line, however, trace to Ch. Perci-Bee's First Impression, who himself sired 15 champions. His producing sons include Ch. Phil-Mar Lugar (one of the top two living sires of the breed still at stud, with 22 champions at the age of 11), Ch. Phil-Mar Emmett with nine, Ch. Phil-Mar Thunderbolt with six, and Ch. Phil-Mar Impressive Lover, who had already sired four when he died at the age of four. The Lugar line is already represented by Ch. Blythewood Main Gazebo with 13, Ch. Dorem Denominator with six and Ch. Mankit's Eager with four. Eager's line is carried further by Ch. Mankit's Moonshot with five and the latter's son, Ch. Mankit's Signal Go, the youngest dog on the producer's list with over ten champions. Gazebo's son Ch. Blythewood Chief Bosun, whelped in 1964, is a top winner and sired four champions in 1967.

Display's second-ranking son, Ch. Diplomat of Ledahof, was the sire of 29 champions of which 13 were sons. The last of them, Ch. Ledahof Ambassador, whelped in 1956, sired a daughter in 1965, Ch. Carolane's Amanda, who finished in 1966, slightly less than 20 years after her grandsire Diplomat's birth. In one of his first litters,

Ch. Fancway Tom Terrific, sire of
6 champions.

Ch. Blythewood Main Gazebo,
Best of Breed winner 85 times.

out of Ch. Sorceress of Ledahof, Diplomat sired four champions, one of which died at the age of two while the other three became top producers: Ch. Marwyck Scenery Road with nine, Ch. Marwyck Brush Cliff with seven, and Ch. Marwyck Penn Hurst with five. Scenery Road's son Ch. Applause of Abingdon also sired nine champions besides being the breed's top sire of obedience winners.

Diplomat's son, Ch. Diplomat of Marienhof, sired 11 champions, of which Ch. Handful's Bantam sired 10 and Ch. Handful's Blue Winged Teal three, including Ch. Handful's Pop-Up with eight. Pop-Up's line continues through Ch. Trayhom Talleyrand with four.

The top-producing Diplomat of Ledahof son, Ch. Delfin Janus, has a record of 34, of which 19 are sons. Of the three appearing on the top producers list, Ch. Mai-Laur Devilish Duke and Ch. Jonaire Pocono Smart Money have each sired four, while Ch. Windy Hill Defiance, at five years old, already has a record of ten.

Ch. Asset of Ledahof, the fifth top producer by Diplomat of Ledahof with ten champions to his credit, including four sons, is best known as the sire of Ch. Marwyck Pitt-Penn Pirate, now credited with 44 AKC champions, the record for the breed. Pirate, whelped in 1954, died shortly before his twelfth birthday. Of his first ten champions, nine were daughters, the son being Ch. Pindar Anfiger. Five more sons finished in 1958, with a current total of 16. Pirate's early show and stud career was in the Pittsburgh area. At about the age of three he was sold to the Glenn Fancys of California and did a large part of his producing on the West Coast, where his progeny are numerous. They also include three Mexican and one Canadian champion. His most successful son to date is Ch. Trayhom Tatters, sire of three champions. Ch. Allaruth Joshua's son, Ch. Allaruth's Jericho, is the top producer of the Pirate male line, with seven champions, six of them daughters. Pirate's best producing daughters are Minchette Maier, dam of six, Ch. Marwyck Gae's Martinette, dam of four, Ch. Trayhom Teaser, dam of three, and Can. Ch. Caldora's Escapade, dam of four Canadian champions.

The third ranking Display son, Ch. Meldon's Ruffian, with 26 champions, was not whelped until late 1950 and died in 1966. Ruffian's most outstanding son, Ch. Helarry's Dark Victory, was whelped in 1958 when his sire was a month short of eight years old. Dark Victory, with 22 champions before his eighth birthday and a twenty-fourth now finished, is now the top living sire at stud. His brother, Ch. Helarry's Danny Boy, is Ruffian's other top producer, with five, while Ch. C-Ton's Bonfire is also carrying on in male line. Two Dark Victory sons already producers are Ch. Helarry's Ruff Stuff with four and Ch. Helarry's Harmony with 13. Ruffian has been particularly successful with Helarry's Delsey, a daughter of Dorem Corsair, brother to Original, while their son Dark Victory and his brother Ch. Helarry's Danny Boy have both produced from the Original granddaughter Ch. Dorem Symphony II. Ruffian's line has surged to the front since 1964, when Dark Victory was still his only top producer, and the latter's record has doubled in the interval. Ruffian is also one of the two sires with three all-breed Best in Show winners, the other being Ch. Dorem Tempo.

Ch. Dorem High Test was Display's first champion son, whelped when his sire was only ten months old. His career was a checkered one. By ten months of age he, too, had sired a litter which contained two champions, one of them his best producing son, Meldon's Mignon. Four more were whelped in 1947, another in 1948, and three in 1949. 1950 was a blank, but in 1951 he sired four who were to finish, including his outstanding daughter Ch. Forest Nod of Mandeville, whose record of two all-breed BIS (in 1952 and 1953) stood until 1966. But this was practically the end. At somewhere about this time he changed hands, and perhaps had fewer bitches available or fewer get shown. There was a gap of nearly five years before his last champion, Liza's William the Conqueror (who finished in 1959) was whelped in 1956, when High Test was nearly eleven. His total of 15 champions makes him fourth of Display's producing sons, but 14 of them were whelped before his sixth birthday.

High Test's male line is still producing champions, but only three are on the top producers list with four or more—Ch. Meldon's Mignon with five, his grandson Ch. Benrook Banning with nine, and the latter's son Ch. Bursche v. Hessen with four, none of them whelped within the past ten years. His best producing daughters were Meldon's Mar Mose (litter sister to Mignon), dam of five champions, and Dorem High Score, dam of three.

The Display son Ch. Benrook Beau Brummell sired 13 U.S. champions, two of them also Canadian, plus six additional Canadian champions. None of his sons was a top producer, but the non-

Ch. Sorceress of Ledahof, dam of 12 champions.

Sorceress's first litter, which contained four champions: Marwyck Scenery Road, Lime Crest, Buena Vista (died young), Brush Cliff and Penn Hurst.

Ch. Meldon's Ruffian, sire of 26
champions with 2 BIS.

Am. & Braz. Ch. Helarry's Dark
Victory, top living sire with 24
champions.

Ch. Tweed Packet of Wilkern,
sire of 15 champions.

champion Cosburn's Admiration sired Am. & Can. Ch. Cosburn's Esquire, sire of 13, through whom the line is carrying on. Esquire's son, Am. & Can. Ch. Esquire of Marienhof, has sired five Canadian champions, and Ch. Andrel's Viceroy was the sire of seven U.S. champions.

The third group of Display sons, all with less than ten champions to their credit, is headed by Ch. Meldon's Merit. He sired nine champions in addition to Morit of Marienhof, who went to Germany after the war, became a Dutch champion, and sired a German Sieger. Meldon's Merit also sired Ch. Handful's Me Too of Marienhof, sire of four champions, and Ch. Kenhoff's I'm It, sire of eight. The latter's line has carried on through Ch. Salt'n Pepper Sampler with three to his son Ch. Glenshaw's Gadget with seven and the latter's son, Ch. Glenshaw Johnny Appleseed, with four, while several others of this line have reached a total of three.

Ch. Gengler's Drum Major follows with seven champions, five of them sons, including Ch. High Potentate of Gengl-Aire with five, one of them a Best in Show winner. Although this line shows signs of carrying on, none of High Potentate's sons or grandsons has yet sired four champions.

Ch. Benrook Zorra has six champions to his credit, but nothing further as yet.

Ch. Delegate of Ledahof, a litter brother to Diplomat, had only one top producer among his five champions, Dorem Tempo. Although privately owned by non-breeders and hence used at stud much less than many of his contemporaries, Tempo sired a high proportion of champions for the number of his get, including three Best in Show winners, and his male line is still found through at least three sons. Ch. Belvedere Gay Boy, sire of six champions, is a son of the untitled Belvedere Andy, and four generations of champions are descended from Ch. Phil-Mars Mr. John. Tempo's top-producing son was Ch. Phil-Mars Gay Knight, with a record of nine. When over nine years old, Gay Knight sired Ch. Phil-Mars Dark Knight, who at slightly past five years old had already surpassed his sire's record.

Another Delegate of Ledahof son, Ch. Rannoch's Rampion, sired Rannoch-Dune Randolph of Appeline, who was exported to England where he made his title and left many winning descendants. (See Chapter 8, The Breed in Great Britain.) Also carrying on in

157

England is the line from the untitled Display son Meldon's Doctor R.R.L. through his son Ch. Nicomur Champagne and the latter's son Ch. Nicomur Chasseur and grandson Ch. Sternroc Sticky Wicket.

By 1953 it was already becoming difficult to find recent champions who did not trace to Display. Today it appears to be impossible, and even non-champions must be rare. One who may be mentioned, Sambo of Cobb, UDT, is now some 13 years old, and each year there are fewer. Even in male line there are few champions finished during the past decade who do not trace to Display. Those who have done so are descended from Ch. Tweed Packet of Wilkern, who was by Display's great-grandsire, Ch. Sandman of Sharvogue, out of Ch. Debutante of Ledahof, a Display daughter. Tweed Packet sired 14 champions by the time he was five, but only one thereafter, due to a serious injury. His producing son, Ch. Wilkern Reveille, sired six, and Reveille's son, Ch. Wilkern Mr. Jackpot, sired five plus the Can. Ch. Belvedere General. The latter sired four Canadian champions including Am. & Can. Ch. Caldora's Returning Ace, who stands second among Canadian sires with 13. Tweed Packet's last son, Am. & Can. Ch. Wilkern Killarney Dandy, has a record of seven Canadian champions. Another Tweed Packet son, Wilkern Tony from America, went to England as a puppy, made his title there, and sired two champion sons and a non-champion who has two champions to his credit. In the United States, however, Tweed Packet has no male line descendants whelped during the past decade who have produced four or more champions, though his line still exists.

The last imported male with a substantial influence on the breed was World Sieger Qualm Heinzelmännchen by RS. Zar Heinzelmännchen (never imported, but sire of six AKC champions). Qualm left many descendants in Germany, and after he was imported around 1939, he sired three American champions as well. His son Ch. Quota of Appletrees, out of Ch. Rosalie of Marienhof, left five non-champion producing daughters. Quota's litter brother, Ch. Rufus of Marienhof I, sired three champions and three producers. Ch. Rufus of Marienhof II sired Ch. Rachel of Marienhof II, who appears in many pedigrees. Ch. Norcrest Enuff carried on through two non-champion sons, Norcrest Enuff's Jupiter and Loki of Appletrees. The latter (out of Ch. Dorem Liberty) sired Exotic of

158

Ledahof, a double Liberty granddaughter who was the dam of Ch. Meldon's Merit. The male line from Rufus I was also continued through Falcon of Palawan, who was out of Myrna of Palawan, litter sister of Ch. Vance. Falcon sired Ledahof's Sentry, another non-champion who sired Ch. Dorem Delegate and Ch. Saladin of Ledahof, the last male champions of this line. Sentry is of outstanding importance, however, as the sire of Saladin's sister, Ch. Sorceress of Ledahof, who tops the list of producing bitches with 12 AKC and one Canadian champion. Sentry's dam, Neff's Risque, carried two lines to Ch. Urian Thuringia, a dog who appears in few other pedigrees, and Sentry was almost a complete outcross to the Dorem line concentrated in Ch. Enchantress, the dam of Sorceress. The Rufus I line is also found through Falcon's sister, Ryta of Palawan, a dam of five producing bitches.

From the breeder's point of view it is interesting and important to observe and study which male lines (and also which bitch families) are the strongest producers. However, it must not be forgotten that these are not the only names in the pedigree. Each generation of the male line likewise had a dam, while the bitches in the family lines had sires. The whole pedigree should be studied, and it may well be in some cases that the emphasis of line or inbreeding is concentrated wholly or in part on individuals to be found in the interior lines rather than either the top or bottom.

While the number of champions produced is only a rough measure of the true breeding value of an individual, it remains a valuable guide. Another, also subject to correction and frequently modified by accidental circumstances, is how the individual breeds carry on beyond the first generation. These points should be weighed, so far as possible, against the opportunities of the individual producer, such as geographical availability, quality of bitches in the locality, prestige to draw good ones from a distance, vigor and persistance of advertising, and even feuds and rumors within the fancy which may create prejudice against one dog or promote another unduly.

Since it takes time for a stud to become recognized as an outstanding producer, and still longer to determine how he will breed on through later generations, it is often too late to make full use of a dog whose value does not become evident in his early years. A notable example of this is the sire of Ch. Dorem Display, who was

159

sold before the latter's reputation was established. He vanished into obscurity and the studbooks reveal only one other litter by him, probably sold as pets.

While remembering how often breeders run after the latest young, spectacular winner, it is nevertheless wise to compare the current successful sires by age as well as descent. In 1966 only two sires whelped more than 10 years earlier had champion get which finished during the year. These were Ch. Cosburn's Esquire, whelped in March 1953 and still living at this writing, and Ch. Marwyck Pitt-Penn Pirate, whelped February 1954, who died in 1966. The youngest dog to have sired at least four champions was Ch. Mankit's Signal Go with 5, whelped ten years after Esquire. Of those whelped in the period between 1953 and 1963 who have achieved a record of four or more, three are already dead at four years old and under, and most of their champion get finished after their sires' deaths. Others made their records a number of years ago and have added nothing recently. On p. 161 the dogs are arranged by date of birth. From 1956 through 1961 the number whelped in each year varies from three to nine. Thereafter there are only five, two in 1962, one in 1963 and two in 1964. Dogs with one or more champions finishing from July 1965 to date are listed in italics and can be considered to form the "active" list. This list, it is interesting to observe, includes three of the six whelped during 1956. The largest increases within that period are shown by Ch. Helarry's Harmony, Ch. Phil-Mar Dark Knight, Ch. Windy Hill Defiance, and Ch. Blythewood Main Gazebo, with Ch. Mankit's Signal Go heading the list.

It is fascinating to speculate on the relative standing of the older dogs five years from now, and on what newcomers whelped from 1962 through 1967 will be added to the list, but so many factors are involved that it would be only guesswork. In the light of present trends, and barring unexpected developments, one could expect Dark Victory to approach or pass the 30 mark and Harmony, Signal Go, Grumpy and Gazebo to stand high. It is interesting to see how many on the list are in California, including Defiance, Ch. Mutiny I'm Grumpy Too, Ch. Melmar's Jack Frost, and the young Ch. Fancway's Tom Terrific. The others are widely scattered, with Rocking Heart Chipper in Washington state, Ch. Dorem Denominator in Massachusetts, Harmony in Tennessee, Ch. High Potentate

Top Sires, 1956–1968

	Date Whelped	Champions
Ch. Handful's Pop-Up	May 10, 1956	8
Ch. Jonaire Pocono Smart Money	July 3, 1956	4
Ch. Phil-Mar Lugar	July 5, 1956	22
Ch. Yankee-Pride Colonel Stump	July 18, 1956	15
Ch. Mai-Laur Devilish Duke	September 29, 1956	4
Rocking Heart Chipper	November 7, 1956	4
Ch. Glenshaw's Johnny Appleseed	January 24, 1957	4
Ch. High Potentate of Gengl-Aire	June 5, 1957	5
Ch. Andrel's Viceroy	July 2, 1957	7
Ch. Trayhom Talleyrand	February 9, 1958	4
Ch. Melmar's Random Rain	March 30, 1958	5
Ch. Mankit's Adam	July 11, 1958	9
Ch. Geelong Little Sargent	September 29, 1958	7
Ch. Helarry's Dark Victory	November 19, 1958	24
Ch. Helarry's Danny Boy	November, 1958	5
Ch. Phil-Mar Impressive Lover	January 17, 1959 (d. 1963)	4
Ch. Phil-Mar Thunderbolt	January 17, 1959	6
Ch. Dorem Denominator	June 12, 1959	6
Ch. Melmar's Jack Frost	August 12, 1959	12
Ch. Allaruth's Jericho	October 9, 1959	7
Ch. Trayhom Tramp-A-Bout	March 29, 1960 (d. 1962)	7
Ch. Mankit's Eager	April 16, 1960	4
Ch. Helarry's Ruff Stuff	June 21, 1960	4
Ch. Blythewood Main Gazebo	September 4, 1960	13
Dorem Minuteman	September 5, 1960	4
Ch. Phil-Mar Dark Knight	February 6, 1961	12
Ch. Adford's Bob White	February 14, 1961	4
Mankit's Hector	March 13, 1961	6
Ch. Windy Hill Defiance	May 8, 1961	11
Ch. Mutiny I'm Grumpy Too	May 25, 1961	10
Ch. Blythewood Blue Salute	July 7, 1961	4
Ch. Winsomor Critique	July 20, 1961 (d. 1965)	5
Ch. Helarry's Harmony	October 31, 1961	13
Ch. Mankit's Moon Shot	December 31, 1961	5
Ch. Fancway's Tom Terrific	May 3, 1962	6
Ch. Mankit's Signal Go	March 13, 1963	11
Ch. Blythewood Chief Bosun	February 23, 1964	4
Ch. Mankit's Xerxes	March 16, 1964	5

161

Ch. Melmar's Jack Frost:
8 champions.

Ch. Mutiny I'm Grumpy Too:
10 champions.

Ch. Windy Hill Defiance:
11 champions.

Ch. Cosburn's Esquire: 13 champions.

Ch. Mankit's Signal Go, BB at 8 specialty shows and sire of 11 champions.

of Gengl-Aire in Texas, Ch. Yankee-Pride Colonel Stump and Ch. Blythewood Main Gazebo in Pennsylvania, Ch. Phil-Mar Thunderbolt in Illinois, and the others scattered within these general limits.

Producing Bitch Families

Most of the outstanding bitches of the breed have been discussed in connection with the male lines to which they belonged or the sires by whom they have produced. Since the maximum number of puppies a bitch can whelp is far less than the number a stud can sire, it is easy to overlook the influence of the dam. No bitch can hope to rival the list of champions by a leading sire, although Ch. Lotte v.d. Goldbachhöhe's and Ch. Sorceress of Ledahof's 12 are exceeded by only a comparative few. The ten champions from Ch. Gladding's Bie Bie and nine from her daughter Ch. Mankit's Augusta, and the same from Ch. Benrook Bona would also be very respectable totals for a male, even today.

While sires achieve renown and impress themselves upon the breed through the number of their winners, the influence of a bitch is generally less immediately apparent. It becomes clearer through the subsequent records of her sons and grandsons, and through the consistent recurrence of producing bitches among her descendants. It is well to remember, however, that in any given litter the influence of the dam almost certainly outweighs that of the sire. Since each contributes an equal number of chromosomes to the mating, the purely genetic effect should be substantially equal (although even here the lack of a second X chromosome in the male puppies may prove important in special cases). To the purely genetic inheritance, however, must be added the fact that once a mating has taken place, the sire's part is over, while the dam can still affect the development of the litter through her health, vigor, and glandular balance while she is carrying them, and through her milk supply and care until weaning. The difference between a healthy, normal litter, capable of developing to the limit of its inherited potentialities, and a weak, scrawny one, easily susceptible to disease or failing to survive at all, depends as much on the dam as on her owner who must supply adequate food and suitable conditions. This is a fact too often forgotten by the owners of good bitches. It is brought

163

home to the breeder with startling force on those infrequent occasions when a bitch's milk fails or she neglects properly to clean and care for her puppies.

When comparing breeding records one should never forget that a great many factors are involved. Luck may play a large part in determining which puppy in a litter is shown and bred or which is sold as a pet, especially in the case of small breeders who must dispose of their stock early for lack of space. The number and quality of bitches available at different times or in different areas can affect a sire's record greatly. Good bitches close at hand help to prove a dog's worth. Without them he must have sufficient reputation to draw them from a distance. To achieve this may require the expenditure of more time and money than his owner can afford. Competition varies in different sections of the country, and this is reflected in the point rating for shows which varies considerably in different areas. Local activity also affects the comparative number of major shows. This makes it difficult to judge the relative worth of dogs from different sections of the country when they have not met in the ring under experienced judges. Owners who can afford to travel long distances or to send their dogs on the circuit with professional handlers have a definite advantage in this respect over those who are restricted to the comparatively small number of shows within a day's driving distance. All this may affect the record of a sire and consequently his reputation. Moreover, bitches, whose ring appearances are always more subject to interruption, face stiffer competition for points than the dogs in three of the five divisions. Accordingly, the sire of outstanding sons would seem to have an advantage over the sire of outstanding daughters. The number of dogs and bitches required to compete for a given number of points varies from year to year. The new ratings are published annually in the May issue of the *American Kennel Gazette* (also known as *Pure-Bred Dogs*) and in the front of all show catalogs for the area in which a show is located. Point ratings are increased or decreased according to the competition in a given district during the preceding year. Hence, if a rating is low, owners or handlers in search of majors may travel long distances to reach such an area. Point adjustments, therefore, do not always reflect local breed activity.

As a guide to breeders and for its intrinsic interest I originally compiled a list of all bitches who had produced two or more AKC champions. These have now become so numerous that only producers of three or more champions are included in the present edition. The list is arranged by families, showing the earliest known bitch in Germany to which they can be traced in tail female line. At the present time all producing lines in the United States belong to only three families. (Additional families are found in England; see Chapter 8, The Breed in Great Britain.) Family IV had produced no dams of two champions for some years before the earlier edition, and was therefore omitted at that time, and Family V has now been traced to the same source as Family III, to which it accordingly belongs. There are also some bitches that do not belong to any of these families, but since they do not as yet include any dams of three or more champions, their lines are not given. Of course, most bitches probably trace back to all the main family lines more than once, but not in tail female.

Family I is decidedly the most important. It contains more than twice the number of top-producing individuals found in either of the others as well as ten of the top 15 individuals who have produced from six to 12 AKC champions, including all but one with eight or more. Very little is known of its origin, an unregistered bitch named Lörchen, whose breeder, owner and date of birth are unknown. By a dog called Sambo (who therefore was very likely black) Lörchen produced the unregistered Christel, whelped no earlier than 1911 and sired by Ulbs (PB 1514), who was whelped in September 1910, and was apparently dark grey.

Christel, whelped between 1911 and 1916, was probably a black like her daughter by Ulbs, Resie Plavia (PB 3336, PSZ 35) whelped in April 1917. Resie, in turn, was bred to the black Stueber Plavia (PB 3270, PSZ 17), both of whom were bred by Max Hartenstein. Stueber was an Ulbs grandson on his dam's side and was sired by the black S. Turko Chemnitz-Plauen, whose brother S. Trumpf Chemnitz-Plauen appears in the male line behind Ch. Dorem Display. Resie whelped several litters, including at least one champion who was sired by Stueber. However, although both parents were blacks, her daughter Peppi I v. Hohndorf (55) was a bicolor. Peppi carried at least three lines to Gift Chemnitz-Plauen, the top sire of his day, and a fourth to Gift's sire, Prinz v. Rheinstein. She was mated to S. Rudi v. Lohr (inbred to the unknown bitch Zecke) tracing in male line to Lord with another line to Cito v.d. Werneburg. So far as is known, Rudi carried no Prinz v. Rheinstein, but his dam, Zecke, a light salt and pepper whelped in 1908, was young enough to have done so. She may also have been the source of the light salt and peppers that appeared when this line was doubled in later generations.

Peppi and Rudi were the parents of AKC Ch. Amsel v.d. Cyriaksburg (716), who had more influence on the breed in this country than any other bitch and perhaps more than any other individual ever imported. (See Pedigree Analysis, p. 110). Whelped June 12, 1921 when her sire was nine years old, Amsel came to this country in 1924 with two puppy daughters, Lady and Ch. Lotte v.d. Goldbachhöhe, and was herself the dam of the first American-bred litter of Miniatures in 1925. While others of her progeny left many descendants, all the Family I producers trace to Amsel through three of her daughters—Lady, Lotte, and a few through Fiffi of Marlou. Because this family is so large, it has been divided into three lines, and the most numerous one, from Lotte, has again been subdivided. Lotte v.d. Goldbachhöhe herself was for a long time the top-producing bitch of the breed, with 12 AKC champions. This record has now been equalled by a descendant of her daughter Ch. Jemima of Wollaton, from whom two of the top producers trace. Ch. Sorceress of Ledahof, dam of 12 AKC champions, is also the dam of one Canadian. The other top-producing line, headed by Ch. Gladding's Bie Bie with ten to her credit, descends from Lotte's daughter Ch. Gretel of Marienhof. Bie Bie's daughter, Ch. Mankit's Augusta, is the dam of nine champions, and Sorceress's dam, Ch. Enchantress, is the dam of eight, thus topping the combined record for a mother and daughter in the breed. In 1967 for the first time a tail female descendant of a third Lotte daughter, Ch. Aennchen of Marienhof, appeared on the list in the bitch Ch. Flintrock's Jakaba, dam of three champions.

Producing Bitches

(The following lists are arranged by number of champions under each line, and where the numbers are the same, with the oldest first.)

FAMILY I
(from Lörchen)

Ch. Amsel v.d. Cyriaksburg	3
Line A: Ch. Lotte v.d. Goldbachhöhe	12
Ch. Jemima of Wollaton	3
Branch 1 *(from Dorem Diva)*	
Ch. Sorceress of Ledahof	12
Ch. Enchantress	8
Ch. Wilkern Ado	7
Ch. Winsome High Style	6
Helarry's Delsey	6
Ch. Dorem Silverette	5
Can. Ch. Cosburn's Deborah	5
Dorem Serenade	5
Ch. Wilkern Smoky Tweed	5
Ch. Fricka von Brittanhof	5
Ch. Cosburn's Beau Brummell Honey	4
Salty Imp	4
Benrook Brillance	4
Ch. Marwyck Maid of the Mist	4
Ch. Marwyck Gaes Martinette	4
Ch. Marwyck SD Comet	3
Lisa v. Kleinwald	3
Ch. Cosburn's Sweet Tribute	3
MacMars Mode	3
Ch. Dorem Escapade	3
Miss Belvedere	3
Jonaire Pocono High Mark	3
Ch. Jonaire Pocono Smart Style	3
Ch. Abingdon Heidi	3
Kummers Dark Hit	3
Branch 2 *(from Ch. Dorem Dubonnet)*	
Ch. Benrook Bona	9
Baker's Cindy of Harbrac	6
Ch. Meldon's Mañana	5
Meldon's Shirley A	5
Ch. Phil-Mars Lady Love	5
Ch. Dorem Symphony II	5
Yankee Dark Drama	5
Ch. Bethel's Original Ember	5
Ch. Dorem Highlight	4

167

Four generations of salt and pepper: Ch. Dorem Shady Lady, CD, Ch. Phil-Mar Gay Lady, Ch. Phil Mar Gay Knight and Ch. Phil-Mar Bright Knight.

Ch. Karen of Marienhof II,
dam of 4 champions.

Ch. Flirtation Walk Tiara,
dam of 6 champions.

168

Ch. Phil-Mars Lucky Lady	4
Meldon's Mar Mose	4
Handful's Doll	4
Handful's Raguletta	4
Ch. Dorem Searchlight	3
Ch. Dorem Shady Lady	3
Ch. Phil-Mars Watta Lady	3
Phil-Mars Lovely Lady	3
Meldon's Machree	3
Dorem Flair	3
Dorem Fame	3
Wilkern Scotch Teviot	3
Ch. Phil-Mars Gay Lady	3
Benrook Beegee	3
Ch. Chuck-A-Luck's Heide	3
Benrook Patricia	3
Ch. Fancway's Blue Magic	3
Ch. Fancway's Jezebel	3
Ch. Phil-Mars Lucy Lady	3
Ch. Phil-Mars Melba	3
Handful's Snow Flurry	3
Hollenwire's Judith	3
Ch. Benrook Bethel	3
Jonaire Pocono Bright Idea	3
Ch. Andrel's Bonne Amie	3
Phil-Mars September Song	3
Ch. Abingdon Elite	3
Dorem High Score	3
Victory's Queen Victoria	3

Via Ch. Gretel of Marienhof

Ch. Gladding's Bie Bie	10
Ch. Mankit's Augusta	9
Ch. Frevoly's Best Bon Bon, UD	5
Weidman's Black Shadow	4
Ch. Barclay Square Becky Sharp	4
Marksman Galatea	3
Ch. Trayhom Terrific	3
Ch. Trayhom Teaser	3
Ch. Mankit's Countess Talleyrand	3
Drummer Girl of Gengl-Aire	3
Ch. Brenhof Katrinka, CD	3
Allaruth's Jolly Anne	3

Via Ch. Aennchen of Marienhof

Ch. Flintrock's Jakaba	3

Line B: Lady v.d. Goldbachhöhe

169

Producing Bitches (*Continued*)

Wild Honey of Sharvogue	8
Debby of Earldorf	5
Mehitabel of Marienhof II	4
Ch. Priscilla of Marienhof II	4
Ch. Hope of Marienhof	4
Galloper of Marienhof	4
Ballerina of Marienhof	4
Fritzi of Marienhof	3
Ch. Imprudent of Sharvogue	3
Ch. Clairedale Lady Luck	3
Ch. Luvemal's Carbon Copy	3
Ch. Luvemal's Victoria	3

Line C: Fiffi of Marlou

Doman Roman Candle	3
Annabelle of Ledahof	3
Marwyck Carlstadt Coco	3

FAMILY II
(*from Hexe Chemnitz-Plauen*)

Via Can. Ch. Nette v. Mümlingtal

Minchette Maier	6
Ch. Gracon's Canis of Kenhoff	5
Trayhom TuTu	5
Ch. Lady Gildae	4
Ch. Sassy Sue of Kenhoff	4
Ch. Queen Mona of Silver Oaks	4
Ch. Marwyck GC Vixen	4
Salt 'n Pepper Scintillation	4
Ch. Silver Belle of Kenhoff	3
Marwyck Princess Augusta	3
Ch. Dixie Belle of Barhelm	3
Brocade of Quality Hill	3
Ch. Dream Girl Moe of Silver Oaks	3
Trayhom Tar and Feathers	3

Via Bässi v.d. Rissener Heide (black)

Dollymount's Agatha	5
Troublesome Lady v.d. Aal	4
Murray's Suzette	3
Junior Miss of Oakridge	3
Ch. Doreen of Oakridge	3

FAMILY III
(*from Alli v.d. Goldbach and Gretel v. Hohenstein, 510*)

Via Christel v.d. Fallerburg

170

Ch. Blythewood Merry Melody	8
Ch. Minquas Athena	6
Ch. Delfin Victoria	6
Ch. Blythewood Sweet Talk	6
Minquas Melita	5
Ch. Minquas Alicia	5
Ch. Jonaire Clarchen	4
Ch. Delfin Lucina	3
Ch. Mutiny Coquette	3
Bon-Ell Bit of Honey	3
Ch. Mutiny Jump for Joy	3
Via Alma v.d. Zukunft (black)	
Ch. Flirtation Walk Tiara	6
Yankee-Pride Cindy	5
Blikaywin Pixie's Peggy	5
Ch. Karen of Marienhof II	4
Ch. Benrook Ben-Gay	4
Ch. Melmar's Rain Song	4
Ch. Woodway Ready	3
Ch. Pal of Marlou	3
Amarantha of Ravenroyd	3
Benrook Bettina	3
Revlis Springtime	3
Ch. Dody's Rhapsody	3
Ch. Rachel of Marienhof II	3
Ch. Andrel's Argenta	3
Ch. Sparks Exotic	3
Via Krabbe Heinzelmännchen	
Ch. Dorem Heather of Eldonhof	3
Via Elfe v. Brentanopark	
Ch. Rosalinde v. Brittanhof II	3
Susi Heinzelmännchen (imported)	3

Short as is the list descended from Fiffi of Marlou, it is worth noting that two of the bitches on it have increased their representation since 1957, while the third is a new name. Also, all three trace back to two full sisters of the dam of the great producing sire, Ch. T.M.G. of Marienhof, through Fiffi's daughter Abigail of Marienhof.

The Lady v.d. Goldbachhöhe line shows the fewest gains comparatively speaking, but a number of bitches with two champions already may easily make the list. How quickly changes can take place is indicated by the Ch. Gretel of Marienhof line, which includes ten new names out of 13. Among the newcomers are two of the five top-ranking bitches of the breed, of whom Ch. Mankit's Augusta is the top living producer.

Ch. Lotte v.d. Goldbachhöhe's other top-producing daughter, Ch. Jemima of Wollaton, was followed by three generations of non-champions, Judy, Jessie and Jill II of Wollaton. The latter produced two champions, and one branch of this line stems from her daughter Ch. Dorem Dubonnet. The other comes from the latter's half sister, Dorem Diva. Each was the dam of two champions.

The longest continuous line of bitches producing three or more champions each is five generations, and they are all champions themselves: Enchantress, Sorceress of Ledahof, Marwyck SD Comet, Marwyck Maid of the Mist, and Marwyck Gae's Martinette. The sisters Ch. Dorem Highlight and Ch. Dorem Searchlight both head lines of four generations. Highlight comes down through Ch. Meldon's Mañana and Ch. Benrook Bona to Handful's Snow Flurry. Searchlight goes through Ch. Dorem Shady Lady who has three top-producing daughters, each in turn the dam of a top producer. Ch. Phil-Mars Watta Lady is the dam of Ch. Phil-Man Lucy Lady; Ch. Phil-Mars Lucky Lady the dam of Ch. Phil-Mars Lady Love; and Ch. Phil-Mars Gay Lady the dam of Ch. Phil-Mars Lovely Lady. Highlight was also the dam of three producers, Meldon's Shirley A, Meldon's Mar Mose, and Ch. Meldon's Mañana.

Family II is descended from Hexe Chemnitz-Plauen, whose breeding is unknown but who must have been whelped by 1908 or earlier. Bred to S. Gift Chemnitz-Plauen, she produced a daughter, Gustel Chemnitz-Plauen (PB 1406), who when bred back to her sire produced a bicolor daughter, Dohle Chemnitz-Plauen, whelped in August 1910. Bred to her half brother S. Fips Chemnitz-Plauen (PB 1377), Dohle produced Hella v. Ruhrtal with at least three lines to Gift. Hella was mated to an apparent outcross, Fritschen (Cito) (PB 1915), a salt and pepper whelped in April 1910 and bred by Hermann Schorr of Velbert, his parents being Hans and Fanny. This Hans may have been the same as Hans Velbert, who sired other litters around 1912 to 1915. Pussel v. Ruhrtal (PSZ 34), a salt and pepper like her sire Fritschen, was whelped August 6, 1914, and in spite of World War I produced seven litters. Two of her daughters, both by Peterl v.d. Werneburg, are represented through descendants in Family II.

Dohle v.d. Werneburg, a bicolor, was the dam of Sn. Heidy v.d.

Hermannsburg and granddam of imported Nette v. Mümlingtal, the first Canadian champion of the breed. Nette's line traces through her daughter Pussel Anfiger and through her granddaughters. The top-producing bitch of this family, Minchette Maier, comes from the bicolor Heidy Anfiger. The rest of Nette's producers come from Isolde Anfiger, Heidy's salt and pepper younger sister. The other line from Pussel v. Ruhrtal traces through the black Satanati v.d. Werneburg and four subsequent generations of blacks: Cariama, Discina and Galera v. Abbagamba, and the imported Bässi v.d. Rissener Heide. Dollymount's Agatha is the top producer of this line, which was mostly located in California. This family also has five generations of top producers, beginning with Ch. Lady Gildae (of the Isolde-Nette line) and running through Marwyck Princess Augusta, Ch. Queen Mona of Silver Oaks, and Ch. Dream Girl Moe of Silver Oaks to Brocade of Quality Hill. (There are only two instances of five generations of bitches producing three or more champions, the other line coming from Ch. Sorceress of Ledahof.)

Family III has now been traced to the unregistered Alli v.d. Goldbach, but is represented by no less than five imported bitches, three of them of slight importance. Nothing is known of Alli except that in March 1902 she whelped a litter by Aeffchen v.d. Goldbach which contained Gretl v. Hohenstein (PB 510). The latter is known to have whelped at least seven litters, from 1903 to 1910, and was bred to both S. Peter v. Westerberg and S. Prinz v. Rheinstein. All the top producers of Family III trace to the Peter daughter Mohrly v.d. Werneburg through her daughter Amsel v.d. Werneburg, by Prinz v. Rheinstein. However, at least one tail female descendant of Mücke v. Hohenstein (out of Gretl by Benno v. Hohenstein) was imported, and the line of Citti v.d. Goetheburg produced a number of champions, but not more than two from one dam.

Mohrly v.d. Werneburg was presumably black like her sire, to judge by her name, and was from her dam's first litter whose sire is known, whelped about 1904. She whelped at least four litters, including one by her sire, but appears to have carried on only through Amsel. The latter, bred to her grandsire Peter, produced Lilli Lehrte, who is found in many pedigrees including a number of Heinzelmännchens. Her Family III descendants in this country are mainly through the imported Christel v.d. Fallerburg. Another

173

Amsel v.d. Werneburg daughter, Mira Lehrte, is behind Alma v.d. Zukunft, one of the earliest blacks imported.

Susi Heinzelmännchen was an imported bitch descended from Mücke Lehrte, and behind her from the same line as Christel v.d. Fallerburg. Three of Susi's imported progeny became champions, and there are still descendants tracing to her via Wilkern Bluette, but none as yet has become eligible for the top-producers list. Krabbe Heinzelmännchen, also tracing to Mücke Lehrte, was another importation of the late 1930's, represented by a single producer. Elfe v. Brentanopark, the only postwar importation in any of the three families with a top producer, appears behind Ch. Rosalinde v. Brittanhof II. Elfe traces back through a litter sister of RS. Zar Heinzelmännchen, Zamba, whose maternal granddam, Grille Heinzelmännchen, was also Susi's maternal granddam. Grille's dam, Dirndl Heinzelmännchen, was the Mücke Lehrte daughter through whom Christel v.d. Fallerburg also traced, so all these bitches are more closely related to each other than to Alma v.d. Zukunft.

Two other families may be mentioned here, one because it has produced champions and may ultimately include some top producers, though there are none as yet; the other simply for the record.

Family IV comes from the postwar importation Vesta Heinzelmännchen. Unlike most of this kennel, who almost without exception belong to Family III, Vesta traces to Nelly (Pabel) (816), a black owned by Ernst Pabel of the Königseck Kennels in Berlin. Nelly was whelped in 1918 and her breeding was unknown—the record was probably lost during World War I. The sixth generation behind Vesta was Pia v. Stolzenburg, a black daughter of S. Egon v. Mümlingtal and Dolly v. Königseck, both blacks. Dolly's dam, Dohle v. Königseck, was out of Grille v. Königseck, who was from Bärbl v. Königseck, a daughter of Nelly (816). Nelly was apparently the foundation of Herr Pabel's kennel (one of the earliest to specialize in blacks) and Dolly carried three lines to her—two through Bärbl and another through a son, Cito v. Königseck. Aside from the line behind Pia v. Stolzenburg, Vesta Heinzelmännchen carries four generations of strong Heinzelmännchen breeding and was sired by General Heinzelmännchen out of a General daughter.

Family VI, originating with Maus v. Höfel and descending through

174

the Dutch Ch. Bärbel v. Dingshaus, one of the first importations into England, seems to be no longer represented in tail female in the latter country and is not known to be so represented in the U.S.

Family V, the top producing line in England, is discussed in the next chapter.

Important Producing Kennels

It is comparatively easy to look back 20 years or more and pick out the breeders and show kennels which have had an outstanding effect on the progress and development of the Miniature Schnauzer, but as we come nearer to the present time this becomes less simple. Breeders and exhibitors come and go for a variety of reasons. Some flash to the top, only to vanish in a few years. Some leave their mark nevertheless, while others might never have existed so far as permanent influence is concerned. Those who remain active for ten or more years are the stayers, and their ranks are studded with the real old timers who have stuck by the breed for 20 or 30 years, or even longer. Among the latter, of course, Mrs. Slattery's Marienhof Kennels hold first rank, with more than 40 years in Miniature Schnauzers. From 1925 through the prewar period this kennel bred and showed extensively and developed a distinct strain, producing in excess of 60 champions and still adding to the list. An exact count is difficult since not all carried the kennel name, but Marienhof stock is still behind *all* of today's champions.

Wollaton Kennels, founded in the late 1920's with a strong infusion of Marienhof blood, likewise bred a distinct type and though ultimately failing in male line played an important part in the formation of the modern breed. They ceased breeding before the death of Mr. Kerns.

Ledahof Kennels began breeding in 1928, the same year as my own Anfiger Kennels, and bred their first champion, Abner of Marlou, in 1930. They developed a recognizable strain based on Ch. Enchantress and her son Ch. Diplomat of Ledahof, one of the top sires of the breed, and Mrs. Martin was still breeding in 1967.

Miss Dorothy Williams of Dorem Kennels began breeding in

175

Ch. Marwyck Pitt-Penn Pirate (left) and his daughter Ch. Marwyck Gae's Martinette.

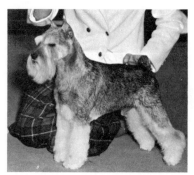

Ch. Blythewood Chief Bosun, a top winner in 1966.

Ch. Yankee-Pride Colonel Stump, winner of 3 BIS, 73 BB and sire of 15 champions.

Ch. Benrook Buckaroo, sire of 17 champions.

176

1935 and her first homebred champion, Dorem Dilletante, was whelped in that year. For over 30 years she has produced consistently good quality and uniform type, with a record for Dorem champions second only to Marienhof, while the top producers, headed by Chs. Dorem Display, Tribute and Favorite are too numerous to mention.

Miss Gene Simmonds' Handful Kennels, going back to the mid-1930's, has produced two dozen champions and is still breeding and showing in 1968.

Mrs. Mae Dickenson's Delfin Kennels, active since about 1950, produced the top living sire Ch. Delfin Janus of a series of champions, the latest, Delfin Do Dona, finished in 1966. Like Mutiny Kennels in California, which began much later, Delfin was founded on Minquas bitches from the small kennel founded in the late 1930's by Miss Marguerite Jones, who only recently gave up breeding. Still another successful show and breeding kennel derived from Minquas is Blythewood, founded about 1952 with Minquas Blithe Spirit and her daughter Ch. Blythewood Merry Elf as the cornerstones. Now a professional handler, Mrs. Joan Huber handles her own dogs and has finished many of them herself.

Another handler-breeder, Mrs. Marguerite Anspach of Phil-Mar kennels, began breeding in 1949 with Ch. Dorem Shady Lady, CD, a litter sister to Display, and her Ch. Phil-Mar Lugar is one of the two top living sires in 1968.

Mrs. Priscilla Deaver is the second generation of Miniature Schnauzer breeders in her family. Her mother, the late Mrs. Joseph Sailer, bred a litter in 1930, but was better known as an exhibitor of top males, the latest being Ch. Yankee-Pride Colonel Stump. Mrs. Deaver bred occasionally from 1936 on, but has recently intensified her activities and finished five champions during 1966 and 1967.

Benrook, a top show and breeding kennel for two decades from about 1947, was widely known as the home of Ch. Dorem Display from about 1952 until his death. They still breed a few litters but have given up showing.

Mrs. Marion Evashwick of Marwyck Kennels finished her first champion in 1946 and is best known as the owner of the record holding producing bitch Ch. Sorceress of Ledahof and also of Ch. Marwyck Pitt-Penn Pirate, bred by Dorothy M. Whitton. Mrs. Evashwick is still active in showing, breeding and club affairs.

177

Mr. and Mrs. Glenn Fancy of Fancway began breeding in 1953 and are best known as the owners of Ch. Marwyck Pitt-Penn Pirate for much of his career at stud. Located in California, they claim to have bred only 26 litters, but are regular exhibitors, though not all the 15 or more Fancway champions are homebreds.

Mrs. Snowdon's Glenshaw Kennels, which turned to Miniature Schnauzers in 1950, has been consistently producing winners of distinctive type for many generations, including nearly 20 champions.

Jonaire Kennels, owned by the Spechts for 20 years from about 1946, has now changed hands but is still breeding and exhibiting. In the course of two decades they bred or finished some 45 champions and were one of the largest scale breeding kennels.

The Randolph Higgins' Geelong Kennels have been operating since at least 1942 and their early bitches, in particular Geelong Peggy, the dam of Minquas Pamela, are behind many present-day winners. During the past decade the male line from Ch. Geelong Playboy has been producing regularly.

The Mankit Kennels of Emanuel and Kitty Miller bred a notable litter in 1958 containing four champions from their Ch. Gladding's BieBie and have been producing winners ever since, with some of them the fifth generation of homebred champions.

Also deserving mention are Mrs. Meiners' Abingdon Kennels, with a string of champions from the early 1950's to the present, and Mrs. Amato's Winsomor, whose winners include the record-breaking bitch Miss Kitty.

In little over a decade Mrs. Wiedenbeck of Helarry Kennels has attained top rank as the breeder of show winners and producers, including the top living sire now at stud, Ch. Helarry's Dark Victory.

The Goulds' Windy Hill, another outstanding California kennel, goes back to the mid-1950's but has come to the front in the last half-dozen years, notably with Ch. Windy Hill Defiance.

One of the oldest California breeders still active is Florence Bradburn of Elfland, who has been producing champions for over 20 years, including the BIS Ch. Samos of Elfland.

As one looks through the current advertisements and the lists of top winners for the year many names meet the eye which could be added to the foregoing list, and some of which will undoubtedly be

178

Ch. Geelong Playboy at 6½ months.

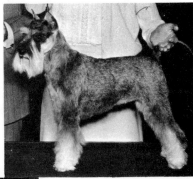

Ch. Gladding's Bie-Bie,
dam of 10 champions.

Ch. Winsomor Miss Kitty,
top-winning bitch for 1967.

Am. & Can. Ch. Jonaire Pocono Rough
Rider, Am. & Can. UDT—a unique
record.

Ch. Orbit's Space Pilot of Janhof, **BB** at the 1967 Chicago International.

Ch. Pickwick's GW Kim Kim, top winner. for the first quarter of 1967 (Phillips System) .

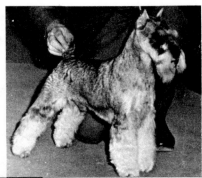

Ch. Samos of Elfland.

on it five or ten years from now. Pickwick in Michigan, Landmark and Orbit in California, Kansho in Texas, Travelmor in New Jersey, Barclay Square in Illinois, E-Narc in Arizona are a few which suggest themselves. Every perusal tempts one to add to the list, but we must draw the line somewhere.

A lucky mating or two does not establish a strain, but only lays the foundation for it. All too often a breeder produces a few excellent dogs but does not know how to continue from this beginning and build upon it. Instead of seeking out suitable studs for his good bitches, or suitable bitches for a potentially excellent sire he is too apt to breed to a big name of the wrong bloodline or to something easily available. Or he may shy away from the bogey of too much inbreeding and dissipate a valuable line by indiscriminate crosses based on no definite plan instead of holding what he has and building further upon it. The result is likely to be a hodgepodge of bloodlines without objective or specific goal. Luck may produce an individual outstanding litter, but it will not give consistently typical puppies year after year and generation after generation. To establish a successful strain and maintain it over any extended period requires good foundation stock plus careful study of individuals and pedigrees. It involves a lot of hard work, and when it is accomplished is indeed no small achievement.

181

Ch. Besernon's Echo.

Ch. Abingdon Authority, a 1966 top winner with 3 BIS.

Ch. Travelmor Witchcraft, BB at the American Miniature Schnauzer Club specialty, October 1967.

7

Postwar Miniatures
on the Continent

THE war ended all contact between German and
American breeders, but the breed was too well established for this
to be of any importance. Breeding in Germany was somewhat curtailed and registrations, which had reached an annual total of 794
in 1938, dropped almost one-fourth during the next two years, only
to increase again to a maximum of 1,245 in 1943. The following
year showed a drop of 27, while the slump in 1945 was so severe
that there were only 310 Miniatures registered. No doubt this was
due at least in part to difficulties caused by the Occupation and
unsettled conditions, for the 1946 registrations included over 400
dogs whelped in 1945 and the total of 1,843 was the largest up to
that time. The peak year was 1948, when registrations actually
reached 2,501. Until recently the decline had been steady, and in
1952 the total registrations for the year were 1,130, only 12 more
than in 1944. In 1944, Miniature Schnauzer registrations in Germany surpassed the registrations of Miniature Pinschers, which 20
years earlier had been 2½ times as numerous. Volume I of the
PSZ, published in 1924, contained 1,505 Miniature Schnauzers com-

pared to 3,970 Miniature Pinschers. By the end of 1965 the Miniature Schnauzer registrations amounted to 45,087 while Miniature Pinschers had reached only 22,863. No figures are available for the total number of Miniature Schnauzers registered in the United States, but in 1967 the breed was in seventh place out of 115 breeds with a total for the year of 26,001 registrations. In 1956 it had been in 24th place with 3,264 individual registrations for the year.

By 1937 the German government had consolidated many breeding operations and the Pinscher-Schnauzer-Klub, formed in 1923 when two earlier clubs combined, had become the *Fachschaft* (Section) *für Schnauzer und Pinscher e. V. in Reichsband für das Deutsche Hundewesen.* The R.D.H. succeeded the old all-breed association, the *Deutsches Kartell für Hundewesen* (D.K.H.) corresponding to the AKC. The earlier *Jahressieger* and *Klubsieger* titles (JS. and KS., or JSn. and KSn. for bitches) became Reichssieger and Fachschaftsieger (RS. and FS.). Owing to the partition of Germany, the RS. or JS. titles, formerly awarded to the winning dog and bitch at the annual Sieger show, are no longer given. The old KS. was revived, and *Bundessieger* (BS.) replaced RS. The KS. and KSn. are awarded to dogs and bitches winning first and "Excellent" ("*Vorzuglich*" or "V") at five shows of a certain size under at least three Klub judges. They must also be at least 12 months old.

The rules have also been tightened in various ways. Only solid black, and gray pepper and salt colors are now recognized. The black and cream or silver dogs can no longer be used for breeding, though they are still entered in the studbook. Moreover, the two remaining colors can no longer be crossed. Black must be bred only to black, and pepper and salt to pepper and salt. The same rule now applies in Switzerland, and, I understand, all over the Continent, though not in England or the United States. In Germany, local "breed wardens" supervise matings and inspect the puppies before they are registered. Unrecognized colors or dogs not considered suitable for breeding are designated in the studbook and cannot be bred. However, the Swiss recognized black and silvers in 1967.

The title of *Weltsieger* (World Champion) was awarded before the war to the dog and bitch going to the top at a designated show each year. This show might be in Germany, France, etc. The *Federation Cynologique Internationale de Beauté,* located in Brussels and recognized by the clubs all over Europe, awards the highly prized title of Champion International de Beauté, or International Bench Show Champion, which is very difficult to obtain. The requirements are four C.A.C.I.B. awards which must be won under three different judges and in three different countries. At least a year must elapse between the first and final win, and the dog must be of exceptional quality. Awards counting toward this title are made only at certain important International shows. The I.C.S. title has been won by a number of Miniature Schnauzers. They include FS. 1935 Marko v. Sachsen, his litter sister FSn. 1936 Mona v. Sachsen, and I.C.S. 1937 Bingulf v. Helluland-Dallacker. WS. winners include Mirko v. Schönhardt (black), the Swiss Artaban du Jorat, Medi v. Sachsen (sister to Marko and Mona), Qualm Heinzelmännchen (exported to America), and Cäcile Heinzelmännchen.

No German titles at all seem to have been awarded in 1939 and 1940. In 1941 there were Reichssieger awards won by Zarewitsch Heinzelmännchen (son of RS. Zar Heinzelmännchen) and Flamme v. Vierlinden in pepper and salts, and by Ratz zum Schlagbaum and Olga v. Burg Heldenstein in blacks. The dates when later titles were won are not given, but it would appear that no all-German Sieger show was held after 1941 and the subsequent KS. and BS. winners were all whelped from 1943 on, with the single exception of Graf v. Sachsen, who was whelped in 1939.

A check of the volume of the PSZ containing the registrations of dogs whelped during 1952 shows some interesting trends. Out of 339 litters, 161 were from solid black parents and with very few exceptions the puppies were all solid blacks. The 178 pepper and salt litters were only slightly in the majority. By 1965 this had been reversed, with 290 black litters against 139 salt and peppers.

Hupp v. Schönhardt played an important role among German blacks. A son of Giff v. Abbagamba (by S. Eros v. Abbagamba), Hupp traced in tail male to the Baltischhort line which went back to S. Zeno Zizlmann, S. Gift v. Chemnitz-Plauen, and Prinz v. Rheinstein. Hupp sired Jörg v. Mümlingtal out of the S. Egon v. Mümlingtal daughter Perle v. Stolzenberg, and Jörg, bred to his litter sister Jette v. Mümlingtal, produced 1941 RS. Ratz zum Schlagbaum and his brother Racker zum Schlagbaum. Udo v. Haus Rupert, who won Best Dog of the Year in 1964, was by Ralf v. Haus

Rupert, a great-great-great-grandson of RS. Ratz zum Schlagbaum. Jörg's line carried on through Nicko v. Nibelungenhort, his son KS. Quick v. Nibelungenhort, and grandson KS. Prinz v. Rauental. Quick also sired Juwel v. Neuhermsheim, who had five litters registered in 1952. Hupp's other sons included Hasso v. Kleinvilliers, from whose line came Wichtel v. Colonia and Peterle v.d. Schwalenburg, whose son Sausewind v.d. Schwalenburg left many male descendants, including Arko v. Haberland and Pitt v.d. Lohrheide. Besides Hupp, the Giff v. Abbagamba line carried on through Giff v. Freyersheim and Eros v. Schönhardt on the one hand, and through Harri and his son Munko v. Burg Heldenstein on the other. Munko's important sons included Voran and Vasko v.d. Schwalenburg and Saturn v.d. Burg Heldenstein. Vasko sired KS. Amor v.d. Schwalenburg and Purzel v. Papenburg, the sire of Axel v. Juchum. Hindrin v. Abbagamba, a full brother to Giff, left a less important male line which goes through Rajah v. Leixenstein for six generations.

S. Fred v. Düsselstein, of the fifth tail male generation from Prinz v. Rheinstein, sired seven German, three Dutch, and one Austrian Sieger, and also left four sons who carried on in male line. Much the most important is through Kurt v. Düsselstein, Lümpli v. Düsselstein, and the latter's two sons, Eros v. Lübeke and the more notable Puck v. Freyersheim. From Puck came Hasso zum Quelle, his son Fred v.d. Fohlenweide, and three generations of Siegers, Dido v. Saumhof, Jackel v.d. Burg Heldenstein, and 1951 BS. Sepp v.d. Burg Heldenstein. KS. Sam v. Liethberg was line-bred to Onyx v. Liethberg, a son of Eros v. Lübeke.

In 1954 the most prominent black line was that of Puck v. Freyersheim, through KS. Dido v. Saumhof's sons. Of these, BS. Alf v.d. Brunnenwiese sired 17 litters, his son Umber v. Nibelungenhort six, and other Alf sons and grandsons six more. Dido's grandson BS. Sepp v. Burg Heldenstein, besides three litters of his own, appears through two sons, with Groll v. Lübeke siring four. Etzel v.d. Heinrichsburg, by Sepp's sire, Jackel, also sired four litters. Arri v. Limburgerhof, a Puck great-great-grandson on a different line, is represented by two sons, Hasso v. Saumhof (seven litters and three by sons) and KS. Bodo v. Riedwald, with six.

Giff v. Abbagamba appears through nine litters by Purzel v. Papenberg's son Axel v. Juchum and through three sons of Immo v.d. Mengener Heide (by KS. Amor v.d. Schwalenburg). The line from Giff through Eros v. Schönhardt and his son Tünnes v. Düsselstein is carried on by two Tünnes sons, Olaf v. Ruschplerski (whose son Ino v. Freudenhall has five litters) and Derb v. Niggelstein, with six litters by Zack v. Skagerak and one by Zack's brother Zeck. Am. Ch. Hupp v. Schönhardt is still represented in Germany over two lines which also trace to Giff. Juwel v. Neuhermsheim is the grandsire of 11 litters, six by Odin v. Burg Weibertreu, three by the latter's brother Orloff, and three by Kuno v. Osterhof. The other Hupp line has four litters by Arko v. Haberland (son of Arko v. Dohlenhorst and grandson of Sausewind v.d. Schwalenburg) and two more by son and grandson.

Less prominent than these lines which trace to Prinz v. Rheinstein, there were still 53 litters in 1952 which went back directly to Peter v. Westerberg. Nine litters descended from S. Arco Heilbronnia and his son Imago v. Abbagamba through the latter's son Apollo v. Liethberg. These nine litters are the only blacks belonging to the Peter line, for the other 44 Peter litters are pepper and salts.

A similar reversal took place in the case of Emir v. Leixenstein, a black son of Benno v. Intzeplatz (by S. Fred v. Düsselstein). At the age of 12, Emir sired the pepper and salt Milan v. Leixenstein, whose son Ulk v. Leixenstein was the grandsire of four pepper and salt litters in 1952.

Only seven pepper and salt litters in 1952 were tail male descendants of Lord v. Dornbusch. All traced via Triple Sieger Zecher v. Dornbusch through his sons Jux v. Schlossberg and Stuss v. Dornbusch. No dog of this line ever sired more than a single litter. A line from S. Don v. Dornbusch and his son Am. Ch. Viktor v. Dornbusch and grandson S. Borzel v. Dornbusch carried down through Hahlo v. Schlossberg, Rauberle v. Helluland-Dallacker, I.C.S. Bingulf v. Helluland-Dallacker, and Zenith v. Helluland-Dallacker to Schnurps v. Helluland-Dallacker, who sired several litters about 1945 and 1946, but seems then to have disappeared.

The majority of pepper and salt litters of 1952 trace to S. Prinz v. Rheinstein. With only seven litters from Lord and 44 pepper and salt litters from Peter v. Westerberg, there remain 123 pepper and salt litters belonging to the Prinz male line. More surprising, however, is the fact that out of the 161 black litters registered in the

187

Franz Leix with ISC Blitz v.d. Neckarburg (left).

Tessie v. Mümlingtal and Favorit Struwelpeter.

188

same year, only nine trace in tail male to Peter, none to Lord, and the remaining 152 to Prinz. Of the entire 339 litters, therefore, 275 trace to Prinz, 53 to Peter and seven to Lord.

By far the greatest number of pepper and salt Prinz lines are descended from RS. Zar Heinzelmännchen, despite the fact that his career was a brief one, as he was poisoned when barely three years old. He had led the breed in number of litters sired during both 1935 and 1936, with a record of 40 during the latter year, and his total including the early part of 1937 was 65. Zar's outstanding son WS. Qualm Heinzelmännchen left 49 litters behind him when exported to the United States in 1938; although his descendants are still numerous, he appears to have left no male line. On the other hand, the Zar son Boris v. Bad Ilmenau had six tail male litters in 1952, and 1941 RS. Zarewitsch Heinzelmännchen inherited the mantle of his sire Zar so completely that no less than 77 litters traced to him. Zarewitsch sired a record total of 202 litters during his lifetime. His most successful son was Markgraf Heinzelmännchen, sire of 69 litters, while Markgraf's son KS. Götterbote Heinzelmännchen had a total of 93.

Götterbote's get included KS. Fridolin v. Köigsstand, KSn. Fulbia Heinzelmännchen, and BSn. Linda v. Lindenplatz. Markgraf also sired KS. Ego Struwelpeter, who sired 65 litters, with others by Ego's son Ass v.d. Niddaperle. Another Markgraf son, Zar v. Diedelsheim, was the sire of KS. and BS. Alex v. Sachsen, and others. The Zarewitsch son General Heinzelmännchen's line was responsible for ten litters in 1952, two of them by KS. Spatz Heinzelmännchen, among the latter's get being Dondeau Favorit Heinzelmännchen, whose third English champion finished at Crufts in 1955. The Zarewitsch Heinzelmännchen line also included Neckteufel Heinzelmännchen and his son KS. Narr Struwelpeter.‘

Aside from the Zarewitsch Heinzelmännchen male lines, Prinz v. Rheinstein is represented in some litters which trace to Am. Ch. Marko v. Beutenberg through Morit of Marienhof, an American-bred exported to Germany to the Heinzelmännchen Kennels and sold to Holland after Herr Walther's death. Morit sired KS. Volker Heinzelmännchen and Nicki v. Königstand, whose son KS. Axel v. Kiebitzbruch was still siring litters in 1965. So, also, was Rauber v. Leixenstein, by the Sieger Volker son Axel v. Holstentor. Finally, there are also litters which trace to Prinz via RS. Major Heinzelmännchen and Balzer v.d. Zwick via Swiss Ch. Blitz v.d. Neckarburg. The Major male line, through his son Crowsteps Hasty, was predominant in England after the war until the recent influx of German and American' stock. In addition to Morit of Marienhof several American-breds have gone to Germany. Ch. Jancy's Accent was shown there a number of times in 1956 and '57, and rated "V" (Excellent). Both Accent and Am. Ch. Delfin Kane sired several German litters.

The 44 pepper and salt litters in 1952 which traced to Peter v. Westerberg were all descended from Zarewitsch v. Leixenstein, a great-grandson of the English-owned Yula v. Leixenstein, who traced ultimately to Arno Heilbronnia. The most prolific of these Peter descendants were Falk v. Muhlgarten, sire of eight litters; Egon v. Gross Niedesheim with five; Muck v. Lindenplatz with five, and his son Sieg v. Lindenplatz with four; and Kautz v. Diedelsheim with three. In 1954 Falk was second for the breed with ten.

Tail male Peter v. Westerberg descendants of recent years include such winners as KS. Lord v.d. Bergheide; KS. Emir v. Spillingseck; ISC., BS., and KS. Wacker Struwelpeter; and his son Barry v. Walterteich.

The popularity of the Miniature Schnauzer has increased steadily in the last few years. German registrations in the latest volume of the studbook are almost double those for Standard Schnauzers. Today, there are also Schnauzer clubs in Switzerland, Austria, France, Belgium, Holland, and Italy. The Swiss club includes both Standards and Miniatures, as well as the middle-sized, smooth-coated Pinscher (quite distinct from the Doberman), but not the Giant Schnauzer. Both solid blacks and pepper and salts are equally popular and have separate classes. Mlle. Louise de Tavel (of the du Jorat Kennels), who has been breeding since 1917, has given up her Standards and now breeds only Miniatures, reporting that she never has enough to satisfy the demand. Her pepper and salt Miniatures won the challenge cup for best Schnauzer team at Lucerne in 1951, defeating both black Miniatures and Standards. She has bred many champions, including Artaban du Jorat, World Sieger and winner of Best of Breed at Frankfurt in 1935 over an entry of 70, in addition to the I.C.S. title. Frau Pfahler, Heljo Kennels, who owned Triple Sn. Annerl v. Hohentwiel, was another successful Swiss

Weisbaden CACIB Show, 1963.

Int. Ch. Atoom v. Neu-Drosedow and daughter, BSn. Marcia v. Neu-Drosedow.

191

Rama v. Neu-Drosedow.

Ch. Morit of Marienhof (Dutch),
American-bred.

A team of Italian champions from Malya Kennels.

192

breeder. A current exhibitor is Frl. Freida Steiger, whose Schnauzis Narzisse recently was best puppy bitch at Innsbruck in Austria.

Black and silvers are now recognized in Switzerland where they have separate classes and championships.

Both German and Italian exhibitors compete at Swiss shows, at some of which C.A.C.I.B. awards are offered. In Italy Dr. Granata, who judged in England in 1953 and won an Italian championship with the English-bred Dondeau Howzat was active in pepper and salts. Another English Miniature, Rownham Baron (by Ch. Gosmore Opening Batsman out of Eastwight Sea-Music) was purchased by the Pozzis of Malya Kennels and won his first C.A.C.I.B. early in 1967.

Italy has been distinguished for its blacks. Mrs. Crippa of the Diavoli Neri (Black Devils) kennels bred numerous winners and her Niks dei Diavoli Neri won the Bundessieger title in Germany in 1966, less than a year before her death. The Pozzis have also bred many winning blacks, including Eng. Ch. Jovinus Malya Swanee and It. Ch. Malya Pixy. The latter is one of the foundations of Mrs. Brivio's del Tornese Kennels which include the English-bred It. Ch. Jovinus Rhythm (a Swanee daughter) and her son It. Ch. Varum del Tornese who finished in 1967. Mrs. Brivio has also become interested in salt and peppers and imported a male puppy, Jovinus Roundabout, by Roundway Amulet ex Ch. Jovinus Ronbacardi.

Several American-bred Miniatures have gone to France at various times, and two English puppies were reportedly sent there in 1965 with the Chambro prefix. However, the breed does not seem to be very active there. A Belgian bitch, Kyrielle des los Robles, was exported to England where she is the dam of Dondeau Hornito, winner of two C.C.'s in 1965 and 1966.

The breed is also gaining advocates in Scandinavia, where the English-bred Ensign Pepper, by Risepark Northern Cockade, has become a champion.

In Holland Mrs. Mary Cloppenburg, owner of the late Dutch and Swiss Ch. Morit of Marienhof, who died in 1964, is an active breeder and exhibitor, with many title winners to her credit. Many in Denmark are Morit's descendants, and others are to be found in Germany.

8

The Breed
in Great Britain

T HE Miniature Schnauzer has been much slower in attaining popularity in Britain than in America. Starting half a dozen years later, at the beginning of the Depression, the timing was bad, and World War II had a more serious effect than would have been the case with a breed already well established. Moreover, British breeders had to contend with two serious handicaps not faced by their American counterparts. The quarantine regulations undoubtedly have added greatly to the difficulty and expenses of importing foundation stock. Otherwise, the nearness of England to the Continent would have been an advantage by enabling more fanciers to select their stock personally while gaining knowledge of the breed through attending Continental shows.

Another prime handicap was the Kennel Club rule forbidding the showing of cropped dogs. This not only increased the interval of waiting already caused by the six months' quarantine, which entails a delay of more than four months before even puppies whelped in quarantine can be shown. It prevented, in most cases, the exhibition of outstanding imported stock, which would have gone far to educate both breeders and public to the correct type and qualities of the breed.

Still another handicap in the early days was the lack of Challenge Certificates (C.C.'s), which were not offered for Miniatures until May 1935. The number allotted depends directly on the number of dogs registered in the breed and is fixed in advance for the year, regardless of competition. Under the American system, on the other hand, championship points are directly dependent on the entry at each show, once recognition is granted. This means that there is a strong inducement to bench the largest possible entry at every show, which helps to keep the breed before the public. While it is true that under the British system a championship very possibly means more in terms of the quality of competition, I do not think it stimulates the entries in a new breed to the same extent.

Another fact which may have played a part in hindering the development of British Miniatures was the establishment of a separate club, the British Miniature Schnauzer Club, in 1933 when the breed was still numerically weak; in the United States both Standard Schnauzers and Miniatures were included in a single organization for several years. While in America this had certain disadvantages in a resultant division of interest, by the time a separate Miniature club was formed in America in 1933, the breed was well able to stand on its own feet. In England, on the other hand, the small group of Miniature fanciers was weakened early by the forced withdrawal of several enthusiastic members who were obliged to curtail or discontinue their activities because of ill health. This resulted in the liquidation of the British Miniature club late in 1936. First the Hancocks of Enstone Kennels, original founders of the British Miniature fancy, then Mrs. Simmons of Crowsteps Kennels (whose importation of 20 Miniatures during the mid-1930's should have established the breed on a firm basis were she to have continued as she had begun), were obliged to withdraw. Then Mrs. Rachel Firth, whose American-bred Dorem Domino won the C.C. at Crufts in 1937, gave up. This left Mr. R. T. Colbourne, Redenhall Kennels, and Mrs. Langton Dennis, Offley Kennels, as the leading supporters of the breed. The war and Mrs. Dennis' death had a further depressing effect, and it was not until after the war was over that a real revival began.

195

Miniature Schnauzers were first imported into England in October 1928, when Mr. W. H. Hancock (Enstone Kennels) imported the black Dutch bitch Enstone Gerti van Duinslust. Following in September 1930 were the German-bred Dutch Ch. Enstone Ador v. Rheinstolz and Enstone Bärbel von Dingshaus. All three appear at the back of the pedigrees of most of today's winning British Miniature Schnauzers.

The Miniatures were registered with the Standard variety from 1929 until May 1932, and this delayed the granting of C.C.'s, for which the requirement was three years' separate registration with a total of at least 80 of the breed registered. By the close of 1934 this minimum had been considerably exceeded and registrations actually numbered 117. The British Miniature Schnauzer Club was formed in July 1933, a month before the American Miniature Schnauzer Club became a separate organization from the Standard Schnauzer Club of America.

In July 1935 the name of the breed was officially changed by the British Kennel Club to "Affenschnauzer" and the Club became the British Affenschnauzer Club, but in August 1936 the name was changed back as the result of protests from the German Klub. This shifting undoubtedly caused some confusion and may have helped to delay the progress of the breed. Late in 1936 the club disbanded, and so far as my records show was not revived as a separate organization until 1953. The breed was included in the Schnauzer Club of Great Britain in 1946, however, and several Miniature breeders were members of the committee in 1947.

The foundation breeding stock falls into several distinct groups within the two main divisions of prewar and postwar. The Enstone importations, already mentioned, produced three of the first four champions. Ch. Enstone Cuno, the first male, whose record of eight C.C.'s was not exceeded till the 1950's, was owned by Miss Humphreys and finished at the L. K. A. Show in April 1936. On the same day the imported German bitch, Mrs. Simmons' Crowsteps Hilvaria Heinzelmännchen, became the first bitch champion. Unfortunately, Hilvaria, an uncropped litter sister to Mrs. Simmons' German RSn. Holde Heinzelmännchen, died suddenly a few days afterwards, leaving no English progeny.

Ch. Enstone Cito was a litter brother to Ch. Enstone Cuno, bred and owned by Mr. Hancock, and the winner of four C.C.'s. Both these dogs were by Ador v. Rheinstolz out of Dutch Ch. Bärbel v. Dingshaus. In spite of their show records, neither seems to have left descendants who carried on to the postwar era. Ch. Enstone Beda, the first English-bred bitch and the only solid black prewar champion, also does not seem to have carried on. She was from a full brother and sister mating of Enstone Erick and Enstone Fanni, both by Ador out of Gerti van Duinslust. Enstone Eros, a full brother to Chs. Enstone Cito and Enstone Cuno, sired Putzi of Offley (out of Ch. Beda's dam, Enstone Fanni) and Bussi of Offley (out of Benta of Offley, a sister to Fanni and Erick). Putzi and Benta were solid blacks, but with the next generation this color disappeared rapidly and seems to be infrequent among postwar Miniatures. Bussi was slate gray or blue—a rare color among Miniatures.

Ador v. Rheinstolz, the double grandsire of Putzi and Bussi, was strongly line bred to Gift Chemnitz-Plauen and to Gift's dam, Ch. Perle v.d. Goldbach, with some Peter v. Westerberg blood but none from Lord v. Dornbusch. Bärbel v. Dingshaus carried a smaller amount of Gift blood with both Lord and Peter through two lines from Friedel v. Affentor in the second and third generations. On her dam's side the pedigree goes back only three generations to the unregistered bitch Maus v. Höfel. Gerti van Duinslust carried many of the same lines as Ador, who was a half brother of her paternal granddam. However, one-fourth of her pedigree was Baltischhort breeding and she carried Schwarze Hexe, a black bitch of unknown pedigree, three times in four generations. Gerti's bitch line went back in the fifth generation to Afra v. Erlenheim, a Standard Schnauzer whose bitch line is further traceable for another five to Kitty v. Kriftel, whelped by 1908 or earlier. Gerti's sire, S. Taps v. Düsselstein, by S. Fred v. Düsselstein, belonged to one of the principal producing black lines. Bärbel's paternal grandsire, Fips v. Hohndorf, is discussed in the chapter on Breed Origins under the male lines from S. Gift Chemnitz-Plauen.

Enstone Anni, sired by Ch. Enstone Cuno out of the Ador–Gerti daughter Enstone Heidi, won a C.C. in 1938, and her dam, Heidi, won in 1937, but this line does not seem to have survived the war. Another Ador–Gerti daughter, Crowsteps Enstone Asta, bred back to her sire, produced Crowsteps Amrei, granddam of Redenhall Baalah. Ador's male line did not carry on beyond Enstone Eros. Ador himself survived until the age of 14 and died in 1936.

Enstone Cuno, the first C.C. winner.

Crowsteps Lydia Heinzelmännchen.

Dutch Ch. Enstone Ador v. Rheinstolz, the first male imported to England.

Simon of Offley, whelped in 1933.

In 1933 Mrs. Dennis imported an American bitch, Gretel of Allsworth, by Jörg v. Dornbusch out of Ch. Gretel of Marienhof (one of the nine champions in the various matings of Ch. Cuno v. Burgstädt to Ch. Lotte v.d. Goldbachhöhe). Before leaving the United States, Gretel of Allsworth was bred to Ch. Porgie of Marienhof and whelped three puppies in quarantine. One male, Simon of Offley, played an important part in the development of the breed, while the bitch Offley Becky Sharp was the dam of Crowsteps Basca. Gretel of Allsworth was a hard-coated bitch of medium size with a moderately good head. She was later sold to Mrs. Simmons and in 1936 passed to Mrs. Hessoll. She was bred several times in England, but none of her other litters seem to have produced anything of importance, although Crowsteps Greta, by Rex Heilbronnia, did some winning. In 1933 another American bitch, Annette of Wollaton, was imported by Mrs. Pope of Moorland Kennels. Annette was bred several times but seems to have left no winning descendants. In 1936 Mrs. Firth visited the United States and took home with her a young male, Dorem Domino, by Ch. Jeff of Wollaton out of Jill of Wollaton II. He was from the same litter as Am. Ch. Dorem Dilletante and Dorem Diva, the latter one of the foundation bitches of the Dorem strain in America. Domino won the C.C. at Crufts in 1937 and was for a time at Mr. R. T. Colbourne's Redenhall Kennels, where he sired several litters. One of his sons, Redenhall Domino, sired the bitch Redenhall Baalah, whose son Redenhall Robert won at Crufts in 1946 when no Certificates were offered. No descendants are known.

The largest prewar group of importations, some 20 in all, was made by Mrs. Simmons' Crowsteps Kennels. The dispersal of this kennel late in 1936, because of ill health, was unquestionably a great blow to the breed. The greatest number of these importations were of Heinzelmännchen stock and several were of very high quality. RSn. Holde Heinzelmännchen whelped a litter of two males by RS. Major Heinzelmännchen in quarantine. One of these, Crowsteps Hasty, won two Certificates before the war and was the sire of Quarrydene Hans, through whose son, Offley Grey Shadow, come most of the male lines which date back to prewar days. Three other Heinzelmännchen bitches left descendants who have carried on to the present time. Lydia Heinzelmännchen, by S. Dieter v. Sachsen, was consequently a granddaughter of S. Marko v. Beutenberg, who played such a decisive part in the improvement of the breed in America, especially in regard to heads. Nudel Heinzelmännchen (a daughter of S. Zar Heinzelmännchen and a granddaughter of Lydia) as well as Ch. Gräfin Heinzelmännchen (half sister to Zar on the dam's side) both went from Crowsteps to Redenhall Kennels, where they left important progeny. Ursel v. Schloss Burgeck was a half sister on the sire's side to Jörg v. Dornbusch, the sire of Gretel of Allsworth. On her dam's side Ursel had additional Dornbusch with some Gift Chemnitz-Plauen lines. Mated to Yula v. Leixenstein (of an elaborately line-bred strain going back strongly to Rudi v. Lohr and Peterl v.d. Werneburg), she produced Crowsteps Ufer, who appears in the pedigrees as Moorland Black Knight, the sire of Gerti of Worth. Knight was a handsome black and cream dog with good body and high withers.

Two other imported Crowsteps sires were Rex Heilbronnia and Wenzel v. Dornbusch. Wenzel, by Triple Sieger Zecher v. Dornbusch, was a typical Dornbusch type, with hard coat, good color, and small size, but not too strong a head. His mating to Offley Becky Sharp, who carried a Dornbusch line on both sides, resulted in Crowsteps Basca, the dam of Quarrydene Hans. Rex Heilbronnia came from an outcross mating of the line-bred Leixenstein and Heinzelmännchen strains. Possibly for that reason, although he sired a number of litters including some winners, he left no champions and apparently no producing get, at least to date.

The last prewar champions were Quarrydene Gretchen (by Crowsteps Hasty out of Crowsteps Basca), who finished at Crufts in 1939, and Redenhall Isaiah (by Simon of Offley out of Bussi of Offley), who combined the American line of his sire with the Enstone strain of his dam, a double Ador v. Rheinstolz granddaughter. Isaiah left two producing sons (Redenhall Ruban, out of Nudel Heinzelmännchen, and Redenhall Graf, out of Ch. Gräfin Heinzelmännchen) and two daughters (Redenhall Olga and Redenhall Zilla, also out of Nudel). Besides Ch. Isaiah, Simon of Offley left Redenhall Phylomena, out of Ch. Gräfin Heinzelmännchen. While the male line has not continued further, Redenhall blood is strong in the postwar champions. Redenhall Phylomena was the dam of Offley Grey Shadow (by Quarrydene Hans) and of Quarrydene Miska (by Redenhall Ruban). Miska bred to Crowsteps Ludwig (by Crowsteps Hasty out of Lydia Heinzelmännchen) was the dam of Quarrydene Smitz, who sired both the outstanding producing bitch Quarrydene Gelda and the dog Gayli of Cluanie, whose male line survived in Ch. Ydrah Quarrydene Gadabout, finished in 1953.

During the war the breed reached a low ebb, for few fanciers were able to carry on and several of the oldtimers died, including Mrs. Dennis and Mrs. Pope. In fact, Mrs. Milsom of Quarrydene, although removed from Yorkshire to Wales, and more recently to Southport, appears to be the only prewar breeder still active. She was interested in Miniatures as early as 1936, finished Quarrydene Gretchen in 1939, and bred several postwar champions out of Quarrydene Gelda, herself a C.C. winner. Mr. R. T. Colbourne (Redenhall Kennels), who was located in Norfolk before the war, and afterwards in Yorkshire, still bred an occasional litter but no longer showed. To his Redenhall stock and the Offley dogs of Mrs. Langton Dennis, who died during the war, trace all the postwar champions which carry prewar lines.

Until 1953 all but one of the postwar champions traced in male line to Crowsteps Hasty, the son of RS. Major Heinzelmännchen and RSn. Holde Heinzelmännchen, whelped in quarantine. Hasty's son Quarrydene Hans continued the male line through Offley Grey Shadow, whose pedigree was half Heinzelmännchen. There was none of the early Enstone strain in Grey Shadow, but this was introduced through most of the bitches bred to him and to Crowsteps Ludwig. Ludwig, by Crowsteps Hasty out of Lydia Heinzelmännchen, was Heinzelmännchen breeding on both sides.

Crowsteps Ludwig was also bred to Redenhall Olga, a sister to Ruban, and produced Solomon of Offley and Hannah of Offley. The latter bitch, bred to Grey Shadow, was the dam of Belinda of Offley, a bitch who figures as the dam of several producers. Belinda traces in tail female to Nudel Heinzelmännchen, one of Mrs. Simmons' imported bitches. By her sire, Grey Shadow, Belinda produced Bobbie of Offley, who carried the male line down through Dondeau Hahn to Ch. Dondeau Harmonika on the one hand, and from Hahn via Dondeau Hansel to Ch. Krass of Crammington on the other. Pickles of Offley, a brother to Bobbie, sired Ch. Dondeau Hamerica out of the American-bred Minquas Harriet, and this line has distinguished itself. Hamerica sired three champions, Dondeau Harvest Time and Dondeau Harvest Moon out of Redenhall Clara

(a daughter of Redenhall Nicholas, another Bobbie of Offley son),
and Ch. Dondeau Hiya Deltone (out of Ch. Quarrydene Gaby of
Dondeau). Ch. Deltone Delestelle, finished in 1953, was a double
granddaughter of Ch. Dondeau Hamerica, being by Harvest Time
out of Hiya Deltone. Delestelle is the dam, by Doughboy, of Ch.
Deltone Delaware, who finished at ten months in three shows.

Still another Grey Shadow son was Tapps of Offley, out of black
Putzi of Offley (by Enstone Eros out of Enstone Fanni). Tapps,
when bred to his half sister Belinda of Offley, sired Joseph of
Talgarth, the sire of two champions out of Quarrydene Gelda. The
male in this Joseph-Gelda litter, Ch. Quarrydene Gabriel of Don-
deau, sired at least three C.C. winners before being exported to
South Africa. Putzi of Offley was also bred to Offley Fredo de
Bayardo, a Miniature Pinscher, and their daughter, Dinah of Offley,
bred to Solomon of Offley, produced Pearlie of Offley, the dam of
Dondeau Hahn.

Quarrydene Smitz, son of Crowsteps Ludwig and Quarrydene
Miska, was another important sire. He is still represented in male
line through Gayli of Cluanie (son of Quarrydene Peggy, a daughter of Grey Shadow's sire, Quarrydene Hans, from the bitch Gerti of
Worth). Gayli's son Quarrydene Ghilli (out of Quarrydene Gertrude, by Smitz out of Gerti) was bred to Ch. Quarrydene Gaynorette (a daughter of Bobbie of Offley and Quarrydene Gelda, the
latter a sister to Quarrydene Gertrude) and produced Quarrydene
Graf. Graf was mated back to his granddam, Quarrydene Gelda,
and this mating, inbred to Gelda and with four lines to Gerti,
produced Ch. Ydrah Quarrydene Gadabout, representing the male
line from Quarrydene Smitz. Aside from his son Gayli, however,
Smitz is also represented through his daughters. Quarrydene Gertrude, already mentioned, is, through her daughter Quarrydene
Guinea, the granddam of Ch. Krass of Crammington. Quarrydene
Sandra, another daughter of Smitz and Gerti of Worth, was the
maternal granddam of Redenhall Clara, dam of Ch. Dondeau
Harvest Time and Ch. Dondeau Harvest Moon. Most notable of all,
Quarrydene Gelda, still vigorous at 11 years old in 1953, was the
dam of five champions by three different sires. This is the most
outstanding record of any bitch in England. All three of Gelda's
champion daughters have been good producers, Ch. Quarrydene
Griselda of Dondeau (by Bobbie of Offley) being the dam of Ch.

202

Eng. Ch. Quarrydene Gaby of Dondeau, litter sister of Gabriel.

Eng. Ch. Quarrydene Gabriel of Dondeau.

Eng. Ch. Dondeau Hamerica.

Eng. Ch. Dondeau Harvest Time.

203

(Offley) Gretel of Allsworth.

Eng. Ch. Rannoch-Dune
Randolph of Appeline.

Eng. Ch. Deltone Appeline
Doughboy.

Dondeau Harmonika; Ch. Quarrydene Gaby of Dondeau, the dam of Ch. Dondeau Hiya Deltone and Dondeau High Hatter, winner of two Challenge Certificates; and Ch. Quarrydene Gaynorette the granddam of Chorltonville Critic. Several others have gone Best in Show at all-breed shows.

Since the war, a new group of fanciers has come to the fore and a number of importations from both the United States and the Continent have made their influence felt. The Dondeau Kennels of Mr. H. D. P. Becker have already owned or bred at least 15 champions, plus It. Ch. Dondeau Howzat and S. Afr. Ch. Dondeau Hiccup. Mrs. Doreen Crowe, owner of Ch. Deltone Appeline Doughboy, finished Ch. Deltone Delestelle, her first homebred, in 1953; Ch. Deltone Delaware, owned by Mr. Peter Newman, finished in 1955.

Many other Deltone Miniatures have since completed their titles. Doughboy had a total of eight C.C.'s, being the first to equal the prewar record of Ch. Enstone Cito. Doughboy was a son of the American-bred Rannoch-Dune Randolph of Appeline, imported by Mr. Douglas Appleton. Uncropped, Randolph made his English title in 1953. Through his son Doughboy, his male line dominated the breed throughout the next ten years and is still carrying on. Doughboy's fourth in line for the supreme award at Cruft's in 1956 also went far toward putting the breed on the map.

Mr. S. E. Whiteley of Chorltonville imported Ch. Chorltonville Quintin Bonus from Germany, a dog who combined strong Heinzel-männchen lines with Leixenstein and other blood. In male line Quintin actually traces to Yula v. Leixenstein, sire of Moorland Black Knight, and so eventually to Peter v. Westerberg. This male line is not otherwise represented among English or American champions today.

Another importation with Heinzelmännchen on both sides is Mr. Becker's Dondeau Favorit Heinzelmännchen, by KS. Spatz Heinzelmännchen out of Farina Heinzelmännchen, a daughter of KS. Götterbotte Heinzelmännchen. Favorit traces in male line to RS. Zar Heinzelmännchen, already represented in England through his daughter Nudel Heinzelmännchen and through several lines in the pedigree of Quintin Bonus. By 1955 Favorit's daughter Dondeau Haphazard had already won six Certificates. In all, he sired four champions including one son, Dondeau Helios.

Also German-bred and the sire of the first postwar English-bred champion not of the Crowsteps Hasty male line, Mr. Becker's Amor v. Ohsen Emmerthal combined Heinzelmännchen in equal parts with Lehrte blood, the latter related on one side to Ursel v. Schloss Burgeck, dam of Moorland Black Knight. Both Favorit and Amor carry some Dornbusch rather far back. Amor was mated to Beta of Bonheur, whose sire, Redenhall Graf, was by Ch. Redenhall Isaiah out of Ch. Gräfin Heinzelmännchen, while her dam was Belinda of Offley, the dam of Bobbie and Pickles of Offley and Joseph of Talgarth. Ch. Dondeau Bessy of Bonheur, the result of the Amor–Beta mating, was bred to Favorit Heinzelmännchen, a combination strong in Heinzelmännchen blood, which produced Ch. Dondeau Tzigane Liza and her sister Dondeau Hertzchen (who died when ten months old, after winning two Certificates). Ch. Dondeau Domingo's Harka was also sired by Favorit. Amor also sired Dondeau High Hatter, who sired Ch. Dondeau Domingo's Hedy and Dondeau Hush-sh, dam (by Favorit) of Italian Ch. Dondeau Howzat.

The postwar American importations began with Minquas Harriet (whelped in 1944 and purchased by a WREN), sired by Am. Ch. Minquas Bimelech, who carried three lines to Am. Ch. Marko of Marienhof and one to Ch. Priscilla of Marienhof II, a litter sister to Simon of Offley's sire, Ch. Porgie of Marienhof. Harriet's dam was Susan of Marienhof, by Ch. Marko out of a Ch. Porgie of Marienhof daughter. Minquas Harriet, when mated to Pickles of Offley (who carried three lines to Simon and two to Simon's sister Becky Sharp), produced Ch. Dondeau Hamerica.

Ch. Rannoch-Dune Randolph of Appeline, owned by Mr. Appleton, was a double grandson of Am. Ch. Delegate of Ledahof (a son of the great Ch. Dorem Display) and carried some of the same lines as Minquas Harriet. Ch. Randolph sired Ch. Deltone Appeline Doughboy out of Deltone Delilah, a double granddaughter of Ch. Dondeau Hamerica (by Dondeau Headlight out of Ch. Dondeau Harvest Moon). Another American bitch imported by a WREN was Minquas Amanda, by Ch. Quota of Appletrees out of Minquas Zorina. Bred to Gayli of Cluanie, she whelped a litter before accompanying her owner to South Africa, and some of her descendants are still extant. Zorina was ex Susan of Marienhof, dam of Minquas Harriet.

Ch. Wilkern Tony from America, who won his first Certificate at

L.K.A. in 1953, was imported for Mrs. Creasy and sired by Ch. Tweed Packet of Wilkern. Tony's dam, Wilkern Nicolette was, like Randolph, a grandchild of Ch. Delegate of Ledahof, while Tweed Packet's dam was Ch. Debutante of Ledahof, a litter sister to Delegate. Tony's dam was also a Ch. Dorem Display granddaughter on her sire's side. At five months of age, the bitch Guenever Anfiger, by the Display grandson Ch. Charlena Sho-Nuff, was imported by Mrs. Milsom. Her first litter produced the Cruft's Best of Breed winning Deltone Quarrydene Felicity, sired by Ch. Doughboy, winner of a Junior Warrant and champion in 1957.

British Miniature Schnauzers are much stronger in Heinzelmännchen blood than are the American dogs. In other respects, too, the pedigrees are decidedly different. The Enstone strain is not found in America. There are, however, sufficient similarities to make it probable that the recent American importations will produce well with the older stock, provided individuals are carefully selected and suitably mated.

There are now a number of Miniatures in Scotland, and the North of England was sufficiently active to have had a breed class scheduled for the first time in 1953. Mrs. Milsom was formerly located in Wales, where there are now several other owners as well (including Mr. Whiteley), and there are likewise breeders in both Ireland and the Isle of Wight. Mrs. Lynch, a pioneer Irish fancier, won with Athboy Dondeau Hero, a son of Dondeau Handeklatschen (by Favorit Heinzelmännchen) out of Ch. Dondeau Domingo's Harka, who became the first Irish champion in 1957.

British Miniature Schnauzers have been exported to various countries, including South Africa, Pakistan, the United States, Italy (where Dottore Granata won with Dondeau Hill Song, and made Dondeau Howzat a champion in 1954), Norway, Australia (since 1961), and Japan.

The Miniature Schnauzer Club of Great Britain, founded in 1953, is actively interested in promoting the breed and in advocating the use of specialist judges for championship shows. The Schnauzer Club of Great Britain continues, however, to include Miniature fanciers among its members. According to the British Kennel Club's ruling, the standard for both breeds is the same except for size, and the Miniature breed standard was reworded during 1954 to conform to this requirement. This is unlike the position in the United States, where the Standard and Miniature Schnauzers are considered completely independent breeds and each club makes its own decisions as to the breed standard of perfection.

The breed standard is substantially the same as the American. The ideal height is set at 13 inches for bitches and 14 inches for dogs, but there is no mention of a disqualification for oversize, nor of any minimum. All pepper and salt colors are approved, as is pure black.

The blacks almost disappeared in England during the war, although there is said to have been a class for blacks offered at Cheltenham in 1936. In 1954 there was a black class at Richmond, where it has since been a regular fixture, as it is at the club specialties.

Mrs. Boubelik of Oddstock has specialized in blacks, combining prewar lines with her Austrian Dyk v. Robertshof, who died in 1966 at the age of 17. By Austrian Ch. Persy v. Schenkenfelden, Dyk went back in male line to S. Oswien v. Königseck, son of S. Egon v. Mümlingtal. Dyk made an excellent record in obedience, and the Oddstock dogs are noted for good temperament. Quisdown Valerian, owned by Miss Maureen Keel, a notable worker and a Dyk son, is a CD (Ex.) and still enjoys performing at the age of ten.

In breed classes Mrs. Joan Reynolds of Surrey has had notable success, including the first black champion since 1937 and several C.C. winners. Her foundation bitch, Redenhall Hella, by the black Redenhall Felix (grandson of Simon of Offley and Gayli of Cluanie) out of Redenhall Gloria (by Redenhall Abel, full brother to Ch. Dondeau Hamerica, ex Redenhall Zilla) carries most of the outstanding prewar lines. Felix traced in tail male to Ch. Porgie of Marienhof, while Zilla was a daughter of (Crowsteps) Nudel Heinzelmännchen. Felix's dam, Gaydon Fann, was out of the American Minquas Amanda, by Ch. Quota of Appletrees ex Minquas Zorina.

Mrs. Reynolds' Italian import Jovinus Malya Swanee, the first black champion since Enstone Beda, has had tremendous influence as a sire. His get include the C.C. winners Barway Bitter Lemon, Jovinus Replica, Jovinus Rigoletto (the first Australian black champion) and exports to Canada and the United States. Still another C.C. winner, Jovinus Risotto (by salt and pepper Ch. Jovinus Roxburgh) is the dam of Replica and Rigoletto. Besides C.C. and

Best of Breed at the Miniature Club specialty in 1961, Risotto was Reserve for Best of Breed at the Schnauzer Club of Great Britain Open Show in 1962 and Reserve C.C. at Cardiff the same year. She is a daughter of Jovinus Ravenna who was ex Redenhall Hella.

In salt and peppers, the American male line from Doughboy, sire of seven champions, was continued through his son Ch. Deltone Deloklahoma, whose only champion son, Deltone Deldiablo, himself sired eight, still the record for the breed. Deldiablo's son, Ch. Deltone Deldomingo, until recently held the record of 17 Challenge Certificates. Deldomingo, his brother Ch. Deltone Deldisplay, and sister Ch. Deltone Delsanta Miranda, were all from one litter out of Ch. Deltone Delsanta Maria, bred by Mrs. Milsom of Quarrydene and sired by Ch. Deloklahoma. Santa Maria and Quarrydene Gelda, bred by Mrs. Milsom and dam of five champions, are two of the top-producing bitches of the breed, a third being Ch. Diablo's daughter Gosmore Peaches and Cream, dam of four.

The male line from Doughboy as of 1967 ends with Deldomingo's son, Ch. Risepark Happy Fella, and the non-champion Quarrydene Fritzi (litter brother to Ch. Deltone Quarrydene Felicity) both of whom have champion daughters.

Ch. Wilkern Tony from America, who finished in 1957 and traces in male line to Ch. Sandman of Sharvogue, sired two champion sons, Roundway Kelpie of Impstown and Jovinus Roxburgh. To date his line is carrying on through the non-champion Rownham's Cavalier, whose daughter Ch. Eastwight Sea Nymph is the dam of three champions, while Cavalier's son, Ch. Rownham's Eastwight Sea Lawyer, finished in 1966, as did his daughter Ch. Rownham's Susique. Roxburgh is the sire of Rhodesian Ch. Jovinus Request.

Beginning in 1960 a new line came to the fore with the father-and-son team of Am. Ch. Nicomur Chasseur and Am. Ch. Sternroc Sticky Wicket, tracing in male line to Display through a minor, non-champion son, Meldon's Dr. R.R.L. and the latter's son Ch. Nicomur Champagne. They are believed to be the only two American champion males so far imported. Chasseur left a champion daughter in the United States and sired three champion sons in England: Dondeau Horseshoe, Dondeau Hunting Horn, and Gosmore Trump Card. Horseshoe's daughter, Ch. Risepark Lucky Choice, and the non-champion Gosmore Contract's son, Ch. Roskill Burns Night, both finished in 1966. Sticky Wicket has sired seven cham-

209

Eng. Ch. Deltone Deldisplay,
winner of 10 C.C.'s.

Eng. Ch. Gosmore Hat Trick,
top bitch with 17 C.C.'s.

Quarrydene Frances of Settnor.

Risepark Northern Cocktail.

pions in England, three of them sons. His get include the top-winning bitch of the breed, Ch. Gosmore Hat Trick, with 17 C.C.'s, Ch. Gosmore Opening Batsman, top-winning dog with 24 and sire of Ch. Gosmore Silver Star of Settnor, and Ch. Gosmore Wicket Keeper, whose son Lichstone Chasseur sired another 1966 champion, Lichstone Pacemaker. Three of Sticky Wicket's seven champions were out of Gosmore Peaches and Cream. The first of these, Ch. Gosmore Wicket Keeper, went to Australia, where he finished in short order, being the first of the breed to do so there.

The year 1966 was a bumper year in which ten champions finished, which appears to be a record. These included a third daughter of Appeline Cosburn's Pickwick Peppers and two by his son Risepark Northern Cockade. Cockade's son, Ch. Roundway Anchor, finished at Richmond, the final show of the year. Pickwick Peppers is a Canadian dog, the first imported from there so far as I know, and was sired by Am. Ch. Cosburn's Esquire (also Canadian-bred), a grandson of the Display son Ch. Benrook Beau Brummell. Besides his three champion daughters out of Eastwight bitches, Pickwick Peppers has sired other C.C. winners. Cockade's third champion, Roundway Annabelle, sister to Anchor, finished in 1967. A full brother is Rhodesian Ch. Roundway Ancestor.

The leading bitch families in Great Britain are limited in number, for many of the importations are no longer represented in tail female, though they appear through other lines. American Family I, by far the most numerous source of top producers in the United States, is understandably the source of nearly all the top-producing bitches from the U.S. Am. Ch. Flint Hill Glitter-bug and the lapsed line from Gretel of Allsworth trace to Am. Ch. Gretel of Marienhof, whose line from Ch. Lotte v.d. Goldbachhöhe has shown a surprising upsurge in America in recent years. Also tracing to Ch. Gretel is Guenever Anfiger, to whom the second largest group of tail female producers at the present time can be traced, with at least 12 champions, several coming through her non-champion producing daughter Quarrydene Frieda. Two of this line, Ch. Scissors of Settnor and Ch. San Marta of Settnor, have each won the English Club trophy for Bitch of the Year. Other Family I bitches with many descendants, although not in tail female, were Minquas Harriet and Minquas Amanda, imported in the 1940's, who both traced to Fiffi of Marlou, a Ch. Amsel v.d. Cyriaksburg daughter not heavily represented in the United States. An additional American import of Family I was Phil-Mars Ritzy Lady, whelped in 1950, by Ch. Dorem Tribute out of Ch. Phil-Mars Lucky Lady. While no English champions appear to be descended from her as yet, Ritzy Lady is the maternal granddam of Roundway Anthony, sire of New Zealand Ch. Dingo Nightlight.

Certainly the most numerous bitch line in England is Family V, derived from the Dutch bitch Gerti van Duinslust, going ultimately to Kitty v. Kriftel, a line as yet unrepresented by any champion in the United States. Most, if not all, tail female descendants at the present time come through Benta of Offley and her daughter Gerti of Worth. The latter is represented through two daughters, the top-producer Quarrydene Gelda, dam of five champions, and Quarrydene Sandra. Sandra traces through Redenhall Carol and Redenhall Clara to Ch. Dondeau Harvest Moon, whose daughter Deltone Delorado produced three champions in one litter. Another Harvest Moon daughter, Deltone Delilah, was the dam of Ch. Doughboy, while a third, Deltone Delnevada, dam of Deltone Delmanhattan, was ancestor of all the Eastwights. Also from Quarrydene Sandra comes Prunes of Noreen and through her a few of the Dondeaus, via her daughter Dondeau Pip Emma. Other Sandra daughters also have descendants but not in tail female.

The largest number of Dondeaus, Deltones, and other lines descended from them trace to Quarrydene Gelda, by way of her daughters Ch. Quarrydene Griselda of Dondeau and Ch. Quarrydene Gaby of Dondeau, and the latter's daughter Ch. Dondeau Hiya Deltone and granddaughter Ch. Dondeau Delestelle, the latter the dam of Deltone Cherokee. Another Gelda daughter, Quarrydene Gazelle, is behind the Sheenharts, including Australian Ch. Sheenhart Honeysuckle.

The other producing family has a common source in Germany with American Family III, which originated with Grethel v. Hohenstein (510) and her unregistered dam, Alli v.d. Goldbach, at the beginning of the century. To this line belong Nudel Heinzelmännchen, imported before the war, as well as others from the same kennel whose tail female lines have lapsed. To Nudel trace the Jovinus blacks and a few of the Dondeaus. Also of this family, but not coming from Nudel, is Ch. Dondeau Hunters Moon out of Dondeau Hxzakly. The latter is the daughter of an American-bred,

Elibanks Cindy, imported about 1957. Cindy's maternal granddam was the German-bred Madel v. Diedelsheim, sired by Dorn v. Batzenberg of the Peter v. Westerberg male line. Madel's dam traced in the fifth generation to Grille Heinzelmännchen, from whom Nudel is descended, but has no U.S. producers.

American Families II and IV are not represented by any English champions, while Family VI, from Maus v. Höfel to the imported Dutch Ch. Bärbel v. Dingshaus, has lapsed in England and is not represented in the United States.

English Champions

(Number of Challenge Certificates won is included so far as known. Males marked "d")

1935–1939

Name	Certificates
Ch. Enstone Cito (d)	8
Ch. Enstone Cuno (d)	4
Ch. Enstone Beda (black)	
Ch. Crowsteps Hilvaria Heinzelmännchen (German)	
Ch. Crowsteps Gräfin Heinzelmännchen (German)	
Ch. Redenhall Isaiah (d)	
Ch. Quarrydene Gretchen	

1947–1967

Ch. Quarrydene Gabriel of Dondeau (d)	6
Ch. Quarrydene Gaynorette	
Ch. Quarrydene Gaby of Dondeau	4
Ch. Dondeau Harmonika (d)	
Ch. Dondeau Hamerika (d)	5
Ch. Quarrydene Griselda of Dondeau	
Ch. Dondeau Hiya Deltone	4
Ch. Dondeau Harvest Time (d)	4
Ch. Dondeau Harvest Moon	5
Ch. Dondeau Bessy of Bonheur	
Ch. Krass of Crammington (d)	
Ch. Rannoch-Dune Randolph of Appeline (American) (d)	6
Ch. Chorltonville Quintin Bonus (German) (d)	
Ch. Quarrydene Gadabout (d)	
Ch. Dondeau Tzigane Liza	
Ch. Deltone Delestelle	
Ch. Deltone Appeline Doughboy (d)	8
Ch. Dondeau Domingos Hedy	4
Ch. Wilkern Tony from America (American) (d)	7
Ch. Dondeau Domingos Harka	

213

Ch. Deltone Delaware (d)	
Ch. Deltone Delsanta Fe	4
Ch. Dondeau Haphazard	6
Ch. Deltone Deloklahoma (d)	5
Ch. Deltone Delpasadena	
Ch. Roundway Kelpie of Impstown (d)	
Ch. Deltone Quarrydene Felicity	
Ch. Dondeau Helios (d)	
Ch. Deltone Deldiablo (d)	12
Ch. Deltone Delwichita	
Ch. Deltone Delsanta Maria	
Ch. Deltone Delsanta Barbara	
Ch. Dondeau Handicap (d)	
Ch. Deltone Deldisplay (d)	10
Ch. Deltone Deldomingo (d)	17
Ch. Eastwight Sea Nymph	
Ch. Gosmore Peach Brandy	
Ch. Risepark Happy Talk	
Ch. Gosmore Hat Trick	17
Ch. Gosmore Wicket Keeper (d)	
Ch. Jovinus Roxburgh (d)	
Ch. Deltone Delsanta Luella	
Ch. Dondeau Hunting Horn (d)	
Ch. Eastwight Sea-Sprite	
Ch. Gosmore L.B.W. (d)	
Ch. Gosmore Sternroc Miss Beachcomber	
Ch. Gosmore Trump Card (d)	
Ch. Quarrydene Frances of Settnor	
Ch. Dondeau Horseshoe (d)	
Ch. Dondeau Hunters Moon	
Ch. Eastwight Spillikins	
Ch. Gosmore Opening Batsman (d)	24
Ch. Jovinus Ronbacardi	
Ch. Eastwight Sea Enchantress	
Ch. Jovinus Malya Swanee (d) (black)	
Ch. Risepark Happy Fella (d)	
Ch. Risepark Karousel	
Ch. Snippet of Settnor	
Ch. Scissors of Settnor	7
Ch. Eastwight Sea Music	
Ch. Eastwight Sea Gala	
Ch. Gosmore Silver Star of Settnor (d)	
Ch. Lichstone Pacemaker (d)	
Ch. Risepark Lucky Choice	
Ch. Risepark Scarlet Ribbons	
Ch. Roskill Burns Night (d)	
Ch. Roundway Anchor (d)	4

Eng. Ch. Eastwight Sea Gala.

Ch. Rownham's Eastwight Sea Lawyer (d)
Ch. San Marta of Settnor   6
Ch. Rownham's Susieque
Ch. Roundway Annabelle
Ch. Sceptre of Settnor (d)
Ch. Sylvia of Symdale

The showing of dogs in Great Britain differs in many ways from exhibiting in the United States. Some of the variations are of minor importance, such as the fact that first prize ribbons are red instead of blue. On the other hand, to become a champion a dog must win three Challenge Certificates under different judges. Certificates are offered only at certain designated championship shows determined in advance by the Kennel Club. The number of Certificates offered annually depends upon the number of registrations in the breed, and no specialty show may receive champion status unless there were at least 750 breed registrations during the previous 12 months.

There are also more types of shows: Championship, Open, Members, Limited, Sanction, Match, and Exemption, with many classes not found at American shows, including numerous Variety classes in which a number of different breeds compete. In one of these classes there are sometimes 30 or more dogs entered. Entry fees are much lower and class prize money is the rule. Consequently, dogs are regularly entered in a number of different classes, and the size of the show is figured on the basis of the number of entries rather than on the number of dogs. Challenge Certificates are awarded regardless of the number of dogs or bitches competing, but since their number is strictly limited, a championship is more difficult to obtain than in the United States. The Schnauzer Club of Great Britain's Open Show is to have Certificates for the first time in 1968, for Miniatures only.

An award peculiar to England is the Junior Warrant. This is granted by the Kennel Club to a dog or bitch winning a total of 25 points at Championship or Open shows before reaching the age of 18 months. Three points are awarded for firsts at Championship shows with C.C.'s, and one point at Open shows.

In January 1967 the large and unwieldly Non-Sporting Group was divided into Working and Utility, and both Standard and Miniature Schnauzers are now in the Utility Group.

9

Miniature Schnauzers in Canada, Bermuda, Mexico and South America

MINIATURE Schnauzers in Canada lagged far behind the breed in the United States. A German male, Morle v.d. Ludwigshöhe, was sold to Mr. MacLimont in 1927, but the first one shown there appears to have been Anfiger Kennels' American-owned but German-bred Nette v. Mümlingtal, who finished her title in 1933. Sired by Ari v. Schillerberg (older full brother to Ch. Bodo v. Schillerberg) out of Sn. Heidy v.d. Hermansburg, Nette left no progeny in Canada, but after a lapse of some generations several of her American-bred descendants, including Ch. Sorceress of Ledahof, the latter's son Ch. Marwyck Penn Hurst, and Ch. Dorem Delegate have likewise made their Canadian titles. Ch. Delegate was owned for a time in Toronto, but later returned to the United States.

The first male to become a Canadian champion was the Canadian-bred Ch. Bendigo of Clearbrook, bred by the Misses Cluff, who purchased Cora of Wollaton in 1935 and bred her to Ch. Rudy of Wollaton. At the Canadian National Show in September 1937 four Miniatures were shown, with the breed centered in Toronto, as it still is. Another early Canadian fancier, Mr. Walter Reeves, owned a Marienhof bitch in 1936 (a black or black and cream). Perhaps one reason for the slow start of the breed in Canada was that it was originally relegated to the Toy Group there. Undoubtedly another factor was World War II, which came just when Miniatures seemed to be getting established, and perhaps on this account the early breeders seem to have discontinued operations, necessitating a fresh start. Difficulties in regard to producing correct size are also said to have occurred.

At any rate, only one more Miniature finished a Canadian championship before the war. Am. Ch. Handful of Marienhof made his U.S. title in 1938 and his Canadian title soon afterwards. Then came Miss Audrey Firman's Ch. Drossel of Furstenhof, whelped in 1940, the first Canadian-owned bitch to finish, although she, too, was American-bred. She was a daughter of Ch. Handful of Marienhof, ex Asta of Fuerstenhof. Mrs. Constable's Am. Ch. Kathie of Marienhof finished in 1944.

Mr. Edwin Wright of Montreal owned the American-bred Can. Ch. Kathie Khan of Marienhof, a half sister to Mrs. Constable's Kathie, and from her bred Can. Ch. Winwel Love-in-Bloom, the second Canadian-bred to complete his title and the first whose parents were both Canadian champions. Love-in-Bloom was sired by Mr. Thomas C. Wylie's Ch. Silvermist of Marienhof. Silvermist sired Mr. Wylie's homebred Ch. Strathburn MP Alpha Cath out of Can. Ch. Princess Pat of Marienhof, who was by Ch. Cockerel of Sharvogue out of Bubbi of Marienhof. From his daughter, Ch. Cath, Silvermist also sired Strathburn MC Alpha Ann, the dam of Am. Ch. MacMar Miniature Model. Ann appears to have been the first Canadian-bred to produce an AKC champion.

Am. & Can. Ch. Neff's Luzon, a younger brother to Ch. Kathie of Marienhof, was by Ch. Kubla Khan of Marienhof out of Rosel v. Neff II. His picture recalls S. Urian Thuringia, a notable show winner from whom Luzon was descended, and he himself compiled a remarkable record, winning 43 Best of Breed awards up to 1947,

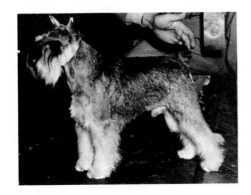

Can. & Am. Ch. Marwyck
Penn Hurst.

Can. & Am. Ch. Esquire of Marienhof,
sire of 6 Canadian champions.

Can. & Am. Ch. Neff's Luzon.

219

and gaining the American Miniature Schnauzer Club annual trophy in 1944. Neff's Luzon was owned in Canada by Mr. Wylie, and was the sire of Can. Ch. Strathburn JP Beta Misty, as well as of four American champions bred by the Schaumburg Kennels in California. Altogether, Mr. Wylie owned six Canadian champions, two of them also U.S. champions and two of them homebreds, but he gave up breeding because of ill health and returned to Great Britain.

In the Toronto area there are a number of active breeders and exhibitors. The Gottschalks (Cosburn Kennels) have bred a number of Canadian champions. In addition, Cosburn's Aristocrat, Cosburn's Esquire, and Cosburn's Sweet Tribute are also U.S. champions. The Gottschalks have also owned Am. Ch. Benrook Beau Brummell and Am. Ch. Dorem Delegate. The MacKendricks owned Ch. Cosburn's Sandman's Kandy and bred her son, Ch. Boxerly Sugar's Sonanaire. Mr. J. Wood's Ch. Cosburn's Karen Jo-Ann was an older sister to Ch. Cosburn's Aristocrat, while the Reids' Ch. Benrook Bally was an American-bred daughter of Ch. Dorem Tribute, and their first homebred, Ch. Oak Gables Affaire du Coeur, was by the Display son Benrook Tradition.

The first Miniature to win the Group in Canada appears to have been Mr. Wylie's homebred Ch. Strathburn JP Beta Misty in May 1948. In June of the same year Mrs. Constable's American-owned Ch. Katydid of Marienhof, another Kubla Khan daughter, was first in the Group at both Charlottetown and Fredericton. In September Mrs. Evashwick's Ch. Sorceress of Ledahof won the Group at Toronto and followed this by the first Canadian Best in Show win at Quebec in October. Her son Ch. Marwyck Penn Hurst, then owned by Mr. Wylie, won the Group twice in 1950, and the American-bred Ch. Hit Parade's Lamplighter won twice, with Best in Show once, in 1951 and 1952. Unfortunately, he died not long after. Ch. Dorem Display, then owned by the Phil Meldons, was Best in Show in 1949, the first male to attain that honor, while Am. & Can. Ch. Cosburn's Sweet Tribute won in 1950.

The Miniature Schnauzer Club of Ontario was founded September 26, 1951. In 1955 the name was changed to the Miniature Schnauzer Club of Canada. It held specialty shows at Oakville, Ontario, in 1951 and 1952, at the Canadian National Livestock Exhibition in 1953, and at the National Sportsmen's Show in 1954.

The original officers were W. Harry MacKendrick, president; E. B. Reid, first vice-president; W. Gottschalk, second vice-president; Mrs. W. Gottschalk, secretary-treasurer. The 1951 specialty show was won by Am. & Can. Ch. Benrook Beau Brummell. The 1952 winner was Am. & Can. Ch. Cosburn's Aristocrat, the first Canadian-bred American champion. The 1953 winner was Ch. Boxerly Sugar's Sonanaire and the 1954 winner, under the American specialist judge R. A. Kerns, Jr., was again Am. & Can. Ch. Cosburn's Aristocrat.

Shows in Canada award points on a basis midway between the American and English systems. Only ten points instead of 15 are required, and points are figured on the basis of the total numbers of dogs of all breeds at the show. However, wins must be made under at least three different judges, and it is no longer possible, as it was in 1933, for a Miniature to complete the title without any competition within the breed. Nevertheless, it is still easier for a Miniature Schnauzer to become a champion in Canada than in the United States. The breed is now classified in the Terrier Group.

The number of Group firsts gained by Miniature Schnauzers during the past few years, not to mention other Group placings and at least three Bests in Show since 1948, should have their effect in making the general public more conscious of the breed and should help to increase its popularity. As yet, only a small group of fanciers are actively breeding and showing, but the increase is steady.

During the 1950's Mr. Paul Delaney of Humphrey, New Brunswick, endeavored to popularize the breed in the Maritime Provinces. His foundation stock consisted of a Canadian male, Ch. Cosburn's Patrick on Parade, and an American bitch, Raphaela Anfiger, by Ch. Jancy's Accent, parents of Can. Ch. Honeywell's Dark Discovery.

The Canadian-bred winners up to 1957 did not show much variety of bloodlines. Lisa v. Klein Wald was by Ch. Dorem High Test out of Exotic of Ledahof. Lisa's sire was a Ch. Dorem Display son and her dam, Exotic, a daughter of Ch. Enchantress, traced in male line through Loki of Appletrees, Ch. Norcrest Enuff, and Ch. Rufus of Marienhof to RS. and Am. Ch. Qualm Heinzelmännchen. Ch. Benrook Beau Brummell was himself a Display son. Beau Brummell sired a number of Canadian champions as well as AKC champions, some of whom have won both titles.

Can. Ch. Yankee-Pride Kandy was by Ch. Sandman of Sharvogue

out of Meldon's Medley, a daughter of Display and Exotic of Ledahof, making Kandy closely related to Lisa v. Klein Wald. Ch. Kathie Khan of Marienhof, like Am. & Can. Ch. Neff's Luzon, was by Ch. Kubla Khan of Marienhof, one of the leading sires of his day. Can. Ch. Silvermist of Marienhof was by Cockerel of Sharvogue, a full brother to Sandman. Cockerel was the grandsire of Jonaire Pocono Compliment, who sired Ch. Boxerly Sugar's Sonanaire. Can. Ch. Princess Pat of Marienhof was likewise a Cockerel daughter. Consequently, her mating to Silvermist resulted in a litter of puppies that were double Cockerel grandchildren. Am. & Can. Ch. Marwyck Penn Hurst, a Display grandson on his sire's side and an Enchantress grandson on his dam's, returned to America. His bloodlines and individual excellence should prove of value to the breed in Canada. Luzon left behind him a Canadian champion son, Strathburn's JP Beta Misty. Penn Hurst's get included Strathburn Joegrau Alpha Anne and Dinah, with American champion descendants. Ch. Dorem Delegate was by Ledahof's Sentry (the grandsire of Marwyck Penn Hurst on his dam's side) and left a champion daughter in the United States.

At least one breeding to Ch. Dorem Tribute in the United States has added further Display blood to the material available for future development of the breed. And with Ontario the principal center of activity it is not difficult to make use of whatever desirable sires are at stud in the Midwest area.

Ch. Cosburn's Esquire, Winners' Dog at the Associated Terrier Club Specialty in New York in 1954 was owned by John R. Graziano, Mount Vernon, N. Y., and later by Travelmor Kennels in New Jersey. He is a son of Cosburn's Admiration, litter brother to Ch. Cosburn's Aristocrat. Esquire has been shown extensively in the United States, and has the most outstanding show record of any Canadian-bred there to date. In 1957 he already had two AKC champions to his credit. His 1967 total is 13.

Appeline Cosburn's Pickwick Peppers, by Ch. Cosburn's Esquire out of Can. Ch. Cosburn's Noranda, was exported to England, where three of his get have finished since 1964.

Of the more recent producers in Canada, Am. & Can. Ch. Jonaire Pocono Gladiator has sired one American and 14 Canadian champions. He is a great-grandson in male line of Ch. Benrook Buckaroo. Close behind him, with 13 champions, comes Am. & Can. Ch.

Can. & Ber. Ch. Rosehill's Poco
Impression.

Can. & Am. Ch. Cosburn's Aristocrat.

223

Can. Ch. Walsh's Frosty Charmer, CD
(black and silver).

Can. Ch. Walsh's Frosty Spaceman.

224

Caldora's Returning Ace, by Can. Ch. Belvedere General, a great-grandson of Ch. Tweed Packet of Wilkern and consequently not of the Display male line. Am. & Can. Ch. Wilkern Killarney Dandy, with one U.S. and seven Canadian champions to his credit, is also of this line. He is, in fact, a son of Tweed Packet from the last litter sired by him, in 1954. Ch. Esquire of Marienhof, by Ch. Cosburn's Esquire, with six Canadian champions (one of them also U.S.) traces to Display via the Ch. Benrook Beau Brummell line.

Among producing bitches should be mentioned Boxerly's Siobhan, dam of five, and Can. Ch. Cosburn's Noranda with four. The former belongs to Family III through Alma v.d. Zukunft, and Noranda to Family I through Lisa v. Klein Wald of the Dorem Diva Branch.

Successful kennels during the sixties include Cosburn, Caldora, Boxerly, Begorra, Rosehill and Sylva Sprite. The last has specialized in black and silvers and has already finished several champions of that color, including Walsh's Frosty Charmer, Sylva Sprite Moon Moth, and Walsh's Frosty Spaceman. Charmer is already the sire of three Canadian champions, including the salt and pepper Can. Ch. Sylva Sprite Tonquin. Another of his sons, Sylva Sprite Benjamin, was Winners at the Paul Revere Miniature Schnauzer Club specialty in August 1967 and is believed the first Canadian black and silver to go winners at an AKC specialty show.

The first black and silver to finish in Canada was the bitch North Wind's Party Doll, in the late 1950's. She was a daughter of Can. Ch. Brigadoon's Little Canuck, by Ch. Jonaire Little Boy Blue, and traces in male line to Ch. Cockerel of Sharvogue, apparently one of the comparatively few champions of the past decade not of the Display line.

At the present time there are several breeders in the Montreal area and there have been a number of English importations reported, although they do not seem to have made their mark as yet.

For those who can afford the time and expense, the Bermuda "circuit" is said to be a fabulous experience.

Shows in Bermuda are held under the rules of the Canadian Kennel Club, but separate championships are awarded. A number of American exhibitors have competed at the Bermuda shows, four of which are usually held during a single week in October or

November, so that lucky owners may go home with a completed title. A number of American champions are Bermuda champions as well.

The first Bermudian champion of the breed seems to have been Jonaire Pocono Top Hit, who completed his American title in 1957 and died in 1966 at the age of 12. Can. Ch. Rosehill Poco's Impression appears to be the only Canadian-bred with the Bermuda title. The full brother and sister Triton's Percy Legend and Triton's Princess Suroya are both triple champions with American, Canadian and Bermudian titles.

No Bermuda-owned champion of the breed has yet been reported, but several English-bred dogs have gone to the Islands, including representatives of the Deltone and Settnor Kennels, one from the latter in 1966. Although owned in the United States, the black Jovinus Rodin of Anfiger made his point show debut in Bermuda in 1964, going Best Terrier Puppy at all four shows plus a Best of Breed and Group 3d over champions.

Bermuda shows also feature obedience, and the Bermuda-owned Deltone Delsantone, bred in England, is both a Bermudian and Canadian CDX as well as an American CD. One of the most outstanding obedience winners, Am. & Can. Ch. Wildwood's Showboat, Am. & Can. CDX and Bermudian CD, who could undoubtedly have added further laurels, died tragically in a traffic accident in 1967 when still under six years old. The top-ranking bitch is the American Valentina of Finebrooke, Am. and Ber. CDX, Can. UD, whose puppy daughter Valentine's Victoria, now living in Bermuda as a house-mate of Delsantone, promises to carry on the family tradition.

Elsewhere in the Western Hemisphere, outside the continental United States and Canada, the breed is still comparatively rare. From time to time service personnel have taken Miniature Schnauzers to Alaska and occasionally exhibited there, but they are not known to have become established among the permanent residents. Am. Ch. Frampton's Beau Geste is reported to be a Cuban champion, and there is said to have been an imported black champion who died young.

Quite a few Miniatures have been exhibited in Mexico and a number of American-breds hold Mexican titles, in addition to several bred in the country. Mex. Ch. Serro v.d. Burg Heldenstein was imported from Germany and is believed to be the only black title holder. Am., Col. & Mex. Ch. Bilco's Replica is a Mexican Best in Show winner. Of the five triple title holders reported, two won in Mexico, Canada, and the U.S.: Ch. Marwyck Pitt-Penn Pirate and the bitch Ch. Rik-Rak Ramie.

Little appears to be known of the breed in South America. However, the top living American sire Ch. Helarry's Dark Victory is also a Brazilian champion. There are said to be two active kennel clubs in Colombia, where the owners of Ch. Bilco's Replica were stationed for several years. Replica's son, Sugarloaf Countdown, was a Best in Show winner there, and the bitch Windy Hill Blue Magic also made her Colombian title.

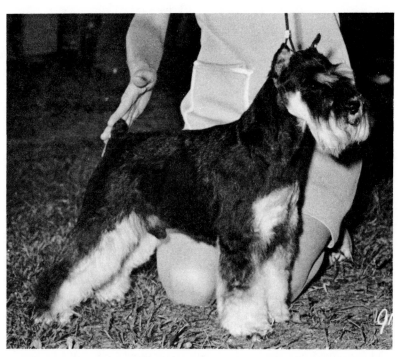

American and Canadian Ch. Sylva Sprite Snowy Mittens was the first black and silver to hold championships in the US and Canada. *William Gilbert.*

10

The Miniature Schnauzer in the Pacific, Asia and Africa

THE breed is comparatively new in Australia, where the earliest recorded importations were made by Mrs. Rees of Casa Verde Kennels in New South Wales. Her first was Gosmore Wicket Keeper, the first English Champion son of Am. Ch. Sternroc Sticky Wicket and Gosmore Peaches and Cream, whelped in September 1960. Wicket Keeper, who died by 1965, does not appear to have left any champion get in England, but a non-champion son, Lichstone Chasseur, sired two champions, Ch. Lichstone Pacemaker, who finished in 1966, and a second son, Ch. Sceptre of Settnor, finished in 1967. Wicket Keeper promptly made his Australian title, and sired several champions there, including Casa Verde Zipper (out of Casa Verde Mary Jane), Casa Verde Mannequin (out of Pickwick Buttons) and Casa Verde Diamond Jim, a full brother to Mannequin. An English-bred C.C. winning son, Deltone Deldario, owned by Mrs. C. V. Cerini, also made his Australian title and went

Best of Breed at the first championship specialty show of the Australian Schnauzer Club in February 1967. At this show the Best Bitch was a Wicket Keeper daughter, Australian Ch. Casa Verde Zipper.

Ch. Casa Verde Handsome (Ch. Gosmore Trump Card–Gosmore Spinners Wicket) is reported to be the first CD winner of the breed in Australia.

Late in 1965 there were said to be about 150 Miniature Schnauzers in Australia, including Tasmania but not New Zealand, with at least 15 champions, of which 5 were in New South Wales, 7 in Victoria, and 3 in Western Australia. The latter included Casa Verde Prancer, Casa Verde Belle Star, and their daughter Wy-Lea Canadian Melody.

In Victoria, Austrl. Ch. Sheenhart Honeysuckle is an English importation and the dam of Ch. Tempo Dasheba, by Mrs. Cerini's Ch. Deldario. Dasheba was the first Victoria-born champion. Other imports include Austrl. Ch. Deltone Deldaryl (by Eng. Ch. Deltone Deldisplay ex Deltone Delsanta Doric) and Austrl. Ch. Deltone Delsanta Delia, a C.C. winner by Ch. Deltone Deldisplay ex Deltone Delsanta Norina. Another importation, shown only occasionally, was Dondeau Hunt Cup (Eng. Ch. Dondeau Hunting Horn ex Dondeau Hxzackly) .

The only black as yet imported, Austrl. Ch. Jovinus Rigoletto, arrived in March 1963 and has sired a number of litters. His get include the young black obedience winner, Koniglich Jason, CD, out of Koniglich Jad Silber (Austrl. Ch. Jovinus Rigoletto ex Austrl. Ch. Deltone Delsanta Delia) , who finished at 16 months old. His full sister, Koniglich Silver Skates, went to the United States along with the black Rigoletto son Koniglich The Groom. Austrl. Ch. Koniglich Silver Three, by Deldario out of Jad Silber, won the Best Miniature Schnauzer award (a club competition over ten designated shows during the year) and Schnauzer of the Year in 1966, with Ch. Rigoletto placing second and Ch. Deldario third. A Deldario son, Koniglich Kaizer (out of a Rigoletto daughter) , was the Dog Challenge winner at the 1966 Adelaide Royal Show in South Australia. The 1966 Royal Melbourne Show had an entry of 22.

Besides the two Miniatures exported to the United States, Mrs. Cerini has also sent a young bitch, Koniglich Deldavinia (by Aus.

Australian-bred Ch. Königlich Deldanilo.
(black and silver)

Australian Ch. Deltone Delsanta Delia
(English-bred) .

Ch. Deltone Deldaryl ex Aus. Ch. Deltone Delsanta Delia) to Honolulu for breeding.

These Australian foundation sires trace in male line almost exclusively to Am. Ch. Dorem Display, as can be seen in the section on English bloodlines. Wicket Keeper and Deldario come from Am. Ch. Sternroc Sticky Wicket, while Deldaryl traces to the American-bred Eng. Ch. Rannoch-Dune Randolph of Appeline. However, the black Ch. Jovinus Rigoletto, by Eng. Ch. Jovinus Malya Swanee ex Jovinus Risotto, goes back through many generations of German dogs to Hupp v. Schönhardt and eventually to Prinz v. Rheinstein.

The bitches probably belong for the most part to Family V, from the Dutch Gerti van Duinslust, since this is by far the most numerous in England. Mrs. Rees' Eng. Ch. Gosmore Peach Brandy belonged to this line, and also Mrs. Cerini's Aus. Ch. Deltone Delsanta Delia, both going back to Ch. Quarrydene Gaby of Dondeau over different lines. Gosmore Spinners Wicket, out of Gosmore Peaches and Cream, and by Ch. Sticky Wicket (and as a result a litter sister to Austrl. Ch. Wicket Keeper) is of the same line as Peach Brandy, a Peaches and Cream sister. Austrl. Ch. Deltone Delsanta Doric, by Deltone Delsan Marko (son of Ch. Deltone Deldisplay) out of Eng. Ch. Deltone Delsanta Miranda, goes back to the American-bred Guenever Anfiger of Family I, and so far as I can tell appears to be the only imported bitch who does so. Australian Ch. Tempo Dasheba's dam, the imported Australian Ch. Sheenhart Honeysuckle, out of Sheenhart Alchera (by Gosmore Middle Stump, a brother to Wicket Keeper), is out of Annalise of Hartland. Annalise's dam, Deltone Delsheena, went back in bitch line through five generations of Quarrydenes (Dodi, Bramble, Sadi, Sally and Gazelle) to Quarrydene Gelda of Family V. Dondeau Hunt Cup, shown only once or twice, is by Ch. Dondeau Hunting Horn out of Dondeau Hxzackly, daughter of the American Elibanks Cindy of Family III, through a comparatively infrequent branch. Another bitch imported by Mrs. Rees, Dondeau Handiness, by Eng. Ch. Dondeau Handicap out of Dondeau High N' Mighty, is by the American-bred Dondeau Handfuls Englan, son of Ch. Dorem Original, but I do not have her dam's family.

Other imported males include Deltone Deldane, C.C. at Hove in 1965 (a son of Ch. Deltone Deldisplay out of Deltone Deldeanna), and Ch. Courtaud Pannyan Pampas Pete, Best of Breed at the Schnauzer Club of Great Britain Show in 1966 and a Junior Warrant winner. Sired by the C.C.-winning Theotone Rudolph, a son of Roundway Autocrat by Roundway Attaboy, Pete traces in male line to the American-bred Eng. Ch. Roundway Tony from America. His dam Ranndune Rebecca, also a C.C. winner, is by Ch. Deltone Deldisplay out of Lichstone Kilsale.

The first New Zealand champion is said to be Peter Beaney's English bitch, Dingo Nightlights. Bred by Mrs. Knight, she is a daughter of the top obedience performer Bingo of Autumnnight, who died in 1967 at the age of 12. This line also belongs to Family V, tracing through Ch. Quarrydene Gaby of Dondeau. Ch. Dingo's sire, Roundway Anthony, is by Ch. Delton Deldiabolo (whose male line goes to Ch. Rannoch-Dune Randolph of Appeline), while her dam, Roundway Antonia, is by Ch. Wilkern Tony From America out of Phil-Mars Ritzi Lady. Besides Dingo, there is at least one other New Zealand champion bitch, Casa Verde Charming, bred in Australia.

As far back as 1933 several American-bred Miniatures were sold by Marienhof Kennels to an American living in Japan, but there is no record of their having been shown, and it is unlikely that any of the line survived the war. However, a seven-month-old male was sent to Japan during the first part of 1967 by Ray Wine of Florida. An Australian Miniature, Casa Verde Up and Atom, bred by Mr. Rees, was sent late in 1965 via Hong Kong to Mme. Chiang Kai-Shek in Formosa.

The breed was at one time fairly numerous in Hawaii, where there was an active club for several years under AKC rules. Charlena Sho-Nuff, bred and owned there by Ena Gillis, was Best in Show at Honolulu in 1950 and completed his title when his owners returned to the mainland. Later a son, Tarquin of Gregglee, went to Hawaii, where he made his championship with a Group first and several other Group placings. Sho-Nuff, a Display grandson and the sire of four champions, appears in pedigrees around the world. His daughter Guenever Anfiger went to England, a granddaughter Am. Ch. Gladding's BieBie was a top American producer with ten champion progeny, and a great-grandson, Eng. Ch. Sternroc Sticky Wicket, has many descendants there and in Australia.

Hawaiian breeders have been handicapped both by the four months' quarantine on dogs brought to the islands and also by the

Can. & Am. Ch. Cosburn's Ensign, sire of S. Afr. Ch. Cosburn's Spicy Skipper.

American-bred Japanese Miniatures in the 1930's.

fact that many fanciers there have been service people who have been transferred elsewhere after a couple of years. This has caused more than the usual turnover of personnel and was probably at least partly responsible for a falling off in show entries. As a result, the Hawaiian Miniature Schnauzer Club recently disbanded.

A number of English Miniatures have gone to Rhodesia, where several have finished their titles. The first recorded, Rh. Ch. Liza of Albright, by Ch. Dondeau Helios, has since returned to England where she won the Veterans Class at the Schnauzer Club Open Show in 1967 when nearly eight years old. Rh. Ch. Roundway Ancestor is a brother to Eng. Chs. Roundway Anchor and Annabelle, while Rh. Ch. Jovinus Request is a daughter of Ch. Jovinus Roxburgh out of Ch. Jovinus Ronbacardi. Ancestor belongs to the male line from Eng. Ch. Wilkern Tony from America (as Request also does). Liza belongs to Family III, through Nudel Heinzel-männchen, and Request to Family V, tracing through Deltone Cherokee and back five generations to Quarrydene Gelda. Settnor Kennels are also said to have exported stock to South Africa and Ghana.

11

Miniatures in Obedience Work

THE obedience record of Miniature Schnauzers goes back to the very beginning of formal obedience work in the United States, and beyond. It was not until 1936 that the AKC set up rules for trials, closely patterned after those in England. Even then, it was some time before obedience wins and degrees were regularly published in the *Gazette* as they are today, nor was there anything approaching the present widespread interest in formal obedience work.

However, even before the AKC's recognition there were a few obedience classes held at shows. In November 1935 Mrs. Slattery's Ch. Mussolini of Marienhof, after only ten days of training, won first in a class of 11 in the Novice class at Philadelphia, followed by a second at Baltimore the same year. At that time only two qualifying scores were required, but since the AKC did not award CD's until the following year, Mussolini never officially gained his title. Unofficially, he was not only the first obedience winner of the breed, but the first combined bench and obedience winner.

The first official CD for the breed was won by Mrs. Marian Shaw's male, Shaw's Little Pepper, who placed fourth at Mt. Kisco with a score of 93 out of 100 (at that time a perfect score), and first in a class of 19 at Orange, N.J. with 99. Pepper later became a bench champion and hence the first official dual titlist.

During the next ten years, which included World War II, there were only 14 CD and two CDX degrees awarded to Miniature Schnauzers. Both the latter were won by dogs with bench show champion parents, Mrs. McCosker's Dorem Extra (by Ch. Normack Fiedler ex Ch. Dorem Dubonnet) and Playboy of Kenhoff, by Ch. Vance of Palawan ex Ch. Gracon's Canis of Kenhoff, the latter also dam of five show champions. Vance, likewise a Ch. Normack Fiedler son, appears in many obedience pedigrees. In 1949 his son Playboy of Kenhoff became the first of the breed to win a UDT, while the first UD bitch, Brunhilde v. Stortsborg, finished the same year. As of 1968, no bitch has yet earned a UDT. Playboy sired at least one litter, in 1946, but his line does not appear to have carried on.

One of the early CD winners, in 1941, was Fred v. Schönhardt of Crystal (by Ch. Hupp v. Schönhardt of Crystal ex Annemie a.d. Vode of Crystal). Besides being the first black winner of an obedience title, Fred seems to be the first American winner with two imported parents, probably because importation ceased during the war, soon after obedience really started.

Since 1946 interest in obedience has increased greatly, along with the popularity of the breed. That Miniature Schnauzers lead the Terrier Group is not surprising, considering their working inheritance from the Standard Schnauzer, not to mention some possible Poodle blood in the background.

By the end of 1964 the breed had earned over 400 CD degrees, 85 CDX, 20 UD and 3 UDT—over 500 in all. To dispel any possible claim that conformation and obedience do not go together, it may be stated that over 50 bench champions hold one or more obedience degrees, including four UD's. Top rank goes to Am. & Can. Ch. Jonaire Pocono Rough Rider, who is both a Canadian and American UDT. He is also the only bench champion with the Tracking title, though at least two others have had training for it. The late Am. & Can. Ch. Wildwood's Showboat was also a triple obedience winner, with Am. & Can. CDX and Bermudian CD degrees. The sole

Ch. Mussolini of Marienhof, first Miniature shown in obedience, 1935.

Hamann's Falla, U.D., the only black U.D. titlist.

Jovinus Royal Rogue, CD, at 4 months.

237

holder of the CDX in all three countries is Valentina of Finebrooke, who has also won highest scoring dog all-breed at ten shows out of 27 times shown.

Besides Playboy of Kenhoff and Jonaire Pocono Rough Rider, the third UDT winner is the black and silver Sambo of Cobb, still active at 12 years old. The first solid black UD, Hamann's Falla, finished in 1964.

Can one show successfully in breed and obedience at the same time? Yes, but it is more difficult. A well-trained dog quickly recognizes the difference between the obedience and show collar. Ch. Mein Herr Schnapps, UD, finished his CD under a year old, was started in breed, and earned his CDX in three straight shows and his UD in four while completing his championship. Once he won the Terrier Group and tied for highest scoring in dog in trial on the same day! His average for the three degrees was 196½, and he was highest scoring Terrier in the country in 1955.

Of the nine top obedience sires, eight have been bench champions. Applause of Abingdon, CD, the only one with a degree himself, sired eight, including a UD, plus six breed champions. His sire, Ch. Marwyck Scenery Road (sire of nine bench champions) was a litter brother to the second ranking obedience sire, Ch. Marwyck Brush Cliff, who had seven obedience winners and an equal number of bench champions. Ch. Dorem High Test, third obedience sire, with 15 champion get and six obedience winners, is followed by his own sire, Ch. Dorem Display, sire of 42 show champions of the breed, with five obedience winners including a UD. Ch. Orchardlawn's Baron (5) and Ch. Benrook Buckaroo (4) were both by Ch. Dorem Tribute, the record-holding sire of show champions among Display's get, while Buckaroo himself sired 17. Ch. Cardot's Citation (4), son of High Test, makes the third generation of this line to appear on the sire list, while Ch. Hollenwire's Staff Sergeant (4), by Ch. Diplomat of Ledahof, gives the latter two sons on the list (Brush Cliff being the other.) The only sire not himself a champion is the solid black Belvedere Caesar, whose four include both a UD and a CDX.

None of the leading bitch producers of obedience winners is herself a champion except Can. Ch. Cosburn's Deborah, a versatile producer of five bench and four obedience winners. Weidman's Black Shadow follows her closely with four of each, while Geelong

Valentina of Finebrooke, Am., Ber. & Can. CDX, receiving Highest Scoring Dog Award at Ottawa, 1963, from Mrs. W. W. Butterworth, wife of the U. S. Ambassador to Canada.

Ch. Mein Herr Schnapps, UD, taking a broad jump.

Sieglinde v. Britanhof, UD, doing scent discrimination.

Sieglinde doing "sit." She finished at the age
of 9.

Tempest's obedience four include a UD. Black Shadow's daughter, Doman Mehitabel, CDX, was the dam of Ch. Frevoly's Best Bon Bon, UD, who produced five bench champions. Another bitch who deserves mention was Sieglinde von Brittanhof, probably the oldest Miniature Schnauzer to finish a UD—at nine years and four months! She gained her first leg at the age of three, after which she was not shown for over five years.

Also of interest is Ch. Rik-Rak Regina, one of the third generation of bench champions who also hold both American and Canadian CD degrees. Her dam, Can. & Am. Ch. Rik-Rak Rebel's Banner, Can. & Am. CD, is by Ch. Richmda's Jaunty Rebel, CD, ex Ch. Brenhof Katrinka, Can. & Am. CD.

Several others have been making outstanding records during the 1960's. Mr. Chips Moler of Finebrooke won both American and Canadian UD degrees with high scores, thereby giving his sire, Benrook Don Wan, CD, the unique distinction of having sired two UD winners. Lo-Mae's Tanzer of Mary-O is the only bitch to hold the UD degree in both Canada and the United States. Valentina of Finebrooke, Am. & Ber. CDX, Can. UD, is also distinguishing herself as a producer of obedience winners. Her young son, Mr. Brandywine of Belvoir, Can. & Am. CD, completed both his titles by the time he was one year old. Another son, Chipper von Manion, CD, has been highest scoring dog in show.

In England a top obedience winner in Miniatures, Gottkernow Tuppence, was still winning in 1962 at the age of 11 years. Deltone Delancy won 14 prizes, including four firsts, in his first year's competition. The black Quisdown Valerian has had a remarkable record, placing less than fourth only twice in three years' competition. He is a son of Oddstock Dyk v. Robertshof, an Austrian black who also did considerable obedience winning and died in 1966 at the age of 17. Valerian and Delancy were both members of the Schnauzer obedience team of five (four of them Miniatures) that competed at Wimbledon in 1961. In 1967 at the age of 10 years Valerian, owned and handled by Miss Maureen Keel, placed fifth in a class of 30 at the A.S.P.A.D. trial and won his CD (ex). This is more difficult than an American CD and is held by only one other Schnauzer—a Standard. Recently a young English black, Jovinus Royal Rogue, completed his American CD in three straight shows.

In England, as on the Continent, obedience requirements differ

Dorem Extra, CDX, retrieving over the high jump.

Ch. Mein Herr Schnapps, UD, retrieving a live duck.

from ours and in certain respects favor the larger breeds. The English CD, which includes "send away," tracking to retrieve an object, and three jumps, is much more advanced than ours. For UD, the requirement of a 9-foot broad jump, 6-foot scaling, and 3-foot hurdle effectively eliminates small breeds.

Though obedience training is work it can be great fun and is well worth the trouble involved. A well-trained dog is a pleasure to have and a credit to the breed. Several of the breed clubs have had their own training classes, and there are now general classes in many areas. While it is possible to train a dog alone, the novice will find it much easier to join a class. Many mistakes and bad habits that are difficult to unlearn can be avoided with the help of a good trainer. Furthermore, a dog who has always worked alone is likely to be distracted the first time he is with a group. Match shows give both dog and handler good experience before entering at regular trials.

Obedience competition offers opportunities for owners and dogs of all types, whether breed winners or not. (Note that spayed bitches, which cannot be shown in breed classes, can compete in obedience trials.) Remember, however, that too much emphasis on mechanical perfection can destroy the dog's enjoyment. Some of the best performers—and those most popular with the spectators—are not above hamming occasionally. Whether you attend a class or try to go it alone, there are excellent books on obedience available, including one especially for children, some of whom have been remarkably successful.

Miniature Schnauzers have also appeared in motion pictures. Hamann's Adolph The Awful, CD, was in a Purina Dog Food documentary around 1962, and four dogs from Elfland Kennels in California took part in the filming of *The Bar Sinister*, by Richard Harding Davis, according to the *American Kennel Gazette* for June 1955.

12

Trimming and Grooming for Show or Home

A wire-coated breed such as the Miniature Schnauzer loses much of its character if not kept in proper coat, even when the dog is only a pet. If he is to be shown, a correct trim is essential. Since each breed has its characteristic trim, the owner should know what to look for. Even today, not all professionals or pet shops that do commercial trimming are acquainted with the breed, and they sometimes turn out a Miniature which resembles a Kerry Blue or some other breed more than a Schnauzer. Even though some owners prefer to have the job done for them, they ought to know what is required. A few, at least, will want to learn how to trim their own dogs. Others will be glad to learn how to keep them looking smart and attractive at home between visits to a professional. Moreover, even the best trimmed coat needs regular grooming and attention.

Growing a good coat and trimming your dog for show cannot be done overnight, nor in a single operation. While individual dogs

244

differ in rate of growth and you should study your own dog to achieve the best results, most coats require about ten weeks after stripping to grow in fully. Accordingly, if you plan to show you must decide well in advance.

Proper care of the coat should begin in early puppyhood, when the coat becomes long enough for gentle brushing. Older dogs require frequent, if not daily brushing and careful combing of the legs and whiskers. When the puppy is a couple of months old (or even less) his coat will usually begin to lengthen and have a slightly fluffy appearance. The outer coat no longer lies flat and close to the body, but begins to stand away a bit, and single hairs scattered over the back and shoulders look longer than the rest. If you are raising a whole litter you may notice quite a difference between various individuals. One puppy may continue to look quite smooth, another's coat may be as soft as a kitten's and even definitely wavy. Others will range between these extremes. At this stage you can judge fairly well what the permanent coat will be like. The close, smooth coat will almost certainly be hard and wiry when the puppy matures. If there is no sign of stubble starting where the whiskers should be, and if the legs are very smooth, the dog may lack furnishings when grown. The very soft, wavy coat is likely to remain soft always, though usually accompanied by plenty of furnishings. Still, one cannot be sure at this age, for the adult coat may be very different from the puppy one.

As soon as you notice the coat beginning to fluff, start work on it. Pull off the long, loose hairs with your thumb and finger as fast as they grow out. The first puppy coat will all have to be removed before your dog is old enough to show in any case. If the puppy coat is not removed early, it blurs the body outline so that it 'is hard to judge what the dog is really like. Also, it often gives an entirely false idea as to the puppy's future color.

The hard-coated puppy will not need as early or as frequent attention, but even he will benefit by at least one thorough going over before reaching six months of age. As he grows older the puppy should be brushed regularly to remove dead hair and keep his coat bright and clean.

When grooming a puppy take care not to hurt or frighten him or he will come to dislike the process, which will create problems later. However, accustoming him early to being worked on without fuss is

An ungroomed puppy at six months.

The finished job: Ch. Pindar Anfiger.

Protecting the coat.

246

very helpful. He should learn to stand quietly, without nipping or trying to play, nor should he be allowed to develop bad habits that he must later unlearn. Often it helps if someone holds him still, so that the person working on his coat can use both hands. Thus an ear, foot or the tail can be held in the best position, or the pull eased on a sensitive spot.

Whether or not you work alone, be careful that a sudden leap does not land your puppy on the floor, with a possible sprain or even a broken bone. Grooming posts attached to the top of a crate or table are best used with older dogs who have learned to stand quietly. Even then, some caution is necessary. Beware of leaving a dog in this position while you answer the door or telephone, lest in trying to jump down he strangle or break his neck.

As you go over the dog's coat, look for fleas, ticks, lice or any other parasites which may have been picked up from other animals or from the great outdoors. (See Part II for instructions for eradicating and controlling external parasites.)

In general, the harder a dog's coat the easier it is to strip and the longer it can be made to last, though there are exceptions. Running through long grass and bushes tears off whiskers and leg hair. Burrs picked up can become so matted that they have to be cut out unless they are removed promptly. Dogs playing together may chew off each other's whiskers, and if kept in runs they may rub and break them on the wire or by digging in the ground. The harder and more wiry the coat, the more brittle the hair. This means that the very dogs whose whiskers and leg furnishings grow most slowly break them off most easily. When the dog spends much of his time in the house this is less of a problem.

After you have stripped a dog once or twice you will have a fair idea how he holds his coat. If it grows faster or slower than the average you can plan accordingly next time, though the time of year and the interval between strippings may cause some modification.

To obtain the best results for show a Miniature Schnauzer should be trimmed in successive stages. This is because the coat on the head and neck grows faster than that on the body, though the latter should be somewhat longer. For pets and breeding stock the entire coat may be done at one time (or at intervals of a day or two). Later you may go over the head and neck again, so that they will not be too long when the body coat is the right length. To do this

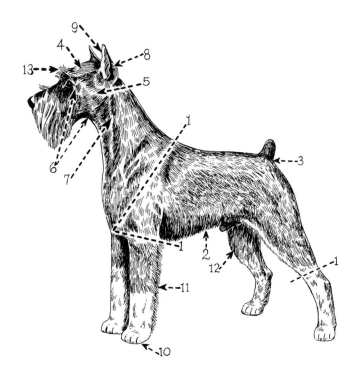

1. Strip back of line indicated, removing outer coat.
2. Remove long hair under and on chest, shaping line to suit dog.
3. Remove all long hair on tail. With scissors, clip closely on "butterfly" beneath tail.
4. Strip or pluck closely on skull.
5. Remove hair closely on cheeks.
6. Remove long hair and pluck or strip on area under neck, in straight line from outer corner of eye to mouth and under throat.
7. Clean neck.
8. Strip outside of ears closely.
9. Using scissors, clip hair on inside of ears; trim hair on edges of ears evenly.
10. Clip neatly around feet.
11. With scissors, even hair on legs to give straight line.
12. Remove long hair on inside of thighs.
13. With scissors, even eyebrows and ends of whiskers.

skillfully enough so that the one blends smoothly into the other requires practice. For show dogs, however, "sectioning" is recommended, as described below.

When using the one-strip method, strip the entire coat except the eyebrows, whiskers and leg furnishings. Keep the ears well cleaned at all times to avoid irritation. The inside of the erect part may be done with scissors, preferably small ones with rounded points. Hair deep in the canal should be removed with finger and thumb or tweezers. Sensitive spots such as under the tail, inside the thighs, and on the stomach should also be done with scissors. Periodic attention to these areas will keep the pet looking tidy for a longer period.

Never use a clipper on a Miniature Schnauzer that is to be shown. Most commercial trimmers and pet shops use an electric clipper because it is quicker and therefore cheaper. Often they do not even know how to hand strip. This is also true of many veterinarians. Clipping softens the coat and usually changes the color because it removes one of the distinctive color bands. It does not remove the roots of the dead top coat, which are left in the skin. Hence a new, vigorous coat does not grow in quickly as it does after hand stripping. Dogs repeatedly clipped are hard to get into good coat afterwards. They develop soft, fuzzy coats not typical of the breed.

In some types of coat the undercoat is easily removed along with the top coat, or it may even be difficult to avoid doing this. The result is a practically hairless dog, unattractive for a brief time, until the new top coat appears. Many professionals use this method. The novice may prefer to leave the undercoat for two to four weeks until it is loosened by the growth of the new top coat and can be more readily removed by finger and thumb or an undercoat stripper. If the undercoat is very thick and hard to remove this may be best, even for show dogs.

Follow the stripping by a bath with mild soap or shampoo, rinse well and dry thoroughly, to avoid colds. If the undercoat has been removed, protect the dog from cold or sunburn until the new coat is sufficiently grown, which may take four to eight weeks. It is debatable whether greasing actually stimulates growth, but if oil or lanolin is used a bath should follow in a couple of days. The greasing is certainly soothing to the skin.

Some owners clip their old dogs when they are retired from shows, or those of strictly pet quality. If this is done, be careful to avoid clipper burns and treat them with lanolin if they occur.

Toenails should be cut regularly from early puppyhood, using sharp scissors. Later, regular toenail clippers are best, or a file if preferred. Trim often to keep the nails short without cutting into the quick. Long nails throw the foot out of position, producing weak pasterns and poor front movement. When trimmed for show, the tips of the nails should be visible after the hair on the foot has been evened.

When stripping, protect your hands with adhesive tape, band-aids, or a rubber office finger as needed. "Moleskin" adhesive gives extra protection. Baby oil may be rubbed onto tender areas on the dog's skin.

If doing a one-strip job but unable to finish in a single session, do not let more than a week elapse or the finished coat will be of different lengths, with a visible line between.

The tools needed to trim a dog for show—or just to keep him looking well at home—vary somewhat according to the taste of the operator, but begin, first and foremost, with the thumb and first finger, which are by far the most important. Choice of a folding stripping knife with two blades, resembling a jackknife, or of a single blade set in a wooden or metal handle (as generally preferred today) is a personal matter. The blades of either vary slightly in size, coarser ones being used for taking off the old coat. They should be rather dull, not sharp, and have a series of nicks along their length, so that not many hairs will be pulled at one time. The blade rests on the forefinger of the right hand and a few hairs are grasped between the blade and the thumb. For the left-handed, single-bladed knives are available, though they are sometimes difficult to obtain. If the coat is "blown" and ready to come out it should pull easily, without great discomfort to the dog. Chalk rubbed into the coat before commencing operations makes it easier to get a good grip, and many top professionals remove the body coat entirely with the thumb and finger.

The coat should be pulled out, not cut off. Some of the tools on the market are really only a razor blade with a handle, and cut the coat instead of stripping it. Besides a stripping knife, some sort of brush (not too hard) and a metal comb are required. A wire brush is likely to tear the coat unless very carefully used, and may hurt the

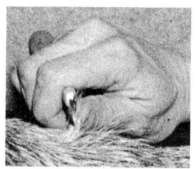

Correct way to hold knife, working in direction hair lies.

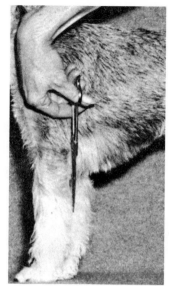

Trimming the elbows and front leg.

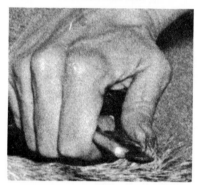

Wrong way to hold knife—pulling may tear skin.

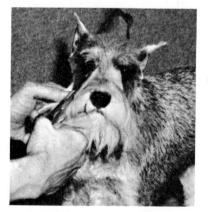

Trimming between the eyes.

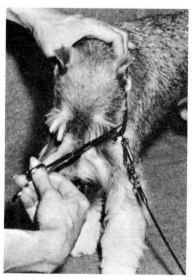

Trimming the eyebrows.

251

dog's skin when his coat is short. A fine-toothed metal flea comb is very useful as is a grooming mitten, though the latter is not essential.

Whiskers and leg furnishings should be combed carefully so as not to pull out the hair. If not combed regularly they may become so matted that the tangles have to be cut out, spoiling the dog's appearance.

Before you attempt to trim a dog, think of how the finished product should look and have in mind a clear picture of what you are attempting to do. Each dog is an individual. Try to bring out his good points and hide his faults. Look at the dogs shown by professional handlers at the shows. Study pictures, if you have nothing better available. If there is a good professional conditioner in your neighborhood who will let you watch him do a few dogs, or even give you pointers, it will be invaluable. Not all professionals are willing to disclose their secrets, however. And do not expect to become an expert at your first attempt, even with professional advice.

When sectioning, start about ten weeks before a show and strip the body, beginning just behind the withers and taking down the back, sides, and thighs to an inch above the hocks. Long hairs under the chest and the chest itself can also be plucked at this time if they have been allowed to grow long. Usually the undercoat becomes fluffy and loose in a short time and should then be plucked, as this will bring the new coat in more quickly. An undercoat stripper is useful for doing this without damage to the new top coat just starting.

After one or two weeks, strip the head and neck down to the withers. At this time the tail and the long hair on the "butterfly" underneath the tail should be plucked, as should the under part of the throat. For best results, the head and ears should be plucked regularly as they begin to grow out and loosen. This does not take long if done regularly. It keeps a dog looking alert and cleancut, even if he is not being shown. Also, it is very important to keep the head coat in good condition. If the hair on the head is allowed to grow long the coat quickly becomes fuzzy and dead. Then stripping produces bare spots which must be plucked several times before a really hard coat can be grown. More Miniature Schnauzers are shown with poor head coat than with any other fault in show preparation. Clipping or razoring is often done to conceal this fault without leaving bare spots, but an expert judge can readily detect the difference.

After two or three weeks more, the cheeks, neckridge (where the hair growing down from the nape of the neck and back from the cheeks and throat comes together at an angle), and the under part of the throat should be plucked closely. The outside of the ears and the skull should also be done as closely as possible. The cheeks are trimmed so that there is a straight line from the outer corner of the eye to the corner of the mouth, with the whiskers beginning at the corner of the mouth but the throat very clean back of a line from one corner of the mouth, around underneath to the other. The closer the skull, cheeks, and throat are trimmed the more whisker and better head a dog will appear to have.

The final touches to the coat may be given a day or two before the show, or even on show day. With sharp scissors the edges of the ears should be evened off (they will not require much if the outsides were properly plucked earlier) and the inside of the ears cleaned as closely as possible. Then even off around the tail, the feet, and the leg furnishings and whiskers. Feet and legs should look straight and solid, with no wisps or tufts sticking out. Be sure there are no tufts at the back of the elbows or hocks. The feet should be neat and trim. The front legs should look as straight as possible from either front or side view.

The dog's head will appear longer if there is not too much hair left between the eyes. A definite division between the eyebrows, though not a deep gouge, is preferable today. From between the eyes to the nose, outstanding hair should be trimmed to a triangular shape blending into the front of the whiskers. The eyebrows themselves should be trimmed close to the outer corner of the eye, gradually curving to their greatest length at the inner corners. The long line of the head is broken when the eyebrows are too long or too prominent. In trimming the skull, the head can be made to appear longer, too, if it is trimmed well forward to the line of the eyebrow. Too much hair left at the outer corner of the eye will make the whole head look rounder and shorter. Never gouge under the eyes, however.

Remember always that the Miniature Schnauzer is a wire-coated breed. The coat on the body, neck and thighs should be hard, with that on the skull, cheeks, and throat tight—all set off by the whiskers and leg furnishings, which while plentiful should not be soft or silky. From any direction the dog should show a cleancut outline, never a blurred effect.

Dogs vary as to the length of time the coat can be kept in good condition. The harder the coat the longer it can be made to last, and the quicker it will grow back in, as a rule. As the coat grows longer, loosened body hairs can be plucked by hand, and the head and neck continually worked over. When the coat finally blows and has to be stripped, a new coat may be already started underneath. A dog having a hard coat of good quality can, with constant attention, be kept in show condition for the greater part of the year. This is naturally a great advantage, whether he is to be shown extensively around the circuit, or handled by his owner at the comparatively few shows within easy reach, which are likely to occur at various seasons of the year. Success depends on both the quality of the coat and the skill of the trimmer, and skill can be acquired only with practice.

It is against the rules of the AKC to "fake" a coat by dyeing it, or by applying any foreign substance to stiffen, straighten, or similarly affect its quality. However, many exhibitors prefer the use of a dry shampoo (which is then brushed out thoroughly) to bathing a dog, especially in cold weather. French chalk or ordinary talcum powder may also be applied to the whiskers and leg furnishings (which should be previously wet). This removes some of the natural oil from the coat and makes the furnishings stand out better, even when the chalk or powder has been thoroughly combed out, as should always be done before a dog enters the ring. Failure to remove any material of this type may lead to a dog's disqualification. After the show whiskers and leg furnishings should be thoroughly washed to prevent their becoming dry and brittle from the effects of the chalk.

In Europe Schnauzers are usually shown with longer body coat than is generally seen in this country. The emphasis on hard coat tends to produce harder and less profuse furnishings, and I believe that leg furnishings are sometimes partly removed on that account.

Reddish stains under the eyes due to an overflow of secretion should be investigated. There may be eye irritation or a blocked duct. Rusty stains on whiskers or leg furnishings may be from food, saliva or urine. Clorox® bleach is sometimes helpful if not too strong. Apply very carefully, so as not to irritate the skin. Washing the legs and whiskers with detergent as often as once a week may be advisable when showing. This should be done routinely the day of a show or the day before.

Fleas or other irritations causing a dog to constantly bite or lick its feet or hindquarters may produce rusty discoloration from the saliva. If the cause is removed the discoloration will eventually disappear. Five Brewer's yeast tablets daily are helpful, presumably by altering the character of the saliva. They are also rich in Vitamin B.

Because the demand for large furnishings has tended to produce softer body coats along with them, many exhibitors seek to disguise their dogs' lack of proper, hard coats by showing them as short as possible. As a consequence, dogs with good coats, of the correct length specified in the standard, are often criticized on the grounds that their coats are too long, or even "blown," and put down to animals that are actually inferior in coat. For the good of the breed, it is high time that more emphasis is put upon coats, since many newcomers, including not a few judges, do not appear to know a good coat when they see one.

You and Your Schnauzer (published by *Schnauzer Shorts,* Drawer A, La Honda, CA 94020) a pamphlet which won the Dog Writers' Award for the best series of articles in a breed magazine in 1962, has a detailed section on stripping, with illustrations.

Pose properly in front
of mirror
at early age

Correct balanced pose as adult

resulting dip

Stretched forward too
far
Back legs out behind too much

Front legs out

Proper
gaiting on loose lead

Dog pulling on lead

Side-winding
to left
Arrow on right
shows correct
path

fat rolled
at withers

Awkward outline from
baiting above dog

Dog incorrectly "hung-up" on lead
causing a paddling, swimming
front action

Baiting correctly
at dog's level

Drawings by Loraine L. Bush, as published in Schnauzer Strips, newsletter of
the Florida West Coast Miniature Schnauzer Club.

256

Part II

GENETICS AND BREEDING

1

Something About Genetics

I_N order to breed intelligently, the dog owner should know something about the mechanics of heredity, the way in which characteristics are transmitted from one generation to the next. If you do not know this, and many breeders do not, there are still certain rule-of-thumb methods and general principles which are helpful, but when they fail you will be at a loss for the reason and hence very likely unable to correct the difficulty.

Why do some characteristics appear generation after generation, while others mysteriously disappear, or perhaps occur as "throwbacks" in the grandchildren or great-grandchildren? Why are some carried only through the dam, though appearing in her sons? Why do littermates sometimes differ so completely in appearance that they appear to be wholly unrelated, and produce so differently also? The answers to these questions are to be found in the science of genetics. Not that we know all the answers, particularly in regard to specific breeds and individuals, but enormous strides have been made in the last 25 years and enough is known to show the general pattern and explain many details. Unfortunately, there are still too many mis-apprehensions rife among breeders.

One difficulty is the fact that the new discoveries constantly being made are usually reported in scientific journals not read by most fanciers. Both these articles and the general books on genetics are written in technical language that the layman may not be able to follow easily. Moreover, so much research has now been done that in reading the ordinary genetic textbooks one must plow through endless details about fruit flies or rabbits in the attempt to glean specific information that may be applicable to dogs. The general principles are lost in the mass of detail, while experiments actually involving dogs may be mentioned only in passing, as scattered references to back issues of scientific magazines not readily available. Even the few books that deal specifically with dog genetics often fail to be as useful as one might wish. They are likely to discuss popular breeds of widely varied backgrounds, and their conclusions are often of limited usefulness.

For these reasons an attempt will be made here to explain the necessary scientific background required for the concrete application of breeding principles in general. Those who do not wish to read this section of this book may attempt to apply the conclusions without understanding their basis.

Every dog develops from the union of two cells, an egg cell or ovum derived from the dam, into which the male cell or sperm, derived from the sire, penetrates. The united cell, or fertilized ovum, formed from the union of the two then divides into two, four, eight, and eventually millions of new cells, all descended from the original pair and carrying the same genetic factors. As these cells are too small to be studied with the naked eye, our knowledge about them has been acquired gradually by means of high-powered microscopes, cell-staining techniques, and experiments of various types too complicated to discuss. The results, substantiated by good evidence, are summarized here.

Each egg cell (smaller than a period on the printed page) contains a nucleus, a small spot or globule which carries the hereditary material or chromosomes, while the remainder consists largely of food stuffs. The sperm is even smaller than the ovum—so small that it is only about 1/2500 of an inch in diameter and several million may be present in a single drop of seminal fluid. They are consequently highly expendable, for only a single sperm unites with the egg to form a new individual. Unlike the egg, the sperm consists of a small, tightly packed head, a spiral body which provides the chief motive force, and a long tail, which aids in propulsion.

Eggs and sperm do not change as an individual does, but remain the same during a dog's lifetime. All the cells in the body are descended by continuous division from the original fertilized egg, but after the earliest stages they begin to specialize. Blood, muscle, bone, brain, skin and other cells develop and reproduce to form different parts and organs. At about the sixth division, during the early growth, one pair of cells is set aside and a special process begins. These divide into the "germ cells" which carry on life to succeeding generations and eventually become the testicles in the male and the ovaries in the female. Ultimately, when the dog or bitch matures, the sperm or eggs will be formed from exactly the same material as the original fertilized egg.

The sperm is formed as needed during the life of the male dog from the existing germ cells, unless disease, accident, or old age reduces or ends its production. The eggs of the bitch are much fewer in number, for she ovulates only twice a year for some seven to ten years. Consequently, at birth her ovaries contain all the eggs, in rudimentary form, which will mature during her lifespan.

Up to this point the inheritance of males and females is alike and all the germ cells of an individual contain similar potentialities. Now it is necessary to consider the role of the chromosomes and why it is that the mating of a single dog and bitch can produce such widely differing offspring.

The chromosomes are almost colorless bodies whose presence was first revealed under high-power microscopes by the use of special dyes, whence their name, meaning "color-bodies," is derived. They vary in number in different species as well as in size and shape. They are always found in pairs, with one of each kind contributed by each parent. Dogs have 39 pairs of chromosomes, or 78 altogether. By the process of division each body cell contains a replica of all 78 chromosomes that were found when the sperm head entered the egg and its 39 chromosomes paired off with their opposite numbers from the egg's nucleus. This is the actual fertilization that starts the puppy on his way.

The chromosomes, small as they are, are far from being alike,

261

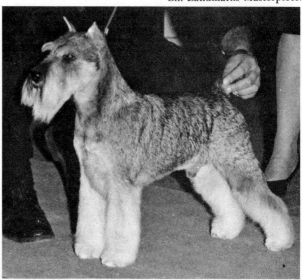

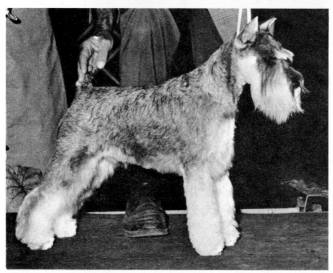

Ch. Blue Devil Sharpshooter, who went BIS the first time shown.

either as a group or even individually. At the time of fertilization they are in a compressed form which requires relatively little space. At certain times, however, they may stretch out into much longer filaments or threadlike forms, when they resemble many gelatinous beads strung together. The "genes," which are the final known breakdown of the hereditary factors, are these "beads" or are contained in them. The rod-like appearance of the compressed stage is due to the coiling up of the chromosomes in close, tight coils. In the stretched-out stage the chromosomes have now been photographed by the use of the tremendously powerful electronmicroscope, showing indications of gene locations, though not clearly indicating specific genes. Each gene has its own particular function, but the genes also work together and modify each other. Many of the methods by which they act are still unknown, but some have been worked out in detail and the results of certain combinations can be quite accurately predicted.

When the egg is fertilized, the corresponding chromosomes, which may be numbered from 1 through 39, pair off—the two number ones together, the two number twos, and so on, up to number 38. Number 39, however, is different from the rest, for the members of this pair are not always alike. The one which came from the dam is known as an X chromosome since it looks like the letter "X." The one which came from the sire may also be an X chromosome, in which case the resulting puppy will be a bitch. But on the other hand it may be smaller and somewhat different from the X with which it pairs, and then it is known as a Y chromosome. In that case the puppy will develop into a male. Whether fertilization results in a male or a female depends upon whether the sperm contains an X or a Y chromosome, and it is therefore the sire that determines the sex of the puppy.

It is apparently because they have only one X chromosome that males are biologically less likely to survive both before and after birth. Consequently, young, healthy bitches are likely to produce more male puppies *on the average* than older bitches, because more of their males survive. Since, nevertheless, about 10 percent more males than females are whelped, it immediately becomes apparent that a good many more males than females must be conceived. The reason for this is concerned with the two types of sperm. One contains a Y chromosome and is male-producing. It is probable that some slight difference between the two types gives the Y-bearing sperm an advantage which leads to more than half the eggs being fertilized by Y sperms. The Y sperms are slightly smaller. They may differ in speed, thus tending to arrive first, or in their chemical reaction to the uterine environment, as a result of which more males are conceived to offset their higher mortality before and immediately after birth. At least one reason for this higher early death rate of the males is that one X chromosome in the female may carry destructive genes that are offset by normal genes in the other X chromosome. The male, having only one X, has nothing but the small Y by way of counterbalance and so is more vulnerable to the action of dangerous genes.

How do the dog's 78 chromosomes act to transmit inherited characteristics and what accounts for individual differences? The answer is linked with the fact that the offspring, like his parents, still has 78 chromosomes instead of double that number. Naturally, if he received the whole 78 from each parent he would have 156. The next generation would have 312, and so on indefinitely. This does not happen because of what is known as reduction division.

In ordinary cell division the chromosomes divide lengthwise, as if they were sliced down the middle. In reduction division, however, the chromosome *pairs* separate, one of each pair going into one half of the cell nucleus and the other member of each pair going into the other half of the nucleus. The nucleus itself then proceeds to divide, leaving each half with 39 chromosomes, one of each kind. In the case of the male, each half becomes a sperm and is ready to fertilize an egg when mature. In the case of the female, however, there is further division and the parts of the divided cell are not of equal size. The smaller portion, called the polar body, does not contain sufficient nutritive material to nourish the fertilized egg until it is firmly implanted in the uterus. Consequently, in each division the polar cell is discarded and excreted from the body. With it go the 39 chromosomes which separated from their opposite numbers remaining in the egg proper. Thus half the chromosomes carried by the bitch are discarded before fertilization, whereas in the male all 78 chromosomes are to be found in one half or the other of the dividing sperm cell and may be passed on to the next generation.

The key to this matter of chromosome division lies in the fact that so far as scientists have been able to determine it is *pure chance*

264

Ch. Rik-Rak Rock Candy.

Ch. Barclay Square Brickbat.

Ready to show: Ch. Blythewood
Ricochet of La May.

how the chromosomes line up before the cell division, and consequently the two halves of the dividing cells may contain chromosomes derived from either grandparent in varying proportions and are *not alike*. This sounds more complicated than it is, as you can easily test for yourself.

Suppose you take two sets of counters (red and white poker chips would do nicely) and number each color from one to 39. Mix them together in a bowl and then draw out one at a time. Arrange them in two piles, with the first of each pair of numbers in one pile and the second in the other. When all have been drawn you will have chips numbered 1–39 in each pile, *but they will not be the same color*. If the red chips represent chromosomes that were derived from the sire and the white chips those derived from the dam, the two mixed piles represent the two halves of the germ cell, in the reduction division, each of which will become a sperm. As you look at the piles you may find that you have 20 red chips and 19 white chips in one pile and 19 red chips and 20 white chips in the other. You *might* theoretically have 39 red in one and 39 white in the other, but that is considerably less likely than a bridge hand of 13 spades. Probably you would have something between these two extremes.

Now put your chips back in the bowl and try again. Whatever your first result, this time it will be different. Even if by any remote chance you came out with the same number of each color you would find that the chips were grouped differently when you looked at the numbers on them. For instance, if you had only one red chip in a pile, you could still have any one of the 39 red chips, making 39 different possible groupings of 1 and 38. If you had two red chips, any number could be paired with any of the other 38, and so on. At the same time, the other pile could also vary. If the first pile contained red chip number 1 and 38 white chips, the second pile would of course contain the other 38 red chips, but it might contain any one of the 39 white chips without changing the overall numbers. A few trials will show that the possible combinations are almost unlimited. A mathematician could figure out the chance of any particular combination coming up; in human beings (who have only 48 chromosomes instead of 78—24 pairs, that is) the chance of a specific chromosome combination occurring is one in 16,777,216.

In the case of the bitch, with only a few eggs maturing at one time, in contrast to the millions of sperms produced by the male, the number of variations possible *in a given litter* would be drastically reduced. The chance of any given combination appearing would be only half as great, however, because half of the chromosomes actually inherited would be discarded with the polar body.

Going back now to our colored chips, suppose we go a step further. Let us take another pair of colors, say blue and yellow, and number them from 1 to 39 as before. They represent the chromosomes of the bitch, while the red and white chips represent the chromosomes of the dog to whom she is to be mated. Separate your blue and yellow chips as you did the red and white ones. Discard one pile (as the polar body is discarded) and arrange the other 39 in order. (Chance decides which chromosomes go into the polar cell, so it does not matter which pile you choose in this case.) Now take your two piles of red and white chips, representing the stud dog's chromosomes and arrange each of them in line, one on each side of the bitch's blue and yellow. Each line of red and white represents one of the many possible combinations of chromosomes in the sperm of a particular dog. Whichever group was combined with the ones from the bitch would give a different result even without considering the endless possible variations.

Now look at the 78 chips which represent the fertilized egg resulting from the mating of dog A and bitch B as above. They will include all four colors. The red chips will be from the stud's sire, whom we will call S, and the white from his dam, whom we will call T. The blue will be from the bitch's sire, J, and the yellow from her dam, K. Well, how do they divide up? Since 39 is an odd number, you cannot possibly get exactly 25 percent from each of the four grandparents, as a widely held theory proclaims. The nearest you could come to this would be 20 each from two and 19 each from the other two (and even that would give various possible combinations, such as 20 red and 20 yellow, 20 red and 20 blue, with their corresponding opposites). Whatever your result, take the whole 78 chips, of the four different colors, and divide them into two piles as you did with each pair of colors in the beginning. Either pile of 39 chips which results will represent *one* of the possible combinations of chromosomes inherited by a puppy from the mating of dog A to bitch B. What color proportions do you have now? How many reds have come down from grandsire S? How many from grandsire J?

Ch. Dardane Priam.

Ch Fancway Pirate Jr. of La May.

How many from each of the two granddams? Already you may find that one of them *is not represented at all!* In that case, of course, one or more of the others would have a heavier representation.

Now suppose that the previous combination of 78 chips in the four different colors were as even as is mathematically possible, that is to say, two groups of 20 and two of 19. An even division (not likely to occur in actual fact, but representing an average) could give three groups with 10 chips of one color in each 39, and one group of 9. If you continue to divide in this manner and figure the *average* number of chromosomes derived from any single ancestor in a given generation, you will find that by the seventh generation the odds are 4 to 3 against a given descendant inheriting *any* chromosome at all from him! Naturally, in that case the dog would inherit more than the average number from some other ancestor. The only case in which one can be sure (granted that the pedigree has been accurately kept) that a dog has inherited at least one chromosome from an ancestor several generations back is the Y chromosome, which is necessarily passed from father to son and so must have been inherited in turn from each ancestor back in the direct male line, no matter how remote. Perhaps this explains the tendency which is found in all breeds of dogs which I have studied, as well as in other animals such as race horses and cattle, for one male line to gradually oust all others, which in time come to appear only through female descendants. However, the Y chromosome has very few genes and it is believed that these are relatively unimportant.

	Generation	No. of potential ancestors	Average chromosomes from each	Odds against receiving even one chromosome
1st	(parents)	2	39	
2nd	(grandparents)	4	19 or 20	
3rd	(great grandparents)	8	9 or 10	
4th	(great gr. grandp.)	16	4 or 5	
5th	(gr. gr. gr. grp.)	32	2 or 3	
6th	(gr. gr. gr. gr. grp.)	64	1 or 2	
7th		128	(at least 50 ancestors	4 to 3
8th		256	would be unrepresented)	8 to 3
9th		512		5 to 1
10th		1024		10 to 1

The table on p. 269 shows the average number of chromosomes that a puppy will derive from any ancestor in a given generation back to the 10th. This would compare with the human generations back to 1620 A.D.

There is a further point to remember, however. Purebred dogs are all more or less inbred. (If they were not, there would come a point when the mathematical number of ancestors would work out to more than the number of dogs existing at that time.) Every time a dog or bitch appears in a pedigree an additional time, the probability that the descendant carries chromosomes derived from him or her is increased. So if a full brother and sister were mated, the puppies would *average* half their chromosomes from each of their common grandparents, in which case they would be as closely related as regards the number of chromosomes as they would be to their own parents. On the other hand, if both the sperm and the egg in a brother-sister mating actually happened to include more than the average number of chromosomes from the same grandparent, the resulting puppy might carry more than 39 chromosomes from that grandparent, and so could be more closely related than to his own sire or dam. Say the sire's sperm had 30 of *his* sire's chromosomes and only 9 of his dam's. Say the dam's egg also had 30 of her sire's chromosomes. Then the fertilized egg would have 60 out of 78 chromosomes from the double grandsire, and only 18 from the double granddam. The offspring of half-brother and sister, with only one parent in common, could also receive just as many chromosomes from the double grandparent as in the above case, but the remaining chromosomes would necessarily be derived from two other grandparents.

From all this it should be clear why even litter brothers and sisters can carry entirely different chromosomes and in consequence can be entirely different in color, size, or any characteristic which is determined or influenced by the genes in the chromosomes. Also, it should be plain that the closer the inbreeding the more likely it is that two dogs will carry similar chromosomes derived from a common ancestor. And so when checking pedigrees reveals that a dog such as the Miniature Schnauzer Ch. Dorem Display, widely used at stud and in subsequent inbreeding, carried 67 crosses to Ch. Amsel v.d. Cyriaksburg in ten generations, with a 68th in the eleventh, it becomes apparent that Amsel must have had a far more profound influence on the breed than would be evident at first thought. To carry this idea still further, Ch. Salt 'N Pepper Salesman, who completed his championship in 1954 and carries Display four times within four generations, goes back to Amsel no less than 586 times, all told, since he also traces to her through other lines in addition to those through Display.

The chromosomes, whose method of transmission has been discussed above, are (with rare exceptions to be discussed later) transmitted as units. However, each chromosome is like a string of beads or a package of assorted Necco candies. It contains a number of genes not yet exactly determined, which are arranged in a definite order. The genes are the smallest unit of life so far as we know. Each gene has its fixed position on the chromosome, as each bead has a different place on the string, and except in rare cases they remain in the same order. Exact replicas of the chromosomes with their genes go into every cell of the body, and accordingly it is probable that each gene plays some part in general development and activities. However, as the process of cell multiplication goes on, certain special genes prove the decisive factor in determining certain specific characteristics.

Like the chromosomes themselves, the genes come in pairs, with corresponding positions and functions. While a number of different pairs of genes may cooperate to produce results in one case and only a single pair may be required in another, only two corresponding genes, one in each chromosome, can occupy a single location on the chromosomes of a given individual. If there are more than two types of genes which belong in this location they are known as alleles or alternates. A number of different alleles form an allelomorphic series, and only two genes of the series may be found in the chromosomes of one individual dog.

One fact most often misunderstood is that only *one* gene of a pair enters the germ cell (egg or sperm) at the time of cell division. When fertilization occurs, this is matched with a corresponding gene from the egg or sperm of the other parent, so that the offspring has *two* and only two of a given pair at a given location on the chromosome. Should this particular allelomorphic series consist of three or four alternative forms (alleles) a specific individual can still only carry two of them. These may be any two transmitted by the parents, but only one from each. Another fact that is frequently

271

Ch. Tiger Bo Von-Riptide, winning black and silver in 1966.

Ch. Rujax Royal Randy, a top winner in 1967.

Ch. Barclay Square Be Glamorous.

misunderstood or forgotten is that where there is such a series a number of characteristics may appear as alternates to each other. The probable number of each type will vary according to a definite rule, as shown by the checkerboard on page 276.

The first real clue to the genes and their functions was provided by Gregor Mendel, an Austrian monk whose carefully tabulated experiments were published in 1866 in a local scientific journal. Their importance was overlooked, however, until 1900, and the whole modern science of genetics has been developed since that date. Although there are many complications of which Mendel never dreamed, and environment plays a part which appears equal to heredity in importance, the basic principles which Mendel worked out hold firm and are reasonably simple.

Mendel made his discovery by confining his studies to one point at a time and keeping exact figures of his results. In his small garden plot he mated peas of a variety which produced red flowers with another type of pea having white flowers. All the offspring had red flowers. This crossbred generation is called by scientists the "first filial" generation. Looking at these red-flowered plants, the influence of the white parent seems to have been entirely lost. But what happens when two of these red first filials are bred together? Then part of the second filial generation is red, to be sure, but part is white, like the white grandparent. By counting thousands of plants, Mendel discovered a definite ratio. One out of four plants was white-flowered, while three out of four were red-flowered. The white factor, although not visible when the two types were crossed, remained hidden, and was carried along to the next generation, reappearing in 25 percent of the second filial generation offspring.

The next step was to discover what happened when the reds and whites of the second filial generation were bred. It was found that white bred to white always produced nothing but whites. The red had been "bred out." On the other hand, the reds proved to be of two different types. Only one out of three of the crossbred reds proved to be "pure" red-flowered. The other two reds were like the crossbreds of the first filial generation and carried the hidden white. Mendel made other experiments. He crossed tall pea plants with short ones, wrinkled seeds with smooth, yellow seeds with green. Invariably, one characteristic was "dominant" when two varieties were crossed, and the first filial generation resembled the dominant parent. However, the second characteristic, although hidden or "recessive" when the two were crossed, was carried on *unchanged* from one generation to another.

The individual characteristics, such as red or white color, tall or short height, smooth or wrinkled seeds, are carried by the genes, which are always found in pairs. And when the two genes of a pair differ in their effects, one dominates the other, and they are known as dominant or recessive. When the chromosomes of a dog divide before fertilization, as has already been described, each egg or sperm contains one gene of a given pair. The fertilized egg, which begins a new generation, has the full set of 39 pairs or 78 chromosomes, each one containing many genes. Like the chromosomes, one gene in every pair is derived from one parent and one from the other.

The results of thousands of experiments show that when two characteristics are crossed in this manner and the first filial generation is interbred, the proportions are always the same. Half of the total number of offspring carries both factors. One fourth of the total carries only the recessive factor, and the other fourth carries only the dominant factor. Either the recessives (which are always pure) or the pure dominants will breed true when mated together, but the mixed individuals, when bred together, go right on producing the same ratio of 1:2:1. Since, however, the pure dominants and the mixed dominant-recessives look alike, it seems as though the proportion was 3 dominants to 1 recessive. This creates one of the dog breeder's main problems: how to distinguish between "genotypes," which carry the same genetic makeup and therefore will breed the same, and "phenotypes," which look alike but may reproduce quite differently. A dog is said to be "homozygous" for a particular characteristic when the pair of genes which produces it are the same. Consequently, we can have either a pair of homozygous dominant genes or a pair of homozygous recessive genes. If the two genes in a given pair are not the same, the dog will be "heterozygous" for the characteristic. ("Heterozygous" comes from the same root as heretic and heterodox, both of which mean *different*.)

Occasionally one of a pair of genes is not entirely dominant and so it is possible to tell by looking at an animal if he is homozygous or heterozygous for a particular quality which the breeder is interested in. This can make selection much easier, but sometimes it complicates breeding operations. In some breeds of animals there are points desired for the show ring which have turned out to be heterozygous. When this occurs *they can never be bred true*. To secure what is wanted, two separate strains must be bred and crossed, or the heterozygous animals in the first filial generation may be bred together and the homozygous ones in each generation (half of the total progeny) discarded. One example of incomplete dominance is found in Shorthorn cattle, where reds and whites if bred together produce roans. When two roans are mated the result is one fourth red, one half roan, and one fourth white, so there is no difficulty in deciding which animals are the homozygous dominants, but the roans will never breed true. There are also certain fancy breeds of poultry in which two separate lines must be bred and crossed in order to obtain the exact color and markings required for prize winning at exhibitions.

An example of this type of heterozygous dominant in dogs is the Norwegian Dunkerhound (a Harrier). This breed comes in three colors, solid black, harlequin (with irregular black spots on a gray or white background), and white with small gray spots. The whites were deaf, often blind with abnormally formed eyes. The typical harlequins were heterozygous for the black color and could never be bred true. After this was established by Norwegian geneticists, breed authorities decided to approve the single-colored black coat in Dunkerhounds. Contrary to most people's expectation, however, it is the harlequin white which is dominant over the solid color, in this case black. Harlequin white is also found in Great Danes, and sometimes in Dachshunds. The dominant form is semilethal when it is doubled (homozygous), so that few of that color survive. Consequently, the best way to breed harlequins is to mate a harlequin with a solid black, thereby producing half harlequin and half black puppies. (More of this later, when color breeding is considered specifically.)

In scientific books and articles the individual genes are represented by letters, with the dominant one of a gene pair written as a capital and the recessive as a small letter. Thus *AA* would represent a homozygous dominant, *aa* its homozygous recessive allele, and *Aa* would represent the heterozygous form. This can be shown most clearly by setting out the possibilities on a checkerboard.

If all characteristics depended on a single pair of genes, breeding would be much simpler. However, inherited qualities may be due to

CHECKERBOARD

Showing inheritance with 2 gene pairs Aa and Bb.

Male sperm types

		AB	Ab	aB	ab
Bitch egg types	AB	AABB 96	AABb 89	AaBB 58	AaBb 51
	Ab	AAAb 89	AAbb 82	AaBb 51	Aabb 44
	aB	AaBB 58	AaBb 51	aaBB 20	aaBb 13
	ab	AaBb 51	Aabb 44	aaBb 13	aabb 6

Figure 1

Male sperm types

		AB
Bitch egg types	AB	AABB 96
	Ab	AABb 89
	aB	AaBB 58
	ab	AaBb 51

Figure 2

Male sperm types

		ab
Bitch egg types	AB	AaBb 51
	Ab	Aabb 44
	aB	aaBb 13
	ab	aabb 6

Figure 3

Where the effect of the genes is quantitative the numerical rating is:
A 40   a 2   B 8   b 1

9 possible genotypes and 9 phenotypes in 16 combinations.

Figure 1. Mating of two heterozygotes with formula AaBb.

Results:

1 each AABB (96), AAbb (82), aaBB (20), aabb (6)

2 each AABb (89), AaBB (58), Aabb (44), aaBb (13)

4 each AaBb (51)

Figure 2. Mating of homozygous dominant AABB to heterozygous AaBb.

Results:

4 genotypes and 4 phenotypes in equal proportions (each 4 in every 16).

Figure 3. Mating of homozygous recessive aabb to h e t e r o z y g o u s AaBb.

AaBb (51)   Aabb (44)
aaBb (13)   aabb (6)

Where the effect of the genes is to produce a specific result rather than to vary the *amount*, the numerical rating should be disregarded. In that case Figure 1 would produce only 4 phenotypes in the proportion of 9:3:3:1, but they would still have 9 different formulas for each 16 puppies. Figure 2 would produce only 1 phenotype, with 4 different formulas. Figure 3 would show 4 types, each with a different formula.

In Figure 2 and Figure 3 the results are the same if the sexes are reversed and the bitch is AB or ab instead of the dog.

276

more than one pair of genes acting together. In the case of two pairs of genes there will be nine possible genotypes, or actual combinations of genes, in a total of 16. The most common combination would occur four times. Four combinations would each occur twice, and four combinations would each occur once. Only one out of 16 puppies would be a pure dominant (homozygous) for both genes. However, the number of *phenotypes* (puppies which look alike in respect to a particular characteristic but may breed differently because they carry different combinations of genes) may be either 9 or 4. This is because there are two ways in which gene pairs may act together. One way, and the most obvious, is when the two affect the same item in different ways. The other is when the two pairs produce the same effect to a different degree, such as size, or the amount of color extension.

For instance, one pair of genes produces short, crooked legs, as in the Dachshund, which are dominant over normal legs. Another pair of genes produces short hair, which is dominant over long hair. When a short-haired, short-legged Dachshund is bred to a long-haired, normal-legged breed, the first generation should all have short legs and short coats. However, when two of these F1 puppies are mated together the results may be not only short-legged dogs with short hair and long-legged dogs with long hair, like the two grandparents, but also short-legged dogs with long hair and long-legged dogs with short hair. The proportions will be 9:3:3:1 for every 16 puppies (if enough matings are made to produce a reliable average), but only one out of each nine having short hair and short legs will be homozygous for both pairs of genes and carry the formula *AABB*. There is no way of telling which of the nine is homozygous, but the one homozygous recessive, with formula *aabb*, is easily recognized, as he alone will have long legs and a long coat. The other 14 out of each 16 will be heterozygous for one or both pairs of genes, but the precise formula cannot be told from their appearance and can only be discovered by further experimental matings.

On the other hand, two or more pairs of genes may work together to produce a characteristic such as the amount of dark color on a particolor dog or the amount of black as compared to tan on a black and tan dog. This is harder to measure, for with only two pairs of genes involved, the color may vary from a very large amount of

277

Am. & Can. Ch. Mutiny Pandemonium
(bitch) .

Ch. Blythewood Evening Star.

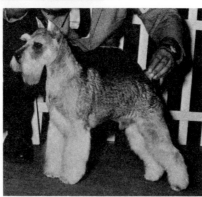

Ch. Mutiny Master Spy.

278

black to a very small amount, with nine different phenotypes or different proportions. The numbers on the checkerboard show the quantitative variations when the gene pairs are given values as indicated. Size variations would follow similar rules but are complicated by the fact that feeding and other environmental factors may intensify or partially offset the effects of the genes.

When three gene pairs are involved, the picture rapidly becomes more complicated. While the F1 generation will, as always when two homozygous animals are mated, be all of one phenotype, there will be eight possible combinations of genes in the F2 generation. Since each gene segregates independently, the complete pattern for possible results in the F2 generation would include 64 individuals. These could exhibit six visible combinations or phenotypes, in the proportion of 36:9:3:12:3:1. Out of the entire 64, there would be nine homozygous dominants and only one homozygous recessive. Naturally, a single litter could include only a few of the possibilities. The triple homozygous recessive which would theoretically appear once in every 64 puppies might not actually occur for even longer.

Now it is evident from this numerical breakdown that the more pairs of genes involved the more complicated this matter of inheritance becomes. It is one thing to deal with fruit flies or plants which can be reproduced quickly and on a large scale. It is through their use that many principles have been worked out. But when it comes to dogs the time and expense necessary has made it practically, though not theoretically, impossible to deal satisfactorily with more than two or at most three pairs of genes at a time. However, once the principle underlying the method of transmission is understood, much of the mystery disappears. Such phenomena as "throwbacks" or "skipping a generation" are simply due to the reappearance of a recessive that has been hidden by the effects of a dominant gene.

Before we go on to apply these genetic principles to actual breeding problems there are a few special instances which must be clarified. The first of these is *mutation*. A mutation is a sudden departure from the parent type caused by a change in a gene or chromosome. It is not always easy to distinguish between a true mutation and the reappearance of a recessive which has been carried along for a number of generations because it did not

279

happen to meet another recessive gene of the same type. However, mutations may be dominant as well as recessive, and in that case they are easier to identify, unless they are mistaken for the combined action of two dominants. Dominant mutations reproduce themselves, and by breeding back to the dominant parent they can be quickly established if desired. Recessive mutations may occur just as often as dominants, for all we know, but are much less likely to be noted. They might be carried along for generations or lost altogether before chancing to meet a similar recessive descended from the same original mutation. Unless this happens they will not appear and their presence will remain unknown.

Mutations are caused by changes in the arrangement of the atoms which make up the genes. How often they normally occur under natural conditions has not been ascertained. However, in fruit flies they can be induced by a variety of means such as X-rays, natural radiation, and certain chemicals and gases. Cosmic rays are among the possible causes. Presumably all differences in genes originated by mutation. The screw tail of the Boston and the short legs of the Dachshund are the results of mutations. Some mutations are favorable and have survived because they gave their possessors a definite advantage in the wild state. Many are unfavorable and usually die out unless artificially preserved by selective breeding. Still others are of no importance either way, and these, too, tend to die out unless deliberately retained through selection. It is now believed that mutations occur more frequently than was formerly thought.

In addition to gene mutation there is chromosome mutation, which is allied to the phenomenon known as "linkage." All the genes in a single chromosome are normally transmitted together. As a result, it is sometimes possible to identify the presence of a recessive by the fact that it occurs in the same chromosome with a dominant gene that is readily recognizable. However, when the chromosomes are in their elongated, threadlike state they sometimes cross, break in two, and rejoin in such a way that pieces from two different chromosomes unite. This is the sort of thing which could happen if two long, thin strips of clay were broken and stuck back together so that a new piece is formed out of parts of the original two. When this happens, genes which were formerly in the same chromosome may be separated.

Genes that are located in the X or Y chromosomes are "sex-linked" and can often be identified fairly easily because they alter the expected ratios. Actually, there are three types of sex-linked genes. The largest portion of the X chromosome contains genes which are not matched by any similar genes in the Y chromosome. If, therefore, a male receives from his dam the gene for a certain characteristic that is carried in this portion of the X chromosome, he will have nothing in his Y chromosome to offset it, even when the gene is normally recessive. Accordingly, whether the gene is dominant or recessive will make no substantial difference to a male in such a case. To be sure, the effect of a dominant gene *may* be more powerful than would be true in the heterozygous form, with a recessive gene also present. If the gene is recessive, on the other hand, one gene derived from his dam is sufficient to affect the male, although two genes (one in the X chromosome from each parent) are required to produce the same effect in the female. When the gene in question happens to be "lethal," all males whose dams are carriers will die, thereby reducing the proportion of males to females.

A smaller portion of the X chromosome is matched by corresponding parts of the Y. The genes in this part, though carried in the sex chromosome, act like the genes in the other 38 chromosome pairs and affect both males and females in the ordinary manner. Finally, there are some exclusively male genes found only in the Y chromosome. These genes can affect only males and are passed on directly from father to son, but their action is still largely unknown.

A dominant factor carried only in the X chromosome will appear in all the daughters of a sire who exhibits the characteristic, regardless of their dam. But since he cannot pass it on to his sons, they can receive it only if their dam carries the factor. If only the dam shows the characteristic, all her sons will show it if she is homozygous, but only half if she is heterozygous and so carries one recessive gene. This makes it comparatively simple to distinguish between homozygous and heterozygous bitches in the case of genes located in the X chromosome. If both parents show the characteristic, all the daughters will show it, but only half the sons when the dam is heterozygous. If she is homozygous, all the sons will show it.

When a recessive factor is located in the X chromosome, if the dam alone shows it, since she must be homozygous all her sons will show it, but none of her daughters, for they would have to receive a

Ch. Gough's Silver Franchise at 11 months.

Ch. Victoria of Mary-O.

dominant gene from their sire. If both parents are recessives, all the puppies will, of course, be homozygous recessive also. If, however, the sire shows the recessive characteristic but the dam is heterozygous, half of their puppies will show it regardless of sex.

Biochemistry today is carrying our knowledge of modes of inheritance, previously based on observation and experiment, much further than ever before. Similarly, the amount of information and observation that can be obtained by the eye alone has increased tremendously as higher powered microscopes become available. In 1944 the discovery of a chemical compound known as DNA (deoxyribonucleic acid) had far-reaching and important implications. DNA was found to be able to change one strain of bacteria into another. Later it was learned that DNA determines the nature of living organisms. Further discoveries have helped to partially break the so-called genetic code.

Protein molecules, the name of which is derived from the Greek word *proteios*, meaning "primary," are the most complicated of the basic organic substances that can be isolated from living tissue. In addition to being highly complex, they are extremely fragile and when in solution can be permanently changed by exposure to gentle heat, acid, alkali solution, strong salt solution, radiation, or even violent shaking. The chromosomes are largely protein in composition, being made up of a "conjugated protein" called nucleoprotein, in which the simple protein is joined to nucleic acid (DNA). To explain the makeup and action of nucleoprotein requires a book in itself, and .the reader is referred to Isaac Asimov's *The Genetic Code* for a more thorough treatment of the subject.

The chemical reactions that occur in the body require the presence of enzymes, or catalysts (substances that cause or accelerate a chemical change without being permanently affected by the reaction). Nearly all the thousands of reactions in the body make use of a specific enzyme, which is different in each case. Every enzyme is a different protein and produces its own specific reaction. Each species has its characteristic proteins and enzymes, found in each individual of the species and in every cell of the individual. Slight variations, such as a difference in the quantity of one enzyme, can produce surprising changes. Such changes may occur not only in the cells making special use of that enzyme but in the entire individual as well. Color variations are an example of this. In human beings, pigment formed by the skin cells in a series of reactions, each controlled by a special enzyme, produces dark skin, black hair and brown eyes. A smaller amount of one of the enzymes reduces the quantity of pigment formed and results in fair skin, blond hair and blue eyes. If the individual is entirely incapable of forming one of the enzymes, the result will be albinism, a condition characterized by a total lack of color in the skin, hair and eyes (although the eyes appear pink since the blood vessels are not hidden by pigment). It would appear, then, that all the characteristics of an individual are visible expressions of his enzyme balance.

A variation in the quantity of a single enzyme can change such visible characteristics as coat color in dogs. Moreover, the absence of an enzyme or the imbalance of several may prevent a normal reaction or cause a reaction which would not ordinarily take place. This in turn may affect the workings of still other enzymes, and may set up a chain reaction. Sometimes a very slight change, such as occasionally occurs in the large hemoglobin molecule which carries oxygen in red blood cells, may result in a serious disorder and early death.

It has been accepted for many years that characteristics are inherited through the genes, and that the genes are carried by the threadlike bodies called chromosomes. While the dog has 78 chromosomes (39 pairs), the number of genes is far greater. One estimate puts the number of genes in each of the 46 human chromosomes at over 3,000. One cause of mutations (new characteristics not found in either parent) may be imperfectly shared chromosomes at the time of cell division. A sperm or egg may then contain one chromosome too many or too few. When this happens, all the cells in the individual share the resulting imbalance, and the consequences can be very serious. Severe disorders, including Mongolism in humans, are believed to be caused by an abnormal number of chromosomes, although few individuals with an abnormal number of chromosomes remain alive for very long. Such chromosome imbalances are also believed to have caused important mutations in plants. More often, however, mutations are caused by chemical changes in the normal number of chromosomes and their components, the genes.

If a gene is damaged by some cause, such as X-rays, it may lose the capacity to manufacture its particular enzyme, which normally catalyzes a specific reaction. Consequently, that reaction would not take place and the expected result would not follow. The importance of the failure to produce this result may vary greatly. It may be of minor importance, such as a slight change in color, or it may be serious, as in the case of hemophilia, where failure of the blood to clot properly may cause bleeding to death from the slightest injury. Or it may interfere with normal development, so that some individuals die before birth or shortly thereafter.

While research during recent years has widened our understanding of the chemical basis of inheritance, the general theory of the descent of characteristics through the genes and chromosomes still applies and should be carefully studied for best results. The chapter on color inheritance is particularly important to breeders interested in blacks.

2

The Practical
Application of Genetics

ALTHOUGH environment, both prenatal and postnatal, can play an important part in producing high-class dogs, the same environment will produce entirely different results when dogs inherit different genes. Acquired characteristics and maternal impressions before birth are not inherited. If a bitch is accidentally mated to a dog of a different breed, later litters will not be affected, although people used to believe that they would and a few still do. This erroneous theory is called *telegony*. There is no actual connection between the bitch and the fetus during pregnancy. The food substances in the dam's blood are strained out, like moisture soaking through blotting paper, by a process known as osmosis. Not even a drop of actual blood from the dam reaches the fetus, and there is no nerve connection. The dam may, however, affect the health or development of the unborn puppy through the lack of certain vitamins, leading to rickets, or through too much of certain proteins, causing allergies. Various drugs may pass from the dam to the embryo, and some diseases in the dam may penetrate the placenta and affect the puppies. Worm eggs, which are too small to see with the naked eye, may also be transmitted before birth if the dam harbors them. On the other hand, some immunities to virus infections may be passed on to the puppies, either before birth or through the milk during the nursing period. In the latter case the immunity ceases upon weaning.

When you are dealing with inherited traits the first problem is to decide how they are transmitted. Are you concerned with a single pair of genes or is there more than one pair? Is the trait you want to reproduce dominant or recessive? Is it one whose mode of inheritance has already been worked out, or must you try to discover this for yourself?

It is characteristic of dominant factors that they do not skip a generation. Once a dominant factor disappears it is gone for good unless it is reintroduced from outside. On the other hand, a relatively large number of progeny usually carry the desired factor. While they may be either homozygous or heterozygous, they do not carry the trait unless they exhibit it. Any individual who exhibits the dominant factor but does not reproduce it in all the progeny is thereby known to be heterozygous if only one pair of genes is involved.

A recessive may skip not merely one generation but several. In fact, in the case of bitches, who have a limited number of litters and only a few puppies each time, it may be almost impossible to prove with certainty that a given recessive is not carried. Unless deliberate selection has been practiced, only a relatively small percentage of a strain is likely to carry a recessive factor, and only those individuals who carry two recessives will show it. Whether a dog is heterozygous and therefore carrying a hidden recessive can usually be ascertained only by mating to a homozygous recessive, or less easily, by breeding to a bitch known to be heterozygous. For a single-factor recessive to appear, it *must* be received from both parents. Consequently, it is unfair to blame only the sire when an undesirable recessive character suddenly appears, for the dam as well must have contributed a recessive gene.

Many valuable qualities such as good temperament or ability to learn easily when trained for obedience work are not inherited as a unit, but are a combination of many factors. Or they may depend upon unit factors which are affected by a number of modifying

287

genes. The great majority of puppies will have good dispositions if they are properly fed, raised, and handled. A few seem to have foolproof temperaments and will take anything in their stride without visible ill effects. The small remainder seem to be "born shy" and the best of care makes little difference. This type should be sternly eliminated from the breeding program no matter how perfect they may be physically. (See Burns' *Genetics of the Dog.*)

Inherited shyness is attributed to a dominant-qualified gene of reduced penetrance. Most dogs with one gene for shyness will show some symptoms. If poorly fed, so that they lack adequate resources for nerve building, or if severely frightened or suffering a painful accident, they may become permanently shy. If, on the other hand, such a dog with one gene for shyness receives only the best of care, it may seem quite normal. Nevertheless, it still has a 50:50 chance of transmitting the hereditary weakness and may at any time be seriously affected by experiences which a normal dog would shrug off. "Fear biting" is one form of shyness, the frightened dog, when cornered, being inclined to bite in self defense.

A dog carrying two shyness genes, one from each parent, will always be shy, and more completely so than the dog with only one shyness gene. As dominant characteristics are easily bred out, there is little excuse for passing on shyness. Since puppies learn much by imitation, the litter of a shy or nervous bitch is likely to imitate the dam's reactions to strangers, aside from any inherited tendency. Therefore a shy dam is more dangerous than a shy sire.

Humphrey and Warner observed in German Shepherds two types of sensitivity that affect temperament and consequently usefulness for training. These are sensitivity to sound and touch, in regard to each of which a dog may be either moderately sensitive, undersensitive, or over-sensitive. Bitches tend to be more sensitive than dogs in both cases, and animals over-sensitive to both sound and touch are likely to be shy and hard to train. Under-sensitive dogs, though not shy, may prove difficult to train, while dogs who are moderately sensitive to both sound and touch have a high percentage of exceptional workers but are easily spoiled by unskillful training. For interesting studies of the inheritance of intelligence and psychological traits in dogs, see *Working Dogs* by Humphrey and Warner.

Individuals who are either too large or too small occur, and may

288

even appear in the same litter. Proper feeding and care is necessary if a dog is to grow to the size his genetic makeup calls for, but most of the difference is due to his genes. A specific factor such as relative length of leg will affect the total size. Results in various breeds seem to indicate that shorter legs are dominant over longer, within the same breed as well as in breed crosses. Overall size probably depends on at least two pairs of genes and very likely more. The checkerboard indication of how two pairs are inherited, with values assigned to each gene, results in nine variations from 96 to 6, with a probability that differences due to environment would make the spread even greater. If three pairs of genes should be involved, more gradations with smaller intervals between them would occur. With three pairs of genes there would be 64 possible combinations.

In the case of two pairs of genes, where both the parents are *AaBb* and intermediate in size between the two extremes, one-fourth of the puppies should resemble the parents and another fourth should be only one degree larger or smaller. This, however, brings up one of the chief problems involved in breeding dogs. With an average of four or five puppies to the litter, it is not possible for more than about half the possible nine types to occur. Even with a single pair of genes involved it might be necessary to breed several litters before a desired recessive would turn up. With two pairs of genes and the *average* probability only one in sixteen, the desired recessive might not appear in half a dozen litters. For three pairs of genes, with an average of one chance in 64, the probability would be so small that a breeder might wait years for it to occur. And remember, too, that sex has a direct effect upon size. When a dog and bitch measure the same, the bitch is larger for her sex, and those of her sons which carry the same genes she does will be a little larger than their dam. Likewise, the daughters of a dog will be smaller than their sire if they have the same genetic makeup as he. Even when the parents are of average size it is possible for puppies in a litter to be either larger or smaller than either parent. On the other hand, breeding a large and a small dog together *might* result in average sized puppies in the first generation, but would probably show substantial variations in later ones.

As the charts on p. 276 show, two bitches with the mean size rating of 51 and the genetic formula *AaBb* of an F1 heterozygous cross would vary in opposite directions, if one were bred to a homozygous

289

dominant dog *AABB* rating 96 and the other a homozygous recessive *aabb* dog rating 6. The first bitch should produce all puppies of her own size or larger; the second, all puppies her own size or smaller. On the other hand, an *AAbb* dog rating 82 when bred to an *aaBB* bitch rating 20, should produce all *AaBb* puppies rating 51. A dog and bitch both *AaBb*, rating 51, when mated together could produce any of the nine phenotypes possible with two gene pairs, as shown in Figure 1 on p. 276. To obtain uniform results between the extremes of a two-gene pair may be extremely difficult. These same charts can be applied to any characteristic dependent upon two gene pairs in which the result is a variation in quantity, such as size, or the relative proportion of dark and light color. If a breed shows slight variation in such characteristics, it may be due to the fact that most individuals are homozygous or almost so, with formulas such as *AABB* or *AABb* on the one hand, or *aabb* or *aaBb* on the other. Or only a single gene pair may be responsible.

Because the number of gene pairs involved and their identification as dominant or recessive has been worked out for only a comparatively small number of the qualities desired by dog breeders, it is impossible to give genetic formulas in most cases, and those that have actually been indicated are often tentative and subject to modification in the light of fuller knowledge. Even if it were possible to work out formulas for most inherited qualities, the great number of genes and chromosomes involved would make it impractical to attempt to apply many formulas in detail. How, then, is the breeder to make use of his genetic knowledge?

It has long been known that "like begets like," and so selection has been one of the breeder's oldest tools. Further experience has indicated that inbreeding tends to perpetuate the desired type. Nevertheless, there have been many instances when like did not beget like, or when inbreeding fell short of setting the type wanted. Now, in the light of modern genetic discoveries, we know at least in a general way why this has been so. We can realize the impossibility of making a heterozygous form breed true. We can explain the sudden appearance of hidden recessives and understand why inbreeding may have both good and bad results, according to circumstances. Selection and inbreeding remain our most potent tools, but through understanding them better we can apply them with greater success.

290

Selection must include a study of what is behind the individuals to be mated. It must consider the dog or bitch as a whole, because the multiplicity of genes involved makes anything else too complicated. At the same time, any particular fault or quality may be chosen for special attention and eliminated or introduced with the maximum of speed and efficiency if its mode of transmission can be ascertained accurately. We cannot breed for everything at once. The most important objective may change from time to time, according to the circumstances existing in the breed at a given moment. But selection should always be done with a view to maintaining the quality at the highest possible level and improving whatever defects may be most predominant at the current time.

Inbreeding is a tool that can produce wonderful results in skillful hands but may do serious harm when used at random. By reducing the number of possible variations in chromosome combinations it tends to fix type. However, the very fact that this is true means that faults as well as desirable qualities may be intensified, and undesirable recessives may be brought to light. It may be to your advantage to discover their presence early, but the puppies which display them should be rigidly eliminated from the breeding program.

Just what constitutes inbreeding? Authorities differ considerably, and experienced breeders as well as novices are often confused in consequence. Crossbreeding is, of course, the crossing of two distinct breeds, or sometimes two varieties of the same breed. Although formerly allowed, Miniature Schnauzers crossed with Standard Schnauzers are no longer eligible for AKC registration. Crossing has often been used, however, for the development of new breeds.

Outcrossing is the mating of purebreds of the same breed which are completely unrelated or only distantly related. It is generally considered that when there is no common ancestor within five generations, the mating is an outcross. In actual practice, I doubt if there are many Miniature Schnauzers of show type in this country today who do not have a single common ancestor within five generations, for most present-day champions trace back to a comparatively small number of imported sires and dams. A few exceptions may be found in dogs or bitches imported since World War II, but even they would almost certainly be related a bit further back. Continual outcrossing, even if it were possible, results in a mixed pedigree with a wide variation in type and great uncertainty as to what will result in ensuing generations. A single outcross may bring in some desired quality or correct a prevalent fault in the first generation, if the quality in question is dominant, whereupon selective line breeding within the kennel's own strain may be resumed. If the desired quality is recessive, however, it will not appear in the first generation of the outcross unless already present as a recessive in the breeder's own strain. Consequently, the outcross may be looked upon at first sight as a failure. To secure the recessive quality, it will be necessary to do one of two things. Either breed back to the original outcross sire or dam, or a near relative who exhibits the desired characteristic, or breed together two individuals resulting from one or more outcross matings. The first method is more likely to produce the desired characteristic, but it also involves increasing the proportion of the foreign strain in the resultant puppies. Once a homozygous recessive with the desired characteristic has been produced in the breeder's kennel, further breeding operations can be carried on through that individual.

Undesirable recessives will not appear in the first generation of an outcross unless both parents carry them. In that case they are even more likely to occur if the individual strain is further line-bred or inbred within itself. However, undesirable recessives may be introduced through the outcross and appear in the second or subsequent generations. Also, either dominant or recessive characteristics dependent upon two or more gene pairs may be introduced through an outcross. In this case, if the animal used for the outcross carried one gene pair and the kennel's own strain carried the second gene pair, the combination might produce undesirable characteristics in the first generation of the outcross. This might be the case with undershot mouths, which are perhaps inherited in this manner.

Both outbreeding and line breeding are terms which have been applied to the mating of a dog or bitch which have one or two common ancestors in the second or third generation. Still others would call this inbreeding. Some fanciers, on the contrary, reserve the term inbreeding for the close matings sometimes called "incest breeding," such as sire to daughter, dam to son, uncle to niece, aunt to nephew, half or full brother to sister. Grandsire to granddaughter and granddam to grandson are sometimes assigned to one group and sometimes to the other. Also generally classified among the closest forms of inbreeding is the mating of double first cousins (where a brother and sister of one litter are mated to a brother and sister of another litter—or two brothers are mated to two sisters—and a dog from one of the litters is mated to a bitch from the other). These close matings should *only* be used where the stock is of extremely high quality. When successful, the result may be uniform litters of excellent puppies. Sometimes there will be one or more outstanding puppies and the rest of little value. Weed out these culls promptly and do not use them for breeding yourself or permit others to do so. They will pass on their poor qualities all the more strongly because they are inbred.

Line breeding is sometimes defined as inbreeding which is not so close as that described in the previous paragraph. It involves the mating of dogs and bitches with ancestors in common two or three generations back, the exact point where one stops and the other begins varying more or less according to the views of the breeder in question. On the other hand, a more accurate definition of line breeding is perhaps that it is a succession of matings of closely related animals with a long-range objective. Line breeding in this sense would not comprise only a single mating. The blood (or more properly the genes) of one or two outstandingly prepotent individuals would be combined in successive generations.

Prepotency is the ability to transmit traits to most or all of the offspring. While usually taken to mean the transmission of good qualities, a dog or bitch may also be prepotent in the transmission of faults. If a dog is to be really prepotent, he must possess many dominant factors. If the qualities sought are recessive they cannot appear unless also present in, or at least transmitted by, the bitch. Bitches as well as dogs can be prepotent, for good or bad, but whereas a bitch produces comparatively few litters during her lifetime, a dog's influence can be much more widespread. It should not be forgotten, nevertheless, that in the case of any specific litter the bitch is precisely as important as the dog. The breeder's old saying that "the bull is half the herd" was true only insofar as the bull actually sired all the calves, while a single cow could produce only one per year.

In planning a breeding program that will be successful over a period of years, the first requirement is to have the type you want to produce clearly in mind. You may start with one bitch, the best you can obtain, and gradually build up your kennel by retaining her best daughters. Or you can start with two or three bitches of closely similar type and breeding. If they vary too greatly in either respect the puppies you raise will also vary and you will not get uniformity of type and quality. Some breeders develop their distinctive strains to a point where it is possible to recognize their dogs at a glance and the kennel name becomes a trademark. Given good bitches, any owner with a good eye for a dog and the will to select carefully should be able to choose good sires from among the many available, and produce good puppies.

Keep as many of your best bitch puppies as you possibly can. If you do not do this you will suffer for it in the long run. This is one place where a very small kennel is at a disadvantage. You should watch how the young bitches develop as long as you can, and try them out before discarding them. Otherwise, the time will come when your foundation bitches grow old and you will find them replaced by the ones which were not good enough to sell for big prices. Your best stock will be producing for your competitors. On the other hand, when weeding out inferior bitches and bitch puppies, make sure they are spayed if they are not good enough to improve the breed. Otherwise the market will be flooded with inferior stock which carries your kennel name in the pedigree.

When you have bred several generations of your own stock and studied the produce of other kennels as it appears in the show ring, you will learn what to look for and what to avoid when selecting a sire. But what of the novice with a bitch to breed and little or no experience? How should he or she go about selecting a sire? It is my belief that the best solution to the problem is to look at your bitch's pedigree and see how she herself is bred. Go back three generations, or further if you can. If she is of open breeding, with few or no ancestors appearing more than once, then select a good line-bred or inbred dog as closely related as possible. This cannot be very close, however, if the bitch is really open bred. Consequently, it might be better to select the best dog in her pedigree within two generations and breed back to him, in the hope of reducing the number of variables. Unless both the bitch and the dog are of unusually good quality the results of such a mating may be disappointing, but a really open pedigree is rare. If there is no really good dog close up, your bitch is probably not worth bothering with.

If your bitch has several common ancestors on one side, but not on the other, breed to the side on which there has already been some inbreeding or line breeding, choosing an outstanding dog who already appears on that side of the pedigree, or a close relative such as a brother, son, or grandson.

If your bitch has common ancestors on both her sire's and her dam's side, then try to select the most outstanding of them. Breed to an outstanding male himself, if he is available, or to a son, brother or grandson, providing they, too, are outstanding. Never forget that the inferior son of a great sire is little if any better than any inferior male. Indeed, where the stud owner will allow it, owners of poor quality bitches may have bred to a great dog in the natural hope of improving their own stock. The son of such a mating may contribute more faults from his inferior dam than can be offset by even close inbreeding to his superior sire.

Finally, if your bitch is herself fairly closely inbred or line-bred, you may look for a dog of similar breeding but not too closely related. This might be a good dog descended from common ancestors two or three generations back, but coming down via different individuals. This type of mating is likely to give better results than an attempt at a real outcross. Or you can, of course, gamble on continuing the inbreeding or line breeding. If the breeder of your bitch will advise you and has been successful over a number of generations, this may be a good choice. Inbreeding should be approached with caution by the novice and attempted only when the stock is of really high quality. Moreover, always try to inbreed to the best individuals in the pedigree, so as to strengthen the qualities you wish to perpetuate.

Above all, be sure they really are the best. Do not fall for a pedigree which is impressive only on paper. There are champions and champions. Some of them make the grade only because they are the best of a poor lot. Some great show dogs have been poor sires. On the other hand, there are also dogs who are greater as sires than as ring performers. Beware of letting a comparatively minor fault, which can be readily bred out, blind you to the value of a dog of outstanding quality overall. No dog is perfect, and the dog with no very noticeable faults may be without noticeable quality, either—just mediocre.

Remember, too, that as long as a male sires puppies at all they should be just as good when he is eight or ten years old as when he was two or three. So do not forget the old champions who have proved themselves top producers. The lovely young winner who catches the eye and gets the publicity is often an unknown quantity as a sire. The older dog who has sired winners consistently in the past has a production record which can be relied on. The old bitch, on the other hand, may suffer from endocrine changes or lowered metabolism, which may affect the quality of her litter. Seven is usually the maximum age for successful breeding of a bitch.

3

Breeding Problems
and Solutions

Ears

So long as a breed continues to be cropped the problem of ears will probably be of minor importance. Winge quotes an earlier investigator, Marchlewski, as claiming that hanging ears are dominant over erect, and as stating that the semi-erect ear, as in Collies, is dominant over the erect. Iljin deduces a case of triple allelomorphs, with the semi-erect ear dominant over both erect and hanging ears, while erect ears are incompletely dominant over hanging ears. There is also considerable difference in the size of ears, both within one type, such as the wide variation between different Hounds, all with hanging ears, and between breeds with entirely different types of ears.

In general, the Miniature Schnauzer seems to have smaller, thinner ears than the Standard Schnauzer. Uncropped Miniatures sometimes carry their ears erect, like a Scottish Terrier. If Iljin is correct, this would be recessive to the drop ear, but partially dominant over the hanging ear. In that case, breeding erect ears to really low-set, hanging ears would not be likely to result in correctly carried uncropped ears.

With cropped ears, too low-set, houndy ears may give a poor expression. While a really low, hanging ear might fail to stand properly after cropping, this is seldom a problem even when the dog is cropped later than the usual age. I can recall one Miniature Schnauzer bitch, whelped during the period between 1929 and 1934 when the Schnauzer Club of America barred the showing of cropped dogs, who was cropped and shown to her championship when six years old.

Too little data is available in this country on uncropped ears to give explicit advice on this point. Erect ears, according to my recollection, are rare but do sometimes occur. Size and placement vary a good deal, and naturally have a big effect upon expression. With Miniature Schnauzers, selecting for small, closely set ears would be my suggestion, plus the keeping of careful records to accumulate sufficient information for eventual compilation and analysis. Experience in other breeds indicates that teething has some effect upon ear carriage, and that the latter may not become definitely settled until the second teeth are cut. Consequently, taping during the teething period may help.

Eyes

Dark eyes are generally dominant over light, and there appears to be some linkage to coat color, particularly in the case of $bbEE$ individuals. Size and placement are also important. In Miniature Schnauzers, large, round eyes and light eyes are comparatively rare and probably recessive in most cases. The main thing is not to feel too secure and allow faults to creep in on that account, for a good eye plays an important part in the dog's expression. The 1957 revision of the breed standard indicates a trend toward smaller eyes in the substitution of the word "small" for "middle sized" in the description of the eyes.

The Animal Health Trust in England conducted studies on night blindness (progressive retinal atrophy) that proved of serious concern in Irish Setter breeding. While this is not a general difficulty among all breeds, it does show how a major fault can become a problem for an entire breed.

Cases of juvenile cataract, probably hereditary, have recently been reported in Miniature Schnauzers. This eye problem is either a recent development in the breed or has become more widespread during the past few years. It has been reported from such varied locations as California, Florida, the Middle West and the East Coast and has been a serious problem in other breeds, such as the Cocker Spaniel. It is true that this type of blindness in babies is believed to be caused by the German measles virus if the mother suffers from the disease during the first three months of pregnancy. Possibly a virus infection in the bitch during the first three weeks may behave similarly, but it has not been ascertained whether or not this is so.

Senile cataract sometimes occurs in old dogs, and veterinarians unfamiliar with the juvenile form have been known to diagnose the latter, when found in dogs four or five years old, as an unusually early case of senile cataract. However, any dog showing indications of cataract before five years of age should be regarded with extreme suspicion.

Juvenile cataract can produce blindness in puppies a few months old. Persons familiar with the condition can recognize it in puppies only three or four weeks old. It has an opalescent appearance, where the lens can be seen through the iris, and thus looks like a small spot, although the whole lens may actually be affected. Dogs with juvenile cataract usually become totally blind within a year or two.

Some of the veterinary schools have become interested in studying this condition, and the Projects Committee of the American Miniature Schnauzer Club is anxious to obtain as much information as possible in regard to the individuals in which it occurs. If a sufficient number of authentic pedigrees of individuals for study can be procured, it may be possible to identify carriers and eliminate them from breeding before the condition spreads further. On the basis of present knowledge, it is uncertain whether hereditary juvenile cataract is a dominant or a recessive. Almost certainly some cases are due to injury or disease, while others are probably inherited, and therefore care should be taken to distinguish between the two types. Research on eye problems in Collies, Cockers and other breeds may ultimately be useful in regard to Miniature Schnauzers, but we should not jump to conclusions.

Mouths

Most Miniature Schnauzers have the correct scissors bite in which the upper teeth just slide past the lower ones without leaving a space between. Cases of really overshot mouths are comparatively rare. Where the teeth meet evenly they wear down badly, while an undershot mouth with the lower teeth protruding beyond the upper is a decided fault. This may be an inheritance from the Affenpinscher, where the undershot mouth is called for by the breed standard.

Undershot mouths should really be divided into two types, one in which the lower front teeth protrude slightly, and one in which the lower jaw itself is too long. The upper and lower jaws do not always grow at equal rates, and until the second teeth are cut and the puppy is about five or six months old, it is impossible to be perfectly sure how his mouth will develop. A perfect mouth at a few weeks of age may change surprisingly before teething is finally completed.

The evidence on the inheritance of poor mouths is confusing. They are sometimes very hard to eliminate and sometimes fairly easy. They may appear, like recessives, from two parents with correct mouths, but even when two undershot individuals are mated, the puppies sometimes have correct mouths. Among various theories which have been advanced, one is that when a long head and a short head are combined, the puppies are prone to be undershot. The linkage between the inheritance of the upper and lower jaw is easily broken, so that a short upper jaw and a long lower jaw may be transmitted.

My own belief is that undershot mouths may be controlled by two pairs of genes, and that the fault is dominant. Crossing two line-bred strains has often resulted in undershot mouths. This could easily be the case if each strain carried the dominant gene of one pair. When the two dominants occurred in the same puppy an undershot mouth would result, but even when two undershot dogs were mated some of the puppies might receive only the recessive factors, or only a single dominant, and therefore might have good mouths. If the two dominant genes are designated A and B, then only dogs which were $AABB$, $AABb$, $AaBB$, or $AaBb$ would be undershot. Two $AaBb$ dogs might produce either $aabb$, $Aabb$,

300

AAbb, or *aaBB,* all of which would have good mouths, in addition to the undershot combinations. Of course, in that case, *aabb* dogs would always produce good mouths unless mated to a dog which was itself undershot.

Blood Groups

Blood groups exist in dogs, as in human beings, and at least three have been determined. However, they do not seem to involve any problems for the breeder, so far as reported. Future increased use of blood transfusion may create problems due to incompatible groups. Possibly something comparable to the human *Rh* factor may account for some deaths of newborn puppies.

Temperament

While tremendously important and undoubtedly including hereditary elements, temperament is not transmitted as a unit. Also, environment (care and nutrition) plays a vital role in the dog's disposition. Numerous studies have been made on the inheritance of particular traits. One of the most useful for the breeder is Humphrey and Warner's *Working Dogs.* In the elimination of shyness it is important to remember that the influence and example of the dam may play an important part. Trainability can certainly be inherited, and breeding from trained parents is consequently desirable. While training itself is not inherited, parents that learned easily are likely to hand on their innate ability. After several generations of untrained stock, the owner can only try and see how the puppy will do. However, most properly reared dogs have good dispositions and are quick to learn. It is clearly to the advantage of breeders to retain this characteristic by eliminating poor temperaments from the breeding program. Since nothing damns a breed more quickly than a reputation for poor disposition, breeders cannot be too careful in this respect. If there is any doubt, eliminate the puppy from your breeding program and be very careful about selling it as a pet. One shy or snappy dog may work untold damage throughout a whole area among laymen who judge a breed by the only individual they happen to know.

Orchidism

Orchidism is something with which all breeders are concerned. A dog with only one normally descended testicle is commonly called a monorchid, while the average fancier uses the term cryptorchid for a dog with neither testicle descended. Actually, both types are correctly called cryptorchids (meaning "hidden testicle") and are more technically described as unilateral cryptorchids (monorchids) and bilateral cryptorchids. The distinction is important because monorchids are usually fertile, while bilateral cryptorchids are almost invariably sterile.

The American Kennel Club in 1955 amended its rules so as to include both types of cryptorchids in the category of unsound or incomplete animals which are disqualified and cannot be shown. They are therefore now classed in the same group with dogs which are blind, deaf, lame, castrated, or spayed. Certain breed clubs had already altered their breed standards to make cryptorchidsm of any type a disqualification, among them the American Miniature Schnauzer Club, which took this action in 1953. Before that time a number of monorchids had been shown and at least two or three had become champions. In England the Kennel Club has now taken similar action.

This disqualification by the AKC applies only to shows and does not at this time affect the registration of dogs who are themselves monorchids, nor does it prevent the registration of their puppies.

The problem which faces the breeder today is this. Cryptorchids cannot be shown, therefore no matter how good a dog may be in other respects he must be written off except as a pet. Even though a monorchid may be fertile, the likelihood that he will pass on his defect, or even complete cryptorchidism with resultant sterility, makes him undesirable as a stud dog. Consequently, the breeder immediately asks three questions: What is the cause of this condition? Is it inherited? How can it be eliminated?

The cause is, of course, a failure of the testicles to develop or descend normally, but precisely why has not been established definitely and may vary in different cases. There appears to be a hereditary basis, and it seems probable that it is the tendency rather than the condition itself which may be inherited. The condition likewise varies in degree. The testicles may remain entirely inside the body cavity. Since sperm is very sensitive to heat this is sufficient to render the dog sterile. Or the testicles may pass through the muscles of the abdominal wall but remain under the skin instead of descending into the scrotum. Such dogs are occasionally fertile even though they are complete cryptorchids, since the temperature outside the body wall is lower, particularly in cold weather. Cryptorchids often develop cancer in the retained testicles or in the prostate gland.

There is some possibility of a relationship between cryptorchidism and slipped kneecap or subluxation, which often seem to occur in the same strain or individual. A possible explanation is that the amino acid tyrosine may be involved in the maturation of germinal tissue in both cases. An inherited inability to break down tyrosine might produce various effects in different individuals. Since sex characteristics begin to develop at a very early stage in both males and females, anything that disturbs them may produce abnormalities. Irregular functioning of the endocrine glands may be the direct cause of cryptorchidism. The point at which this occurs or the degree of hereditary susceptibility may determine the type or degree of the defect which will become apparent when the puppy reaches maturity. While cryptorchidism sometimes yields to hormone therapy or may even be corrected surgically by an operation, the remedial treatment would not prevent such a dog from passing on the condition to his puppies if it is actually inherited.

While there seems fairly general agreement that orchidism does "run in families" and is inherited in some way, there is wide disagreement among authorities as to just how it is transmitted. Some claim it is a simple recessive, others that it is a dominant characteristic. Matters are greatly complicated by the fact that while the dam is certainly involved in the matter of inheritance, there is no way of telling whether or not she is affected except by a study of her progeny. This is somewhat similar to the case of dairy cattle in which a bull passes on to his daughters the ability to produce a high yield of milk or butterfat, but cannot, of course, be judged except indirectly through them.

Two studies on cryptorchidism give substantially different conclusions. A report prepared by the British Veterinary Association, and published by the British Kennel Club in its Gazette in 1955,

303

stated that expert opinion held that the evidence pointed to a recessive factor. This view was based upon observations in other species, including pigs and goats, and upon breeders' records in Germany. On the other hand, a study of Collies made by the Society for the Advancement of Canine Genetics in this country, involving some 250 dogs and including some specific test matings, concluded that cryptorchidism is caused by a sex limited dominant gene. Both studies accept the condition as due to a single gene, but the method of transmission would vary in an important way. If the defect is dominant it would normally be transmitted by the dam, unless the sire was himself a monorchid. Few monorchids are used at stud and this source could be easily eliminated. If the sire is a normal male, according to this theory, the dam would necessarily be responsible. She would transmit the defect to half her sons (on the average) and half her daughters would be carriers, unless she herself were the daughter of a monorchid and a carrier and so carried the characteristic in both genes of the pair. In the latter case, all her sons would be monorchids (or cryptorchids) and all her daughters carriers. By eliminating as breeders all bitches who produced any type of cryptorchid, the fault could be largely reduced. However, there would still remain the dams, sisters, and daughters of such bitches. Particularly in the case of a small litter or one that included mostly females, a carrier bitch with only one gene of the pair affected may easily produce several litters before she was identified. While theoretically half of her sons would be monorchids or cryptorchids, all males might be normal were there only one or two. Even with half the litter carrying defective genes, as expected, there would be only one chance in four that a puppy with the "black" gene would likewise be a male. Accordingly, a bitch bred once a year might have daughters who were bred before she herself had happened to produce a monorchid male.

On the other hand, if cryptorchidism is due to a recessive gene it would show itself only when a male received one of the genes from each parent and so had a pair of them. In this case both parents would be carriers, though the sire might appear perfectly normal. The mating of a dog and bitch each carrying one of these recessive genes for cryptorchidism should result in an average of one puppy with two normal genes, two carriers, and one puppy with two recessive genes. If the one puppy in four with two recessives happened to be a male he would be a monorchid or a complete cryptorchid. As a result, only one male out of every four produced from two carriers would be theoretically expected to be a monorchid or cryptorchid (and only one puppy in eight when both males and females are included). Actually, of course, in a small number such as one or two litters there might be more or less than this average.

Taking the theoretical number as typical, however, in addition to the one male actually showing the defect, we could expect to get two normal puppies and four carriers plus one bitch with two defective genes. There would be no way of telling which normal-appearing male might be a carrier, and the females would be completely unknown quantities. Any particular one might have two, one, or no defective genes.

Even when dealing with an ordinary recessive factor, one litter may not be enough to establish with certainty whether a bitch carries the characteristic in question. In the case of orchidism, the difficulty is greatly increased. While one monorchid is enough to prove that the defect is carried, to prove that it is *not* requires the production of a number of males, all normal, sired by a monorchid or a known carrier. Probably the whelping of four to six males sired by a monorchid would give reasonable certainty, but this may require two or more litters. Then if the bitch is cleared, there would still remain the problem of her progeny from those litters, all of which, if by a monorchid, would be certain carriers. This makes the use of test matings impracticable in this case. The problem is somewhat similar to that of inherited subluxation, apparently a recessive, which does not develop until several months after birth. However, when subluxation does appear, it is recognizable in either sex.

For the average breeder to eliminate monorchidism would seem to be extremely difficult, for the necessary information is not available. If every case were reported to some central collection agency the mode of inheritance might eventually be settled. However, many puppies die young or are sold and lost track of before the condition is recognized. Even the breeder may not be aware that it has appeared and the owner of a dog or bitch can be totally ignorant that a close relative of his dog was a monorchid or has produced one. If a popular stud dog carries the recessive, he may greatly increase the number of carriers in the next generation and when these are mated to other carriers the proportion of defective males will increase. Inbreeding to such a carrier may unknowingly have serious results.

The best advice which can be given at this time is (1) never breed to a monorchid male, regardless of how good he is otherwise. (2) Discard any bitch who produces a monorchid or cryptorchid, as she is certainly a carrier, whether the gene be dominant or recessive. (3) If the gene is recessive the sire of a monorchid or cryptorchid must be a carrier, but until this is established with certainty it is possible that he may not be responsible if normal himself. (4) The daughters of a bitch who has produced a monorchid have at least one chance in two of being carriers, whether the gene is dominant or recessive. (5) The normal sons of a carrier bitch will be carriers only if the gene is recessive. By discarding known carrier bitches and breeding only to normal studs the prevalence of monorchids may be somewhat reduced, but the results will be much less satisfactory if the gene is a recessive.

A method of testing for recessive subluxation suggested by Dr. A. L. Hagedorn (*Journal of Canine Genetics,* January 1955, p. 20) might be of some help, though less effective than when the defect is recognizable in both sexes. If a male to be tested is bred to his daughters and is himself a carrier the chances are three to one that out of two daughters there will be at least one carrier. With three daughters, the odds are seven to one, and with four, they are fifteen to one. Consequently, if a stud is bred to four of his daughters and produces an average of four puppies per litter, the test should be fairly conclusive if all the puppies are normal. In this case, however, if half the puppies are males theory would require no more than two defectives and these numbers are too small for certainty. Nevertheless, such a test would give a fair indication that a dog was probably not a carrier. If careful records of such test matings were kept by some organization such as the Society for the Advancement of Canine Genetics or even the specialty club for the breed, it might be possible to award a certificate to the owner of any stud dog whose record was satisfactory. Once a fair number of dogs had been tested, breeders who used them would have reasonable assurance that they would not introduce the fault into their strain. Any such system, however, would take time to establish and could not be of immediate use.

The inheritance of this condition may be more complicated, since it may not be entirely the result of a single gene. There might be an inherited tendency to monorchidism and cryptorchidism which would develop only when another factor is present as well. This is now believed to be the case with baldness in human beings, which is very rare in women but can be transmitted by normal women to their sons. Even when the tendency is present in a man, however, baldness develops only if certain male hormones are not present in normal quantity. Similarly, an inherited tendency to retain the testicles in the body cavity might become evident only when some glandular disturbance or inability to properly absorb or convert some substance in the diet was also present, just as occasional individuals show an inability to assimilate calcium or can do so only when fed abnormally great amounts of vitamin D.

If there is actually a connection between monorchidism and subluxation, as suggested earlier, it might be that a like inability to break down tyrosine could produce either of these defects (or even both) only when a particular inherited tendency was also present.

There are various faults that are found in some breeds but are not common among others. These need not ordinarily concern the breeder, but he should be alert to notice any signs which might indicate their presence and to eliminate them before they become widespread.

Deafness has sometimes been linked with white color, but this is by no means always true. Clever dogs may compensate by their alertness so that the breeder does not realize they are deaf, but thinks them stupid or stubborn. Deafness is probably inherited as a recessive, and may be complete or partial. It is not a typical Schnauzer fault.

Blindness can also be inherited. I have heard of one or two cases where close inbreeding resulted in puppies with malformed eyes. This is also probably recessive. Dogs or bitches that produce such puppies should be watched carefully. Even though they do not produce the fault when not inbred, they may perhaps transmit it to their descendants. In some breeds such as Norwegian Dunkerhounds and Harlequin Great Danes, where the harlequin color is semilethal when homozygous, puppies appear regularly with eye defects apparently due to related effects of the color genes.

Subluxation is an inherited condition of the hip joint in which the bone of the socket is eroded and the ball head of the femur (thigh bone) is also worn away. This causes lameness which becomes progressively worse until the dog is completely crippled. The condition is said to be more common in medium-sized breeds than in either very large or very small ones. The results of careful study and experimental research conducted by the Society for the Advancement of Canine Genetics over a two-year period, published in the January 1955 issue of the *Journal of Canine Genetics,* indicated that subluxation is a recessive trait that occurs according to Mendelian expectations. It does not appear to be influenced by diet except that where the hereditary weakness already exists a poor diet may possibly make the subluxation more severe.

A recent study by Dr. Wayne H. Riser at the University of Pennsylvania School of Veterinary Medicine indicates that many puppies with normal hip joints at birth develop dysplastic changes during the first $4\frac{1}{2}$ to 5 months. Hip dysplasia and a genetic lack of muscle mass are closely associated. Those breeds and individuals that show less aggressive vigorous eating habits, with less rapid gain in weight, are not so prone to dysplasia. While a puppy's bones are soft and growing, the head of the femur needs to be held in the hip socket under sufficient muscle tension so that the socket cannot develop too shallowly. This requires a greater pelvic muscle mass than the heavy, fast-growing puppies have available. This relationship of weight to pelvic muscle doubtless accounts for the relative scarcity of this defect in smaller breeds, including the Miniature Schnauzer.

Early loss of teeth is a condition sometimes encountered in Miniature Schnauzers that may have a hereditary basis. Many individuals retain all their teeth in good condition to an advanced age, while sometimes dogs no more than two to four years old may develop serious mouth problems. It is probable that the condition is at least partially the result of inherited factors, but no study has yet been made to show what genetic factors are involved. Correct diet and care of the mouth, with regular removal of tartar deposits, are natural recommendations. It would doubtless be advisable not to mate two individuals who both suffer from early loss of teeth.

The Projects Committee of the American Miniature Schnauzer Club is interested in studying the prevalence of bladder stones in the breed. Anyone whose dog is operated upon for the removal of such stones is requested to send them to Dr. Robert J. Huber, 1240 Snyder Road, MR-2, Lansdale, Pa. 19446.

Recent medical research indicates that the dividing line between genetic causes and the effects of outside influences is less sharply drawn than was formerly supposed. It is sometimes difficult to tell where inheritance stops and other causes begin. Indeed, both may often be involved.

There seems little doubt that some breeds are more susceptible than others to certain diseases or defects. This is apparently due in some cases to the physical structure of a particular breed. In other cases it may be accidental. Since most if not all modern breeds are descended from a small group of ancestors, which were used to fix the desired type, it is clearly probable that any faults or weaknesses of such a group would be handed down to their descendants. The corresponding ancestral group in another breed could easily possess and hand on an entirely different group of faults and weaknesses. The same thing, of course, can occur within a single breed when individual strains or families are compared.

A particular characteristic, good or bad, may be directly due to the genes that a dog inherits. But sometimes a quality or characteristic may be suppressed entirely, modified, or brought to the surface by some circumstance that has little or nothing to do with the genes the dog inherits. Since sexual development depends on the action of numerous glands, it seems probable that if stresses occurred at the precise period when these glands or the sex organs themselves were forming, they could produce defects which would become evident later on. Heredity might perhaps determine the weak point which would yield to abnormal pressure or how great the resistance would be, but if the required stress did not occur at the required time, development would be normal. This may account for the fact that some defects that seem to "run in families" do not show the expected genetic pattern. The defect itself may not be inherited, but only a low resistance to some special pressure at a particular moment. Or some local condition in a kennel where the dogs are more or less related may suggest that the defect is a family one when this is not actually the case.

Various medical experiments and studies carried on at the Harvard School of Public Health during the years from 1947 to 1956

309

indicate that not all defects and deformities formerly assumed to be inherited are actually carried by the genes. A variety of diseases and other critical stresses may produce defects if they occur during the early stages of pregnancy. The embryo develops according to a definite pattern. A given stress occurring at a particular stage of development will produce a certain result, while the same stress at a different stage of development will produce a different result. In mice, the ninth day was critical for defects of the brain and skull, the fifteenth for cleft palate. Cleft palate can be produced by any one of a number of stresses, such as X-ray, vitamin deficiency, or cortisone intoxication, provided they are operating at the time when the two halves of the palate normally fuse. In man, rubella (German measles) at five weeks may cause congenital cataract, but at nine weeks causes deafness.

Eye, brain, bone, tooth, and heart defects may be due to a temporary stress during pregnancy. Undescended testicles very definitely have environmental facets of this type. Such defects are on the borderline between genetics and superimposed environmental influence, and the exact relationship is not yet clear. Even where a particular stress is the primary cause, it is still possible that an inherited susceptibility may increase the likelihood of defective development.

Apparently, little has been done as yet in the application of these findings to dogs. A few possible stresses which deserve consideration as possible sources of congenital defects are: atmospheric pressures encountered in high altitude flying (applicable to dogs with the increase of air shipment of bitches for breeding) ; lead or carbon monoxide poisoning; virus disease of the dam; blood or endocrine disorders; kidney disease; food and vitamin deficiency; reaction to medication or inoculation against rabies early in pregnancy. Vitamin supplements and antibiotics added to dog foods during manufacture may need recognition and study.

In a matter such as the prevalence of monorchidism and cryptorchidism, where some authorities claim that the condition is due to a recessive gene and others that it is dominant, it might be well to watch developments before taking too drastic action.

Defects and conditions that occur only rarely are likely to be overlooked and hence may attain serious proportions before notice is taken of them. Even in the case of those not commonly found in the breed it is wise to be on guard against any feeling of over-security. Beware of allowing any fault to creep in unnoticed, for it may then become firmly established and widely distributed. The time to eliminate a fault is before it takes root.

4

Color Inheritance

THE color inheritance of any breed is much more involved than appears at first glance, for it is not governed by a single pair of genes. The whole genetic makeup of the dog plays a part, and the effectiveness of any one gene may depend on its interactions with others. Environment, too, can make a difference. Breeders often notice a variation in color as well as density between winter and summer coats. Scientists have observed that the time at which the dark markings develop in Himalayan rabbits varies with the temperature. In both horses and dogs, certain colors regularly change as the animal grows older. Sometimes a single gene seems to have its full effect and produce a definite color. Sometimes two or more act together to produce a blend or entirely different effect from the action of either one alone, instead of either being an outright dominant.

A true dominant gene produces its full effect in the presence of a rival allele. Confusion very often arises in the minds of laymen who do not realize a very important fact. A gene that is recessive in its own allelomorphic series, and so requires the presence of two genes (one from each parent) to enable it to act, may still be able to affect, or even nullify, the action of a dominant gene in another series. This can happen even though the second gene is dominant in its own series. A gene that overcomes the normal effects of genes in another series is said to be *epistatic* to them. A gene whose action is modified by one of another series is *hypostatic*. It is very important to make this distinction between a dominant and an epistatic gene on the one hand, and between a hypostatic and a recessive gene on the other. Failure to do this is responsible for much uncertainty and confusion, not only in popular accounts of genetics but even in supposedly scientific literature.

In addition to the ordinary dominant and recessive genes with fairly simple action, the term multiple genes is used where several or many genes are needed to produce a given effect, or where their action is cumulative, as in the case of size.

During the last 30 years there has been a good deal of material published with regard to color inheritance in dogs, much of it in studies of single breeds or of related groups such as Hounds or gun dogs. Frequently this has dealt with crosses between breeds. There has been comparatively little, however, concerning variations within breeds in two main categories. These are the breeds in which the breed standard allows very little color variation, and the opposite group where color is of small importance.

To avoid confusion, I will start by describing the appearance of the colors usually found in Miniature Schnauzers, so that the terms used will be clearly understood, and then proceed to discuss how they are transmitted.

Solid Black, without any light markings except perhaps a small white spot on the chest, is recognized in all countries. Separate classes and championship titles for blacks are offered in Germany, Switzerland, Italy, and elsewhere on the Continent, just as black Cocker Spaniels have separate classes in this country. Formerly, Miniature Schnauzers of any colors were mated together at the whim of the breeder, but today in Germany blacks must be bred to other blacks or the progeny will not be registered.

Bicolor is a convenient term which includes all combinations of two colors with the pattern arrangement popularly called "black and tan." In the case of Miniature Schnauzers such dogs are usually black and cream or black and silver (sometimes the markings are so light as to be almost white). In bicolor dogs the back, sides, neck,

313

part of the head, and the tail are black. The feet and legs, belly, insides of ears, lower jaw, spots over the eyes, around the anus, and the underside of the tail at the root are light. A similar pattern in some breeds produces so-called blue and tan or liver and tan dogs. Real black and tan seldom if ever occurs in Miniature Schnauzers, but black and cream or silver used to be common and still appears from time to time. The American standard includes bicolors among the desired colors, although in Germany they were eliminated a number of years ago, while the Swiss standard only recently reinstated them.

Pepper and salt is the usual color in this country, but in Germany blacks now outnumber them in the total of annual registrations. It is a loose term covering every gradation from very light to very dark, with various amounts of yellow, brown, or red included. Pepper and salts are distinguished by the fact that the individual hairs are of more than one color. Usually the tips are dark (either black or almost black) with a lighter colored band toward the body and a second dark band toward the root. According to the amount of dark on the tips of the hairs where it shows most the coat will be darker or lighter. Solid dark hairs or unbanded light ones scattered at intervals also modify the general effect. This also changes as the coat grows in after stripping, with the dark tips showing first. Some pepper and salt Miniatures have a solid dark stripe down the center of the back. Further variations in appearance are caused by the undercoat, which is usually unbanded and lighter in color. Some dogs with a good outer coat have a yellowish undercoat, while sometimes the undercoat is quite dark. After a dog's topcoat has been stripped, his color may appear entirely different on this account. As the outside coat grows in through the undercoat the original color will usually return. However, a puppy's first coat may be quite different from his adult color, and even adults sometimes vary considerably for reasons which are not always clear. Sunburn certainly, and perhaps temperature, age, and changes in body chemistry, may be at least partly responsible.

The term *chinchilla* is sometimes used to designate a clear gray pepper and salt in which the dark portions of the hairs approach jet black and the light ones are white or silver, without yellow or brown tinge. *Agouti* or *wild color* is frequently applied by writers on genetics to the mixture with brown or yellow which is usually considered to be the original wild type, of which chinchilla is a recessive mutation in various animals.

White is a show disqualification according to the present American standard as amended in 1953, but does not prevent a puppy's being registered. Pure whites with dark eyes and noses appear occasionally in a number of lines. They are *not* albinos, which would be white with pink noses, and no albino Miniature Schnauzer has ever been brought to my attention.

Yellow is also a color not allowed in the show ring. Many early German dogs were registered as *gelb* (which is translated yellow). Some of them may have been yellowish pepper and salts. Others were probably cream verging on white, according to some of my German correspondence years ago. About 1935 I owned a puppy that might be described as wheaten and had a white litter brother. This color is certainly very rare and of interest chiefly because of the bare possibility of its reappearing as an occasional recessive.

Particolor is also contrary to the standard (which condemns spotted or white markings other than a small spot on the breast), but it does occur from time to time. Particolor dogs are basically white, with large patches of color on the head, neck, and body, such as are found in Cocker Spaniels, Fox Terriers, Hounds, etc. The colored patches may vary from a few fairly small markings to large areas covering a great part of the body. The color of the markings depends on what would be the normal color of the individual if the white were not present. Hence particolors may be black and white when they come from black stock, or pepper and salt and white when from pepper and salt stock. Theoretically, a bicolor dog with the spotting factor added should be considered a tricolor, as is the case in a number of other breeds. In practice, I have never seen a real tricolor Miniature Schnauzer, the nearest being a bicolor with white front feet, though a few registrations of "black and tan and white" might conceivably be actual tricolors.

Students of color inheritance have adopted a formula for expressing the different genetic combinations in simple form by the use of letters, usually accepting those employed in the first publication of that particular gene, with modifications when necessary. I have tried to follow this practice so far as possible. Genes that affect color fall into several classes. Pigment genes are naturally basic and without them no color can be present. Pigment is composed of

315

Three whites with dark eyes and black noses.

A mixed litter: 3 whites, 2 blacks, 2 pepper and salts and 1 black and silver, by a salt and pepper sire out of a white dam.

chemical substances deposited in the hair and skin in the form of granules and known as melanin. Beginning before birth, the process continues thereafter. Variations in the amount and rate of deposit, plus growth of the hair so that a greater amount of it is visible, account for the sometimes startling changes in coat color from whelping to maturity. Pigment is deposited at the root, where the hair grows. A change in the pigment-forming process while the hair is only partly grown out produces the typical banding found in agouti dogs, where the individual hairs are partly of one color and partly of another. Slighter changes doubtless account for variations in a dog's color from one coat to the next and may be due in part to temperature changes, gland irregularities, or other factors that change the amount of melanin deposited.

There seem to be two types of black pigment in dogs. In one, all the granules are small and similar in type. The more common kind varies from small to large granules, with fairly large ones the most numerous. The pigment granules of black dogs, when bleached by hydrogen peroxide or a similar agent, resemble those of yellow dogs, indicating that black may be formed from yellow by some further chemical process. Yellow dogs normally have black pigment in the skin of the nose and eyelids, the nails, etc. If black pigment is not present in these areas, both skin and hair become chocolate or liver-colored rather than yellow. Chocolate hairs under the microscope show a difference in size as well as color. The granules are smaller than in black hairs, very regular in size, with a special cluster arrangement, while the pigment is light brown. Chocolate, like black, can be oxidized to yellow. Partial bleaching by strong sunlight may temporarily affect both coat and nose color, so that black or blue dogs tend to become rusty in hot summer weather.

Besides the pigment genes themselves, there are genes which produce various patterns in dogs that are not all of one color. Extension genes or combinations of multiple genes may determine the relative amount of the different colors when more than one is present. Intensity or dilution genes may affect the strength of a color, which can thus vary from light to dark, while restriction genes may inhibit a color from showing, although the genes for it actually are present.

An apparently simple color, such as a solid black, may involve the interaction of a large number of genes. Some of these are necessary

317

to produce any color at all and are found in all or most breeds. Others make the difference between black and other colors. Though no more essential than the first type, they are more specific. Accordingly, writers on the subject of color inheritance often speak of genes for certain colors as if they were the only ones involved, without repeating the entire formula. Most students agree on certain genes but differ on others. Several allelomorphic series have been suggested but have not gained complete acceptance. In some series there appear to be only two alleles, one dominant and one recessive. In others there are several mutations, and in a number of instances there has been apparent confusion, on the part of the writers, between epistatic recessives of one series and hypostatic dominants of another.

The following list, based on various authorities and my own studies, has been revised in this edition to conform as much as possible to C. C. Little's *Inheritance of Coat Color in Dogs* (Howell Book House, 1967).

A^s—Dominant allele allowing dark pigment to extend over entire body area. There are four or five alleles at this locus, at least three occurring in Miniature Schnauzers.

a^y—Tan or "sable" yellow, as found in Collies, is placed here by Little and may have been present in Miniature Schnauzers up to the 1920's and early 1930's. If so, it has been largely if not completely bred out.

a^w—(called a^g in the first edition) "Wild color" or "agouti," producing banded hairs with dark tips, usually black. Called "pepper and salt" in the breed standard. Recessive to A^s and probably to a^y.

a^t—Bicolor or "tan-point." A pattern gene in which the body is typically black, with light markings on the chest, belly, feet, legs, sides of the muzzle, over the eyes, inside the ears and around the anus, when BE is present. Recessive to all the preceding.

B—A dominant gene necessary to produce black pigment in either coat, nose or foot pads.

b—Recessive allele of B. Dogs with bb have chocolate or liver coats, brown noses and light eyes. Very rare in Miniature Schnauzers if found at all.

C—This genetic series is necessary in some form to produce the pigment melanin, and C is believed to be present in all deep-red or tan breeds and at least some of the blacks.

c^{ch}—Recessive to C but apparently with little influence on solid black. It reduces yellow-tan to cream or off-white and is probably responsible for the "chinchilla" color of many Miniature Schnauzers as compared to the older color types. In bicolors it produces black and

318

silvers. Blacks of the real jet type are probably C, but others are c^{ch}. Although Little ascribes c^{ch} to certain black breeds, including Labrador Retrievers and Giant Schnauzers, it is probable that most solid blacks were originally C. The breeding of black Miniature Schnauzers to chinchillas probably accounts for the relatively poor color of many blacks in this country, and is doubtless one reason the Germans have forbidden color crosses. In the days before chinchillas were frequent, blacks were regularly bred to salt and peppers without apparent ill effects.

c^e—Extreme dilution of red-yellow pigment has been suggested, as perhaps producing puppies from yellow-tan dogs which would be white at birth and remain so light that traces of color would be hard to find. Burns calls this c^r. The existence of this gene is not definitely proved, and I do not believe that white Miniature Schnauzers are caused by it.

c^a—Complete albinism is extremely rare in dogs and not known to occur in Miniature Schnauzers. A $c^a c^a$ dog shows *no* pigment in hair, skin or eyes except where the blood vessels on the retina allow the blood to show through pink or red. Whites with dark eyes, black noses and foot pads are emphatically not albinos.

D—A dominant gene causing intense pigmentation of whatever color is present It is found in deep reds, such as Irish Setters, and in all blacks (in association with B and E). It was formerly nearly univerversal in Miniature Schnauzers.

d—The only known recessive to D is a dilution factor, producing "blue" or Maltese in the case of blacks. (The "silvery" color occurring in Weimaraners is a dilution of liver, with the formula $bbdd$). Blue is rare in Miniature Schnauzers, though a very few have been reported among blacks. Possibly this gene may be responsible for the very pale salt and peppers, lacking proper contrast in the banded hairs, which seem to be on the increase.

E—Dominant gene for formation of dark pigment over the whole coat, or "extension." Produces solid black, provided B and A^s are present.

e—Recessive yellow or fawn in which dark pigment is restricted to the eyes, nose and footpads. An $A^s ee$ yellow mated to a gray or sable with EE can produce solid blacks.

E^m—The gene for "mask," believed to be epistatic to E but not, of course, visible in the case of solid blacks. It covers the face and ears with dark pigment, even in otherwise red or gray dogs, and in bicolors the tan area disappears from the head. The combination of mask with bicolor (E^m and a^t) may produce near-blacks with light markings only on the feet and lower legs. While more or less dark on the forehead, around the eyes, and on the top of the nose, few if any adult Miniature Schnauzers have the completely dark muzzle of the typical "masked" breeds. It is doubtful whether E^m actually occurs and it would certainly seem to be rare in this breed.

319

e^{br}—Brindle, exhibiting light and dark stripes, which is distinct from the banding of individual hairs and not normally found in Miniature Schnauzers. Its place in the E series is between E and e.

G—This gene is dominant over the g gene found in most breeds, and its behavior needs further study. It is believed to produce progressive graying from birth to maturity, or through life, whereas normal dark pigmented animals with g maintain their color unchanged. Puppies with Gg that are born black may become silver in the case of Poodles, or bluish in Kerry Blues, whereas dd blues are so from birth. G can also act on brown dogs, but whether it affects the banded hairs of a^w and others in the A series is not stated by Little. However, the fact that Miniature Schnauzers of the chinchilla type are often nearly black at birth, with light points and undercoats, suggests that they may carry G. Pepper and salts of a reddish or yellowish color indicating the presence of C and/or a^y show much less change. Either they are gg or the G gene has less effect when they are present.

m—Recessive to the M gene which produces merles in Collies and several other breeds; appears to be universal in Miniature Schnauzers.

S—Dominant gene for expression of pigment in the coat. It is found in all dogs that do not have sizeable white markings. (It is claimed that no dog is without a few white hairs. Even SS individuals may have a small white spot on the breast, the tip of the tail, or the toes. These are thought to be caused by "minus modifiers" of the regular genes.) The S locus is believed to contain several different alleles which determine the amount of white, and together with the addition of plus and minus modifiers produce a whole series ranging from complete pigmentation to complete or almost complete white. The alleles are known as spotting or piebald genes and vary considerably in different breeds. The appearance of white is not due to an absence of the normal genes for color, however, but to restriction of their expression to larger or smaller areas.

s^i—The gene next below S in epistatic order, producing a distinct pattern known as "Irish spotting," with a few definitely located white areas on the feet, legs, chest, tail tip, and sometimes on the muzzle, belly, and neck, producing a white collar. It is typical of Basenjis, Boxers and Collies, but is extremely rare in Miniature Schnauzers.

s^p—Piebald spotting or particolor, varying greatly in the proportion of white to colored area. Like Irish spotting, it is affected by plus and minus modifiers. Actually, the basic genetic color pattern of a dog with s^p remains unchanged, but the particolor gene acts to restrict the deposit of this pigment in certain areas, which remain white. If $s^p s^p$ is replaced by SS or Ss^p, however, the normal pigment reappears. Black Miniature Schnauzers with two s^p genes are black and white particolors. Salt and peppers with $s^p s^p$ genes have large

320

patches of salt and pepper on a white background. While parti-color is a disqualification in this breed (as is also complete white) a number of individuals do carry this recessive, and when two of them are mated, a quarter of the puppies can be expected to be particolors. Another allele of this series, which Little calls s^w (extreme-white piebald), is believed to produce dogs with almost entirely white coats with very small colored areas, usually on the head. Intermediate types, with some overlapping, are attributed to plus and minus factors.

s^{wh}—This gene, which I called s^w in the first edition, has been changed to avoid confusion with Little's s^w. It produces complete white, with dark eyes and a black nose and footpads. While it may possibly be Little's $s^w s^w$ with strong minus modifiers, I prefer to consider it a distinct allele. The particolor Miniature Schnauzers thus far reported are nearly all of the fairly heavily marked s^p type and quite distinct from the whites. The inheritance of both whites and particolors is discussed in greater detail later.

T—A dominant gene for ticking (small pigmented spots or flecks on a white ground) not known to occur in Miniature Schnauzers, but if present could be observed only in whites, particolors, or perhaps on the light portions of black and silvers. The normal gene for non-ticking is tt.

In the first edition of this book I used the designation T for a self-colored coat of a single color, which I considered dominant to various patterns and necessary to produce solid black. In this edition its place is taken, to some extent, by A^s, and its recessive bicolor t^{bi} has become a^t. My original a^{ch} has here become c^{ch}. I disagree with the suggestion that c^{ch} or a further allele c^e might produce whites, which I think belong to the S series as explained above. I am still not wholly convinced that there is not a dominant gene for single colored hairs, to which banded hairs are recessive.

Having defined the terms to be used, let us now see how these genes combine to produce the various colors. (Additional genes found in other breeds but not known to appear in Miniature Schnauzers have been omitted except where they help to clarify the action of those that do appear). Readers are reminded that a dog must have two genes of every pair, one in each chromosome. When one gene of a pair is a dominant and it is not known whether the second is the same or a recessive allele, this is expressed by the dominant symbol followed by a dash. For instance, B- could represent either BB or Bb, but bb is always given in full and the form bB or b- is never used.

321

For convenient reference the various dominant genes were arranged in alphabetical order, but they actually fall into several groups which produce similar results. They may be classed as (1) pigments, or qualitative genes; (2) quantitative or intensity genes; (3) individual hair pattern genes; and finally (4) coat pattern arrangement genes or restriction genes.

To begin with, any dog not an albino must have C or one of its alleles other than $c^a c^a$. Many modern salt and pepper Miniature Schnauzers are probably $c^{ch} c^{ch}$. Others, particularly the darker types, may be $C c^{ch}$, or even CC, though in the latter case the light portions of the coat would tend to be cream or yellowish rather than silver or off-white. However, even the bicolors do not show real tan markings such as occur in tan-point breeds like Doberman Pinschers. Possibly this is due to some unidentified allele of C, or to modifiers such as are believed to affect size, or the amount of spotting in particolors. Real jet blacks, particularly from recently imported stock, may have CC or $C c^{ch}$.

B and E are practically universal in Miniature Schnauzers, whether black, salt and pepper, or even white or particolor. When A^s is present the color becomes black, while $a^t a^t$ produces bicolor (tan-point or black and silver). To prevent the color restriction which produces white or particolor, S is necessary. The normal formula for a salt and pepper Miniature Schnauzer thus becomes:

$$
\begin{array}{ccccccccc}
a^y & & C & & & G\,? & & & \\
a^w & B & c^{ch} & D & E & g & m & S & t
\end{array}
$$

The same formula with the first gene changed to a^t produces bicolor, while the substitution of A^s gives black, the latter being more likely to have C. The litter of eight shown on page 60, consisting of two blacks, three whites, two pepper and salts and a black and silver, came from a salt and pepper sire with formula $a^w a^t S s^{wh}$ and a white dam with formula $A^s a^t s^{wh} s^{wh}$. Three of the puppies were homozygous for s^{wh}, which was received from both parents, and thus were white. (Theoretically half the litter should have been so, but three out of eight is quite close.) The other five would carry $S s^{wh}$ and so could transmit a white gene to half their progeny. The two blacks would be $A^s a^w$ or $A^s a^t$ and would transmit A^s to half their puppies and a^w or a^t to one-fourth of them. The two salt and peppers would be $a^w a^t$ and would transmit these genes in equal numbers. The single black and silver would be $a^t a^t$ and would transmit this to all puppies. One would expect half the litter to be black and a quarter (two) to be black and silver were it not for the presence of the s^{wh} genes. In theory, at least, the three white puppies should have been two blacks and a black and silver.

Bicolor is no longer a recognized color on the Continent and has been largely eliminated here by discarding most bicolors for breeding, although there have been several champions of the color. Among producers, Ch. T.M.G. of Marienhof's granddam, Abigail of Marienhof, was a bicolor. There has been a recent revival of interest in them, with a Canadian champion, Walsh's Frosty Charmer, finishing in 1964 and others since. They are unquestionably flashy in appearance and add variety to the breed. Two bicolors should produce all bicolor puppies.

What does all this mean to the breeder? It means black seldom occurs unless one or both parents are black, although it is not impossible. Many reddish dogs frequently found during the 1920's and early 1930's were doubtless heterozygous dark sables ($a^y a^y$, $a^y a^w$, or $a^y a^t$), as in Collies. Since yellow was early rejected and a^y is dominant over the other two these could have been easily eliminated from salt and pepper lines but less easily from blacks, which could carry them down unobserved.

There seems to be a definite tendency for some chinchillas to show brown or yellow, particularly on the back of the neck and along the spine, but why this happens is not clear. It may in some cases be a temporary phase, due to sunburn or partial oxidation of black pigment and so be non-genetic. It could also, perhaps, indicate a heterozygous condition of some of the other factors such as Ee, but this is by no means certain. Still another possibility is that light pepper and salt dogs that show a tendency to brown in the saddle area may carry both the chinchilla factor c^{ch} and a heterozygous (and therefore incompletely dominant) Bb. Since bb would produce chocolate on the dark area, a tendency to brown might show through. If that is the case, mating two such dogs should produce some recessive bb chocolates. However, a breeder desiring to obtain a pure pepper and salt would naturally breed to a dog that did not show any brown and would therefore, presumably, be BB, with all the puppies BB or Bb. In such a case it would probably be advisable to breed to a very dark chinchilla or to a strongly

323

colored dog of the agouti type, even though he may carry some yellow in the light portion of the banded hairs, so long as the dark portion showed no indication of a dilution factor.

Solid black might also be useful as a correction for dilution factors, especially if a true jet black. The rusty black which is sometimes found may indicate a heterozygous condition such as *Bb*, perhaps emphasized by oxidation. Any tendency toward a smoky black or "blue" would suggest heterozygous *Dd* in either blacks or chinchillas.

A gene which was ignored when the full formula for black was given is the dominant merle *M*, because it does not seem to occur in Miniature Schnauzers, all of which appear to be *mm*. However, it should be mentioned here because it has caused some confusion in the past. Heterozygous *Mm* produces merles or harlequins, but is also semilethal. When two *Mm* merles are mated together the expected 25 percent of *MM* puppies are not only almost white but show various abnormalities, including deafness, blindness and structurally abnormal eyes. Consequently, many fanciers hold the opinion that breeding white to white or particolor to particolor is unsafe. This may also be connected with the fact that in some breeds and strains white has been associated with deafness, and that some writers claim albinos are deaf, although this has been disputed.

Actually, the merle white is caused by entirely different genes from either the dark-eyed white or the usual particolor found in many breeds. Even in Collies, where the other types occur in addition to the merle, ordinary whites may be bred to white successfully for generations without ill effects.

Many Miniature Schnauzer breeders are unaware that either whites or particolors are ever found in the breed and immediately suspect a mismating when puppies of those colors appear. They have, indeed, been distinctly rare in the past, but have been occurring lately in increasing numbers. I have been told on good authority that they are fairly numerous in Germany, but are now always destroyed at birth. Particolors also occur in England in some lines.

While it has not been finally determined whether particolor spotting and complete white belong to the same allelomorphic series or not, I am increasingly inclined to believe that they do. This does

324

not, however, mean that they would occur at random, but only that they are both mutations of the same normal color-expression gene *S*. From this it follows that a dog of normal color could carry only one recessive gene for some one of the various alleles. As a result, particolor and white could not both occur in the same litter from two normal parents. In actual fact, I have never come across a case in which they did, although in several instances of closely related dogs one line has transmitted particolor and another white.

After studying the transmission of white spotting in various breeds I am inclined to agree with Leon Whitney that completely dark dogs without a single white hair are virtually nonexistent. (See also Part III.) Almost all dogs seem to carry a gene that produces a minimum amount of white, in the form of a few hairs on the chest, toes, belly, or tail tip. This gene has the homozygous dominant form *SS*, in which the amount of white is so slight as to be disregarded. It bears no relation to such special forms of spotting as harlequin in Great Danes, merle in Collies, or the peculiar Dalmatian spotting. However, *S* has a number of alleles. Just how many has not been definitely determined, and they are very likely cumulative in their effect, giving results similar to those shown in Figure 1 (p. 276) for the action of two gene pairs, if numbers are taken to indicate the relative size of the white and colored areas. In addition to this, the inhibiting factor which produces the white area meets with more resistance in the case of black than of the lighter colors. Consequently, black-and-white particolors, regardless of the alleles involved, show heavier dark markings than do particolors that exhibit lighter colors. Most Miniature Schnauzers are homozygous for *S* or may possibly carry an allele which produces a very limited amount of white. The occasional dog with a nearly white foreleg may be suspected of being heterozygous for particolor, though such comparatively small markings tend to become smaller with age and may even disappear completely. Since particolor is due to variation in a single allelomorphic series, the dark markings are of whatever color is determined by the rest of the formula. The only difference is that instead of being *SS* or *Ss^{wh}*, the particolor carries some combination of *s^p* genes. It could, for instance, be *s'p s'p*, *s'p s''p*, or *s''p s''p*, with varying amounts of white to correspond. There may even be a further allele *s''p'*, which would allow for additional combinations. Since most particolor Miniature Schnauzers seem to be rather heavily marked, they may not carry as many alleles as some other breeds.

The first particolors of which I have specific record were three out of a litter of seven whelped in Germany at the Abbagamba Kennels in 1929. They came from solid black parents, and so were themselves black and white. They were registered in the PSZ as *Schecken* or *Platenfarbe*. The male was mated to his litter sister and to a sister of his sire, and several generations were produced. The matings of two particolors invariably gave all particolor puppies. Particolors bred to blacks gave some blacks and some particolors when the black parent was a carrier, and all blacks when it was not. About 1934 the PSK refused to continue registering the particolors. Gräfin Kanitz (Abbagamba Kennels) gave up breeding and was later killed in a motor accident. Whatever German particolors may have been whelped since were presumably destroyed.

I have had only one report concerning black and white particolors in this country, and this appears to have been due to s^p genes derived from salt and pepper grandparents. There are numerous cases in which pepper and salt markings of precisely the same type have appeared. The first litters occurred in 1946, the sire of one litter being the grandsire of the other, while on the other side the two litters had a common grandsire. I heard of no more until 1952, when I was told of two bitches in a litter of four. One of these particolors, experimentally mated to her uncle and later to her own sire, had two particolors out of four in the first litter and three out of four in the second, clearly indicating a single gene recessive.

This started me on a hunt for the source of the particolor variation, and inquiry turned up several more examples. The method of transmission proved unexpectedly hard to identify. So many dogs in the various pedigrees were inbred that many possible sources had to be discarded because they appeared too often. Had they been responsible, particolors should have occurred constantly, and they were decidedly rare, even assuming that a number of instances had not been reported.

Careful checking back for generations finally led to the conclusion that certain of the early Dornbusch dogs must be responsible. In each case the line had survived through only one or two individuals in a generation, and for a long time the lines in question had not been crossed so as to bring two carriers together. When this

Ilfis v. Abbagamba, a German black particolor
of 1930.

A genetic black at the age of 6½ with
grizzled whiskers.

finally did happen, the particolors put in an appearance. This deduction was confirmed when subsequent inquiry in Germany brought the statement that Lord v. Dornbusch had been known to sire particolors.

Since the chance that a given son or daughter of a carrier mated to a normal dog will likewise be a carrier is only one in two, it is often impossible to be sure which lines have transmitted the recessive in cases where there is more than one possibility. By accumulating material and comparing the pedigrees of various particolors, however, I have come to the conclusion that Schnapp v. Dornbusch was one of the importations involved, in all likelihood through his sire, Hupp. Jörg v. Dornbusch, a Hupp grandson on his dam's side, was probably another; and possibly Viktor v. Dornbusch as well. An alternative possibility would be Viktor and his sire, Don v. Dornbusch, but this seems less likely. Ukase du Jorat, whose great-granddam, Gaya v. Abbagamba, was a sister to the sire of the 1929 particolors, is also a possible candidate. Both sides of this Abbagamba litter traced to a Lord descendant who does not otherwise appear.

Today there are several champions who carry a particolor recessive, while a number of their close relatives must do so as well. Consequently, it is probable that particolors will occur more often in the future than they have in the past. When this does happen, both parents must have carried a recessive s^p gene. A carrier bred to a homozygous SS dog or bitch will not produce any particolor puppies. It should not be forgotten, however, that half the progeny in such a case can be expected to be carriers also, and there is no known way to determine which they are except by breeding back to a particolor. This method has the disadvantage of inevitably producing more carriers from the particolored parent, even if the colored parent turns out to be SS, and a single litter, especially a small one, is not enough to give absolute certainty. Six or seven normal puppies and no particolors would be indicative, but even that is not positive proof. A mismating to another breed, such as a Fox Terrier, should *not* produce particolors in the first generation unless the Miniature parent is itself a carrier.

Whites, as distinct from particolors, appeared from pepper and salt parents in this country as early as 1933 or 1934. The source appears to have been Bodo v. Schillerberg. Christel v.d. Fallerberg and, in one instance, Achill Heinzelmännchen were also involved, and probably also Mücke Heinzelmännchen. In 1936 Gräfin Kanitz of Abbagamba wrote of a litter of white from white parents, and in the same year a white occurred in California from Abbagamba stock, probably tracing through Heimia v. Abbagamba. The descendants of this dog, bred for close to 30 years, have proved invaluable in working out the white inheritance. Gräfin Kanitz seemed to consider whites as variations of yellow or cream. She stated that many of these "yellows" were registered in the early days of the breed, a fact substantiated by the studbooks. A majority of whites in this country show a faint cream or yellow tinge, especially on the back and ears. All the original importations that produced white in this country can be traced to daughters of Peterl v.d. Werneburg and Pussel v. Ruhrtal; two of these daughters were owned by the Abbagamba Kennels. Peterl's dam, Mucki v.d. Werneburg, was actually registered as *gelb* (yellow), so she may have been the source, although this is far from certain.

White is clearly due to a single recessive gene. It is probably recessive to all the color alleles of the S series, since it acts like s^p to inhibit color, only more completely. Accordingly, I have called it s^{wh}. Eventually I hope to determine by a test mating whether this theory is actually correct, or whether the gene for white is independent of the S series. As I mentioned previously, I have never heard of a white and a particolor occurring in the same litter. If they are alleles, this could only happen if an $s^p s^{wh}$ particolor was bred to an $s^{wh} s^{wh}$ white, for two colored individuals would have to be Ss^p and Ss^{wh} in order to carry both alleles, and so could not produce $s^{wh} s^{wh}$. They could, of course, produce $s^p s^{wh}$ particolors. In a recently reported case, a dog sired whites from one bitch and particolors from another. This would be possible if the first bitch carried a white recessive while the second carried parti. The latter would be dominant over Ss^{wh}, which would be carried by the male.

White has occurred in this country over a longer period than has particolor pepper and salt, and rather more often as well. Although still rare, white also appears to be increasing, and several champions are certainly carriers.

I have heard it claimed that there is a connection between bicolor and particolor or white. I do not agree with this theory. When any degree of white spotting or particolor is found on a bicolor dog the result is a tricolor, or black, white and tan. This coloration frequently occurs in Collies, which are homozygous for a varying degree of white. Sable is the dominant color, and the combination results in either sable and white or tricolor (when the recessive bicolor combines with the usual white markings.) I have never come across a true tricolor Miniature Schnauzer, but it should be easy to produce tricolors by breeding bicolor to particolor and backcrossing to another particolor. In one or two instances a bicolor with white feet might perhaps have been considered a tricolor but was probably a bicolor that was possibly heterozygous for particolor.

White bred to white, when of the dark-eyed, black-nosed type, appears to breed true and produces only dark-eyed whites. Consequently, it would be a simple matter to develop a white strain of Miniature Schnauzers from stock now available, although they would not be eligible to show according to the present standard. The elimination of white and particolor from our breeding stock, on the other hand, is likely to prove a much more difficult matter which can only be solved by cooperation. Otherwise, only the breeder who keeps strictly to his own strain, generation after generation, can be reasonably sure of not introducing these recessive genes, which can arise to plague later generations. Merely destroying white or particolor puppies, while continuing to breed from their parents, brothers, and sisters, will not solve the problem.

I have not discussed the genes for brindle and mask, as their relationship to the various series has been questioned. Brindle is seldom found in Miniature Schnauzers, but it seems possible that it sometimes does occur. It may be the cause of certain "dirty colors" which occasionally appear among dark pepper and salts, but not enough evidence is available at present to place it definitely in the scheme as outlined. Brindle appears to have some relationship to yellow e of the extension series. In other breeds (German Shepherds for instance) it occasionally appears on the light areas of bicolor dogs, presumably as a recessive to the normal color. Brindle in the smooth-haired breeds such as Great Danes and Boxers is believed to be dominant over fawn (yellow) and is given the formula e^{br}. It obviously requires the presence of black pigment to become visible. It takes the form of narrow, irregular black stripes on a yellowish ground, so that it would seem to belong, logically, among the pattern factors. An agouti Miniature Schnauzer with considerable yellow in the coat, as opposed to a "chinchilla" that has lost the yellow tone, might easily produce the cloudy, "dirty-colored" effect if brindle were added to the genetic make-up. This may be tested by breeding such a dog to a bicolor. If Little is right the legs should show brindle markings. Since most Miniature Schnauzers appear to be EE, an occasional Ee^{br} may transmit a gene for brindling over many generations before it would have the opportunity to show itself upon encountering another Ee^{br}.

The fawn with black mask as found in Boxers and Danes does not seem to be relevant. There is, however, a distinct tendency among Miniatures to a dark-faced type comparable to the mask of other breeds, although it is most often found in dogs with at least moderately dark body coats. Miniature Schnauzer whiskers may vary from almost white to really dark. Though as a general rule the lighter the dog the lighter the whiskers, this is not invariably the case. I incline to the belief that the dark face is dominant, for it usually occurs where at least one parent exhibits it. However, there is almost certainly an allelomorphic series involved, unless some other gene acts as a modifier, for the variations are not clear-cut.

As a rule, undercoat resembles topcoat but is apt to be lighter. It is often yellower than the outside coat, but some dogs show dark when stripped. The dog's age and the time of year appear to cause considerable differences. Dogs with light undercoats darken as the guard hairs with dark tips grow in, while dogs with dark undercoats may grow much lighter as the light bands on the outer coat become visible.

The linkage between under and outer coat appears to be some-what loose and is therefore rather easily broken. I can recall a Standard Schnauzer seen in 1937 who was solid black at first sight but had a white undercoat on his legs and feet where the light markings show on a bicolor. The rest of his undercoat was dark. This dog's dam was a very light pepper and salt Swiss bitch. I have heard of a similar condition in a black Miniature. It might be due to crossing of the chromosomes, with broken linkage, or to incomplete dominance of A^s over a^t, since only one parent was black.

Double-coated breeds tend to shed twice a year, losing the outer coat mainly in the fall and the undercoat in the spring. This difference is less pronounced in wirehaired breeds than in those with longer coats. However, this tendency, plus stripping at the

331

requisite intervals, makes Schnauzers less inclined to shed around the house than the short-coated breeds, which lose a little hair constantly the year around. Whitney states that in particolor dogs the pigmented hairs are frequently longer than the white portions of the coat, and that black hairs grow longer than yellow. Chocolate hairs are said to grow longer than black but to be softer in texture, while yellow or red is finer and more silky. Such differences that are actually associated with color and not merely coincidence may be caused by the chemical effects that play a part in pigment formation and deposit.

The possibility of an infusion of Poodle blood in the Miniature Schnauzer at an early date is pointed up by the investigation of color in the breed, as well as by statements of German writers. Black Poodles would have been a possible source of the black color in Miniature Schnauzers around 1900. Silver poodles, which are born black and begin to turn silver by six or eight weeks old, show their full adult color by six or eight months. While length and quality of coat are of course different, the dark-tipped hairs which are light toward the body seem to belong to the same color group as the chinchilla Miniature Schnauzers. Although newborn Schnauzers are not as jet black as newborn silver Poodles, the comparison is at once obvious and suggests the probability of a relationship and perhaps G genes.

Eye color shows less variety than coat color. Some colors seem closely related to coat color, while others are independent or loosely linked. In the ordinary dog with E-, B-, D- and mm genes, the eyes are said to depend on three alleles which are dominant in the order dark (Ir), medium (ir^m) and light (or yellow) (ir^y). Incomplete dominance may give intermediate shades in heterozygotes. Though these are generally inherited independently of coat color, certain genes affect both. The dilution factor dd is said to produce smoky eyes and slaty noses as well as dilute black or "blue" color. Also bb, which produces brown or liver coats turns Ir eyes dark chestnut, ir^m eyes hazel, and ir^y eyes pale yellow. Most Miniature Schnauzers appear to have Ir or ir^m.

White dogs may have either pigmented or unpigmented skin, but when the hair is pigmented the skin beneath usually is pigmented too, although the color is not necessarily the same. (Some solid blacks have very white skin.) The pads of the feet are generally similar in color to the nose and eye rims. Toenails may vary on different toes of the same dog, but are usually dark unless the toe is white, and may then be either white or colored.

The color history of the Miniature Schnauzer appears to agree with the foregoing analysis. Early German writers on dogs in the nineteenth century state that the old German Pinscher stock, from which the Doberman Pinscher was likewise descended, was generally black and tan or *rehfarbig* (reddish). These dogs are said to have been crossed with German black Poodle and wolfgray Spitz (or perhaps, judging from pictures, with the forerunners of the German Shepherd) about 1850 to 1855. This presumably produced the Standard Schnauzer, after selective breeding. A subsequent cross to Affenpinschers or perhaps to the smooth-haired Miniature Pinscher, around 1885 to 1900, reduced the size of the Miniature and reintroduced the greater color variety which had largely been eliminated from the Standard Schnauzers.

When the first Miniature Schnauzers were imported into the United States and bred here during the late 1920's, the red color was still predominant. Even as late as 1935 a prominent Swiss breeder could write, "The Baltischhort type is still the best, but the brown color is no more wanted. It is not easy to have good color with good type." In a number of recorded cases Standard Schnauzer bitches were bred to Miniature males, a practice which doubtless improved color while causing wider variation in size.

The gray pepper and salt or "chinchillas" appeared in this country during the late 1920's often, as recessives from agouti parents. Grey Girl of Marienhof is an example. Certain imported strains, notably von Dornbusch and the related Bodo v. Schillerberg, excelled in color. These dogs were popular at stud on that account, but many of their puppies were bicolors. The dogs from the Chemnitz-Plauen strain, as represented by the early Marienhof and Wollaton stock, surpassed the others in the show ring and soon began to rival them in color. By 1936 the owner of Wollaton Kennels was able to write, "I have been getting 80 percent pure salt and pepper color in all my pups for the last year, with about 10 percent brown and 10 percent black with silver markings. My 1936 show string are all salt and pepper color excepting Jeff." Breeding a sufficient number of litters annually to allow a fairly wide choice, and then selecting young bitches of good color who were usually bred once or twice and then sold, retaining their best puppies, was the method employed by him. This resulted, in a few years, in a strain which was fairly uniform in blood and type, and soon had three or four generations of gray ancestors behind it. Most of the sires used after the first year or two were either bred in the kennel or purchased with a view to their suitability for Wollaton bitches. By combining color and type in the early generations the quality was good, and once the desired color was fixed the entire emphasis in selection could be placed on quality.

Marienhof Kennels employed a slightly different method. Starting with Chemnitz-Plauen stock which produced high quality show type from the beginning, the primary emphasis was placed upon conformation. Color improvement was also desired, and various experimental crosses were made with this end in view. However, they were often unsatisfactory. Instead of retaining only the best salt and pepper stock and going on from there, the best quality puppies were retained, as a rule, regardless of color. This method frequently resulted in a considerable number of bicolor and reddish puppies, but it produced some outstanding winners. Later uniformity in color developed more gradually. Other kennels of this early period that purchased and bred to Dornbusch and similar stock with a sole eye to color soon found themselves outclassed.

Not all color problems have been eliminated, however. Many dogs today are so light that they can hardly be called salt and pepper and are frequently registered as "silver" or "grey and white," colors not mentioned in the breed standard. It is unfortunate that in the 1957 revised standard the phrase "very light, whitish colors" was left out of the list of color faults. Many novices apparently do not even know that "salt and pepper" means a mixture produced by banded hairs, as described on page 314 of this section. Some of the very light colors often found today may be due to dilution factors such as d, or even b. Solid blacks or salt and peppers with one or both black parents might help correct too pale coloring but should be used with discretion. The black could also hide other recessives. The time to eliminate unwanted characteristics, whether old recessives or new mutations, is before the genes become widely distributed. For there may come a point of no return when it becomes difficult or impossible to find enough individuals who do not carry the undesirable fault.

334

We still have much to learn about color inheritance. I have made some tentative conclusions and suggested improved possibilities in the hope that they may be helpful and suggestive. Further observation and experiment will, it is to be hoped, confirm or disprove them. Though I differ with some of his conclusions and he gives less on the Schnauzers than on a number of other breeds, I have found Clarence C. Little's *The Inheritance of Coat Color in Dogs* the best book on the subject. Asdell's *Dog Breeding* gives useful summaries and indicates where authorities differ.

5

Puppy and Litter Size

PUPPIES vary in size at birth and also in rate of development. There are few actual statistics available, for not many breeders trouble to keep weight records and ordinary scales are not sufficiently accurate when the puppies are very small. Five to 6½ ounces at birth appears to be average.

While as a general rule the biggest puppy in the litter can be expected to grow large, this does not always happen. The rate of growth may vary greatly. Final size depends as much on how fast the puppy grows and for how long a time as it does on birth weight. Vigorous puppies often gain as much as one-half to one ounce per day during the first week and double or triple their birth weight in that time. Up to the age of three or four months they grow very fast, then begin to slow down. Small puppies do not grow quite so quickly and stop growing sooner. The puppies which go oversize usually grow rapidly during the first months and continue to grow more slowly for several months longer. A puppy with large feet can be depended on to grow into them, and a bitch usually continues to grow until her first heat, except when it is unusually delayed, but not much thereafter.

Weight charts compiled by Barclay Square Kennels indicate that puppies maturing at a correct size weighed from 13 oz. to 1 lb. 3 oz. at two weeks old. At four weeks they weighed 1 lb. 9 oz. to 2 lbs. 4 oz. Six-week-old puppies of correct size weighed 2 lbs. 8 oz. to 3 lbs. 5 oz. Most consistent of all were the eight-week-old puppies, ranging from 4 to 5 lbs. Bitches 4 to 4½ pounds and dogs 4¼ to 4¾ pounds at eight weeks seemed preferable. Puppies should be weighed at the same time of day and always either before or after the same meal. At three months start measuring shoulder height. This should be about 10 in. at three months, 11 in. at four months, and 12 in. at five months, give or take a small fraction. Weight at birth is of minor importance.

It is probable that a small bitch will have smaller puppies at birth than a very large bitch, but they may be no smaller when fully grown. If there are only one or two puppies in the litter they may be unusually large at birth, since they will have had the full benefit of the dam's food supply, but this effect is usually temporary. Even a big litter may consist of puppies fully up to the normal size if the dam is healthy and well fed.

One point to be noted is that the rate of growth is rapid just before birth, and consequently even two or three days make considerable difference. If a bitch whelps on the 58th or 59th day, instead of the 62nd or 63rd, her puppies will be proportionately smaller. In such a case, however, the difference is soon made up and by three weeks old the puppies whelped a few days early will have caught up with those that went full term.

Some litters are very even in size at birth and may remain so as they grow older. Sometimes a small puppy remains a runt, but if the difference in size is due to a less favorable location in the uterus, it may soon be made up. It is wise to watch the smallest puppy and make sure it gets its full share of milk. Otherwise the larger, stronger members of the litter may leave the small one only the dregs. If the small puppy has to work hard to obtain enough milk, instead of receiving first chance at a full nipple from which the milk runs easily, he may have to use more strength than he can afford. Also, the smaller puppy will have a smaller capacity and cannot hold as much milk at a time, so he will need to nurse more frequently than his larger littermates.

If the puppies of one litter are not uniform in size, the differences

337

All one litter, at 11 weeks. Barclay Square Brickbat and Becky Sharp (left) became champions.

tend to increase as the puppies grow older. It is not unusual for above average and below average puppies to occur in the same litter.

Litter size depends on many factors, including the age, condition, feeding and heredity of both parents, especially the dam. The bitch determines the maximum size of a litter, which naturally cannot be larger than the number of mature eggs available for fertilization when the mating takes place. (Of course, there is a possibility that some fertilized egg may divide into identical twins, but if identical twins do occur in dogs they are apparently rare.) The number of mature eggs that are available probably depends to a major degree upon the heredity of the bitch but may also vary according to the date of service.

When the eggs are already mature at the time of service a later service normally has no effect. Once the egg is fertilized a change immediately takes place in the covering of the cell so that no other sperm can enter. It is possible that an egg which matured later than the rest may be fertilized a couple of days later than the others. This is a possible cause of one or two very small puppies in a litter. However, eggs normally cease maturing very shortly after fertilization occurs.

Two matings within a few hours of each other certainly *can* both result in fertilization. Hence the need to be careful of the bitch *after* mating as well as before. Should she be accidentally bred to a different dog it would be impossible to tell which is the sire of the litter (unless the puppies are crossbred or of a color which would only be possible from one of the sires), and if the matings were not long apart some puppies may be by one male and some by the other.

If a bitch produces very small litters it may be advisable to try waiting a day or two and breeding her later in her heat. Young bitches bred for the first time seem to be inclined to produce slightly smaller litters, although this is not invariable. Bitches that are decidedly small for the breed also frequently have somewhat smaller litters than the average.

Aside from the maximum number as determined by the number of mature eggs available, various causes can operate to reduce the size of the litter. Authorities claim that many fertilized eggs do not develop to full term. In addition to puppies born dead or whelped only partially developed, many probably are lost at such an early date that the breeder is unaware of the fact. Sometimes a bitch fails to carry her entire litter beyond the early stages. She may begin to show in whelp, then go back to normal size. The partly developed embryos are resorbed, and the owner thinks she has missed or talks of a "false pregnancy." Actually, the bitch was in whelp but did not carry the litter to term. This is said to happen if a bitch contracts Carré's distemper soon after being bred, which may easily happen in the course of shipment by express to be mated. The bitch shows no signs of the disease superficially but loses her litter. Afterwards, however, she is permanently immune. On the other hand, if infection occurs not long before the whelping date, the bitch becomes seriously ill after whelping and the puppies are not immune and almost always die.

The failure of some of the fertilized eggs in a litter to develop sufficiently for their loss to be evident can be due to various reasons. The age, health, and nutrition of the bitch undoubtedly have some influence. Old bitches may resorb their entire litter unless treated with hormones, although bitches as old as ten or 12 years have been known to whelp living puppies. Very fat bitches often miss entirely. Probably the eggs do not mature normally. Some of the fertilized eggs that do not develop may not be firmly planted in the uterus. Other fertilized eggs may contain lethal factors which prevent their developing properly. A number of causes may operate together to reduce the size of the litter from the theoretical maximum. The best way to insure a good-sized litter is to select a healthy bitch from a reasonably prolific line, see that her food includes all necessary elements as well as being of the right amount, and exercise her well before she comes in season. It is true that some bitches seem to produce sizeable litters regardless of condition or care; however, they are the exception.

The sire as well as the dam plays a part in determining the number of puppies in a litter. The very fact that millions of sperms are emitted in one ejaculation indicates that an enormous quantity fail to reproduce at all. If the sperm swarm is too dilute, or many sperms are abnormal, a dog may fail to sire any puppies whatever. Or he may sire smaller than average litters. Studs vary, and some can handle a much greater number of services than can others. A dog that is inclined to miss may do better if bred to fewer bitches.

How a puppy changes: Frick Anfiger at 6
weeks, uncropped.

Frick at 3 months, after cropping.

Frick at 10 months.

Wilkern Scotch Teviot with a litter two hours old.

Studies made with fruit flies and laboratory animals indicate that the genes carry many lethal factors which prevent the development of living or normal offspring. A few lethal or semilethal factors have been recognized in various breeds of dogs. These often seem to be connected with color (perhaps these are easier to identify), like the lethal yellow found in mice, and include the semilethal harlequin of Great Danes, Dunkerhounds and blue merle Collies. If a stud dog carries more than the usual number of lethal factors, the size of his litters is likely to be smaller. Since the embryos often die too early for their loss to be noted by the owner, there is no visible evidence of the fact except in reduced litter size. The more lethal factors a dog carries the greater the likelihood that a bitch to whom he is bred carries some of the same lethals. Hence, the more likely it is that a double dose will prevent the embryos' development. In strong inbreeding there is even greater likelihood that a closely related bitch will have several of the same lethal factors as the dog. For this reason, highly inbred litters may be somewhat smaller than outcross matings. This may be one cause of the "hybrid vigor" that is claimed to result from outcrossing. Naturally this result would hold good only if there were a considerable number of lethal factors present in the closely related parents. In the case of a strong outcross, an equal number of lethal factors may actually be present, but if they were not the same ones the resulting combination would not lead to the doubling of identical factors which makes them lethal. Unquestionably, certain bitches seem to have large litters regularly, and this tends to run in families.

It is difficult to obtain information on the number of puppies actually whelped per litter in this country. Probably there is no substantial difference here and abroad. For a period of eight years, from 1934 through 1942, the German studbook (Miniature Schnauzer) contained full information as to the number of puppies actually whelped, plus figures as to stillbirths, puppies intentionally destroyed and those that died before registration. Occasionally it is stated that part of a litter was raised by a foster mother. A spot check of the last volume indicates that if this is typical, about one litter in 11 is likely to contain a stillborn puppy. Only three litters out of 283 had two puppies stillborn, and none had more than two. However, it should be noted that any litters in which all the puppies died before or immediately after birth would not have been registered at all. Therefore, there would be no records of one puppy which was stillborn or of two puppies both stillborn. Since there was no indication as to how soon after birth the additional deaths occurred no count of these was made.

The German figures show an average for the eight years of 4.1 puppies per litter, distributed as follows:

Puppies in litter	Number of litters
1	48
2	136
3	379
4	495
5	392
6	212
7	65
8	20
9	0
10	1
Total: 7174 puppies	Total: 1748 litters

There were no litters of nine puppies and the sole litter of ten was out of Assi v. Kobelberg. In the United States the breed record was for many years held by Abigail of Marienhof, with two litters of ten. Then in 1958 and again in 1960 Doman Copy whelped litters of eleven but did not raise all in either case. Another bitch, Nordot Dazzle, whelped nine, eleven and ten puppies in three successive litters, raising eight, ten and ten to weaning age. The thirty puppies were by three different sires. Abigail of Marienhof and a dam of nine, Woots of Sharvogue, are both in Ch. Dorem Display's pedigree.

The eight volumes of the German studbook for which detailed figures are available contained 1,748 litters, of which the largest number contained four puppies (495 litters or 28.31 percent of the total number of litters). There are more litters of five puppies (22.36 percent) than of three (21.68 percent). Nearly three-quarters (72.35 percent) of the total number of litters, or 1,266 out of 1,748, consisted of from three to five puppies. Litters of six, though less common than litters of three, are over 50 percent more common than litters of two, and litters of seven are over 25 percent more common than litters of only one. Litters of eight are comparatively rare, averaging only 2½ per year for the eight-year period, while over eight occur so seldom as to be negligible.

344

More than half the number of litters (1,058 litters out of 1,748) contained four puppies or less, making 3,317 puppies altogether. This was 60½ percent of all litters but only 46.23 percent of all the puppies. Of all the litters, 39½ percent (690 litters) contained five or more puppies (3,857), which was 53.77 percent of the total number of puppies. Consequently, there were more puppies from the larger litters than from the smaller ones.

By selecting breeding stock from large litters it might be possible to raise the average, though there is always a tendency for extremes to revert to what is normal for the breed. There is too much variation, however, to lay down any hard and fast rules. Litter sisters may vary consistently, and the daughters of a bitch who produces average-sized litters may have large ones. Or the reverse may be true. The record-holding Abigail of Marienhof was from a prolific dam, but the latter, Fiffi or Marlou, came from a bitch who never had more than four to a litter. The German Miniature Schnauzer dam of ten, Assi v. Kobelberg, came from a litter of five, and her dam was one of only three. Some bitches regularly have large litters, while an occasional big one may be whelped by a bitch whose litters are usually average. Nevertheless, unless the dam has a large supply of milk or a foster mother is available, the puppies are likely to get a better start if there are not too many of them. Since it is usually a matter of luck deciding which is best at birth, it is hard to choose which puppies to keep if the dam has more than she can handle. Consequently, there is no great advantage in very big litters.

Small litters are likely to go full term, or even over, when the individual puppies may be big enough to cause the bitch trouble when she whelps. Large litters frequently come early, but this is not always the case. If the bitch is very distended the uterus may be so stretched that it loses its elasticity and does not contract properly. Then it may be necessary to have the assistance of a veterinarian to avoid the risk of a ruptured uterus.

A new litter, eyes closed and tails uncut.

Bibliography for Genetics and Color Breeding

Asdell, Sydney A., *Dog Breeding: Reproduction and Genetics.* Boston: Little Brown & Company, 1966.

Asimov, Isaac, *The Genetic Code.* New York: Grossman Publishers, Inc., 1963.

Burns, Marca and Fraser, M. N., *Genetics of the Dog: The Basis of Successful Breeding.* Philadelphia: J. B. Lippincott Company, 1967.

Frankling, Eleanor, *Practical Dog Breeding and Genetics.* New York: Arco Publishing Company, Inc., 1963.

Hutt, Frederick B., *Animal Genetics.* New York: The Ronald Press Company, 1964.

Little, Clarence C., *The Inheritance of Coat Color in Dogs.* New York: Howell Book House Inc., 1967.

Whitney, Leon F., *How to Breed Dogs.* New York: Howell Book House Inc., 1966.

Winge, Ojvind, *Inheritance in Dogs.* Ithaca, N.Y.: Comstock Publishing Associates (Div. of Cornell University Press), 1950.

It. Ch. Jovinus Rhythm, English-Bred.

Part III

BLACK MINIATURE SCHNAUZERS

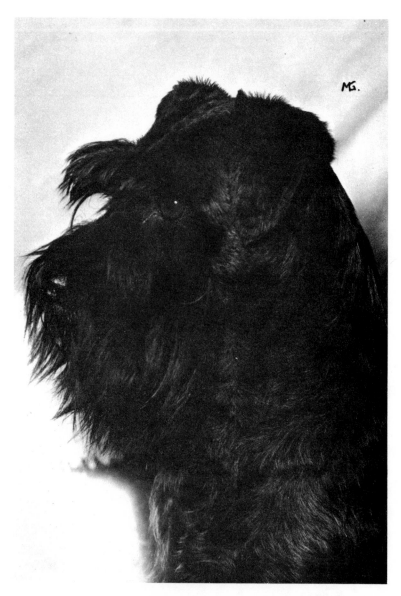

Head study of Australian Ch. Jovinus Rigoletto.

1

The History of Black
Miniature Schnauzers

Black Miniatures played a major role in the
formation of the breed in Germany. Peter v. Westerberg, whelped
in 1902, was one of the three main pillars of the breed, although
today most of his tail male descendants are salt and peppers. Modern blacks derive their color in part from Peter's female descendants; from the black bitch Nettel v.d. Goldbach, whelped before
1904; from Schwarze Hexe (breeding unknown), whelped in 1914;
and from Nelly (Pabel), also of unknown breeding, whelped in 1918.

Blacks were imported to the United States in the middle 1920's
but were few in number and attracted little attention. Most of the
black bitches were mated to salt and pepper males and have left
only salt and pepper descendants. The first American-bred black
recorded was Medor Black Lady, out of Alma v.d. Zunkunft (PSZ
2268). Through a salt and pepper daughter, Sue of Marlou, Alma is
the tail female ancestress of many Family III producers (tracing to
Grethel v. Hohenstein and her dam Alli v.d. Goldbach), with
substantial additions in recent years.

Ch. Turko Chemnitz-Plauen,
whelped 1912.

Karat v. Abbagamba at 3 months, 1930.

KS. Taps v. Düsselstein, 1928.

Another early black with numerous salt and pepper descendants, though not in direct tail female line, was Bässi v.d. Rissener Heide, whelped in 1930.

The first serious attempt to breed blacks was made by Mrs. Willia N. Maguire of California, now an honorary member of the Black Miniature Schnauzer Fanciers' Association. Mrs. Nion R. Tucker had imported a black pair, Heliaster and Heimia v. Abbagamba, who produced a litter of seven in October 1930. They were litter brother and sister, by S. Eros v. Abbagamba ex Filanda v. Abbagamba, both blacks, and had three black grandparents. The fourth, S. Fatzke Baltischhort, gave a male line to the salt and pepper Prinz v. Rheinstein.

Standard–Miniature crosses were still technically allowable at that time, so Tuckaway Bambisito, a son of Heliaster and Heimia, was mated to Vinci of Tuckaway, a small Standard double granddaughter of the famous Ch. Claus v.d. Fuerstenwall. From this mating, which produced solid blacks and black and silvers, came all the old Bambivin strain. Tuckaway Bozra, brother of Bambisito, was also used once. A black and silver bitch, Isandra Anfiger, was bred to Heliaster and his grandson, Gnome Claus of Bambivin, and a black Austrian importation, Diavolo v. Rotherz, was also used.

The first black AKC champion, and as of 1967 the only American-bred one, Cunning Asta of Bambivin (whelped January 15, 1935), was by Heliaster out of Inky of Bambivin, a Bambisito–Vinci daughter. Asta went Best in Match all-breeds at the age of 4½ months and finished her title in July 1936 with a Group third at Santa Cruz, California. She remained with her breeder-owner until her death in September 1951 at the age of 16 years and 8 months. Never a prolific producer—she was well under 12 inches in size—only four of Asta's puppies out of three litters lived to maturity. Although her daughters Fiji and Honey Lamb of Bambivin both had litters, and her son Jung Diabolo of Bambivin sired several, her line appears to be extinct. The last known descendant, a male called Ebony whelped in 1950, was still living in 1961, but an attempt to obtain a litter by him failed.

The old Bambivin male line continued down to Edric of Bambivin from Heliaster through Gnome Claus and his son Yeppo. Whelped in February 1949, Edric sired a litter at the age of 11 and is represented today through four daughters. Frou Frou Isa of

Eng. Ch. Enstone Beda, 1937.

Mrs. Dennis with Putzi of Offley, about
1935.

Bambivin (out of her sire's litter sister Emmy Lou of Bambivin) was owned by Windy Hill Kennels and appears in the pedigrees of the salt and peppers Ch. Windy Hill Jiminy Cricket and Am. & Can. Ch. Howtwo Here's How. Hunie and Von Gearin's Buttons, from Edric's last litter, have both been bred; however, it is through Topsy of Paradise, a daughter of the salt and pepper Tykhof's Emmi (by Ch. Neff's Scoop ex Ch. Sindi v. Rogar) that the old Bambivin line has played an important part in the blacks of today.

The mating of Edric and Topsy produced two daughters who were both bred to Heigo v. Neuhermsheim, who was acquired in Germany by Lt.-Col. Earle P. Schouten. Heigo, who was sired in 1948 and died in 1956, was a son of Hasso z. Quelle, by Puck v. Freyersheim. He thus belonged to one of the principal German black lines, that of S. Fredi v. Düsselstein, going back eventually to Bendor Chemnitz-Plauen, son of Gift Chemnitz-Plauen. There is no record that any of Heigo's sons were used for breeding, but his daughter ChoCho, and their daughter Bambi of Bambivin, have been major factors in the blacks produced in America during the past ten years. Heidi of Belvedere's line, though still producing, is not very numerous.

The second black AKC champion was the imported male, Hupp v. Schönhardt of Crystal, whelped April 19, 1936 and imported late in 1938. He left a number of litters in Germany, where his descendants are numerous, and a number have subsequently been imported. Although Hupp headed William F. Kubach's Crystal Kennels in Berlin, Conn., and finished his title in 1942, he has few American descendants and most are salt and peppers. Mr. Kubach was the first Eastern breeder to specialize in blacks and continued to breed them until about 1950, when he gave up breeding because of poor health. The last black tail male descendant of this line, Iolaus Anfiger, whelped in 1957, sired two litters in 1964 but no black sons.

The third black AKC champion, the imported bitch Dirndl v. Schloss Helmstadt, completed her title in 1950 and is the only German import since World War II who has finished as of 1967. She left at least two litters in Germany, and among her European descendants are It. Chs. Malya Titbit and Malya Uebi, Eng. Ch. Jovinus Malya Swanee, his son Australian Ch. Jovinus Rigoletto, and ISC., KS. Cosi v. Waldrautenschlösschen. From her two American litters, Dirndl's sole producer was the daughter Heathcote

Black Beauty, by Ch. Wilkern Clickety Clack. Through four daughters and a son, Beauty has a considerable number of black descendants, and her grandson Harter's Black Joe is the great-great-grandsire of the 1965 salt and pepper Ch. Ty-Bets Mr. Talisman.

Two additional bitches who have produced a number of litters and have numerous descendants in the United States are Karen v. Scheffeleck and Iris v. Mittelrhein, the latter by S. Dorn v. Bexbach. Both were owned by Allen C. Ade, who has been one of the most active black breeders in the East.

In England, the Jovinus Kennels have successfully combined the winning Italian line of Signora Pozzi's Malya Kennels with descendants of the prewar Enstone blacks which produced Eng. Ch. Enstone Beda in 1936. The Jovinus foundation black bitch, Redenhall Hella, traced back to the Dutch Enstone Gerti van Duinslust, imported by Mr. Hancock of Enstone in 1928 and believed to be the first of the breed to reach England. The other principal source of blacks in that country is Mrs. Boubelik's Austrian Dyk v. Robertshof, mated to several descendants of the prewar Enstone blacks.

Up to 1967, all the blacks in Australia were still the get or grandget of Jovinus Rigoletto, the first black imported, who finished his championship in November 1965—the first black to do so in that country. A black son, Koniglich the Groom, came to the United States in the summer of 1965. With Rigoletto's three brothers—Jovinus Rodin of Anfiger, Jovinus Royal Rogue and Camoli's Island Jovinus—and a sister, Jovinus Rebel Rouser, all by Eng. Ch. Jovinus Malya Swanee out of the winning Jovinus Risotto, there is a nucleus of this line in the United States. These trace in tail male to Am. Ch. Hupp v. Schönhardt through his German son Jörg v. Mumlingtal. The Italian male Piper del Tornese, imported in 1968, is closely related, but goes in male line via Ch. Blitz v. Vogelwoog to Puck v. Freyersheim.

Comparatively few German imported males thus far have had an appreciable influence on the breed, but some others should be mentioned. Lump v. Lubeke's daughter, Lubeke's Wilhelmena, has had several litters, at least one by Gero v. Niddertal, a son of the popular sire Firbo v. Nägelhof, who also traces to Hupp v. Schönhardt. Bogey v.d. Rennenburg, with 12 lines to Hupp, traces in tail male to Hupp's sire, Giff v. Abbagamba. His son, Jimarlo's Blue Beard, may carry on this line.

Eng. Ch. Jovinus Malya Swanee, 1964.

Continental blacks of the 1940's.

The C.C. Winner Jovinus Risotto and puppies, 1961.

Arri v.d. Bärenfeste, who has sired several litters, is the sixth generation from Hasso z. Quelle, sire of Heigo v. Neuhermsheim; and Heiko v. Rodenstein is the seventh from Hasso's sire, Puck v. Freyersheim. Lump v. Lubeke and Golo v.d. Saarschleife also belong to this line, as do Benno v.d. Bärenfeste, Juno v. Schwanental (a male!), Barri v. Bernstein and Faruck v. Murgtal. Itzig v. Muhlgarten traces to Giff v. Abbagamba, while Job v.d. Burg Heldenstein and the Italian-bred Nelson dei Diavoli Neri go to Hupp v. Schönhardt. The Swiss pedigree of Bambo-Espero, by Zitto-Espero, traces to Puck via S. Alf v.d. Brunnenwiese. Hannes v. Heidenhorst, CDX, who went Winners Dog at Dubuque in 1965, traces to Puck through BS. Igor v. Saumhof. Darry v. Nibelungengold, another recent import, is a son of triple Ch. Dorn v. Bexbach, also tracing in tail male to Puck.

The imported black males who have been used for breeding during recent years belong to either the Hupp–Giff v. Abbagamba line or the Puck v. Freyersheim branch of the Fredi v. Düsselstein line. However, the great majority of American blacks trace to salt and pepper lines, most of them going back to Ch. Dorem Display. The most numerous of these are the descendants of Belvedere Caesar, with at least eight sons who have sired litters, including Little Black Sambo, Hamann's Falla, UD, Aswad ben Bambi and Chester's Yago. Besides the Display lines, there is at least one through Ralwick's Resolute to Ch. Tweed Packet of Wilkern and Ch. Sandman of Sharvogue. So long as the breeding of blacks to salt and peppers continues, there is likely to be a variety of male lines and many open pedigrees. It is still too early to predict what will turn out to be the outstanding black producing lines.

In Germany during the past decade the top producers seem to have belonged to the Puck v. Freyersheim line. Puck's great-great-grandson, Arri v. Limburgerhof, left many descendants through BS. Igor v. Saumhof and other sons. Most notable of Arri's get, however, was KS. Bodo v. Riedwald, sire of WS. Gin v. Rosengarten and triple Ch. Dorn v. Bexbach. Gin's son Coni v.d. Batschka has been very popular. Dorn sired three international champions, all of which have in turn produced title winners—BS. '64 & KS. Owid v. Termeerhofen, Int. Ch. & KS. Blitz v. Vogelwoog, and KS. & Belg. Ch. Klaus v. Bexbach, the latter sire of BS. '62-'63 & KS. Droll v. Kurfürstenplatz, who sired BS. Bodo v.d. Weihrichshöhe, the fifth generation of Siegers in male line. Blitz sired the 1966 BSn. Kitty v. Einsiedlerhof and KS. Jokeli v. Einsiedlerhof, and Owid sired the 1967 Bundessieger.

Another outstanding line comes from the Puck grandson KS. Dido v. Saumhof. One of Dido's sons, BS. Alf v.d. Brunnenwiese, sired BS. Dolf v. Rosengarten and KS. Basko v. Mittelrhein, who in turn sired KS. Groll v.d. Schurwaldhöhe. Another Dido son, ISC. Jackel v.d. Burg Heldenstein, sired KS. & BS. Sepp v.d. Burg Heldenstein and BS., KS. & ISC. Etzel v.d. Heinrichsburg. Etzel sired KS. Fredachs v. Mittelrhein and KS. & BS. Mohr v. Gross Wiesbaden, another four-generation male line. Sepp was the maternal grandsire of Dorn v. Bexbach, but his tail male descendants are through the untitled sons Eliot v.d. Burg Heldenstein and Groll v. Lubeke. Eliot's son Scheich v.d. Burg Heldenstein sired BS. & KS. Yopo v.d. Burg Heldenstein. Groll sired Wulf v. Lubeke, sire of KS. Wiggi v. Aichelehof. KS. Gollo v.d. Burg Heldenstein, by Eliot, was the top black sire of the breed in number of litters whelped during 1963 (as published in the 1964 studbook).

The most successful producing line from Hupp v. Schönhardt is that from Jörg v. Mümlingtal, whose grandson KS. Quick v. Nibelungenhort sired Juwel v. Neuhermsheim, sire of KS. Prinz v. Rauental. Another Juwel son, Kuno v. Osterhof, sired Karo v.d. Grafschaft Oberndorf. Karo's son Firbo v. Nägelshof was for a time the most popular black sire in Germany. His son KS. & BS. Enzo v.d. Burg Heldenstein ranked next to Gollo v.d. Burg Heldenstein in popularity in 1963 and sired KS. Karo v.d. Burg Heldenstein. Another Firbo son is KS. Zio v.d. Burg Heldenstein.

It should be remembered that the opportunities to win German or ISC titles are comparatively limited. In 1960, for instance, five black Miniature Schnauzers won eight titles among them. Hence the top German sires and dams have few title-winning progeny compared to those in the United States. The leading bitch in recent years appears to be Alma v.d. Grafschaft Oberndorf. Her sire traced to Hasso z. Quelle, and her dam was a Hasso granddaughter with considerable Burghausen and Schönhardt blood. It is interesting to note that a younger full sister, Dora v. Grafschaft Oberndorf, was the dam of Karo and granddam of Firbo v. Nägelshof. Alma produced four title winners—Dorle, Ella, and Fredachs v. Mittelrhein, by Etzel v.d. Heinrichsburg, and Basko v. Mittelrhein, by Alf

ISC., KS. Cosi v. Waldrautenschlösschen, 1964.

It. Ch. Malya Uebi.

v.d. Brunnenwiese. Nelke v.d. Nibelungenhort was by KS. Quick
v.d. Nibelungenhort of the Hupp v. Schönhardt male line, and
both her granddams were Burg Heldenstein breeding. Nelke produced BS. & KS. Bessie v. Rosengarten and BS. & KS. Dolf v.
Rosengarten by Alf v.d. Brunnenwiese, and WS. & KS. Gin v.
Rosengarten by KS. Bodo v. Riedwald. Yalta v.d. Burg Heldenstein, younger than Alma or Nelke, was by Scheich v.d. Burg
Heldenstein; she produced KS. Gollo v.d. Burg Heldenstein by her
half brother Eliot and KS. Karo v.d. Burg Heldenstein by Enzo v.d.
Burg Heldenstein.

While in Germany there is a flourishing male line of salt and
peppers descended from Peter v. Westerberg, his black line has
almost disappeared there. Only 17 litters have been registered in the
past six years, although there were five in 1960. All these blacks
trace to Apollo v. Liethberg, a son of Imago v. Abbagamba, through
either Hallo v. Mazeppa or Giff v. Liethberg. Hallo's line via Bubi
v. Osning, whose dam was strong in Peterl v.d. Werneburg blood,
comes down through Darius v. Haindlhof, whelped in 1957. Darius'
sons Amor and Axel v. Fahninghof together sired three litters in
1964, and Axel placed third with the rating of "Excellent" at the
Düsseldorf show that year. The Axel son Arko v. Hinterhof sired a
litter with four males in 1966. Giff v. Liethberg's line comes through
Giff v. Rade, Arko v.d. Münde (who sired a number of litters),
Dodo and Fritzi v. St. Pauli, to Ali Baba v. Träberhof, who sired
two litters in 1964.

The Peter black line does not appear to have produced any
Siegers in Germany since before World War II, but S. Oswien v.
Königseck and his son S. Radi v. Königseck seem to have gone to
Austria, where Oswien's great-grandson, Persy v. Schenkenfelden,
made his title. Persy's son, Dyk v. Robertshof, went to England in
the late 1940's, and Dyk's brother Dero had grandchildren whelped
in Italy in 1958, so there may well be others of this line in Austria,
Italy, or Switzerland. Since S. Egon v. Mümlingtal was sold to
Switzerland, there may also be some of his descendants there, or
even among the small number of Swiss imports during recent years
whose descent I have been unable to ascertain.

As previously mentioned, Diavolo v. Rotherz, son of S. Radi v.
Königseck, has no known living descendants. He seems to be the
only imported black male of the Peter line used at stud in the U.S.

At the close of World War II, very few blacks remained in this country, and there was almost no interest in breeding them. However, they were steadily gaining popularity in Germany, where the number of blacks registered annually was soon to equal and then to surpass the salt and peppers. (In 1965, more than twice as many blacks as salt and peppers were registered there.) Many service people acquired them as pets while overseas and brought them back when they returned home. Undine v. Salzland, a black imported bitch owned by Mrs. Vera Kantor of Sugar Grove, Pa., produced several litters by salt and pepper males and has black descendants from at least five daughters: Flirtation Walk Melissa, Mona Lisa, Pixie, Whimsey, and Winsome. By far the most numerous are from Pixie, whose daughter Waggs Wiggles was the dam of Belvedere Caesar. Acquired as a puppy by Lt.-Col. Schouten, Caesar undoubtedly appears in the pedigrees of a majority of American-bred blacks at this time. A son of the salt and pepper Ch. Belvedere Sensation, he traces in male line to Ch. Dorem Tempo, Ch. Delegate of Ledahof and Ch. Dorem Display. He was bred repeatedly to ChoCho and Bambi of Bambivin, whose progeny thus combine three black lines—the old prewar Bambivins, Heigo v. Neuhermsheim and Undine v. Salzland. Caesar was also a successful sire of obedience winners, including the first black UD, Hamann's Falla.

Breeders of black Miniatures in the U.S. face a different situation from that encountered by breeders of salt and peppers. Nearly all the latter are descended from prewar stock derived from a comparatively small number of imported individuals, as discussed elsewhere. Even "outcross" matings go back sooner or later to related lines. The prewar blacks likewise had a common background, but so few of them remained by the late 1950's that it was necessary to begin all over again with postwar importations.

By the 1950's, German and American type in all colors had come to vary considerably. The German preference for rather sparse, hard furnishings combined with a tendency toward lighter bone and lower-set tails proved to be a handicap to imported salt and peppers in the American show ring. Blacks faced the additional handicap of a color unfamiliar to most breeders and judges. Even today there is a tendency for the average judge to disregard the blacks, no matter how good they may be. Or he may spend an undue amount of time going over a good one looking for nonexistent faults and end by

362

Hummel v. Falkenberg and his daughter Butzi v. Murten-
stern (Swiss).

It. Ch. Malya Titbit, brother of Malya Uebi.

Jovinus Rodin of Anfiger as a puppy.

A litter of blacks by
Jovinus Rodin of Anfiger.

putting the black down anyway. Very few seem to have the courage of their convictions. The breeder of blacks, then, requires a dog of exceptional quality to stand a chance of winning, while most of the imported blacks are not of the type which is desired.

Many of the blacks brought back to this country since the war were purchased as pets by novice owners who knew nothing of the breed, and hence the dogs were not of show quality. If they were bred, it was usually completely at random to any black available, just because he was black, or to a salt and pepper even more casually selected. Breeders being few and widely scattered, even a good black from a top producing line was unlikely to find a mate of suitable type and breeding readily available. Partly for this reason, many black bitches were bred to salt and pepper males. On the other hand, since comparatively few owners of salt and pepper bitches wished to breed them to blacks, the black males had fewer opportunities.

Because of the wartime interruption, no postwar importations were closely related to American-bred stock, while the blacks were complete outcrosses for the salt and peppers with no common ancestors for many generations. Even the imported German blacks (since registrations there had increased so enormously) were usually so remotely related to each other as to make linebreeding difficult. Any improvement in type gained by selection would be difficult to fix and retain.

The Black Miniature Schnauzer Fanciers' Association was founded in March 1958 through the instigation of Mrs. Pauline de B. Bninska of Florida, with Earle P. Schouten as the first president. It now includes approximately 60 members from 29 states, including Hawaii, as well as England, Canada, Australia, Italy, and Switzerland. The object of the association is to improve the quality of the blacks being produced by giving advice, information, and encouragement to breeders. It publishes a newsletter, *The Blackboard,* and has supported several special "black" issues of *Schnauzer Shorts* magazine, the latest was in February 1974. Information is available from the secretary, Mrs. Frank T. Eskrigge, 482 Whiting Street, Hanover, Mass. 02339.

Blacks Since 1967

Up to 1969 there had not been a black champion finished in the USA since 1950. In June 1969 the bitch Johnson's Ebony Kwicksilver went Winners at the Paul Revere Miniature Schnauzer Club specialty, and went on to complete her title the following December,— the first American-bred black champion since 1936. An increasing number of good quality blacks began to appear in the show ring, some of them shown by top handlers.

In 1972 the first black American-bred male, Woodhaven's Black Gough Drops, finished his title and subsequently won two Group Firsts—a record for the color. "Lucky" is a son of Gough's Ebony Knight Longleat, a half-brother to Kwicksilver. Both of them were sired by the late Gough's Ebony Royal Guardsman, a son of the English-bred Jovinus Rodin of Anfiger.

The next year Arbury Gay Uncle Sam, a tail male descendant of the English-bred Australian Ch. Jovinus Rigoletto (Rodin's full brother) became the second American-bred black male to finish. Sired by Tammashann's Black Onyx out of an imported German black, Sam's pedigree is the most consistently black-bred of the current winners, with no salt & pepper and only one black & silver in three generations.

In 1974 still another black male finished, Aljamar Tommy Gun, who went Winners at Westminster and topped the breed at the Chicago International. Tommy Gun is by the imported Italian Ch. Malya Gunter, who traces in tail male to the Puck v. Freyersheim line, but also goes twice to Ch. Malya Quiz, who is out of Eng. Ch. Malya Swanee's full sister, Ch. Malya Uebi, and also to Swanee himself, through his daughter, Italian Ch. Jovinus Rhythm. The Jovinus blacks all trace to Am. Ch. Hupp von Schönhardt of Crystal through the latter's German get.

Several blacks have finished in Canada during the past two or three years, the first being the late Winsor's Jon Martinique, by Winsor's Johann B. The latter was sired by Kafka, a son of Harter's Black Joe (by the salt and pepper Ch. Hit Parade's Blacksmith Blues). He therefore traces in male line to Ch. Dorem Display, through the latter's son Ch. Diplomat of Ledahof. The first Canadian champion black bitch, Halland's Black Rose, is also by Johann B., making him the only black sire with two Canadian champions to his credit. Black Rose finished in 1973. In early 1974 the first Canadian-bred black to finish, Killock's Red Toby Anfiger, by Aymar Anfiger out of Girly Carmen, was followed by his half-brother, Killock's Theophilus, a son of the salt and Pepper C. Killock's Theodosius and Girly Carmen, making her the first black bitch with two title winners to her credit. Girly is a daughter of Am. & Can. Ch. Kansho Play Boy's Replica and the black Alador's Kadarwina Anfiger. Both Red Toby and Theophilus are owned by Mrs. Mary Summers of Newfoundland, who is also the latter's breeder. Through their dam they carry a line to Jovinus Rodin of Anfiger, while Red Toby's sire is a grandson of Rodin's younger brother, Jovinus Royal Rogue, CDX. The latter is the top black sire of Obedience title winners in the US.

Several other blacks of both sexes have been doing considerable winning during 1974 and some at least will probably be added to the growing list of champions in the near future. Interest in blacks has been increasing steadily, but they are still at a disadvantage in the show ring under many judges who seem reluctant to put them up or not sufficiently self-confident to do so. Breeding and showing blacks is still a challenge requiring hard work and careful planning.

2

The Genetic Makeup
of Blacks

IT is easy to say that black is dominant over other colors, but this does not explain why, nor does it explain precisely what happens when colors are crossed. Our knowledge of color inheritance has certainly increased during recent years but is still far from complete, and there are many factors involved that are far from clear. When we speak of a "gene for black coat" we are actually using a verbal shortcut to express a fairly complicated situation, for there is no single gene that will produce black by itself. Certain genes are found in most dogs and therefore can be assumed to be present in blacks. Others are found less generally and vary from breed to breed. Another group of genes must be present to produce black, but even so can only do so in combination with still others.

The various genetic series and their effects have been discussed in the chapter on color inheritance in Part II. Most Miniature Schnauzers, regardless of color, carry the following genes, usually in homozygous form: BB, $c^{ch}c^{ch}$, DD, EE, mm, SS, and tt. It is possible that some jet blacks or even dark salt and peppers may be CC

or Cc^{ch}, but this is not certain. It seems highly probable that many salt and peppers carry the dominant G for progressive graying from birth to old age, rather than the recessive gg found in normal dark-pigmented dogs which show no such change. The main difference in color, however, results from the various alleles of the A series. It is true that B, D and E are all essential for the production of black in any breed, and solid-colored dogs that carry bb, dd or ee will accordingly be of some other color such as red, yellow or liver, but these recessive forms are very rarely found in Miniature Schnauzers.

A black Miniature carries much the same combination of dominant genes as a black Newfoundland, Cocker Spaniel or Labrador Retriever. On the other hand, the recessives carried may vary widely according to whether color selection in the past has encouraged a considerable variety or frowned on all but one or two colors. Until shortly before 1938, blacks and salt and peppers were interbred at will. Why the German Club then prohibited this is uncertain, but presumably it was believed that too many intermediate or un-wanted colors were produced. Consequently, in Germany and else-where on the Continent blacks can now be bred only to blacks. Continental imports may therefore have seven, eight or more gener-ations of blacks behind them and are unlikely to carry recessives for either salt and pepper or black and silver, although this is not wholly impossible even after so many generations. Hence puppies from a German (or other Continental) black parent are almost invariably all black, regardless of the color of the other parent.

Going back to the A series of genes, only the top allele, A^s, pro-duces solid color, and since no other solid color but black is nor-mally found in the breed it is usually this gene that determines whether or not a particular dog is to be black. Lower alleles of this series are a^y, a^w and a^t, in that order. It is probable that a^y produced many of the reddish grizzle salt and peppers that were common in the 1920's and early 1930's but have since largely disappeared. The normal salt and pepper is a^w, produced by the typical banded hairs in contrast to hairs of a single color throughout. Recessive to all three of the above is a^t, known as bicolor or tan points and more commonly called black and silver. In this the whiskers, spots above the eyes, chest, lower legs, abdomen and around the anus are light and the rest of the dog black. Since this allele is the lowest of the series, black and silvers are necessarily $a^t a^t$, and two black and silvers

Ch. Woodhaven's Black Gough Drop is the first American-bred male black champion. He is also a group winner. *Olson photo*.

Canadian Ch. Winsor's Jon Martinique, the first black Canadian champion. *Bill Francis*.

should produce all black and silver puppies. Of course, any of the higher colors that carry a^t (whether $A^s a^t$, $a^y a^t$ or $a^w a^t$) can transmit it, and the black and silver will appear when two carriers are mated. This means that two blacks, two salt and peppers, or a black and a salt and pepper may produce black and silver puppies if both carry a^t. In fact, a majority of black and silvers have had at least one parent of another color, and very often two. It is only recently the increased interest in them has led to matings of two individuals of this color. Theoretically it should be easy to produce black and silvers that would breed true.

When breeding solid blacks there are two principal requirements: (1) superiority of physical type, as with any individual, and (2) jet black color, without markings or shading of any sort. While the German standard formerly permitted a small white spot on the chest (as does the American standard today) this is not desired. The former ruling does indicate, however, that such markings must once have been too frequent to ban them outright.

The improvement of type depends primarily on selection of quality foundation stock and the choice of suitable matings. If not enough good blacks are available, the obvious remedy would be to mate the best blacks to top salt and peppers. It is here that color problems are likely to begin. Since black is dominant over salt and pepper, the result in the first generation should be all solid blacks indistinguishable in color from the black parent, if indeed such parent is a homozygous black. However, it is in the second generation that the problems arise. If the heterozygous black offspring are bred back to a homozygous black, any improvement in type gained from the cross can easily be lost. This leaves the breeder with two further alternatives: to mate two heterozygous blacks, or to breed one of these blacks to a salt and pepper in order to hold, and possibly intensify, the improvement in type that he has already obtained.

How will this mating affect the color? In general, the result in either case will be some blacks and some salt and peppers. If the breeder is lucky, the mating of two heterozygous blacks should result in three black puppies out of four, and one of the three blacks should be homozygous. A heterozygous black bred to a salt and pepper should in theory give one-half heterozygous blacks and one-half salt and peppers.

370

How will the resultant salt and peppers compare in color to those from a mating of two sal. and peppers? They may be darker, and since many present-day salt and peppers show an undesirable tendency to fade out and lose the characteristic sharp bands of color, this return to better markings may be advantageous. On the other hand, the black color may hide other factors, such as a black mask rather than the light whiskers that most people prefer. Or, should the black carry C rather than c^{ch}, the light portions of the banded hairs may revert to a yellowish color such as used to be common, for c^{ch} affects the red and brown colors and makes them paler but does not produce any visible effect on black.

While the effects of color crossing upon the salt and peppers produced are only indirectly related to the breeding of quality blacks, their relation to the breed as a whole deserves consideration. Such salt and peppers mated to salt and peppers will produce only salt and peppers. This is because black is dominant, and therefore can be transmitted by a single A^s gene. Thus if the dog is *not* black it cannot transmit that color. A salt and pepper with one, or even two, black parents is as much a salt and pepper as one with no black ancestors for ten generations.

It is true that an occasional puppy from salt and pepper stock may be born completely black at birth, and even remain so for some weeks or months. This condition may be due to the presence of G, perhaps even of GG. One such puppy still appeared absolutely black at several months but eventually turned out an indubitable black and silver. The appearance of a real black from two salt and pepper parents could be due to one of three things: (1) an accidental mating, unknown to the owner, with a solid black male—this is the most likely, if such a male is on the premises; (2) a mutation from a^w (or possibly a^y) to A^s—such mutations are considered by geneticists to be very rare, and consequently most unlikely; (3) the presence of other genes, unusual for the breed, which may recombine so as to produce black. This last possibility seems to have happened fairly often in the early days of the breed. A dog with ee, for instance, would have black restricted to the nose, foot pads, eyes and eye rims. Such a dog would be some shade of red or yellow, and "yellow" appears fairly frequent in the old German studbooks. If such an ee dog, whose parents might both have been Ee, also carried A^s for solid color, it would still not be black, for the

371

Three Australian blacks (l. to r.) : Austr. Ch. Jovinus Rigoletto, Königlich Kipps Kitt and Königlich Jason, CD.

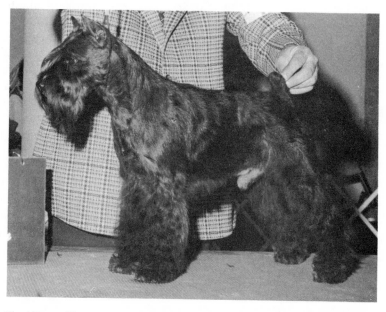

Ch. Aljamar Tommy Gun, owned by Aljamar Kennels, made some outstanding wins enroute to his title. He was Winners at Westminster 1974 and Best of Breed at International 1974. *Earl Graham.*

ee would prevent any black pigment being deposited in the coat. However, were this dog mated to a dark salt and pepper carrying *EE* or *Ee,* a puppy receiving *E* from one parent and A^s from the other could have the formula $A^s a^w Ee$ and would therefore be black.

It is unlikely that many Miniature Schnauzers today carry *ee* or even *Ee.* If they did, yellows or reds without dark banding would appear as recessives now and then, which does not seem to be the case, or at least is extremely rare. Accordingly, very few blacks are likely to be a result of this combination of genes. In the vast majority of cases, then, blacks will occur only when they have at least one black parent. Furthermore, the salt and peppers from black parents quickly become absorbed into the general population.

Turning now to the blacks with salt and pepper behind them, what problems, if any, will be encountered? As stated above, imported blacks are usually homozygous, and may be expected to sire all black puppies of good, pure color. Theoretically this should continue in later generations, and sometimes does so, but more genes are likely to be at work then simply those that deposit black throughout the entire length of the hair instead of merely in bands. The two principal types of faults likely to arise are mismarkings and poor color in the case of the black itself.

"Self color" dogs, in which the coat is of one color throughout, are genetically *SS* when homozygous and are typically without any white markings. However, in the presence of minus modifiers even *SS* dogs may develop a small amount of white, showing as no more than a small patch on the chest, white toes or toenails (particularly on the hind feet) and a small amount of white on the stomach. Markings of this sort are quite common in salt and peppers but usually grow smaller or completely disappear by the time the puppies are two or three months old. Anything that remains blends into the very light furnishings so that it hardly shows.

Such slight markings do not indicate the presence of recessive particolor or white spotting, at least in the majority of cases, but they are naturally more conspicuous on solid blacks and are accordingly less desirable. Because such minus modifiers do not express themselves consistently, and because a number of different modifiers may be involved, getting rid of them by selective breeding may be difficult. If introduced into a black line by crossing with salt and peppers, they may be hard to eliminate.

373

Recessive to the dominant S for solid color is a gene known as "Irish spotting" for which the symbol is s^i. This is typical of Basenjis and some other breeds in which the tip of the muzzle, the throat and chest, tail tip, a strip on the stomach, and the feet up to about the hocks or pasterns are white. Plus modifiers may result in a smaller amount of white, resembling an SS solid with minus modifiers, while minus modifiers may increase the white to the point where it overlaps with s^p particolor. In a number of breeds that do not appear to carry the gene for Irish spotting (including Miniature Schnauzers), occasional puppies may show "pseudo-Irish" patterns which represent incomplete dominance of normal salt and pepper or black over particolor (Ss^p). Since theoretically S should be completely dominant over s^p, it is more likely that such incomplete dominance is due to the presence of minus modifiers. One reason for rejecting the possibility that such markings indicate the presence of true Irish spotting is the fact that the latter nearly always shows a white tail tip and a considerable amount of white on the muzzle, or even a blaze on the face. While Miniature Schnauzers do sometimes show a very small amount of white on the chin (which usually disappears like the white toe tips) and very occasionally a white tail tip, both these markings are rare.

I know of several litters that have included puppies with white legs up to or near the elbow or hock and fairly large white areas on the chest and stomach. These dogs were discarded for breeding, but later a brother or sister of apparently normal color was found to carry a particolor (s^p) recessive and produced particolors when mated to another carrier. The pseudo-Irish mismarked puppies appear to have had only one parent that carried particolor, but when an Ss^p combination of genes coincided with minus modifiers, the dominance of S was incomplete.

The presence of pseudo-Irish markings in puppies of any color, whether black or not, is a danger signal, and it should be remembered that littermates or parents that show no such indications themselves may nevertheless be carriers. True $s^p s^p$ particolors do occur when two carriers are mated and so do $s^{wh} s^{wh}$ complete whites. Both genes are scattered throughout the breed and are carried by a number of individuals, including some champions.

The crossing of salt and peppers with blacks has nothing to do with the production of particolors as such. Both parents must be

374

Dyonyx Anfiger, owned by Anne F. Eskrigge (breeder) and Jane Scanlon. *Dianna H. Cooney.*

Dynamo Anfiger, owned by Carolyn T. Urban. *William P. Gilbert.*

Ch. Arbury Gay Uncle Sam with his sons Dynamo Anfiger and Dyonyx Anfiger. *William P. Gilbert.*

Italian Ch. Varum del Tornese.

Vassili del Tornese, who won the **CAC** award at his first show.

carriers to produce them, and it makes no difference whether such carriers are both blacks, both salt and peppers, or one of each. The same is true of plus and minus modifiers, except that because even small white markings show up more on a black, there may have been more effort made to eliminate them from the blacks by rigid selection. In consequence, more salt and peppers may carry minus modifiers which could be transmitted to the blacks when the two types are interbred.

The color fault that may appear relates to the quality of the black itself. This should be a clear jet black with a black undercoat, but this is not always the case. The black may be of a reddish tone, or of a flat, dull color—even a slate or "blue." There may be a sprinkling of light hairs on the body or head. There may also be light areas on the hocks or elbows, and occasionally an otherwise black dog may have a light undercoat on the legs or body.

The origins of these conditions vary. Normally, a black dog has a black undercoat and a salt and pepper has a light undercoat, although it may vary quite a bit from the shade of the top coat. It seems probable that different genes control the color of the top coat and the undercoat but are carried on the same chromosome so that they are transmitted together, resulting in what is called "linkage." Sometimes this linkage breaks down. Before or during the division of the sex cells which precedes mating, two chromosomes in a pair may break at the same point and a piece of one unites with a piece of the other. If one chromosome carried the gene for black top coat and black undercoat and the other carried genes for salt and pepper top coat and light undercoat, presuming that the chromosomes broke between the locations of the undercoat and top coat genes the piece carrying black top coat might be united to the piece carrying light undercoat. How often this would happen would depend partly on how often such a break occurred and where. If the two genes in question were at opposite ends of the chromosome, *any* break would separate them. Should they be located next to each other on the chromosome they would remain in the same piece unless the break occurred exactly between them. The farther apart the two genes, the greater the likelihood of a break in the linkage between top coat and undercoat. Unquestionably such breaks in linkage do occur, but when black is bred to black a crossing over of the chromosome would make no difference. Therefore this condition must result from a color cross some time in the past. When, as is sometimes the case, the light undercoat appears only on the legs of a black dog, it may be that there is some connection with the a^t gene for bicolor.

Some solid blacks appear to have a sprinkling of white hairs through the top coat, though not enough to consider the dog a roan. If these hairs are pulled with tweezers and carefully examined they will usually be found to have a small dark tip which does not show against the black coat, and that such hairs are actually salt and pepper. This condition has been found to occur in a dog whose litter brother was an excellent black throughout. Their sire was a black and their dam a fairly dark salt and pepper. Whether the sprinkling of banded hairs was the result of incomplete dominance of A^s over a^w in one case, and if so, why it was not evident in the other, is not clear. The dog with the sprinkling of banded hairs also carried particolor (Ss^p), which his brother may have lacked. This may have operated to interfere with the complete dominance of A^s, but that is only a guess.

Slate or "blue" color in a black may result from a pair of the recessive genes dd which reduce black by dilution. This is rare among blacks in general, but a few early blacks were registered as blue, and some of the very light salt and peppers may carry d and could transmit it in case of a color cross. The dominant G gene for progressive graying may also be present in a good many salt and peppers and could be transmitted to a black even in the first generation after a cross. Salt and peppers with G are born almost black, except for light areas on the face and feet, but become lighter as they get older, much like silver Poodles. Dilute blacks caused by dd would show the dilution at birth.

What causes certain dogs to show silvery hair on the elbows, hocks, or the top of the head is not wholly clear. All these areas are usually scissored when a dog is touched up for shows. One breeder reported that her black male became greyish on the top of his head after being scissored there for a considerable period, and that after she hand-stripped the area he grew a lovely, hard black head coat. This makes one wonder whether more black pigment is deposited in new hairs, and less and less as the hairs grow out. Scissoring the ends would leave only the less heavily pigmented portion toward the roots. This, again, is guesswork and not established fact. However, it is worth remembering that in the case of salt and peppers the banded hairs have dark tips and then a light band, varying in length. This makes one wonder whether incomplete dominance of A^s over a^w, possibly due to minus modifiers, might be responsible. But in that case the question could be raised as to why the effect should be limited to a few areas.

When the black coat as a whole is not of the desired jet color it may be due to several possible factors. The occasional presence of d, which produces "blue" in dd animals, has been mentioned. In his book, Little speaks of a peculiar flat, dull quality as characteristic of this color. While in theory Dd should not differ from DD in appearance it is possible that a slight difference may be apparent, especially in dogs that also carry $c^{ch}c^{ch}$. Although the latter gene is supposed to have little or no effect on black, but confines its influence to red, it could conceivably have a cumulative effect when combined with the two other recessives in Dd and A^sa^w.

The distinction between black (BB) and liver (bb) seems to depend chemically on two distinct stages in oxidation of the dark pigment involved. The recessive bb does not appear to be present in Miniature Schnauzers (at least I have never come across a liver or solid brown, nor heard of any). However, strong sunlight, particularly when a dog has been stripped practically bare and a new coat is in process of formation, may also cause some oxidation, resulting in a slightly reddish cast to an otherwise black coat. Little mentions an indistinct reddish undertone as apparent in blacks—sometimes only in certain lights and sometimes more generally—when A^s incompletely conceals a^y in A^sa^y animals. In the case of A^sa^t he states that the reddish tinge is found only where tan occurs in bicolor animals. While he does not mention a^w in this connection, A^sa^w might well produce similar results. Why such incomplete dominance occurs only in some cases he does not say, but it might be due to the combined effects of other genes such as c^{ch} or minus modifiers. Since the effects of a gene are not limited to one specific characteristic and they can react with other genes, some of the results which occur may be comparable to the "side effects" of antibiotic drugs which affect some individuals but apparently do not affect others.

With more specific cases of color crossing available for study it may be possible to confirm or disprove some of the suggestions made above. For example, the presence of C in jet-black homozygous

German blacks might be confirmed by the appearance of tan or yellow furnishings and whiskers in second generation salt and peppers resulting from color crosses. The presence of *dd* in very light salt and peppers might also be confirmed by the appearance of blues among the second generation blacks. The incidence of minus modifiers producing small amounts of white on *SS* dogs may likewise be further studied.

Now that what is known or surmised regarding the genetic makeup of blacks and the possible or probable results of color crossing has been set forth, the question remains as to how to make best use of this knowledge. To say that matings should be carefully planned and only the best individuals retained for breeding is to oversimplify the problem. That should go without saying. Nor should it be really necessary to warn against expecting too rapid results. Success will not come overnight. There will be many disappointments. It may even be necessary to go back and start over again.

Four of Mrs. Brivio's blacks at Turin, 1967.

3

Breeding Blacks for Color and Type

WHY, indeed, try to breed blacks at all? Because one likes their color. Because they add variety to the breed. And because it is a challenge to produce blacks good enough to compete with salt and peppers on even terms. It is the last reason, of course, that demands careful thought and selection.

The first step in planning a color cross is to consider what each color can contribute and how to go about choosing the individuals to be used. Regardless of color, German breeders demand very hard coats with harsh, somewhat sparse furnishings. They dislike "all that spinach" and are reported to strip out what they consider superfluous. A result of their preference for hard coats and sparse furnishings is that most German imports lack furnishings by our standards. Since few German salt and peppers have been shown here since before the war, and since so many blacks have been imported or are from imported parents, this has given the blacks a reputation for lacking furnishings. Sparser furnishings may also give the effect of less bone, and the German dogs also appear to have a tendency to slightly roached backs and low-set tails.

As previously mentioned, all recent German imports, whether line-bred, inbred, or open in pedigree themselves, are virtually complete outcrosses to all American Miniature Schnauzers derived from prewar stock. The only partial exceptions are a few individuals descended from American dogs taken to Germany and bred there. Of these, Dutch Ch. Morit of Marienhof is the leading example. There is also quite a considerable amount of American blood in England—probably enough to give a degree of compatibility to the black Jovinus importations mentioned earlier.

The principal contribution of the German blacks to color-cross matings can therefore be seen to be their color. Of less importance, although not without value, is their really hard body coat, which some American salt and peppers seem in danger of losing. And for what it may be worth, the German blacks can provide a more complete outcross than can American Miniatures descended from a relatively small group of importations during the 1920's and 1930's. On the other hand, any top-quality salt and pepper with the desired color should fulfill a black breeder's dream.

When selecting foundation stock for breeding blacks, the best plan is to choose one or more black bitches. If they are imported, or from imported parents, color is of the utmost importance as it will be their greatest asset. If they are from stock in which some color crossing has already been done, care should be taken to see that such crossing has resulted in improvement of type without serious loss of color quality or, so far as can be ascertained, the introduction of undesirable recessives. It is advisable in most cases to start with black bitches rather than males because there is an almost unlimited choice of top salt and pepper studs available for breeding at a normal stud fee. On the other and, to secure salt and pepper bitches of the highest quality would probably be very much more expensive and by no means always possible, regardless of the financial aspect. Therefore, assuming the black dogs and bitches were of equal quality, the average combined contribution of a black bitch bred to a top salt and pepper male would probably be considerably greater.

As when planning any mating, the male should be chosen for his individual quality, his suitability for the bitch in question (so as to minimize faults and emphasize good points), his record as a producer of quality puppies, if he has one, and his pedigree from a producing angle. Where a mating is of necessity an outcross, it is most important that line breeding or inbreeding should help to give prepotency to the sire chosen and make the planning of future combinations easier. Other qualifications being equal, then, choose a male who is not only outstanding himself but has one—or still better, several—top-quality relations within a reasonable distance.

It will be easier and quicker to achieve the desired results if you have two or three black bitches available when you start operations, or if some neighboring breeder will cooperate. You can then try more than one combination and compare the results. Also, there is less possibility that you will lose time because your bitch presents you with an all male litter, or one in which the only female is the poorest of the lot; for once again, it is better to choose a bitch for the next step in your program.

Obviously, since you are seeking to establish the American show type in blacks, you will want to select a female puppy who represents an improvement over her dam in this respect. At this stage, type is of greater importance, but if the choice between two puppies is otherwise equal, or the variation a minor one that can easily be corrected, always choose the better colored one.

In order to fix the desired improvement of type if it is obtained, the bitch (or bitches) selected from the first generation cross should be mated back to a salt and pepper closely related to her sire and of equally good quality. This might be his own sire, making a grand-sire–granddaughter breeding which is often very successful. Or it could be his uncle, a full or half brother, a nephew or even a son or grandson. In any case, the emphasis should be upon the most prepotent lines in the pedigree.

The result of this second generation color cross is decidedly less predictable than was the first as far as color is concerned. Approximately half the litter will be salt and pepp r, or perhaps there may even be one or more black and silvers. Also, if any recessives have been introduced there may be mismarkings or other color faults to a greater degree than is likely in the first generation. Then, considering the sex ratio, especially if the litter is small, there is a good possibility that there may be no more than one black bitch, if any. Unless other litters are available, either within the kennel or through cooperation with another breeder, this may mean waiting in the hope of better luck in the next litter.

If a good black bitch does appear in this litter, she will of course be three-fourths salt and pepper breeding. At this point there is a choice between a further mating to a salt and pepper, once again selected to maintain quality and continue the line breeding, or if there is one available, breeding to a black male of similar breeding. The decision depends on the judgment of the breeder and the results so far obtained. If the black color continues to be good, continuing the line breeding to the salt and pepper side may be the best decision in the long run. Even if the quality of the black is not all that it might be, this may still be the best choice.

After establishing a uniform type, with a number of individuals at hand for further breeding, emphasis in selection may then be shifted to color. The problem then becomes one of retaining the desired type while using the strongest colored individuals to improve the black color. If the type is sufficiently established, one may then try going back to one of the first generation cross. To return to the original or some other imported black would certainly be likely to help in the matter of color but would have no advantage over the first generation cross other than that. The mating of a homozygous to a heterozygous black should result in half the litter being homozygous. Which individuals are homozygous can then be established by test matings, preferably with salt and peppers, to see whether any salt and peppers are produced.

The alternative choice of a heterozygous black from the first color-cross generation, while theoretically producing an average of one salt and pepper to three blacks out of every four puppies, would be more likely to retain the improvement in type that we are assuming has been established and would not involve another complete outcross. Moreover, there would still be the chance of obtaining one homozygous black out of every three whelped. When test-mating to salt and peppers has identified a homozygous black of acceptable quality, the breeder will have come a long way toward accomplishing his objective. Several such blacks of both sexes should make it possible to breed black to black and obtain 100 percent black puppies. The problem from that point on is to maintain both type and color quality. This requires sufficient available stock to allow for proper selection and culling of inferior specimens.